JL
27
. N48
1995

S0-BNV-354

NEW TRENDS IN CANADIAN FEDERALISM

NEW
TRENDS

in Canadian Federalism

EDITED BY FRANÇOIS ROCHER & MIRIAM SMITH

broadview press

Langsdale Library
University of Baltimore
1420 Maryland Avenue
Baltimore, MD. 21201

©1995 the authors

All rights reserved. The use of any part of this publication reproduced, transmitted
in any form or by any means, electronic, mechanical, photocopying, recording,
or otherwise, or stored in a retrieval system, without prior written consent of the
publisher — or in the case of photocopying, a licence from CANCOPY (Canadian
Copyright Licensing Agency) 6 Adelaide Street East, Suite 900, Toronto, Ontario
M5C 1H6 — is an infringement of the copyright law.

Canadian Cataloguing and Publication Data

Rocher, François
New trends in Canadian federalism

Includes bibliographical references.
ISBN 1-55111-019-9

1. Federal government — Canada.   2. Federal-provincial relations — Canada.★
I. Smith, Miriam Catherine. II. Title.
JL27.R63 1995   321.02'0971   C95-931431-8

Broadview Press
Post Office Box 1243, Peterborough, Ontario, Canada K9J 7H5

in the United States of America:
3576 California Road, Orchard Park, NY 14127

in the United Kingdom:
B.R.A.D. Book Representation & Distribution Ltd., 244A, London Road,
Hadleigh, Essex SS7 2DE

Broadview Press gratefully acknowledges the support of the Canada Council, the
Ontario Arts Council, the Ontario Publishing Centre, and the Ministry of
National Heritage.

PRINTED IN CANADA

5 4 3 2 1 95 96 97

Contents

Introduction / *François Rocher and Miriam Smith*   7

PART ONE: CONSTITUTIONAL DEVELOPMENTS AND CANADIAN
POLITICAL IDENTITY

CHAPTER 1
The Political Uses of Federalism *Alain-G. Gagnon*   23

CHAPTER 2
Four Dimensions of the Canadian Constitutional Debate *François
Rocher and Miriam Smith*   45

CHAPTER 3
The Unsolvable Constitutional Crisis *Jennifer Smith*   67

CHAPTER 4
The End of Executive Federalism? *Kathy L. Brock*   91

CHAPTER 5
Living with Dualism and Multiculturalism
Kenneth McRoberts   109

CHAPTER 6
The 1982 Constitution and the Charter of Rights:
A View from Québec *Robert Vandycke*   133

CHAPTER 7
The Federal-Provincial Power-grid and Aboriginal
Self-Government *Radha Jhappan*   155

PART TWO: PUBLIC POLICY AND THE DIVISION OF POWERS

CHAPTER 8
Federalism and Economic Policy
Robert M. Campbell   187

CHAPTER 9

Global Economic Restructuring and the Evolution of Canadian
Federalism and Constitutionalism
François Rocher and Richard Nimijean   211

CHAPTER 10

Trade Policy, Globalization, and the Future of Canadian
Federalism *Ian Robinson*   234

CHAPTER 11

Fiscal Federalism: The Politics of Intergovernmental Transfers
Gérald Bernier and David Irwin   270

CHAPTER 12

Social Policy and Canadian Federalism:
What Are the Pressures for Change?
Leon Muszynski   288

CHAPTER 13

Retrenching the Sacred Trust: Medicare and Canadian Federalism
Miriam Smith   319

CHAPTER 14

Federalism and Training Policy in Canada:Institutional Barriers to
Economic Adjustment *Rodney Haddow*   338

CHAPTER 15

Regional Development: A Policy for All Seasons
Donald J. Savoie   369

CHAPTER 16

Conflicting Trends in Canadian Federalism
The Case of Energy Policy / *Michel Duquette*   391

CHAPTER 17

Federalism, Environmental Protection, and Blame Avoidance
Kathryn Harrison   414

Contributors   439

Introduction

François Rocher and Miriam Smith[1]

IN CANADIAN POLITICS COURSES, A TRADITIONAL JOKE IS SOME-
times used to introduce the topic of federalism. In an international essay
competition, students are asked to write on the subject of the elephant.
The American student writes a paper entitled "The Elephant and the Free
Enterprise System." The French student writes on "The Love Life of the
Elephant." The British student writes of "The Elephant in the British
Empire." The Canadian student writes on "The Elephant: Federal or Pro-
vincial Jurisdiction?"

The purpose of this book is to introduce students to the changes of the
last decades that have shaped the role and functions of Canadian federal
institutions as well as federal-provincial relations. If the Fathers of Confederation visited us today, they would hardly recognize the political system they helped establish over a century ago. Similarly, the political and
economic factors that shape federalism have changed markedly and have
created new constraints: globalization of markets, the fiscal crisis, and
problems related to the clash of multiple loyalties (at territorial, national,
and community levels). These limitations generate new challenges for the
Canadian political structure. The controversies surrounding the patriation
of the constitution in 1982 and the negotiations leading to the failure of
the Meech Lake Accord in 1990 and the Charlottetown Accord in 1992
clearly illustrate divergent visions of the future of federalism. That Jean
Chrétien's Liberal government as well as a strong majority of the Canadian intellectual, economic, and political élite have indefinitely postponed

---

1   Parts of the Introduction were translated from the French original by Maya
     Berbery.

any reopening of constitutional negotiations does not mean that federalism is stuck in the status quo.

On the contrary, the emphasis on constitutional change from the early 1980s to the early 1990s may have obscured the fact that Canada's constitution has always been imperfect. Under the pressure of Québec governments since 1960, the federal government and the other provinces began to consider the need to "modernize" the Canadian constitution. The difficulties of securing the consent of all provinces (not to mention the population) to a project of constitutional reform demonstrate underlying conflicts. Québec's "secessionist threat," the reinforcement of regionalism, and the decreased fiscal flexibility of governments may be difficult to resolve by constitutional means; in this sense, then, the constitutional crisis was only an epiphenomenon.

Several political analysts have emphasized the flexible nature of the Canadian political system. This much-praised flexibility means that it has been possible to implement new programs in health care, the environment, education, and social assistance without formal constitutional changes. Informal changes to the division of powers have been made either through administrative agreements between the federal government and the provinces or, alternatively, through the federal government's *de facto* capacity to shape policy in areas of provincial jurisdiction via the use of its spending power. Even such informal changes did not occur without conflict. The political and institutional restructuring generated by the implementation of new mechanisms for intervention required intense negotiations between the federal government and the provinces, or the imposition of federal priorities through the spending power. The provinces defended often contradictory interests because of their own distinct economic and/or social priorities. As for the federal government, since the end of World War Two it has followed an increasingly centralizing course. Centralization responds to the desire for policy consistency and harmonization – if not homogenization – and for the development of a sense of "national" identity. The recent evolution of Canadian federalism has not prevented a resurgence of the sovereignist project in Québec, the election of a large number of sovereignist members of Parliament in the 1993 federal election, and the re-election of a sovereignist Québec government. Similarly, outside Québec, some provinces have attempted to increase their leeway (if not their autonomy) in areas of provincial jurisdiction while, for lack of financial and economic resources, other provinces prefer the strengthening of federal jurisdiction because of the benefits they receive from it.

This book aims to outline the major changes in different areas of Canadian federalism over the last decade and to identify some of the consequences of these changes for future developments. Two major considerations must be kept in mind. First, it must be recalled that the federal structure adopted in 1867 took into account the national, regional, and linguistic diversity that characterized the era. A basically pragmatic agreement between elites, the federal bargain was designed to equip the central government with the capacity for economic intervention while giving the provinces (Québec in particular) sufficient latitude to ensure their cultural, linguistic, and religious development. The new state was founded on the assumption of national dualism. The recognition of dualism, at least at the level of political discourse and practice, permitted French Canadians to embrace the project. However, the Canadian political and social context has changed in ways that make political and institutional arrangements based on binationalism increasingly difficult to accept for many Canadians, particularly outside Québec. Québec's evolution since the early 1960s has only exacerbated tensions. The adoption of the federal multiculturalism policy, the entrenchment of a Charter of Rights centred on individual freedoms, and the quest of the First Nations for political, cultural, economic, and social recognition have contributed to the delegitimation of Québec's political discourse based on the idea of two founding peoples. Problems related to the quest for a pan-Canadian identity became clear in the constitutional discussions. These focused not only on the restructuring of the federal framework itself (the division of powers, the capacity of each level of government to intervene, the recasting of institutions such as the Senate and the Supreme Court, coordination mechanisms such as the first ministers' annual conferences) but also on the symbolic aspects. The constitutional negotiations revealed much more than a crisis of institutions and of intergovernmental relations. They brought out the magnitude of the identity crisis that is shaking the country. In this sense, the crisis of Canadian federalism involves the clash of competing identity projects. The solution to this crisis would require flexibility in acknowledging a diversity that goes beyond the issue of institutions.

The second consideration pertains to the workings of Canadian federalism. The history of federal-provincial relations in the post-war period was marked by an unprecedented increase in economic and social intervention at both levels of government. In different areas – health, education, the environment, economic policy, and regional development – the federal and provincial states implemented programs that required mutual adjustments in terms of financing and goal-setting. Some saw a greater decentralization of federalism in this; others emphasized federal intervention in areas of provincial jurisdictions.

The concepts of centralization/decentralization are essential to the analysis. However, there is no consensus on their meaning. One approach focuses on formal and institutional dimensions. The centralization/decentralization problem is therefore nearly always linked to the issue of the division of powers between the two levels of government, which in turn refers to the capacity of each level of government to intervene independently in specific areas. A decentralizing trend would emerge when provincial governments obtain new constitutional responsibilities or increase the areas of federal intervention that are subject to provincial consultation. Other cases would be when provinces increase their fiscal resources (by increasing their own revenue or through unconditional federal transfers), when they intervene in areas of federal jurisdiction, or when they exert control over central government institutions, as would have been the case if senators were appointed exclusively by the provinces.

On the other hand, a centralizing trend involves the exercise of power in Ottawa at the expense of provincial governments, even in jurisdictions formally reserved to the provinces. Centralization also means that there is an explicit hierarchy between orders of governments, the federal government taking the upper floor of the pyramid while provincial governments, at a level below the federal government, are subordinated to its will and authority. Finally, political centralization makes Ottawa the voice and the representative of all Canadians regardless of their differences. In this perspective, Canadian "national" political institutions must not only reflect the diversity that characterizes Canada, but must also contribute to the creation of national unity. Taken to its extreme, this centralizing dynamic is such that the federal government appropriates the authority to define a "national" interest. Provincial governments are relegated to a position of secondary importance and are no longer viewed as legitimate representatives of economic, social, and cultural differences. This is the traditional meaning of the concept of centralization.

Another approach to the concepts of centralization and decentralization downplays the legal and institutional dimensions. Instead, it focuses on the actual capacity to intervene of each level of government. Supporters of this approach centre their analysis on the growth of provincial budgets compared to the federal government, the scope of responsibilities entrusted to each level, the capacity of provinces to shape decisions made by the federal government, and the primary loyalty of citizens. This new dichotomy highlights the extent to which policies and tendencies favour provincial intervention (in which case we talk about provincialization) or federal intervention (in which case we talk about Canadianization). In this perspective, a *de facto* centralization of power can be observed when the federal government tightens its control over policies, as when the federal government defined "national objectives" in health care while increasing the provinces' capacity to intervene. Centralization of power combined with Canadianization was also observed in cases such as the National Energy Program. Furthermore, a provincialization of federal institutions would occur if, for example, Supreme Court judges were to be appointed from lists prepared by the provinces, or if senators were to be elected within each province. Finally, there are no examples of formal decentralization of power, i.e. where the federal government surrenders its responsibilities in favour of the provinces.

✢ ✢ ✢

Both sections of this book use these cleavages, emphasizing one or the other of the dimensions. The first section deals with constitutional developments and the fundamental question of Canadian political identity. The issues raised are both institutional and societal in nature. In the first chapter, Alain-G. Gagnon explores the concept of federalism. He suggests that federalism must be examined from two different points of view. The institutional dimension refers to arrangements that structure relationships between communities, regions, and levels of government. Sociological dimensions, with various processes favouring either homogeneity or diversity, must also be considered. Federalism must therefore be examined as a conflict resolution mechanism and as a tool to be used by minority groups who might otherwise be threatened.

The search for a balance between the pressures of centralization and decentralization brings into play the two dynamics sustaining federalism: the pursuit of autonomy versus the emphasis on unity. Two representational logics can also be observed within a federal system: social pluralism upon which the central government is based, and territorial pluralism put forward by the provinces. Federalism can encourage innovation by favouring competition between levels of government in popular, regional and community support. In Gagnon's words, "federalism brings amicably competing arrangements. It is therefore essential for a federal society to maintain tolerance of other communities. In addition, the pursuit and respect of consent among the various constituent units is a must in the pursuit of democracy and the quest for justice."

Chapter 2 examines conflicting views of the recent constitutional debates. In this chapter, François Rocher and Miriam Smith describe four divergent approaches to constitutional change, each emphasizing a particular view of the kind of relationships that should exist between governments and communities in Canada. The first approach rests on the principle of equality of the provinces. In this view, the original federal bargain was the product of provincial agreement, and thus an equal relationship between the two orders of government should be privileged. Inspired by a classical definition of federalism whereby each level of government is considered to be autonomous in its own area of jurisdiction, the Canadian political community is made up not only of individual rights-bearing citizens but also of provinces that have equal rights. The second approach is that of dualism and asymmetrical federalism. This view is based on the perceived need to manage diversity, particularly with respect to minority groups. In direct opposition to this view, the third approach – the nationalizing vision in its different versions – sees the entire country as the basis of a national identity and favours the strengthening of the federal government's powers. The last approach – the most recent one – emerged in the wake of the social and political changes following the adoption of the Charter of Rights and Freedoms in the 1982 constitution. It defines identity in terms of equally shared rights (either individual or collective). The constitutional debate, it is argued here, not only concerns legal and institutional change; it also raises fundamental questions about the parameters that should shape Canadian identity. The clash of these competing views, based on mutually exclusive principles, makes it difficult if not impossible to reach constitutional agreement.

In the third chapter, Jennifer Smith examines the two failed constitutional accords, Meech Lake and Charlottetown, and analyzes in detail their most contentious aspects: the distinct society clause, the Canada clause, and the proposed rules for representation in the Senate and the House of Commons. These agreements, especially the Charlottetown Accord, attempted to respond to competing demands without taking into account the fact that principles at stake were not always compatible.

Smith explains that the Charter encouraged the adoption of a uniform, homogeneous citizenship based on equal rights, thus opposing the specific recognition of certain groups in the constitution. The debate centred on the constitutional status of different communities, not only Québec, but also Aboriginal peoples and minority ethnic groups. According to Smith, the mistake of the Charlottetown Accord was to abandon the traditional neutrality of the constitution in favour of a normative approach. In addition, the agreement's institutional aspects ran counter to the notion of justice associated with the representation by population ("rep by pop") principle. This principle was abandoned for the sake of the equality of the provinces in the new Senate and the rearrangement of seats in the House of Commons with a guarantee of one-quarter of the seats for Québec. Québec's population would not have been willing to accept a double minority status (in the Senate and in the House of Commons), which would have broken the 1867 compromise based on the equality of the regions. In short, the "rep by pop" principle seems to have prevailed over the equality of provinces. Smith maintains that the constitution affects citizens more than the powers of governments, and citizens must be taken into account in the process of constitutional change.

In Chapter 4, Kathy Brock explores the constitutional process and the impacts of the constitutional debate on the future of executive federalism. She emphasizes that, unlike Meech, the road to Charlottetown was characterized by significant public input. Brock disagrees with many of the criticisms that have been levelled against executive federalism, arguing that these were both premature and exaggerated. Agreements involving first ministers and bureaucrats remain an important dimension in the working of federalism. On the other hand, the way institutions are defined must change. With regard to constitutional negotiations, Brock draws two lessons from past attempts. First, negotiations behind closed doors render the whole process vulnerable to the charge that elites have shaped the process to serve their own interests; the relationship between popular consultations and formal governmental agreement must be clarified. Second, the role and responsibilities of political leaders have been significantly altered; leaders must display greater consistency with principles dear to Canadians. Nevertheless, Brock maintains that, as a general rule, executive federalism will continue to serve as a widely used mechanism for major policy developments. She concludes by arguing that Canada does need an efficient mechanism to negotiate intergovernmental arrangements but that such mechanisms require greater public legitimacy.

Kenneth McRoberts, in Chapter 5, examines how the Canadian state has managed cultural diversity. He discusses two crucial issues: how the Canadian state defines and recognizes newly mobilized cultural identities; and the ways that the state has attempted to accommodate previously recognized cultural differences. According to McRoberts, the main reason for the original adoption of federalism stemmed from the necessity of accommodating cultural differences by allowing certain groups to control state structures. Federalism gave significant support to cultural dualism. On some issues, Québec francophones were considered a linguistic majority. However, linguistic boundaries did not correspond to political boundaries so that, outside Québec, French-Canadian culture did not receive support or recognition. Political demands, as well as Québec's language legislation, radicalized the reality of dualism. The central government attempted to put forward a new conception of dualism, one that undermined the role of the Québec government in favour of a greater role for the federal state in the strengthening of minorities outside Québec. Multiculturalism was first presented as a federal response to Québec's desire for the recognition of Canada's binational nature. Yet multiculturalism policy seemed to call into question the country's dualistic nature, which was the initial rationale for a federal system. Multiculturalism issues were at the centre of the constitutional debates of the eighties and nineties. "The federal formula of bilingualism and multiculturalism was clearly designed to reduce historical linkage between cultural difference and Canadian federalism," concludes McRoberts.

Writing from a Québec perspective, Robert Vandycke asserts in Chapter 6 that the conception of Canada that developed after 1982 as a result of the Charter of Rights and Freedoms is rejected by a majority of Québécois. The Canadian Charter modified some provincial powers pertaining to language policy. He examines the issue of collective rights vs. individual rights as defined in the Charter and addresses the ideological debate on the rights of minorities from a theoretical perspective.

In Chapter 7, Radha Jhappan analyzes the division of powers and its impact on the First Nations. The rise of Aboriginal issues constitutes the most recent significant trend in Canadian federalism. The potential establishment of Aboriginal self-government would represent a fundamental restructuring of the federation to accommodate a completely new order of government. Jhappan rejects the idea that this new political order would be based strictly on ethnicity. Nevertheless, it would deviate from traditional constitutional practice. This chapter provides an overview of

roles and responsibilities of federal and provincial governments with regard to the First Nations; it assesses how these roles have changed in the
last twenty years and explains why Aboriginal peoples are not satisfied
with existing arrangements. Finally, the chapter reviews changes that have
occurred in negotiations pertaining to self-government as well as territorial claims. Jhappan stresses that the future of self-government may depend on piecemeal negotiations or amendments to the Indian Act rather
than on constitutional amendments.

The chapters in Part Two analyze the evolution of federal and provincial roles across different areas of public policy. Each chapter outlines the
formal division of powers, the actual evolution of federal/provincial roles,
especially over the past fifteen years, and provides insights into directions
for the future. In Chapter 8, Robert Campbell addresses federalism and
the evolution of macroeconomic policy in Canada, especially with respect
to price and employment stability. As monetary policy is under federal
control and fiscal policy is in part a provincial responsibility, both levels of
government have played a role in increasing state intervention in the post-
war period. Campbell explains the origins of Keynesian economic policy
and the key role played by the federal government in its development. He
notes, however, a decline in centralized economic management as provincial revenue has increased and provincial taxation has been broadened.
These shifts have contributed to the view that provinces must play a role
in economic stabilization, making further centralization unlikely. Campbell evaluates mechanisms for coordinating fiscal policy and assesses the
impact of the neo-conservative change in policy direction on federalism
and the management of the economy. The perception that the federal
government is an inefficient economic manager has encouraged provinces
to manage their own economies, weakened attempts at centralization, and
called into question the Keynesian paradigm. According to Campbell, intergovernmental relations with regard to economic policy will continue
to be shaped by cuts in federal transfers. If the neo-conservative trend persists, the federal government will remain the main actor in managing the
Canadian economy.

Another critical aspect of economic policy is explored by François Rocher and Richard Nimijean in Chapter 9, which focuses on the implications of globalization of the international economy on federalism. Rocher
and Nimijean examine how issues related to globalization, competitiveness, and economic restructuring have surfaced in the constitutional debate. The authors note that the globalization process affects the division of

powers, either by decreasing state-imposed constraints on the economy or by increasing the need for a decentralization of power. They then point out that recent constitutional history has clarified, among other things, the ways in which governments respond to new economic challenges. Constitutional negotiations focused in particular on ways to reinforce the Canadian economic union. Ottawa's goal was to maintain its control over the Canadian economy in an increasingly competitive environment. Negotiations addressed deconcentration of power more than decentralization, allowing the federal government to remain the prominent political authority in economic matters.

Chapter 10 examines another dimension of globalization. Ian Robinson here focuses on the significance of the recent North American Free Trade Agreement (NAFTA) as well as the conclusion of the recent Uruguay Round of world trade talks (GATT). Although these agreements do not constitute formal constitutional changes, they will have significant consequences for intergovernmental relations. The chapter analyzes the extent to which trade agreements will intensify intergovernmental conflicts and contribute to the emergence of a residual-type federalism. Finally, Robinson sketches two approaches to globalization and argues that a "communitarian globalization" would be more compatible with the spirit of Canadian federalism.

In Chapter 11, Gérald Bernier and David Irwin set out the historical and economic dimensions of intergovernmental transfers in comparative perspective. Tracing the origins of the transfer system, the authors analyze differences and similarities among three major transfer programs – equalization, Established Programs Financing (EPF), and the Canada Assistance Plan (CAP). Bernier and Irwin then explain the relevance of using specific criteria to compare the impact of transfers and assess provincial dependence on the transfer system. The degree to which provinces benefit from transfers varies greatly, and, according to Bernier and Irwin, it would be wrong to look for winners and losers. They argue that the transfer system can be understood as a response to constitutional constraints inherent in a federal structure. It should be seen as a mechanism designed to mitigate centrifugal effects that may stem from disparities in provincial governments' fiscal capacity.

A similar dynamic has affected intergovernmental transfers in other fields of social policy. In Chapter 12, Leon Muszynski provides an overview of federalism and social policy. He points out that the improvement of social protection rests on the federal government's capacity to maintain its power and leadership over the provinces (with the exception of Québec, where the government has preferred to preserve its autonomy in this area of jurisdiction). This accounts for the reluctance of many Canadians to support the provisions of the Meech Lake and Charlottetown Accords that would have changed the methods of developing new social programs. However, Muszynski explains that constitutional discussions addressing this issue did not go to the heart of matters. The criticisms of Meech Lake and Charlottetown overstated the impact of the decentralization of power as well as the pro-statist character of federal intervention in social policy. Despite the appearances, the Canadian welfare state is not a paragon of social justice and progress. Constitutional discussions, analyses of administrative decentralization, and even debates on Québec's sovereignist project avoid the fundamental issue of the real benefits citizens receive from social programs. In addition, Muszynski provides a critique of the dominant neo-conservative vision and suggests an alternative approach. Finally, he argues that the history of the welfare state is the history of the struggles of social movements against the devastating consequences of a market-oriented approach. He contends that the welfare state aims primarily at forging social solidarity.

Chapter 13 addresses major trends of federal involvement in the medicare system. Miriam Smith discusses the impact of cost increases in the health system on the role of federal government. Because of the manner in which the financing system was implemented, the federal government is in a strong position to impose difficult fiscal choices on provincial governments. The federal budgetary process and the complexity of the intergovernmental transfer system hinder the growth of an opposition to cutbacks. However, Smith points out the limits on the federal government's capacity to impose unilateral restrictions on transfers. Whether or not the erosion of the financing of health programs managed by the provinces is irreversible remains to be determined. The main obstacle to the strengthening of the federal government's role is the fiscal pressure exerted by the size of the deficit and the public debt.

In Chapter 14, Rodney Haddow addresses training policy in Canada, which he argues is determined to a large extent by complex federal-provincial relations that hinder the labour market adjustment process. Provinces invoke their formal jurisdiction over education while the federal government intervenes in the name of the spending power. Haddow traces the history of government intervention in the area of manpower training from the early 1960s to the Charlottetown Accord. He wonders whether Canada is heading for a new form of administrative asymmetry and questions the consistency of federal policy. In 1982, the central government attempted to limit the influence of provinces, while in the last constitutional round it tried to increase their capacity to intervene. The author points out that since conflicts vary from one province to the other, a *de facto* asymmetry should be considered. He emphasizes the conflicting approaches advocated by the provinces and the lack of coherence found in federal policy. By and large, the prospects for a Canada-wide strategy adapted to economic problems are not very encouraging.

Regional development is a crucial issue in Canadian federalism. In Chapter 15, Donald Savoie assesses the multiple turnarounds that have characterized regional development policy in recent decades. These changes are attributable both to the complex nature of the problems and to the attempts to find easy solutions or to give governments greater visibility. Savoie reviews the evolution of regional development policy and various programs that have been implemented, taking into account the role played by each level of government. He points out that, in terms of the constitution, neither of the two levels of government is explicitly entrusted with responsibility for the reduction of regional disparities. Nonetheless, the federal government has claimed a major role through the use of its spending power. This role was not contested by the provinces; on the contrary, they requested it. Savoie emphasizes the flexibility of regional development policy. Without guidelines provided by the constitution and the division of powers, federal intervention was developed in cooperation with the provinces. The federal government was considered primarily as the supplier of funds, and "in trying to be all things to all regions, Canadian regional development has thus lost its way." According to Savoie, the fiscal crisis and market globalization will prompt a redefinition of relations among regions in Canada. A global economy reinforces regional fragmentation and decentralization so that provincial jurisdictions, particularly in education and infrastructure, will become key instruments in the promotion of regional development. However, provincial governments benefiting from regional development programs lack financial resources. According to Savoie, the pragmatic approach will continue to shape trends in this field and will support a redefinition of goals in a context of scarce resources, though without calling into question the need to reduce regional disparities.

In Chapter 16, Michel Duquette explains to what extent major changes in the international economy have destroyed the balance between federal and provincial jurisdictions in the field of energy policy. Previous federal-provincial conflicts developed in a political and economic dynamic between centre and periphery. The author distinguishes two periods: the first, from 1973 to 1982, was characterized by the exaltation of pan-Canadian nationalism rooted in a self-sufficiency approach; the second, starting in 1983, was characterized by intergovernmental conflicts that resulted in the decentralization of power and the implementation of policy rooted more in interest accommodation. Duquette analyzes provincial involvement in energy policy; he addresses the issue of the National Energy Program; he considers the implications of continental trade agreements; and he examines the impact of hydroelectric development in Québec on the Aboriginal question. It is too early to foresee whether the ascendance of peripheral provinces at the expense of federal authority will lead to the balkanization of Canada. On the one hand, the potential for conflict remains serious, especially considering the uncertain implications of continental trade agreements. On the other hand, energy-producing provinces agree with the federal government on the need to support the industry, develop new projects, and stimulate exports. Duquette argues that the struggle of Aboriginal communities against hydroelectric projects paves the way for the internationalization of internal economic and political conflicts.

Finally, the evolution of federal-provincial relations in the environmental field is discussed in Chapter 17. According to Kathryn Harrison, these relations have been marked by numerous conflicts recently, especially with Alberta, Saskatchewan, and Québec. This contrasts with the era of cooperation of the 1970s and 1980s. This shift was caused in part by greater public awareness and the desire of both levels of government to reap the political credit for action in the environmental field. The author reviews the involvement, retreat, and reinvolvement of the federal government since 1960, and assesses the impact of these changes on the policy capacity of each level of government. She argues that the federal government has attempted to evade its responsibilities in an area that is particularly sensitive in the public opinion. The federal government has refrained from intervening in order to avoid the blame as companies resisted regulation at a time when public opinion was less aware of environmental issues. Provinces, on the other hand, wanted to maintain their authority over their natural resources. In short, the fact that the federal government did not attempt to provoke the provinces accounts for the climate of federal-provincial cooperation that marked most of the seventies and eighties.

19

More recently, the 1990 Green Plan put forward the need for national standards and for an increased federal role in environmental issues while giving some leeway to provinces in the environmental assessment process.

Taken as a whole, the policy chapters emphasize several important points for the student of Canadian federalism. First, they highlight the difference between formal jurisdictions (as laid out in sections 91 and 92 of the Constitution Act, 1867) and the working reality of Canadian federalism. For various fiscal, economic, and social reasons, Canadian federalism does not operate in "watertight" compartments as classical theories of federalism would suggest. In practice, overlap has developed between federal and provincial jurisdictions as the Canadian states (federal and provincial) have enlarged their roles and responsibilities in the post-war era. Untangling federal and provincial roles in each policy area is a complicated task. Because of the practical overlap of jurisdictions, informal administrative and funding mechanisms are an extremely important dimension of the system. The specific arrangements vary across policy areas, thus involving different dynamics of federal-provincial conflict and cooperation.

Moreover, these chapters suggest that two new forces are at work in shaping Canadian federalism in the nineties. One is the fiscal pressure exerted by deficits and debt, which have restricted the choices of federal and provincial states. A second important dynamic is the impact of the globalizing political economy and the ways that this force is shaping (*de facto* and *de jure*) the capacity of each level of government to intervene. In this sense, then, the question may no longer be "federal or provincial jurisdiction?" In many areas, governments (federal and provincial) may be displaced by international market forces and international regimes (such as trade agreements) that regulate and govern in areas that were once the domain of the state.

Part One:

Constitutional Developments

and Canadian Political Identity

CHAPTER ONE

The Political Uses of Federalism

Alain-G. Gagnon

FEDERALISM MAY BE CONCEIVED AS A POLITICAL DEVICE FOR establishing viable institutions and flexible relationships capable of facilitating interstate relations (e.g., division of powers between orders of government), intrastate linkages (e.g., representation at the central level), and inter-community cooperation. With an emphasis on process, institutions can be seen as arising out of politics, the genesis of institutions resulting essentially from the conflicts and power struggles of economic, societal, and political actors. However, the question of territory is also central to any study of federalism, as it allows for the expression of both diversity and unity.

The following discussion moves principally between two planes of analysis: institutional and sociological. At the institutional level, the chapter centres on arrangements that structure community or regional relations either within central institutions (e.g., the German Bundesrat) or between orders of government (e.g., the interlocking fiscal and policy arrangements in Canadian, German, or Swiss federalism). The sociological level focuses on the issues of homogeneity and diversity, as seen in various federal practices and the reaction of groups and communities who feel threatened or who see greater potential in alternative arrangements that give broader expression to community or regional interests.

In this chapter, several avenues are explored. Federalism is examined as a conflict-solving mechanism, that is, as a shield for minority groups that would otherwise feel threatened. Federalism is also seen as an expression of democratic practices encouraging innovation in policy preferences and political choices at the territorial level. This chapter highlights many contributions federalism has made in the areas of representation and innovation, suggesting that it has the propensity to ameliorate living conditions, to provide additional opportunities for access to the system, and to create favorable conditions for the initiation of new programs to meet people's needs.

Following a brief discussion of the concept of federalism, the chapter will focus on the themes of conflict management, protection of minorities and social engineering, the issue of representation, and the politics of innovation. In my view, these four elements constitute the main tenets around which federalism is capable of making a strong contribution to humankind and to the furthering of democracy and democratic traditions.

DEFINITION

Federalism means different things to different people. Canadian federalism is influenced greatly by American federalism, which stresses the one-nation concept, and no less profoundly by European traditions of federalism, which encourage the expression of many different political streams in the body politic. Canada, then, constitutes a unique laboratory for students of comparative politics, in that varying political traditions compete with one another for political relevance and, by extension, for political power.

From the American perspective, there is a tendency to view federalism in a hierarchical way, with a central government controlling the principal levers of power and the provinces being subordinated to its authority. There has been a tendency to emulate this model in Canada, though not without challenge. To many decentralists, the American model is detrimental and should be revised to improve power relationships between the centre and the regions. This confirms Robert C. Vipond's view of two competing traditions of federalism in Canada.

One is built on a liberalism that emphasizes individual liberty, views the state as a means to protecting liberty, and typically looks to the national government for leadership. The other stresses the value of community, is more likely to encourage collective choice, and tends to recognize the importance of provincial governments as the guardians of regional identities (Vipond, 1991: 2).

Federalism implies a commitment to a contractual arrangement between political units that decide to create a new political space. As James Tully put it, following the failure of the Meech Lake Accord, "what touches all must be approved by all" (Tully, 1992). This is one of the most established principles of federalism, a principle ensconced in the Western judicial tradition.

Many experts on federalism support such positions. Daniel Elazar argues that "In a larger sense, however, federalism is more than an arrangement of governmental structures; it is a mode of political activity that requires the extension of certain kinds of cooperative relationships throughout any political system it animates" (Elazar, 1984: 2). The notion of partnership is central to federalism and represents an element without which plural societies may easily fail the test of time. Federalism suggests the presence or establishment of bridging mechanisms[1] for communities to be able to operate in a climate of respect and trust.

CONFLICT MANAGEMENT VERSUS CONFLICT RESOLUTION

The political uses of federalism are first seen in the area of conflict management. Explanations of how federal systems have managed significant crises, whether economic, political, or structural, most often emphasize cross-cutting cleavages, political elite behaviour, and political instrumentalities or, alternatively, administrative arrangements.

Conflict management is not solely the preserve of federal systems, though social diversities are frequently associated with this type of political structure. The success of federal systems is not to be measured in terms of the elimination of social conflicts but instead in their capacity to regulate and manage such conflicts. It is completely misleading to expect federalism to resolve conflict. Rather, it can only ease tensions and be sensitive to diversity (Gagnon, 1989: 147-68). Conflicts must be viewed as an inherent component of all federal societies. Paradoxically, the capacity of a federal system to reflect diversity constitutes a built-in weakness since it allows for conflicts to emerge and be politicized.

Maureen Covell, an expert on Belgium and Canada, observes that "Many writers on Canadian federalism argue that the existence of a provincial level of government has exacerbated the country's regional and language divisions by giving the groups involved an institutional power base and creating political élites with a vested interest in bad relations with the national government" (Covell, 1987: 75). Covell puts things in perspective by arguing:

> On balance, it seems that federal institutions should ease the process of conflict resolution, at least of low- to medium-level conflicts. At the simplest level, federalism may lower the temperature of élite

competition by multiplying the number of available political and bureaucratic posts.... When lack of Liberal representation in the west [western Canada] lowered the capacity of national-level institutions for handling Canada's regional tensions, the possibility of federal-provincial negotiations provided a useful alternative. Federalism also reduces the number of topics on which it is necessary to arrive at interregional and inter-community agreement.... (Covell, 1987: 75)

Particularly sensitive to issues of social conflicts in Belgium, Covell is well placed to understand how these can be successfully managed. It rapidly becomes obvious to any serious analyst that federalism can be used to express conflicts, to provide avenues for solving them, and to give incentives for reaching compromises that otherwise would jeopardize the survival of many polities.

Federalism does not evolve in a void. It is crucial, therefore, to examine the dynamics of political economy to have a fuller understanding of the forces present. Garth Stevenson has influenced students of federalism in advocating this approach. Building on the work of historians, this view gained respect and prominence in Canada during the late 1970s with the emergence of neo-Marxism.[2] In his classic study, *Unfulfilled Union*, Stevenson argues:

> More frequently, federal-provincial conflict has represented class fractions within the dominant world of corporate capitalism.... Each fraction identifies its interests with a level of government where it finds a sympathetic hearing, and the economic conflict becomes institutionalized as a federal-provincial one, complete with the usual ideological justification on both sides. (1989: 212)

This suggests that institutions may not matter as much as we have been led to believe. Such an understanding is somewhat qualified by the fact that federalism offers to political elites added access points for conflict management. This interpretation stands in sharp contrast with Pierre Elliott Trudeau's view:

> One way of offsetting the appeal of separatism is by investing tremendous amounts of time, energy, and money in nationalism, at the federal level.... Resources must be diverted into such things as na-

tional flags, anthems, education, arts council, broadcasting corporations, film boards; the territory must be bound together by a network of railways, airlines; the national culture and the national economy must be protected by taxes and tariffs; ownership of resources and industry by nationals must be made a matter of policy. In short, the whole of the citizenry must be made to feel that it is only within the framework of the federal state that their language, culture, institutions, sacred traditions, and standard of living can be protected from external attack and internal strife. (1968: 193)

What must be stressed again is that federalism is not there to resolve conflicts but to manage them. Insofar as federal systems seek to accommodate diversity, conflicts must be recognized as inherent to the federal setting. Diversity invariably produces some conflicts, but this does not have to be conceived as a weakness. Canadians, at least until 1982, have tended to respect the conflictual nature prevalent in their federal system and to view diversity as a beneficial feature of federalism.

The multiple access points that federalism provides to political elites ensure many safety valves for the expression of dissatisfaction with government policies, and thus federalism encourages proposals and solutions to the crises that erupt from time to time. A case in point is provided by the West German construction industry. Streeck argued that in the German case business associations assisted in coordinating, and at times in bringing together, both federal and *Land* governments.[3] In light of this example, the idea too often expressed that federalism pits government against government is worth reconsidering.

FEDERALISM AS A SHIELD FOR MINORITIES AND TERRITORIAL INTERESTS

The political uses of federalism have been particularly notable with respect to the protection of minorities. For most ethnic groups and territorially structured communities, federalism has the potential to respond adequately to problems occurring in multicultural and multilingual settings. Formal constitutional studies have tended to ignore the place of and the role played by political and economic challenges, often failing to understand the deep transformations taking place in society.

The importance of territory has too often been neglected in studies of federalism. The "bias of mobilization," to use E.E. Schattschneider's formulation, favours political regions rather than societies or ethnic groups *per se*. What needs to be underscored is the centrality of the spatial interactional dimension, as well as the sociological differences that prevail between territorial divisions of the federal state. The dynamics of federal states are constituted by the interactional and interrelational modes allowing for consideration of relations between local, regional and central orders of government. This view results in increased sensitivity to intergovernmental cooperation and confrontation.

Central to any view of federalism is the respect for diversity, which implies the maintenance of territorially based communities with specific identities. As Alan C. Cairns argues, "the provinces, aided by secular trends that have enhanced the practical significance of their constitutionally based legislative authority, and by the deliberate improvement of their own bureaucratic power and capacity, have given a new salience to the politics of federalism and the territorially based diversities it encompasses, reflects, and fosters" (Cairns, 1988: 165). The Canadian experience is particularly interesting since it is influenced by both individual and collective aspirations. In countries where a minority or economically subordinate ethnolinguistic community is capable of commanding the politics of a specific region, the questions of territory and, by extension, federalism become central to political life. A case in point is provided by Québec in the Canadian context. In countries where ethnic or linguistic groups are dispersed evenly throughout a number of territories, shifting political coalitions and group politics generate conflicts that often do not necessitate federal institutions.

The late Donald V. Smiley argued that in Canada the federal government has tried to elaborate "national policies" that are territorially blind. Examples include the entrenchment of a Canadian Charter of Rights and Freedoms, the elaboration of the Free Trade Agreement between Canada and the United States, and the adoption of government policies that tend to be more concerned with issues such as the environment, gender, and Aboriginals than with territory, as was the case in the past.

In an attempt to attenuate regional/territorial conflicts, several scholars have proposed a focus on class politics. In Canada, this dates back to the early 1960s when John Porter and Gad Horowitz suggested adopting a creative politics that would organize politics around class and no longer differentiate citizens in terms of linguistic, ethnic, religious or regional characteristics. Based on this reading, federalism would tend to accentuate long-established political cleavages. Andrew Petter offers a complementary point of view. According to Petter, "What writers like Porter [and Horowitz] fail to note is that, while federalism serves to reinforce traditional cleavages at the national level, it creates a second tier of political action decision-making at the regional level in which traditional cleavages are minimized and which therefore is more conducive to the development [of] class-based politics" (1989: 471, n.67). The fundamental difference between their positions centres on the governmental level at which the class-based politics would tend to develop.

Recent societal transformations are challenging the relevance of the federal system in managing new power relations. Alan C. Cairns argues that, in Canada:

> An ethnic constitutional discourse dominated by French-English relations, which could be translated into a federalism discourse by Québec's political power, has lost ground. The ethnicity of the new non-aboriginal, multicultural, and multiracial Canada largely concentrated in metropolitan centres cannot be "managed" by federalism. Federalism can contribute to interethnic harmony or civility only when the ethnic groups in question are territorially concentrated and thus capable of escaping from each other by exercising limited powers of self-government in provinces or states. For the emergent ethnicity of metropolitan Canada, federalism provides no solution.... Canadians are becoming a new people for whom the past of Wolfe and Montcalm is truly another country and for whom federalism has declined in instrumental value. (1992: 112)

Different mechanisms have been invented to cope with territorial vested interests. In Germany, for example, the Bundesrat has proved to be an essential mechanism for ensuring the protection and promotion of territorial aspirations within the federation. The Bundesrat possesses an absolute veto in all legislative matters affecting interests of the Lander. These interests are determined by the constitutional enumeration of legislative fields requiring consent of the Bundesrat (e.g., amendments to the basic law, laws affecting state finances, and legislation affecting the administrative sovereignty of the Lander). In contrast, the experience of Australia's Triple E Senate reveals that centralist intrastate changes have little positive impact in attenuating conflict arising from territorially or regionally defined interests. This makes the effectiveness of the Bundesrat in protecting the regional interests of the *Länder*, in a relatively homogeneous context, a significant achievement to be emulated by other federal countries.

From a Canadian perspective, an important political use of federalism is found in its long-term capability to manage "antagonistic cooperation,"[4] Ivo Duchacek argues that:

> A federal constitution may therefore be seen as a political compact that explicitly admits of the existence of conflicting interests among the component territorial communities and commits them all to seek accommodation without outvoting the minority and without the use of force. Or, in other words, a federal constitution expresses the core creed of democracy, pluralism, in territorial terms. (1970: 192)

While retaining the concept of an antagonistic relationship, this interpretation suggests that political groups can join forces to achieve some purposes. Federalism does not entail the elimination of political conflicts. Rather, it permits the full expression of diversity. In a sense, this view reveals that federalism is not achieved once and for all; rather, it is always in the process of being ameliorated. In short, federalism is about social engineering and political ingenuity.[5]

In his study of Canadian federalism, Garth Stevenson remarks that federalism "protects minorities and enables cultural, linguistic, religious, and ideological diversity to flourish" (1989: 16). This, I would suggest, represents a dominant view among students of Canadian federalism. Writing from this tradition, Ronald Watts links the construction of provincial autonomy to political safeguards provided by a federal system, arguing that the degree of success is measured by the degree to which the different internal linguistic and cultural groups have been given an opportunity to express their cultural distinctiveness through this autonomy. At the same time, the central institutions, political parties, and official language policy must foster federal cohesion by giving the different cultural groups an opportunity to participate in central policy-making and administration (Watts, 1975: 585).

Fundamental to federalism is the need to respect diversities and to encourage them to blossom. A significant caveat, however, is offered by Maureen Covell:

> federalism is not always a guarantee of protection for minorities at

the national level. The existence of Québec as a political unit has not allowed the Québécois to prevent the perpetuation of the British connection, participation in two world wars, and, most recently, the explicit denial of a Québec veto over future constitutional revision. The existence of the prairie provinces as institutions did not protect farmers against the effects of eastern economic domination.... Federal institutions provide a tool for self-defence but no guarantee of success. (1987: 76)

With hindsight, the success of federalism in ensuring the protection of minorities and territorial interests is something that can never be taken for granted due to the dynamic forces competing for political resources. What is essential is the capacity of these forces to strike a deal that has the potential to satisfy communities sharing a common territory.

A SEARCH FOR BALANCE

An essential element of federalism, according to A.V. Dicey, is that people desiring to find an equilibrium between forces of centralization and decentralization, or else between provincial and federal powers, "must desire union, and must not desire unity" (1908: 141). A central feature of federalism has been its ability to establish varying balances between centripetal and centrifugal forces. Difficulties emerge only when a sense of unfair treatment, perceived or real, is being felt by communities.

Federalism has been used to achieve different ends. It has been used not only to fight regional disparities but to cope with deep societal cleavages in plural societies. This has led, for instance, to federal and provincial governments striking deals on sharing power based on the many differences of culture, religion, and language that colour a country. In Canada, these cleavages tend to overlap, giving provincial government a more pronounced responsibility in making policies for its constituents. Once again, Québec is unique in that its population is 80 per cent francophone, of Catholic background, and influenced by a civil law tradition while the rest of Canada is mostly anglophone, tends to have a Protestant background, and has a common law tradition.

It is with this background in mind that the Report of the Royal Commission of Inquiry on Constitutional Problems, also known as the Tremblay Commission, set up by the Québec Legislative Assembly (later National Assembly) in 1953, should be examined. The notions of autonomy and coordination were emphasized, with the understanding that if one of these two elements is challenged, this may call for an end to federalism. Therefore, it is possible for a member state of a federation to refuse assistance and to exercise fully its responsibilities as agreed to in the original compact. The Tremblay Commission was influenced largely by the social doctrine of the Catholic Church and built on the principle of subsidiarity, meaning that higher levels of authority cannot take on tasks if these can be dealt with at levels closer to the individual. In the Canadian context, the commissioners argued in the best tradition of the social doctrine of the Church:

> Only federalism as a political system permits two cultures to live and develop side by side within a single state: that was the real reason for the Canadian state's federative form.... So, therefore, there can be no federalism without autonomy of the state's constituent parts, and no sovereignty of the various governments without fiscal and financial autonomy. (Kwavnick, 1973: 209, 215)

This interpretation of federalism takes its inspiration from Europe (e.g., Switzerland) as it builds simultaneously on two pillars, autonomy and union. Neither of these two pillars can take precedence over the other without endangering the maintenance of a federal system. Federalism is therefore perceived as a balance between union and diversity, as well as between autonomy and sovereignty or, if one prefers, a balancing act between polarized views, conveyed by the image of checks and balances so dear to Lord Acton. Many Anglo-Canadian experts on federalism have come to believe that this state of equilibrium has outlived its usefulness and should be replaced by something more stringent. David Milne makes the argument that following the separatist threat from Québec in 1980 and important challenges from the oil-producing provinces, the federal government no longer had any choice and "was finally driven to insist that there had to be a 'preponderant power' at the center in the event of fundamental conflict in the Canadian state" (1986: 209).

The risks of such a view were noted many years ago by J.A. Corry: "Because power alone can balance power, the provinces and states have to keep strong and vigorous bodies of opinion on their side if they are able to stop the aggrandizement of national governments" (Corry, 1958: 115). This statement gives credence to the opinion that forces of federalism are continually being threatened by forces of unitarism, and that people need to be aware of such challenges. To allow one order of government to take precedence over the other is to render federalism a fiction.[6] In this sense, it is essential to the survival of the spirit of federalism that political parties, think tanks, and territorial as well as interest groups continue to find support with either order of government. Were such groupings to stop finding support, federalism would be threatened and in all probability its continuance would be an aberration.

Federalism, under normal circumstances, constitutes a balancing act. Vested interests can, however, challenge this *modus operandi* from time to time, as is suggested by the political economy literature. For instance, Garth Stevenson developed the argument that:

> important sections of the ruling class have an interest in strengthening the provinces in relation to Ottawa. The primordial basis of the distinction is the existence in Canada of a largely resource-based economy, plus the provincial jurisdiction over the resources themselves.... Provincial jurisdiction over resources makes control over the provincial state apparatus important to certain sections of the bourgeoisie and gives them an interest in strengthening the provincial state and providing it with the wherewithal to carry out its functions effectively. (1977:78)

The act of balancing power relations and power claims on the part of the main protagonists is subject to a fair amount of pressure, as reflected in the many of political forces influenced by the political economy of a country.

From time to time, dynamic forces throw the balance off in one direction or the other, forcing political elites to elaborate political arrangements that better fit the changing realities. According to Trudeau:

> The compromise of federalism is generally reached under a very particular set of circumstances. As time goes by these circumstances change; the external menace recedes, the economy flourishes, mobility increases, industrialization and urbanization proceed; and also the federated groups grow, sometimes at uneven paces, their cultures mature, sometimes in divergent directions. To meet these changes, the terms of the federative pact must be altered, and this is done as smoothly as possible by administrative practice, by judicial

33

decision, and by constitutional amendment, giving a little more regional autonomy here, a bit more centralization there, but at the same time taking great care to preserve the delicate balance upon which the national consensus rests. (1968: 193-94)[7]

J.A. Corry was disenchanted with the way the federal government had modified power relations in Canada: "No constitution however good will supply us with resourcefulness and mental adroitness. Look at what we did without the aid of war powers from 1950 on! The centralizing trend begun in the war was continued by imaginative use of the fiscal, monetary and spending powers.... Nevertheless, by 1970 the long reach and the preservative influence of the federal government were striking features of Canadian federalism" (Corry, 1978: 7-8). According to Corry, whatever changes occur it is essential to establish a process that would reflect a state of "constitutional morality." Failing to maintain such a high level of morality and trust between the member states negatively affects the relevance of federalism for plural societies.

It is because of these transformations that instruments have to be invented to respond to pressing needs. As B.C. Smith appropriately puts it: "Federalism involves special techniques for managing a changing equilibrium between national and regional levels of government" (1985: 15-16). Central to this process, however, is the requirement that consent of all partners is required to modify operative constitutional principles. Failure to obtain such consent jeopardizes the continuity of a country. Once again, the Canadian example is illustrative of such a case, where the consent of a province, Québec in this case, the only territory where francophones have a majority in Canada, was not obtained before making fundamental changes to the Canadian constitution: the Charter of Rights and Freedoms was added with little consideration given to Québec's distinct character, and an amending formula was imposed that, in most cases, recognizes no right of veto for that province.[8]

Federalism has been viewed and used by the provinces as a political device for encouraging provincial economies to attend to the needs of the citizenry more appropriately. In the Canadian context, Québec economic policies since the Quiet Revolution of the early 1960s reflect attempts by the Québec state to limit economic peripheralization in North America by using state instruments. Similar economic strategies were emulated by provinces in western Canada where the level of alienation has been running high and the natural resources have been of benefit mostly to out-of-region people. One of the more appealing aspects of federalism for the provinces has been an increase in jurisdictions.

THE POLITICS OF REPRESENTATION

The question of representation is central to any understanding of federalism. Indeed, in his 1977 presidential address to the American Political Science Association, Samuel H. Beer indicated that two distinct logics of representation are usually at play in federal countries since "the voter views the political world from two perspectives, one shaped by the social pluralism of the general government, the other shaped by territorial pluralism of state government" (1978: 15). Beer added that:

> [the voter's] state perspective affects his choices and decisions in federal politics as his federal perspective affects his choices and decisions in state politics. One may call this process "representational federalism" because it gives representation in the general government to the territorial pluralism of the states and representation in the state governments to the social pluralism of the general government. (1978: 15)[9]

According to William Riker, the advocates of state rights believe that too much power is threatening and can be used to impose unwelcome measures. This view is founded on the premise that "concentrated power is dangerous, a position best expressed in Acton's aphorism that power tends to corrupt and absolute power corrupts absolutely. Federalism is said to be a device to prevent absolute power and therefore prevent tyranny." However, Riker believes that the opposite could frequently occur, since "there is no assurance that separating power is the appropriate way to prevent tyranny" (Riker, 1964: 140).

One should be careful not to confuse "representational federalism" of the kind defined by Samuel Beer with Reg Whitaker's interpretation of "cooperative federalism." The issue here is not about direct linkages between governments but rather the extent to which each order of government can exercise some influence on the other. Federalism is clearly about representation and, by extension, democracy. Whitaker correctly remarked that, in the Canadian context, "The essential organizational principle of federalism is territoriality.... Federalism as a system of repre-

35

sentation remains formally silent about the economic and class content of the nation, but is predicated along the axis of space and its political organization" (Whitaker, 1992: 193).[10] In one of the clearest statements about federalism to date, Whitaker maintains that:

> Modern federalism is an institutionalization of the formal limitation of the national majority will as the legitimate ground for legislation. Any functioning federal system denies by its very processes that the national majority is the efficient expression of the sovereignty of the people: a federation replaces this majority with a more diffuse definition of sovereignty. It does this not by denying the democratic principle, as such, but by advancing a more complex political expression and representation in dual (sometimes even multiple) manifestations which may even be contradictory and antagonistic (Whitaker, 1992: 193).

Whitaker's contribution to our understanding of federalism situates the concept in its proper context. He gives credence to the expression of different majorities in the same nation-state. Instead of arguing that such an understanding challenges the principle of democracy, Whitaker makes the point that federalism allows for a more sophisticated kind of representation whereby sovereignty is more diffused and imaginative than under a simple majority rule.[11]

In more recent years, parliamentary democracy has been challenged by the emergence of functional representation, as expressed by meetings of key actors such as unions, business interests, and the state. This has led some to believe that territorial representation, via the parliamentary branch, is vanishing, if not simply becoming obsolete, making functional representation necessary for the smooth functioning of the economy and to maintain legitimacy with the citizens.[12]

THE POLITICS OF INNOVATION

It is widely acknowledged that federalism allows for policy innovations. The most important contribution federalism can have on societal developments is indeed at the level of innovation.

Several political scientists tend to equate decentralization in a federal system with policy innovations, whereas others associate centralization with efficiency and rationalization. Richard Simeon and Ian Robinson (1990: 234-35) summarize the two sides of the argument and conclude that support can easily be found for both, but they make no direct link between decentralization and inefficiency or between province-building and unhealthy interprovincial competition. According to the public choice literature, competition between the two orders of government may have proved beneficial:

> Modern governments face an almost impossible range of demands. The "reach" of the state has in many ways outrun both our administrative and technical capacities, and our capacity to ensure democratic accountability. One approach to minimizing this problem is to try to limit the range of state interventions: to encourage the state to do less, but to do it better. Another is to recognize the advantages of sharing power and responsibilities among governments. No one government has to try to do everything, or to be responsible for everything. No one set of institutions has to try to do everything, or to be the focus for all demands and expectations of citizens, or to try to resolve all divisions and conflicts of society. In a country as diverse as Canada, centralization would be a recipe for paralysis. (Simeon and Robinson: 148).[13]

The point here is that uses of federalism are particularly noticeable at the level of competition between orders of government, creating a situation in which federalism provides for added flexibility in the system. Indeed, Albert Breton makes the point that:

> Federalism ... provides greater stability by diffusing conflict and expectations throughout the system. It offers the opportunity to tailor economic policies to the specific needs and concerns of citizens and groups in different parts of the country.... In a world of uncertainty and rapidly shifting economic challenges, where there is little understanding of what is likely to work best, it provides the opportunity for experiment and learning, for flexibility and inventiveness.... We can try different models for improving labour relations, for integrating education and training, for stimulating the flow of investment, and for diffusing technology. (1964: 148)

In short, federalism possesses the necessary elements to become a social laboratory in order to put in place new programs, to experiment, before proposing them to other partners in the federation. Similarly, Vincent Ostrom argues that overlapping and fragmentation lead to more effective public policies: "Conflicts among public jurisdictions in a highly federalized political system will elucidate larger amounts of information about alternative solutions to public problems" (1973: 230).

Federalism encourages competition between orders of government for popular support. Such a situation is not detrimental in itself. It becomes damaging when the two governments are constantly at odds with each other. Alan C. Cairns remarks, however, that:

> Canadian federalism contributes to the generation of pressure for government action in other ways. The nature of the federal system, with its fuzzy lines of jurisdictional demarcation and extensive overlapping of the potential for government response, means that in innumerable fields there is, in fact, an intergovernmental competition to occupy the field, and slackness by one level of government provides the occasion for a pre-emptive strike by the other. Further, the prevailing French-English crisis of Canadian federalism, with the federal and Québec governments vying for the allegiance of the Québec voter, encourages an elaborate competition between governments not just for party support but for regime support. (1988: 184-85)

Provincial governments are responsible to the citizens residing on their territories. This fact may lead them from time to time to refuse policy directions adopted by the central government because these may not correspond to the demands made by the provinces. Following a major study on the implementation of industrial policies in Canada, Allan Tupper concluded that "the provinces are unanimous in their rejection of market forces and federal policy as the exclusive determinants of provincial economic development" (1982: 26).

Richard French's study of industrial policy is of particular interest here, as it points to the many contradictions within the federal system itself. Competition within the government leads to different approaches, e.g., technological sovereignty versus free trade. Tupper supports the analysis proposed by French. Reviewing French's book, he states that "the federal bureaucracy is a complex and heterogeneous entity replete with internal controversies about the scope of state intervention and the content of an industrial strategy" (*ibid*: 101). This reveals the extent to which provinces have to achieve their ends by insisting on the importance of "politics" as a means to attenuate negative impacts of market forces on their economic bases.

In light of the fact that regionalism became a permanent feature in Canadian politics, it would not be wise for the federal government to neglect the provinces. Provincial governments tend to focus on perceived negligence on the part of the federal government and structure their economic plans to counter policies said to have had deleterious effects on the provinces.[14] The failure of the federal government to elaborate policies that could satisfy every region has led to a desire on the part of the provinces to take into their own hands economic development policies. This is further compounded by widespread nationalism in the province of Québec.

CONCLUSION

This chapter has assessed the many political uses of federalism through an examination of conflict management devices and measures adopted for the protection of minorities, as well as efforts made to maintain some equilibrium between unity and diversity. In addition, the politics of representation and innovation have been viewed as having the most potential for future developments of the democratic principle.

Federalism is a process offering a variety of options to cope with many conflicting cleavages. It is also used as a political instrument for communities to express themselves and be included in the political process. Federalism does not have clear delimitations on all sides. This grants political actors more flexibility in finding acceptable solutions. We have seen that federalism possesses the necessary elements to manage situations of social heterogeneity provided that political leaders decide not to throw off course the goals federalism was called upon to achieve.

The meanings given to federalism by its users are clearly about power. E.E. Schattschneider has perceptively argued that "the definition of alternatives is the supreme instrument of power; the antagonists can rarely agree on what the issues are because power is involved in the definition. He who determines what politics is about runs the country, because the definition of the alternatives is the choice of conflicts and the choice of conflicts allocates power" (1983: 66).[15] In other words, institutions are never value-neutral. The types of cleavages that make it to the forefront of the political agenda are very revealing in this regard.

Real federalism is comprised of a special fibre that allows for the respect of clear spheres of jurisdiction, and real federalism would find unacceptable any distancing from those spheres. Federalism brings amicably competing polities under the umbrella of a free, willingly accepted political arrangement. It is therefore essential for a federal society to maintain tolerance among its constituent communities. In addition, the pursuit and respect of consent among the various units is a must in the pursuit of democracy and the quest for justice. The political continuity of any democratic regime depends on the respect for these conditions.[16]

NOTES

1   On the importance of bridging mechanisms, see Throburn (1989: 183).

2   It is not without interest here to mention the work of Charles Beard. First published in 1913, *An Economic Interpretation of the Constitution of the United States* constitutes the most important anti-conventional analysis of American federalism of this century. Beard concluded that "The members of the Philadelphia Convention which drafted the Constitution were, with a few exceptions, immediately, directly, and personally interested in, and derived economic advantages from, the establishment of the new system" (p.324). Beard's work is particularly important since he was introducing political economy to the United States. For Beard, "The social structure by which one type of legislation is secured and another prevented – that is, the constitution – is a secondary or derivative feature arising from the nature of economic groups seeking positive action and negative restraint" (p.13).

3   W. Streeck, "Die Reform der beruflichen Bildung in der westdeutschen Bauwittschaft 1969-1982. Eine Fallstudie über Verbands als Trager offentlicher Politik," Discussion paper IIM/LMP 82-83, Berlin, Wissenschftszentrum Berlin, 1983, cited in Coleman (1987: 172). Young, Faucher, and Blais (1984: 818) made the key point that conflict is as important to the effective functioning of federalism as cooperation.

4   Grodgins (1966: 327); also mentioned in Duchacek (1970: 192).

5   David Kwavnick (1975: 71) has remarked that "depending on the basis upon which they are organized, pressure groups may serve to further integrate a federal society or to further fragment it."

6   See Gagnon and Rocher (1992: 29-33); also, see *ibid.*, note 3, on the concept of "façade federalism."

7   Trudeau was always a better theoretician than a committed practician of federalism.

8   I have dealt with this question more fully in "Everything Old is New Again: Canada, Québec and Constitutional Impasse" (1991).

9   Beer (1978: 15). See, for a similar interpretation, Huntington (1959: 192). For Beer and Huntington, federalism is more about political interaction between the two orders of government than about equilibrium.

10   It should be mentioned, however, that federalism can sometimes take on non-territorial forms, as was the case with both Austro-Hungary and Estonia. See, Friedrich (1975: 227-42). Taking note of this point, Kenneth McRae indicates, with regard to Belgium, that "If we define federalism in terms of entrenched, independent levels of legislative authority, the Belgian political system, as set out in the 1980 reforms, can be categorized as a unique combination of territorial and non-territorial federalism, each with its own assigned list of legislative powers" (1986-171).

11   Is democracy being eroded? It is not without interest to refer to Pierre Elliott Trudeau on issue of the "power of the purse." Trudeau discusses "the eroding effect that the 'power of the purse' will have on Canadian democracy if the present construction continues to prevail, and in particular what chaos will result if provincial governments borrow federal logic and begin using their own 'power of the purse' to meddle in federal affairs." Trudeau mentions also that, "Indeed the federal 'spending power' or so-called 'power of the purse' is presently being construed as a federal right to decide (at the taxpayers' expense!) whether provincial governments are properly exercising any and every rights they hold under the constitution" (Trudeau, 1961: 382, n. 4). For a more recent account, see, Petter (1989: 448-79).

12   For a fuller account of this transformation, see Bickerton (1990: 328).

13   The influence of Albert Breton is particularly evident in this section of the *Report*; see "Supplementary statements," especially pp. 493, 506.

14   See Julien (1992: 424-39); Simeon (1975: 499-511).

15   Schattschneider (1983: 69), remarkably, argues that "Some issues are organized into politics while others are organized out."

16   This chapter is a shortened and revised version of Gagnon (1993).

REFERENCES

Beard, Charles (1960 [1913]). *An Economic Interpretation of the Constitution of the United States.* New York: Macmillan Company.

Beer, Samuel (1978). "Federalism, Nationalism and Democracy in America," *American Political Science Review,* 72, 1: 9-21.

Bickerton, James (1990). *Nova Scotia, Ottawa and the Politics of Regional Development.* Toronto: University of Toronto Press.

Breton, Albert (1964). "The Economics of Nationalism," *Journal of Political Economy,* 72, 3: 376-86.

Cairns, Alan C. (1988). *Constitution, Government, and Society in Canada: Selected Essays by Alan Cairns,* edited by Douglas Williams. Toronto: McClelland & Stewart.

Cairns, Alan C. (1992). *Charter Versus Federalism: The Dilemmas of Constitutional Reform.* Montreal and Kingston: McGill-Queen's University Press.

Canada (1985). Royal Commission on the Economic Union and the Development Prospects for Canada. *Report.*

Coleman, William (1987). "Federalism and Interest Group Organization," in Herman Bakvis and William Chandler, eds., *Federalism and the Role of the State.* Toronto: University of Toronto Press: 171-87.

Corry, J.A. (1958). "Constitutional Trends and Federalism," in A.R.M. Lower, eds., *Evolving Canadian Federalism.* Durham, N.C.: Duke University Press: 92-125.

Corry, J.A. (1978). "The Uses of a Constitution," *Special Lectures of the Law Society of Upper Canada 1978, the Constitution and the Future of Canada.* Toronto: Richard de Boo Limited: 1-15.

Covell, Maureen (1987). "Federalization and Federalism: Belgium and Canada," in Bakvis and Chandler, eds., *Federalism and the Role of the State:* 57-81.

Dicey, A.V. (1908). *Introduction to the Study of the Law of the Constitution.* London: Macmillan.

Duchacek, Ivo (1970). *Comparative Federalism: The Territorial Dimension of Politics.* New York: Holt, Rinehart and Winston.

Elazar, Daniel (1984). *American Federalism: A View From the States,* Third Edition. New York: Harper & Row.

Friedrich, Carl (1975). "The Politics of Language and Corporate Federalism," in Jean-Guy Savard and Richard Vigneault, eds., *Multilingual Political Systems: Problems and Solutions.* Québec: Les Presses de l'Université Laval: 227-42.

Gagnon, Alain-G. (1989). "Canadian Federalism: A Working Balance," in Murray Forsyth, ed., *Federalism and Nationalism*. Leicester: Leicester University Press, 1989: 147-68.

Gagnon, Alain-G. (1991). "Everything Old is New Again: Canada, Québec and Constitutional Impasse," in Frances Abele, ed., *How Ottawa Spends 1991: The Politics of Fragmentation*. Ottawa: Carleton University Press: 63-105.

Gagnon, Alain-G. (1993). "The Political Uses of Federalism," in Michael Burgess and Alain-G. Gagnon, eds., *Comparative Federalism and Federation: Competing Tradition and Future Directions*. Toronto: University of Toronto Press: 15-44.

Gagnon, Alain-G., and François Rocher (1992). "Faire l'histoire au lieu de la subir," in Alain-G. Gagnon et François Rocher, eds., *Répliques aux détracteurs de la souveraineté du Québec*. Montréal: *VLB* Editeur: 27-48.

Grodgins, Morton (1966). *The American System: A New View of Government in the United States*. Skokie, Illinois: Rand McNally.

Huntington, Samuel (1959). "The Founding Fathers and the Division of Powers," in Arthur Maass, ed., *Area and Power: A Theory of Local Government*. Glencoe, Illinois: Free Press.

Julien, Paul-André (1992). "L'incidence de la souveraineté du Québec," in Gagnon and Rocher, eds., *Répliques aux détracteurs de la souveraineté du Québec*: 424-39.

Kwavnick, David, ed., (1973). *The Tremblay Report: Report of the Royal Commission of Inquiry on Constitutional Problems*. Toronto: McClelland & Stewart.

Kwavnick, David, ed., (1975). "Interest Group Demands and the Federal Political System: Two Canadian Case Studies," in Paul Pross, ed., *Pressure Group Behaviour in Canadian Politics*. Toronto: McGraw Hill: 70-86.

McRae, Kenneth (1986). *Conflict and Compromise in Multilingual Societies: Belgium*. Waterloo, Ont.: Wilfrid University Press.

Milne, David (1986). *Tug of War: Ottawa and the Provinces Under Trudeau and Mulroney*. Toronto: James Lorimer.

Ostrom, Vincent (1973). "Can Federalism Make a Difference?" *Publius*, 3, 2: 198-237.

Petter, Andrew (1989). "Federalism and the Myth of the Federal Spending Power," *Canadian Bar Review*, 68: 448-79.

Riker, William (1964). Federalism: Origin, Operation, Significance. Boston: Little, Brown and Company.

Schattsscheider, E.E. (1983). The Semi-Sovereign People: A Realist's View of Democracy in America. Chicago: Holt, Rinehart and Winston.

Simeon, Richard (1975). "Regionalism and Canadian Political Institutions," *Queen's Quarterly*, 82: 4: 499-511.

Simeon, Richard, and Ian Robinson (1990). *State, Society and the Development of Canadian Federalism*. Toronto: University of Toronto Press.

Smith, B.C. (1985). *Decentralization: The Territorial Dimension of the State*. London: George Allen & Unwin.

Stevenson, Garth (1977). "Federalism and the Political Economy of the Canadian State," in Leo Panitch, ed., *The Canadian State: Political Economy and Political Power*. Toronto: University of Toronto Press: 71-100.

Stevenson, Garth (1989). *Unfulfilled Union*, Third edition. Toronto: Gage.

Thorburn, Hugh (1989). "Federalism, Pluralism, and the Canadian Community," in David P. Shugarman and Reg Whitaker, eds., *Federalism and Political Community: Essays in Honour of Donald Smiley*. Peterborough, Ont.: Broadview Press: 173-85.

Trudeau, Pierre Elliott (1961). "The Practice and Theory of Federalism," in Michael Oliver, ed., *Social Purpose for Canada*. Toronto: University of Toronto Press: 371-93.

Trudeau, Pierre Elliott (1968). *Federalism and the French Canadians*. Toronto: Macmillan.

Tully, James (1992). "Multirow Wampum, the Charter and Federalism," paper delivered to the Conference on the Charter Ten Years After., University of British Columbia Civil Liberties Association and the Department of Philosophy, Simon Fraser University, May 15-16.

Tupper, Alan (1982). *Public Money in the Private Sector*. Kingston: Institute of Intergovernmental Relations.

Vipond, Robert (1991). *Liberty and Community: Canadian Federalism and the Future of the Constitution*. Albany: State University of New York Press.

Watts, Ronald (1975). "Asian Multicultural Federations," in Jean-Guy Savard and Richard Vigneault, eds., *Multilingual Political Systems: Problems and Solutions*. Québec: Les Presses de l'Université Laval: 561-91.

Whitaker, Reginald (1992). *A Sovereign Idea: Essays on Canada as a Democratic Community*. Montreal and Kingston, McGill-Queen's University Press.

Young, Robert, Phillippe Faucher, and André Blais, (1984). "The Concept of Province-Building: A Critique," *Canadian Journal of Political Science*, 17, 4: 783-818.

CHAPTER TWO

Four Dimensions of the Canadian Constitutional Debate

François Rocher and Miriam Smith[1]

OVER THE COURSE OF THE 1980S, CANADIANS ENDURED THREE rounds of constitutional negotiations. The first, in 1980-81, led to the patriation of the constitution with an amending formula and a Charter of Rights and Freedoms in 1982. The second round, under the Mulroney Conservatives, ended in failure in June, 1990, when the deadline for ratification of the Meech Lake Accord passed without achieving of the unanimous consent of the provinces. The third round, again under the Mulroney Conservatives, resulted in the Charlottetown Accord in August, 1992, which was rejected by voters in most parts of Canada in the referendum of October, 1992. While the first round did result in the successful achievement of constitutional change, it did so only because the federal government was willing to proceed with the consent of nine provinces rather than ten. But in the two subsequent rounds, Meech Lake and Charlottetown, aimed at remedying the exclusion of Québec in 1982, the unanimous consent of all provinces was achieved – at least for a time. In the case of Meech, new governments were elected in some provinces that opposed the Accord, while in the case of Charlottetown, despite the agreement of governments, the Accord was rejected by voters when, for the first time in Canadian history, constitutional changes were put to the people.

Through this modern constitutional odyssey, as Peter Russell has termed it, there have been different and conflicting visions of what the Canadian constitution should reflect and the kinds of constitutional

---

1   Parts of this chapter were translated from the French original by Maya Berbery.

change that are needed (Russell, 1993). A number of classifications of federalism in the literature have been wedded to constitutional positions. For example, a classic delineation of the types of federalism is Mallory's "Five Faces of Canadian Federalism" (1977). This classification, ranging from emergency federalism through cooperative federalism, covered the historical development of Canadian federalism in terms of power relations between levels of government. However, topologies of this type, while useful in understanding the historical evolution of Canadian federalism, are inadequate as a basis for understanding the complexities of the modern constitutional odyssey, at least as it has developed over the course of the 1980s and early 1990s.

When we consider these modern visions, from Pierre Trudeau's nationalizing vision through Québec nationalism to the demands of western Canadians for a Triple-E Senate, one of the most striking dimensions of these conflicting views of the constitution and of constitutional priorities is that each is based on different underlying definitions of political identity.

Political identity refers to the way individuals perceive their membership in the community upon which political institutions are built. This notion goes beyond the simple scope of legitimacy. It includes the acceptance of the norms and rules of behaviour applicable to all, as well as the parameters by which individuals recognize themselves within the political whole and in the institutions to which they belong. The political community must not only be recognized; it must also be accepted and shared. Political identity is a fluid and many-sided reality; identities can multiply and overlap. Nonetheless, a political community must in part be based on convergent conceptions of relations that unite its members. The members of the political community contribute to its definition but are also influenced by the actions, discourse, and symbols offered by political actors themselves. In the same way, members of the political community can contest the behaviour of the political elite, especially if it no longer accords with the articulated definitions of shared identity.

In what follows, we identify four key constitutional visions: the compact theory, asymmetrical federalism, nationalizing federalism, and the rights-based constitutional vision. For each, we attempt to delineate its bases of political identity and the social, economic, and political forces that underlie it. The four dimensions of the constitutional debate are not mutually exclusive; while at times they seem to be in irreconcilable conflict, there are also some interesting commonalities and links between them. Thus, while we will emphasize the different dimensions based on national identities and those based on rights-based identities, all of the modern nationalisms – Canadian, Québécois, and Aboriginal – have a significant rights component.

THE EQUALITY OF THE PROVINCES

From Confederation, the idea was put forth that the Canadian political regime should reflect an equality between the provinces and the federal government. This debate has largely been perceived as pitting centralizers against decentralizers. It should be noted, however, that beyond the legal parameters defining the powers of each order of government, it is the nature of the federation itself that has been debated. The notion of the equality of the provinces was articulated, as one would expect, by provincial politicians. The quest for provincial autonomy was, from the start, the cornerstone of their reasoning and their strategy for achieving political recognition. As Stevenson (1982) notes, in its most lasting version the approach stressing provincial autonomy took the form of the compact theory.

In this view, Canada is first and foremost the creation of the provinces. The "Fathers of Confederation" were the spokesmen of already existing political entities. Besides the representatives of Canada (present-day Ontario and Québec) as created by the Act of Union of 1841, there were delegates from the colonial provinces of the Maritimes, who wanted to protect the rights they had acquired from Great Britain. Hence, the very existence of the federal government itself could be attributed to the provinces.

On the political level, this notion of federalism refers to a relationship of equality between the two orders of government. Initially, on the constitutional front, this approach was inscribed in the classical notion of federalism. At least theoretically, it implies that each political entity (i.e., the provinces and the central government) is recognized as sovereign in its areas of jurisdiction and can act independently of the others. The creation of a federal system of government presupposes that the provinces had an independent existence prior to the creation of the new state. This was obviously the case in what would become Canada, even if the extension of Canadian territory and the addition of new provinces were almost exclusively the result of federal government actions. It is important here to note the primary argument that each order of government has the latitude to legislate in the jurisdictions granted by the constitution. In this sense, ac-

47

tions by the central government must be limited to the areas granted to it by the constitution. Where this is not the case, the provinces must give their explicit consent to all federal intrusions into provincial jurisdiction. Moreover, because the very existence of the federal regime is perceived as the result of a contract between pre-existing states, the original contract – the constitution – cannot be altered without obtaining the consent of all parties, i.e., all provinces.

At the economic and fiscal level, this conception of federalism implies that the provinces can count on a certain financial independence. This independence means not only that the provinces must have a fiscal base sufficient to allow them to meet their obligations in their areas of jurisdiction, but also that the benefits of the federation must be shared between the affluent and less affluent provinces.

The theory of the equality of the provinces is laden with consequences for the way the Canadian political community is perceived and, therefore, for the nature of the relations between the central government and the provinces. In this view, the provincial premiers have as much right to represent citizens as does the Canadian Prime Minister. In short, the total is not more or less than the sum of its parts. The first community of belonging is provincial. Thus, the central government is not in a position to speak for provincial interests.

From the beginning of Confederation, this approach led to the provincial rights movement. The Ontario Premier, Sir Oliver Mowat, who led the province from 1872 to 1896, was a defender of provincial autonomy. More preoccupied by provincial autonomy than by the need to reduce provincial inequalities, Mowat, as well as the premiers who followed him, stressed fiscal autonomy and the right to levy taxes and to spend without being subject to central government control (Armstrong, 1981).

A more contemporary expression of the compact theory is the effort to ensure that the political institutions of the central government better represent the provinces and that mechanisms favour a more equitable if not equal representation at the centre (Smiley and Watts, 1986). Thus, the provincial and regional diversity that characterizes Canada must be reflected in the composition of federal institutions as well as in how they operate. It is now the provinces outside of central Canada, particularly those west of Ontario, that want the central government to take their interests into account. While western alienation based on economic and political grievances is by no means new, many provinces currently are demanding a redefinition of Canadian political institutions. According to this view, because the recognition of diversity is a cornerstone of federalism, all of the provinces possess, by definition, a distinct nature that not only must be taken into account by the federal government but must also condition how the central government's institutions operate. Hence, it is not a question of granting special status to one province; this would deny the fact that Canada is created out of its diversity. Even at the symbolic level, how is it possible to recognize one of the partners as distinct without acknowledging that all other members of the federation are also, to varying degrees, distinct?

Adherents to the equality of provinces theory find little support in the British North America Act of 1867. For example, the number of senators was defined in terms of regional rather than provincial representation; representation in the House of Commons follows demographic distribution; the federal Parliament was granted the powers of reservation and disallowance, giving it a dominant role vis-à-vis the provincial legislatures. However, section 92 of the bna Act, which lists the jurisdictions exclusive to the provinces, does not make distinctions between provinces, thus strengthening compact theory.

In addition, the Constitution Act, 1982, in keeping with the practice of federalism over the past decades, has strengthened the conception of the formal equality of the provinces. The Charter of Rights and Freedoms as well as the amending formulas in the 1982 Act were based on the principle of provincial equality. The general amending formula does not grant a veto to any province; the Charter is applied to all governments, federal and provincial. Moreover, the possibility of negotiating federal-provincial agreements was always offered to all provinces, even though in reality Québec chiefly took advantage of this, notably in the areas of pensions, family allowances, health, and immigration. Thus, in part, the modern notion of the equality of the provinces was articulated as a reaction to numerous requests by the Québec government to obtain a *de jure* special status in the Canadian federation.

The tenacious political roots of the equal provinces view partly explains the defeat of the attempts of the Meech Lake and Charlottetown Accords to entrench recognition of Québec's distinct character in the constitution (Blais and Crête, 1991). In the same way, the rejection of the Charlottetown Accord by a majority of Canadians outside of Québec stemmed from the inability to modify substantially the institutions of the central government so that regional interests could be better represented, notably in terms of a Triple-E Senate that would have explicitly reflected the principle of the equality of the provinces (McRoberts, 1993a). First put forth by the political elite in the West, this vision seems to have become widespread and is now held by a majority of the Canadian population.

The equal provinces view was also expressed at the Citizens' Forum on Canada's Future (Spicer Commission). Initiated after the defeat of the Meech Lake Accord, it sought to take the pulse of the population on constitutional issues. While the Forum was ignored by francophone Quebecers, for many Canadians it appeared that there was no longer any reason to negotiate a special status for Québec that would give it privileges denied to other provinces. Special status cut against the concept of the equality of the provinces and would constitute a departure from fundamental Canadian values. For example, the following reflected the sentiments of many who expressed their views to the Commission: "Québec's continued presence in Confederation cannot be bought at the price of damaging or destroying those things they value most about the country, and in particular, must not be bought by sacrificing individual or provincial equality" (Canada, 1991: 53). These sentiments hardly differed from the results of public opinion polls. For example, In May of 1991 Gallup asked, "Would you prefer to keep Québec in Canada by giving it the power it requests, or should the federal government turn down these requests and risk Québec separating?" Between 61 per cent (Ontario) and 76 per cent (the Prairies) preferred to turn down Québec's requests. In the same way, a May, 1992, Gallup poll showed that except for Ontario, the proportion of the population of all the provinces who expressed their preference for a transfer of powers exceeded those who preferred the status quo. Interestingly, only 10 per cent wanted a transfer of powers from the provinces to the central government (*Gallup Report*, May 28, 1992).

In short, the vision of the Canadian political community that revolves around the notion of the equality of the provinces has its roots in federal-provincial relations. First put forth to promote provincial autonomy and to ensure that all constitutional changes would be ratified by the provinces, this vision subsequently changed to reflect the new dynamic of Canadian federalism, a dynamic that is not restricted to the political elite. Thus, the compact theory has expanded to reflect in a much more fundamental way a shared definition of the nature of the Canadian political community. In this sense, the provinces must possess the same powers in order to guarantee their capacity to act in their jurisdictions of responsibility. This vision is explicitly rooted, in a positive way, in the desire to take account of the profound diversity of Canada and thus the unique character of each province; in a more negative way, it is rooted in the desire to prevent Québec from receiving special powers.

THE DUALIST VISION

A second constitutional vision – dualism – views Confederation as a pact between the two founding nations. This vision, which many do not hesitate to qualify as mythical, refers to the bicultural character of Canada. Nevertheless, this approach continues to inform the debates on the nature of Canadian federalism and continues to pit Québec and Ottawa against each other.

The fact that Canada adopted a federal system is explained by the presence of two cultural, linguistic groups, demographically unequal but still geographically concentrated. Thus, following the conflicts and the political instability that characterized the Union government after 1840, it was acknowledged that only a federal system would be suitable for the marked regionalism of the Maritime provinces and also able to respond to the aspirations of Lower Canada. To use Lionel Groulx's words, it was the form of government best suited for a small population too diverse to merge, and it would allow for the greatest autonomy possible. Canada was thus more than a federation of provinces; it was also a federation of nationalities and beliefs. On this matter, the remarks of John A. Macdonald before the Canadian Assembly in 1865 are revealing. He recalled that while he had always preferred a legislative union, adopting a federal system was the condition required to gain the consent of Lower Canada. Hence:

> I have again and again stated in the House, that, if practicable, I thought a Legislative Union would be preferable.... But in looking at the subject in the Conference, and discussing the matter as we did, most unreservedly, and with a desire to arrive at a satisfactory conclusion, we found that such a system was impracticable. In the first place, it would not meet the assent of the people of Lower Canada, because they felt that in their peculiar position – being a minority with a different language, nationality and religion from the majority – in case of a junction with the other provinces, their institutions and their law might be assailed, and their ancestral associa-

tions, on which they prided themselves, attacked and prejudiced; it was found that any proposition which involved the absorption of the individuality of Lower Canada – if I may use the expression – would not be received with favour by her people. (Cited in Simeon and Robinson, 1990: 22.)

Macdonald therefore explicitly recognized that his unitary project met with opposition from French Canada, thus making it impractical. Moreover, in 1892 the Judicial Committee of the Privy Council (JCPC), in what has been considered by many to be a "True charter of Canadian federalism," put forth the constitutional basis of the compact theory:

The goal of the Act was not to merge the provinces into one nor to subordinate the provincial governments to a central authority, but to create a federal government in which they would all be represented and to which would be exclusively entrusted matters in which they shared a common interest, each province preserving its independence and its autonomy. (Cited in Patenaude, 1992: 8; our translation.)

Among other things, provincial autonomy sought to ensure not only that the cultural and linguistic diversity was recognized as one of the fundamental characteristics of Canada, but that it could also be protected by the Québec government. Section 133 of the BNA Act, which deals with the use of language in the Canadian and Québec legislatures and in the courts, and section 93, which gives the provinces autonomy in education, are two examples. As well, the recognition of the two legal traditions in Canada (common law and civil law) confirmed the distinct nature of Québec.

However, it was only with the Quiet Revolution and the emergence of modern Québec nationalism that the two nations thesis took full force. While Premier Maurice Duplessis was an advocate of provincial autonomy, the position of the Lesage government on constitutional matters marked a deep change in perception and strategy. Thus, political autonomy was seen less as a means of limiting the growing presence of the central government in provincial jurisdictions than as a means for the political, economic and social restoration of francophone Québec. The autonomist discourse thus took on a new tone, marked by the need to affirm the fact that only Québec was in a position to protect and promote the interests of French Canadians because it was the only state in which they constituted a majority. Historically, French Canadians saw themselves as being members of a minority in Canada, but this unavoidable reality was now associated with a political project that translated into a desire to increase — and no longer simply to preserve — the capacity of the Québec state to act. Jean Lesage linked the place of Québec in the federation to the problem of the survival and development of French Canadians. From this time on the question was raised of revising the division of powers and of studying the relations between the two ethnic groups that made up Canada. In response to the question, "What does Québec want?" Daniel Johnson, the Union Nationale Premier who took power in 1966, gave the following answer:

> As the base of operations of a nation, it wants to be the master of the decisions that deal with the human growth of its citizens (that is, education, social security, and health in all its forms), with their economic affirmation (that is, the power to establish the economic and financial levers they believe necessary), with their cultural flourishing (that is, not only arts and literature, but also language) and with the extension of the Québécois community (that is, relations with some countries and international organizations). (Québec, 1966: 2-3; our translation)

This approach, stressing one of the dimensions, would be followed by all Québec governments, from Robert Bourassa to René Lévesque's "beau risque" (Rocher, 1992).

Québec's pursuit of special status has never been presented as a desire to deny the specific character or the multitude of interests in the rest of Canada. Rather, dualism can be seen as the pursuit of a status allowing a minority community to have the political and economic instruments likely to guarantee its development. The reasoning is relatively easy to understand: the Québec government is the only one where francophones can constitute a majority. Everywhere else in Canada, including the federal government, which became sensitive to this issue following the report of the Royal Commission on Bilingualism and Biculturalism, francophones are a minority facing, in many cases, indifference if not hostility. In this context, it is not surprising that francophone Quebecers identify themselves with the Québec government. Their adherence to the federal system was based on practical reasoning, what Robert Bourassa called "profitable federalism" in the early 1970s. At a strictly logical level, there are no contradictions between being Québécois and Canadian at the same time, on the condition that the federal system demonstrates enough flexibility to accommodate the Québécois identity.

Whether by a more general decentralization of powers or by the granting of special status – what is called asymmetrical federalism – Québec has continuously sought to increase its room to manoeuvre. Contrary to many of the opinions expressed to the Spicer Commission in the early 1990s, the commissioners themselves emphasized that the uneasiness felt with respect to Québec was essentially attributable to a "dangerous lack of knowledge of each other" (Canada, 1991: 123). Moreover, they latched onto the idea of the equality of provinces, which does not convey either the complexity of the Canadian political reality or the recognition in the constitution of the specific needs of many provinces, including Québec. This is why they stated that "[g]iven that provinces have entered Confederation on different terms and operate under different provisions, we believe that special arrangements in provinces based on special needs are a fundamental principle of Canadian federalism. This principle would apply where needed to all provinces" (ibid.: 124). It appears nevertheless that this necessity creates problems in Canada. Beyond the division of powers, the symbolism associated with the definition of the Canadian political community that is at issue. Must Canada be perceived as a practical arrangement in order to accommodate its communities or must it be based on a common definition of values, taken here in its uniform meaning, leaving little room for implementation that could vary from one community to the other according to their own needs?

Many people have linked the survival of the Canadian federation to its ability to adapt to profound diversity. In this view, asymmetry seems to be the path to follow (Resnick, 1991; Taylor, 1991; McRoberts, 1993b). Others, however, have stressed the impossibility of coming to a compromise on the basis of this principle (Dufour, 1992; Monière, 1992; Bariteau et al., 1992). This acknowledgement was at the root of the Parti Québécois plan for sovereignty-association at the end of the 1970s. In its 1979 White Paper, the PQ drew up a highly negative account of the Canadian experience. It claimed that francophones had not been perceived as a society with their own history, culture, and aspirations. Assimilation, stated the authors of the document, had always been the driving force of the rest of Canada with respect to francophones. Hence, the history of federalism since 1867 was one of the invasion of provincial jurisdictions by the central government. The White Paper explained this centralizing tendency by the fact that it responded to the aspirations of the rest of Canada, which saw in the central government the principal instrument of development. This tendency had its roots in the fact that the BNA Act favoured the expansion of the central government by granting it all powers not explicitly given to the provinces and by further bestowing it financial resources not granted to the provinces. Thus, the desire of Québec governments to resist this tendency has led to permanent conflicts between Québec and Ottawa. The "renewed federalism" advocated by English Canada would mean only superficial alterations of the role and powers of the central government. The reforms would not lead to the recognition of the Québécois "nation," nor would they give Québec a special place in the federation.

More than a decade later, the work of the Commission on the Political and Constitutional Future of Québec (popularly known as the Bélanger-Campeau Commission), created following the defeat of the Meech Lake Accord, arrived at the same conclusions. The Commission's report, retracing the evolution of the Canadian constitutional debate, noted the consequences of the Constitution Act of 1982 for Québec. It reinforced the political vision of the Canadian political community, which was irreconcilable with the effective recognition and political expression of the Québécois identity. Three dimensions of this new Canadian identity were given: the equality of all citizens, which does not allow special constitutional recognition for the Québécois collectivity; the equality of cultures and of cultural origins in Canada, which would undermine the French language and the cultural origins of francophones; and the equality of the provinces, which would forestall the granting of special status for Québec (Québec, 1991).

The question asked by Québec since the mid-1960s refers not only to a symbolic recognition of its distinct nature but also to the capacity to act in order to assure the development of its society. In this, it is opposed to the centralizing logic that has driven federal constitutional plans since 1968. The decentralization of powers or asymmetry is seen as the necessary condition to take account of the deep diversity of Canada.

Arguments favouring asymmetry have not only been put forth by francophone Quebecers. Aboriginal groups have also lately demanded the recognition of their difference in the constitution. Centred on the notion of the inherent right to self-government, the asymmetry demanded by the Aboriginal groups refers to a different conception of the political community as defined elsewhere in Canada. The mobilization of Aboriginals "is characterized by an emerging sense of nationalism which presents a number of challenges to traditional notions about the nation-state in Canada.... [including] the legitimacy of a constitutional order based upon a division of powers between the federal Parliament and the provincial Legislatures" (Jhappan, 1993: 232). The nation in question here is based on cultural, ethnic, linguistic, historic, and territorial characteristics, and because of these unique characteristics Canada's Native peoples seek powers to manage their social, economic and cultural institutions. Moreover, in contrast to the disagreement between Québec and Ottawa, which is framed in terms of the traditional discourse of federalism, the Aboriginal nations want a new order of government in the constitution, although its institutions, powers, and financing remain to be defined.

The rise of a pan-Aboriginal nationalism has rendered obsolete the dualist vision of Canada. More and more people now contrast the concept of two nations to that of three (or many) nations. This discourse recalls that the Aboriginals occupied the territory well before the Europeans arrived and that they must be considered as the First Nations and, in many ways, as much more distinct than other communities in Canada. Thus, Aboriginal claims have greatly altered our understanding of the idea of asymmetry. Viewed from an Aboriginal perspective, it is less a question of the devolution of powers from the central government to already existing political entities than of the creation of a new order that would force the federal and provincial governments to recast the government of Aboriginal communities.

In summary, whether for francophone Quebecers or for Aboriginal peoples, the idea of asymmetry extends well beyond the legal dimensions of the division of powers or of the institutional dimension related to changes to federal political institutions. A new division of powers – decentralization or special status for Québec or the First Nations – is but the reflection of the need to recognize that some communities, because of their minority status, may need particular political levers to ensure their development. This has been contested by the central government, for whom the state must above all be of service to all citizens, regardless of their differences. The community approach favoured by adherents of one form of asymmetry or another is contrasted with the equality of individuals and the universal nature of state action.

A NATIONALIZING VISION

The nationalizing vision of Canadian federalism and the constitution, like asymmetrical federalism and the compact theory, is founded on a territorially based political identity. In this case, the territorial base is Canada itself, and in this view the nation is more than the sum of its parts. As this privileges the federal level of government, a nationalizing constitutional vision tends also to be centralizing. Based on a Canadian political identity, nationalizing federalism seeks to deny other sources of political identity, particularly those based on region, province, or Québec or Aboriginal nationalism. In terms of historical development, there are at least three different versions of the nationalizing vision: the original view of the Fathers of Confederation; that of the English-Canadian social democrats of the thirties, whose political and economic project for an interventionist state was based on a nationalizing federalism; and, by far the best known version of centralized federalism, the Trudeau Liberal view during the 1970s and early 1980s that culminated in the patriation and amendment of the constitution in 1982. We will deal with each in turn.

It is believed that the Fathers of Confederation favoured a centralized federalism in which, in MacDonald's view, the provincial governments would be nothing more than glorified municipal governments. As MacDonald put it, in avoiding the mistakes made in the design of the U.S. constitution, "We should thus have a powerful Central Government, a powerful Central Legislature, and a decentralized system of minor legislatures for local purposes" (cited in Waite, 1963: 156). While the BNA Act itself is an ambiguous document, the result of political negotiation and political compromise, we can find evidence that the federal government was intended to be the senior level of government and that the Fathers of Confederation (or some of them at any rate) expected that power within the federation would be relatively centralized. For example, the federal level of government was given the unlimited power to tax and spend while the provincial governments had their financial hands tied by the original Act. The federal government appointed the lieutenant-governor of each province, who in turn had the power to reserve provincial legislation for a year after its passage by the provincial assembly. Such legislation could then be disallowed by the federal government. All residual powers were given to the federal government under the original Act. The political purpose of this vision of Confederation and this view of nationalizing federalism was nation–building. The federal government had to be the stronger level of government to ensure that the economic and political project of creating a new state in British North America would be successful (Simeon and Robinson, 1992).

A second version of centralized federalism developed in English Canada during the Great Depression. Like the first version, this view argued that the federal level of government needed to have certain powers in the interests of all Canadians. However, the economic and political agenda of the nationalizers during the thirties was quite distinct from that of the Fathers of Confederation. The liberal-left social democrats of the thirties favoured centralizing power in the federal government to enable the Canadian state to intervene in the economy and society in such a way as to alleviate some of the worst effects of the Great Depression and to get Canada back on the road to economic recovery (Scott, 1989). Thus, these nationalizers were very critical of the decisions of Canada's highest constitutional court at the time – the JCPC – which consistently placed key elements of social policy and the modern welfare state in provincial jurisdiction. Criticism of the JCPC reached a head when the JCPC struck down the so-called Bennett "New Deal" as *ultra vires* federal jurisdiction in 1935. English-Canadian critics of the JCPC argued that it was tying the hands of the federal government and preventing it from acting in the face of the economic catastrophe of the Great Depression (*ibid.*).

A third version of nationalizing federalism arose during the seventies and early eighties as the Trudeau Liberals responded to the rise of Québec nationalism and the election of the Parti Québécois in 1976. This version was the first explicitly to include the concept of citizenship as part of its vision. In this view, Canadian political identity overrode regional and national political identities. In part, this type of federalism and the view of political identity on which it was based were aimed at other political identities that were competing with the federal government for citizen loyalties, in particular Québec nationalism and the centrifugal forces of regionalism that were particularly strong during the province-building seventies.

According to the nationalizing vision, then, the federal government could act against the will of the provinces who were the guardians of narrow regional interests. This constitutional vision was strongly opposed to any kind of special status or asymmetrical federalism. Concretely, certain policies accompanied this view. First, the Trudeau government pursued a broad range of economic policies, from the National Energy Program to the Foreign Investment Review Agency, designed to strengthen the hand of the federal government but also to "Canadianize" the economy. As in the two previous historical iterations of nationalizing federalism, once more there was a link between nation-building and the centralization of power in the hands of the federal government. The Liberal government's policies were relatively interventionist, thus recalling the social democrats' critiques of a powerless federal government of the thirties. Once again, economic nationalism went hand in hand with centralized federalism.

On the constitutional front, Trudeau's nationalizing federalism was specifically aimed against the centrifugal forces of regionalism, province-building, and Québec nationalism. The 1982 Constitution Act reflects this vision both in its content (especially the Canadian Charter of Rights and Freedoms) and in the process by which the constitution was patriated. At various points of negotiating the constitutional amendment of 1982, the Trudeau government threatened to proceed with constitutional change unilaterally, without the consent of the provinces. In doing so, Trudeau appealed explicitly "over the heads" of the provinces to the people. This strategy stressed the symbolic dimension of the federal government's role as the sole government of all Canadians and depicted the provinces as spoilers in the system. In making this appeal, the Trudeau government attempted to undercut the provinces and to solidify citizens' loyalty to the federal level of government. Finally, the Trudeau government did patriate and amend the constitution in ways that fundamentally affected provincial powers and did so without the consent of one of the provinces – Québec. The Trudeau government offered the nationalizing constitutional vision as a defence of this move – that a "separatist" government of Québec would never have signed the 1982 constitution in any case and that the federal Liberal Party represented the interests of Québec. Hence, the Trudeau Liberals argued that the 1982 constitutional change was legitimate, even without the consent of Québec (Banting and Simeon, 1983; Cairns, 1991; McWhinney, 1982).

In addition to the process of constitutional change, the substance of the 1982 constitution to some extent reflected the nationalizing vision. In particular, the Charter of Rights was intended to cement the attachment of Canadians to the federal level of government as the grantor and guarantor of the rights contained in the Charter. All Canadians enjoyed these rights equally, thus strengthening national sentiment. Of course, the Charter also contained specific rights protections for particular groups in addition to guarantees of equality of individual rights. In particular, the nationalizing vision of Trudeau included a strong commitment to the equality of the two official language communities in Canada, especially in terms of access to federal government services in the official language of choice and also to official language minority educational rights. This bilingual dimension of the nationalizing vision was entrenched in section 23 of the Charter of Rights, which rendered parts of Québec's Charter of the French Language (Bill 101) unconstitutional. The nationalizers thereby asserted federal intervention in matters of language policy, reflecting their view that the federal level of government, as the government of "all Canadians," could provide for and guarantee (through the Supreme Court of Canada) official language rights throughout Canada. That this section of the Charter interfered with Québec's ability to set is own course in language policy was one of the main reasons why Québec did not accept the 1982 constitutional deal.

The nationalizing dynamic had a major impact on the Meech Lake and Charlottetown debates. In fact, the "nationalizers" were critical in galvanizing opposition to both Accords. For example, in Meech, the provisions for provincial input into the selection of senators and Supreme Court justices and the potential for decentralization in the clauses governing opting out and the spending power were seen as preventing the future adoption of new shared-cost programs. The distinct society clause was viewed as potentially undermining Charter rights and as giving special protections to collective rights. The distinct society clause seemed to give political weight to the great political enemy of the nationalizers – regional dynamics and Québec nationalism. By privileging Québec nationalism, the clause created backlash regional demands in the rest of the country. Of course, by privileging Québec to begin with, the clause cut at the very heart of the nationalizers' goal – the strengthening of Canadian national identity rather than the particularistic identities of Québec and other provinces. The tension between the nationalizing vision and the decentralizing vision of Meech could be seen in the opposition of Trudeau himself to the Meech Lake Accord (Trudeau, 1989).

In the Charlottetown Accord, this vision once again animated at least some of its detractors, especially those who felt that, once again, the federal government would be weakened by the potential transfers of power to the provinces, by the potential limitations on the federal spending power, and by the potential weakening of the Charter of Rights by the Canada clause, which included a scaled-down version of the distinct society clause (Rebick, 1993: 102-06).

As the Fathers of Confederation were interested in state-building and wanted to make sure that the federal government had the tools necessary to accomplish this task, so, too, the social democrats of the thirties were concerned with the state-building – in their case, the modern Keynesian welfare state. For the Trudeau Liberals, state-building and even nation-building were the goal, in this case, against the threats of regionalism and Québec nationalism. In all three instances, the core of this vision of the constitution has not been just the privileging of the national level of government (hence "centralized federalism") but also the political project that accompanies it, which in all cases had at its roots the project of creating or expanding the federal state, not just for economic and social reasons, but also as the symbolic cradle of national citizenship.

RIGHTS-BASED CONSTITUTIONAL VISIONS

The rights-based constitutional dimension is the most recent to arise in the constitutional debate because it has its origins in the 1982 Charter of Rights. This dimension differs from the other three in that it is not based on a territorial political identity but, as its name implies, on the basis of rights. Rather than anchoring a constitutional vision in a territorially defined political identity such as nation or province, the rights-based approach anchors its vision in individuals and groups as rights-bearers and envisions the constitution as a mechanism for entrenching and protecting rights rather than national or territorial identities and interests. As well, the rights in question are often based on political identities such as race and gender that have traditionally had little place, if any, in either Canadian politics generally or constitutional politics specifically.

The rights-bearers stake their claim to constitutional participation on the basis of the rights that they hold as individuals and as members of groups, such as racial or ethnic minorities, Aboriginal peoples, and women. As Alan Cairns has pointed out, these groups have been brought into the constitutional conversation in part by the Charter of Rights and Freedoms (Cairns, 1991b). Although the Trudeau Liberal government had proposed a constitutionally entrenched bill of rights during the Victoria Charter constitutional round in 1971, the government's 1980 proposal for a restricted bill of rights served to galvanize ethnic minority groups and the women's movement into the constitutional fight. Of course, Aboriginal peoples were involved in the 1982 round both on the issue of the Charter and on many issues connected quite precisely to their unique status. The women's movement and ethnic minorities were deeply implicated in the process leading to the patriation of the constitution in 1982 and succeeded in achieving stronger protection for women's rights and the rights of racial and ethnic minorities than would otherwise have been the case. This was the first constitutional recognition of the importance of the rights-bearers and it gave these groups both the constitutional recognition and the constitutional foothold that ensured their further involvement in constitutional amendments.

There are several different versions of the rights-based constitutional vision, some of which overlap with and reinforce the territorially based political identities already discussed. First, the Trudeau nationalizing vision of the Canadian constitution contains a significant rights component. This has put a new twist on an old idea by giving some constitutional content to Canadian identity. For some constitutional actors, Canadian identity is now based on "equal rights," that is, the idea that all Canadians have the same individual rights. To put it another way, according to this view, all Canadians have become individual rights-bearers and constitutional proposals that would somehow threaten or minimize these equal rights are seen as a threat to Canadian identity. Once again, this dimension was at work in the opposition to the distinct society clause in the Meech Lake Accord and to the Canada clause in the Charlottetown Accord.

A second rights-based dimension emphasizes collective rights, such as the rights of women, minorities, and Aboriginal peoples. These are the groups that struggled for constitutional recognition in the 1982 constitutional round and who became increasingly important actors in the constitutional process over the course of the eighties. For these groups, the protection and expansion of their rights in the constitution are paramount. Unlike the territorially based political identities, these identities represent the politicization of non-territorial cleavages in Canadian society and the entry of non-territorial equality concerns into constitutional discourse. These rights-based constitutional actors can be linked to the nationalizers. They see the role of the federal government as very important because only it can create a level playing field for equality-seeking groups throughout the whole country. For these groups, the federal level of government is the natural one at which to seek redress, in part because the Charter itself is a federal creation but also because these new constitutional actors represent cleavages that are nation-wide and non-territorial, thus politicizing new constitutional cleavages. Their vision of the constitution is that their political identities are paramount and that anything that could potentially undermine the rights they gained in the 1982 constitution and in the Charter of Rights, in particular, cannot be supported. Thus, this constitutional vision gives primacy to the Charter of Rights, although major organizations representing both the women's movement and Canada's ethnic communities have developed positions on many other constitutional issues. For these groups, the protection of their existing Charter rights is paramount.

A third type of rights-based constitutional discourse ties collective rights to national communities. In the Aboriginal case, these rights-bearers are potentially tied to a "three nations" view, as the rights they claim are at times national or collective rather than individual. In the case of Québec, the defence of collective rights is clearly linked to nation.

Thus, at certain points during the debate, it appears that non-Canadian nationalisms (Québécois and Aboriginal) are potentially threatening to the rights-bearers. If nation is the primary political identity and if nationalisms are given pride of place in constitution-writing and in constitutional politics, then the other cleavages of Canadian society and the interests they reflect and represent will tend to be suppressed in the name of the nation. So it was with the Meech Lake Accord when the women's movement in English Canada worried that the distinct society clause might be used to undercut women's rights, and with the Charlottetown Accord when both racial and ethnic minorities and the women's movement were concerned that the Canada clause created a hierarchy of rights because, seemingly, it gave stronger protection to linguistic minority language communities and to the protection of Québec's distinct society than to the rights-bearers. In this way, rights have come to conflict with nationalisms in the Canadian constitutional debate.

On the other hand, it is important to note the common links as well as the tensions between rights and nationalisms as sources of political identity in the constitutional debate. We have already suggested the link between the nationalizers with their territorially-based political identities and the rights-based vision centred on equal individual rights for all Canadians. This is an example of the way in which nationalism and the rights-based constitutional dimensions can work together. Another case would be the women's movement and Aboriginal claims oriented around either collective rights or Aboriginal nationalism. Rather than pitting rights claimants against nationalism, in this case, the English-Canadian women's movement has developed a "three nations" position that attempts to accommodate nationalisms within an equality-seeking strategy and discourse.

CONCLUSION

Although current classifications of Canadian federalism are valuable, they tend to stress institutional aspects (intrastate vs. interstate federalism) or historical aspects (from emergency federalism to executive federalism), while too often forgetting that these dimensions reflect more fundamental constraints. Canada's contemporary political dilemma goes beyond the constitutional question. Along with divergent views of the constitution, there are also, perhaps to a greater extent, divergent conceptions of the Canadian political community. The four dimensions of the constitutional debate identified above are always present in Canada. The notions of the equality of the provinces (compact theory), of the equality of national communities, of a political community that subsumes differences, or of the recognition of particular identities are engaged in an endless struggle from which there can emerge no winner. Each vision is held by important groups who are players in the constitutional debate. Each of these groups offers its own conception of the Canadian political community and of the elements that comprise its identity.

If the constitutional debate was simply about legal and institutional rearrangements, these differences eventually could be worked out. Negotiations would pit players who know the rules of the game against each other, as in the industrial relations world where negotiations take place as if the final result will be halfway between the demands of each party. However, it is very different when it is a matter of agreeing on matters of political identity. It is difficult to compromise about issues and interests that have come to be defined as affecting one's core political identity. Thus, the conflict between nationalisms as well as the new conflict between collective rights-bearers and nationalisms is a very thorny one to resolve. Whatever one might think of "politics as usual," even for groups willing to participate in the traditional political process, such an approach quickly degenerates into non-compromisable political positions. Unlike the jurisdictional conflict, political identity is not divisible; therefore, it is inherently difficult, if not impossible, to negotiate, bargain, or compromise.

REFERENCES

Armstrong, Christopher (1981). *The Politics of Federalism: Ontario's Relations with the Federal Government, 1867-1942.* Toronto: University of Toronto Press.

Banting, Keith, and Richard Simeon, eds. (1983). And No One Cheered: Federalism, Democracy and the Constitution. Toronto: Methuen.

Bariteau, Claude, et al. (1992). *Les objections de 20 spécialistes aux offres fédérales.* Montréal: Éditions Saint-Martin.

Blais, André, and Jean Crête (1991). "Pourquoi l'opinion publique au Canada a-t-elle rejeté l'Accord du lac Meech?" in R. Hudon et R. Pelletier, eds., *L'engagement intellectuel. Mélanges en l'honneur de Léon Dion.* Sainte-Foy: Presses de l'Université Laval: 385-400.

Cairns, Alan C. (1991a). "An Overview of the Trudeau Constitutional Proposals," in Cairns, *Disruptions: Constitutional Struggles, from the Charter to Meech Lake,* edited by Douglas E. Williams. Toronto: McClelland & Stewart: 58-67.

Cairns, Alan C. (1991b). "Citizens (Outsiders) and Governments (Insiders) in Constitution-Making: The Case of Meech Lake," in Cairns, *Disruptions:* 108-38.

Canada (1991). *Citizens' Forum on Canada's Future.*

Dufour, Christian (1992). *La rupture tranquille.* Montréal: Boréal, 1992.

Jhappan, C. Radha (1993). "Inherency, Three Nations and Collective Rights: the Evolution of Aboriginal Constitutional Discourse from 1982 to the Charlottetown Accord," *International Journal of Canadian Studies,* No. 7-8 (Spring-Fall).

Mallory, J.R. (1977). "Five Faces of Federalism," in J. Peter Meekison, ed., *Canadian Federalism: Myth or Reality?* Third Edition. Toronto: Methuen: 19-30.

McRoberts, Kenneth (1993a). "Disagreeing on Fundamentals: English Canada and Quebec," in Kenneth McRoberts and Patrick Monahan, eds., *The Charlottetown Accord, the Referendum, and the Future of Canada.* Toronto: University of Toronto Press: 249-63.

McRoberts, Kenneth (1993b). "English-Canadian Perceptions of Quebec," in A.-G. Gagnon, ed., *Québec. State and Society,* Second Edition. Scarborough: Nelson, 116-29.

McWhinney, E. (1982). *Canada and the Constitution, 1979-1982.* Toronto: University of Toronto Press.

Monière, Denis. (1992). L'indépendance. Montréal: Québec/Amérique.

Patenaude, Pierre (1992). "LAO," in Patenaude, ed., Québec-communauté française de Belgique: autonomie et spécificité dans le cadre du système fédéral. Montréal: Wilson & Lafleur.

Québec (1966). Déclaration de l'Honorable Daniel Johnson. Quatrième réunion du comité fiscal. 14 et 15 septembre.

Québec, Commission sur l'avenir politique et constitutionnel du Québec (1991). *L'avenir politique et constitutionnel du Québec*. Saint-Romuald: Imprimerie St-Romuald.

Rebick, Judy (1993). "The Charlottetown Accord: A Faulty Framework and a Wrong-headed Compromise," in McRoberts and Monahan, eds., *The Charlottetown Accord*: 102-06.

Resnick, Philip (1991). *Toward a Canada-Québec Union*. Montreal and Kingston: McGill-Queen's University Press.

Rocher, François (1992). "Le Québec et la Constitution: une valse à mille temps," in Rocher, ed., *Bilan québécois du fédéralisme canadien*. Montréal: VLB éditeur: 20-57.

Russell, Peter (1993). *Constitutional Odyssey*. Toronto: University of Toronto Press.

Scott, F.R. (1989). "Centralization and Decentralization in Canadian Federalism," in Garth Stevenson, ed., *Federalism in Canada: Selected Readings*. Toronto: McClelland & Stewart: 52-61.

Simeon, Richard, and Ian Robinson (1992). *State, Society and the Development of Canadian Federalism*. Toronto: University of Toronto Press.

Smiley, Donald V. and Ronald L. Watts (1986). *Intrastate Federalism in Canada*. Toronto: University of Toronto Press.

Stevenson, Garth (1982). *Unfulfilled Union*. Toronto: Gage.

Taylor, Charles (1991). "Shared and Divergent Values," in R.L. Watts and D.M. Brown, eds., *Options for a New Canada*. Toronto: University of Toronto Press.

Trudeau, Pierre (1989). "Who speaks for Canada?" in Michael Behiels, ed., *The Meech Lake Primer: Conflicting Views of the 1987 Constitutional Accord*. Ottawa: University of Ottawa Press.

Waite, P.B., ed. (1963). *The Confederation Debates in the Province of Canada*. Toronto and Montreal: McClelland & Stewart.

CHAPTER THREE

The Unsolvable Constitutional Crisis

Jennifer Smith

THE REFERENDUM ON THE CHARLOTTETOWN ACCORD, HELD on October 26, 1992, produced a decisive No. The size of the No majorities in the Yukon and six of the provinces ranged from a mere 51.1 per cent in Nova Scotia to a startling 68 per cent in British Columbia. In Native communities, No majorities were larger than anyone had been led to expect. On the other hand, the heftiest Yes majorities were confined to the three least populous provinces and the Northwest Territories, while in the most populous province, Ontario, Yes votes edged past No votes by a hair.[1]

In the context of liberal democratic politics, results like these are unambiguous. To suggest otherwise is either creative interpretation or wishful thinking (Tully, 1994). But the results are not very easy to explain. What was it about the Charlottetown Accord that so many voters disliked? The Accord was a comprehensive and complex document that contained an array of constitutional proposals touching everything from the division of powers between Parliament and the provincial legislatures to Native self-government, to a series of commitments on economic and social matters. In this paper I deal exclusively with the distinct society and other provisions of the Canada clause and the representation rules of the Senate and the House of Commons because these are the matters on which so many Canadians focused their attention. My argument is that their resistance to these provisions can be understood to be shrewd and intelligent. In other words, they zeroed in on proposals that mattered a great deal, and in doing so evinced a sounder sense of constitutionalism than the authors of the Accord.

The other side of the coin, which I also want to stress, is that these authors demonstrated too little in the way of what might be called a constitutional sensibility. There are two crucial things to notice about a constitution. One is that it supplies the decision-making rules under which political institutions operate. If a constitution is to endure, these rules must reflect principles of justice or a mix of competing principles arranged in the form of a compromise acceptable to the political forces in play and therefore reasonably consistent with their political position. The result cannot be a mere record of the heft of the contending political forces, since that might amount to no compromise and a single, dominant principle favouring one party. Neither can it be unhinged from or unanchored in political realities – up in the sky, so to speak, with no support other than someone's dreamy theorizing. There needs to be a balance, and the authors of the Accord were unable to strike it. They could not get the right adjustment of competing principles, certainly not one acceptable to enough Canadians. Indeed, it is not even clear that they were thinking about the proper mix of principles, because if they were they never said so. Instead, they were mired in *ad hoc* responses to the competing demands of the leading interests of the day.

The other point about a constitution is that not everything is fit to put into it. Once the shape and the powers of the institutions of government and the rights and freedoms of individuals are covered, there is not a whole lot more. To decide what is fit for a constitution and what is not requires a theory of constitutions (Ajzenstat, 1993). Lacking, it appears, both a theory of constitutions and a sense of how to mix principles in the formulation of decision-making rules, the authors of the Accord made two serious errors in judgment. One was to underestimate just how settled some of the decision-making rules of the constitution already are, and why that is so. The other was to pursue a new type of language in the constitution, a language of evaluation of specified groups, thereby abandoning explicitly what many would regard as constitutional neutrality. The second of these two errors was the spectacular feature of the Meech Lake round of constitutional negotiations that preceded the Charlottetown round, and so it is necessary to turn first to Meech Lake.

THE MEECH LAKE ACCORD

In 1982 the Canadian constitution was buttressed by the addition of the Constitution Act, 1982, which contains, among other things, the Charter of Rights and Freedoms and a general amending formula. The Charter was an immediate hit with almost everyone in the country except an insignificant number who doubted the wisdom of entrenching rights in the first place and the infinitely more important nationalists in Québec, whose party happened to be the governing party of the province at the time. In an important, symbolic gesture of disapproval the Premier, René Lévesque, refused to sign on the dotted line. Ever since, or at least since 1984, when the federal Progressive Conservative Party took office, the federal government pursued Québec's signature with tenacity (Simeon, 1990).

The first opportunity arose when the Québec Liberal Party, under the leadership of Robert Bourassa, defeated the incumbent government in the provincial election in December, 1985. The Liberal Party had worked out the conditions of its acceptance of the revised constitution, and these included an explicit recognition of Québec "comme foyer d'une société distincte et pierre d'assise de l'élément francophone de la dualité canadienne" (Cook, 1989: 151). In a speech at Mont Gabriel in May of the following year, the new Intergovernmental Affairs Minister, Gil Rémillard, formally outlined five conditions: constitutional recognition of Québec as a distinct society; increased powers for Québec over immigration; limitation of the federal spending power; changes to the amending formula that would strengthen Québec's hand in future amendments; and participation in the appointment of judges to the Supreme Court of Canada (Leslie, 1987). In the round of negotiations that followed, the Québec government skilfully parleyed these conditions into the text of the Meech Lake Accord. But they were not unmodified.

Under the terms of Canada's amending formula, the agreement of Parliament and of all the provincial legislatures is required for changes to specified items, including the amending formula itself and the composition of the Supreme Court. This meant that the other provincial leaders, no matter how sympathetic they might be to Québec's demands, were operating from an irresistibly strong position, particularly if Québec's requirements were treated as a package, one and indivisible, which they were. Moreover, the federal government was anxious to get an agreement. It is hardly surprising, then, that in the course of negotiations Québec's conditions, where possible, were transformed into provincial gains. The exception, of course, was the distinct society clause, which by definition resisted nation-wide application.

The distinct society clause of the Meech Lake Accord would have required the constitution to be interpreted in accordance with "the recognition that Quebec constitutes within Canada a distinct society." The role of the Québec government and legislature to preserve and promote this distinct identity was affirmed. Another interpretive clause described the French- and English-speaking components of the country as "a fundamental characteristic" and affirmed the role of Parliament and the provincial legislatures to preserve it (Canada, 1987a). The twofold effect of these section 2 clauses – they were meant to be located in section 2 of the Constitution Act, 1867 – was to distinguish one society and to underline the centrality of linguistic dualism. In popular debate, these clauses were not usually treated separately, although when they were, those who opposed the one often opposed the other. The phrase "distinct society" proved to be a handy surrogate for the section as a whole (Canada, 1987b: 32). Indeed, as a lightning rod for everything that was wrong with the Accord, the distinct society clause was in a class by itself. Why?

In his study of the use of symbols in politics, Murray Edelman wrote: "It is characteristic of large numbers of people in our society that they see and think in terms of stereotypes, personalization, and oversimplifications, that they cannot recognize or tolerate ambiguous and complex situations, and that they accordingly respond chiefly to symbols that oversimplify and distort" (1967: 31). On this account it can be argued that in the distinct society clause, the federal government found itself in the worst possible situation, that is, backing an ambiguous constitutional clause with Janus-faced symbolic effects – good in much of French-speaking Québec, bad almost everywhere else. Precisely because of its ambiguity, people could read into the clause either their fears or their hopes. Of course, there was no way that the federal government could dispel the problem without worsening the division. This is illustrated easily by the question of whom the distinct society in Québec was meant to include. There were only two logical possibilities: everyone in the province, or the francophone majority alone. Since the first answer was guaranteed an unwelcome reception among the majority and the second among the minority, leading supporters of the Accord naturally retreated from logical rigour (Canada, 1987b: 41) and critics had a field day (Cook, 1989: 15-20; Breton, 1988: 7; Schwartz, 1987: 8-9).

The definitional question had an immediacy for putative members of the distinct society in Québec. Elsewhere, people persisted in debating the implications of both the distinct society and linguistic duality clauses for themselves, that is, for their own standing in the national political community. Again, the debate was fuelled by ambiguity, and the federal government was hardly better off. To take an obvious example, people hotly debated whether the distinct society clause did or did not confer additional powers on the Québec government and legislature to preserve and promote the distinctness. Critics feared it did while advocates either did not care or certainly hoped so. Faced with this dilemma, the federal government was able to avoid an answer by retreating into the fog of the "interpretive" clause, which essentially means that ultimately the courts will decide the matter. Thus ambiguity persisted, and the clause remained a source of reassurance to some and a threat to many. In the end, the perception of threat was widespread among English-speaking Canadians.

There are a number of explanations of the hostility, beginning with prejudice, and no doubt there was some of that.[2] A better explanation is rooted in Edelman's comment, cited above, on the difficulties many people have when they encounter complex or ambiguous situations. Preferring clarity, they scan for cues, which turn out to be easily available because the political value and legal potential of symbolic statements are widely appreciated by political actors (Breton, 1988: 10). Thus in the public debate about an ambiguously worded constitutional clause, groups battle one another over definition. The winner of the definitional debate is the one whose interpretation comes to be accepted by the majority of the public, as determined, say, in an opinion poll. Members of the public need not follow the intricacies of an argument supporting a particular interpretation in order to accept the normative gist of it. They only need to know that there is an argument in which their own doubts, however vague, can be articulated.

In the case of the Accord, opponents of the section 2 clauses on distinct society and linguistic duality won the definitional debate hands down. Their point was that these clauses were somehow potential threats to people's rights and/or status. On the question of rights, for example, various women's organizations measured the potential weight of both clauses against gender equality rights in the Charter and concluded on the basis of close textual analyses that they posed a real threat to gender rights (L. Smith, 1988; Greschner, 1988). Although these critics were interested primarily in gender equality rights, the argument they made was easily applicable to the equality rights of other minorities and, ultimately, to Charter rights generally (Brock, 1990: 81–84). Given the public esteem in which the Charter is held, this was no small thing. Even those with no particular interest in the fate of gender equality rights might be led to wonder about the security of their own rights should the section 2 clauses be entrenched in the constitution.

There was also an argument about status. Alan Cairns summed it up in this observation, penned before the demise of the Accord: "For the ethnic and aboriginal minorities who feel left out by Meech Lake the latter's provisions are experienced as a sense of loss, of status deprivation, of non-recognition, of being rebuffed" (1989: 124). The rebuff was rooted in language that established exclusive categories: distinct society; official language minorities and majorities. Brock reports the words of Joe Guy Wood to the Manitoba Task Force: "This section [2] is offensive to the First Nations of Canada in Island Lake and it should also be offensive to other nations of people in Canada. We live in the multicultural mosaic of Canada and I think we should all be recognized as a fundamental characteristic of Canada" (1990: 89).

These are the responses of people immediately engaged in the debate, and they do not necessarily embody a theory of constitutions, although they certainly indicate ideas of what is constitutionally appropriate, which is the start of theory. Cairns's analysis of the constitutional failures since 1982 has led him to suggest that more attention be paid to constitutional theory in general, and the concept of citizenship in particular (1992: 2). In this vein he explores the relationship between the Charter and objections to the Accord, beginning at the most general level with the Charter-driven idea of equal rights that has taken hold outside Francophone Québec. The Charter, he writes, encourages a view of citizenship based on equal rights, a view that is hostile to proposals to distinguish between citizens and to treat them constitutionally in different ways (Cairns, 1991: 243-44).

On the other hand, and shifting to the conduct of politics in the constitutional arena, Cairns notices the constitutional identities that the Charter confers on some groups, for example, the social category groups that can be derived from the grounds of discrimination listed in section 15, the equality rights section. He refers to a "minoritarian counter-culture ... which comprises a variety of interests and social categories and is endowed with organizations and elites, each of which sees the constitution as a vehicle to advance or protect particularistic concerns" (1991: 244). Since the Charter is the relatively new-found basis of their power, the representatives of such groups can be expected to scrutinize carefully constitutional proposals that reach it and reject any that might weaken it. Thus they supply a powerful, conservative force in the face of change. Finally, there is the notion of the status of collectivities, and that, too, is thought to have roots in the Charter as well as in other sections of the

Constitution Act, 1982. In a passage on ethnic and Aboriginal constitutional discourse, Cairns writes: "the constitution is now an arena within which competing ethnic and aboriginal Canadians battle for relative status vis-à-vis each other and with the two founding peoples privileged by past history and, even now, by the contemporary constitution" (1989: 120).

It is this last idea that is central. Cairns' argument is that the Constitution Act, 1982 established the arena of competition in the multicultural heritage and language clauses of the Charter and the sections on the rights of Aboriginal peoples. Thus the drafters of the section 2 clauses of the Accord were following a path already broken. However, this interpretation of the 1982 Act cannot easily be sustained. Consider the multicultural heritage clause, which requires that the Charter be interpreted in a way that is "consistent with the preservation and enhancement of the multicultural heritage of Canadians" (Reesor, 1992: 374). The lead noun is "heritage" and everyone has one, a point not effaced by the adjective "multicultural," which logically includes "multiracial." How could it not? Moreover, there are no evaluative phrases that yield a pecking order. There is only the implication that heritages must be good things because good things are enhanced and preserved.

What about the Charter section on Aboriginal rights? Again, the language is practical — it is about powers, rights, and freedoms — rather than evaluative. The purpose of section 25 is to ensure that Charter rights and freedoms are not interpreted so as to diminish Aboriginal rights and freedoms arising out of existing treaties and existing or future land claims agreements. One other section on Aboriginal rights, also located in the Constitution Act, 1982, but outside the Charter of Rights, is similarly non-evaluative. Section 35 recognizes existing Aboriginal and treaty rights and defines the term "aboriginal peoples," gives rights arising out of existing or future land claims agreements the same constitutional status as treaty rights, and guarantees Aboriginal and treaty rights equally to male and female persons. In short, there are no adjectives that evaluate Aboriginal peoples in relation to others.

The language provisions of the Charter present a slightly different case (Reesor, 1992: 358-67). There are two official languages of Canada — French and English — and everyone has rights in relation to the use of them in specified circumstances, for example, in the debates and proceedings of Parliament and in the education of children. Obviously, other languages are unofficial, and no entrenched rights of usage, with the associated expenditures of public monies, are attached to them. So there is a constitutional ranking of languages, but it does not imply a corresponding ranking of peoples. At least that is the assumption that harnesses the otherwise incompatible notions of bilingualism and multiculturalism. As Rainer Knopff explains, such an assumption requires a theory according to which language and culture, while understood to be related intimately, are not collapsed. In this way language can be understood to serve a utilitarian or communications purpose in addition to its prime function as the vehicle for the acquisition and transmission of a culture. On the basis of the utilitarian function, it is possible for governments to legislate official languages without legislating official cultures (1979: 66-67).

Whatever the merits of the utilitarian language theory backing the policy of official bilingualism, it is enormously important that such a theory is available. After all, the rival theory posits that language and culture stand or fall together, in which case a public policy of official bilingualism is a public policy of unofficial biculturalism (*ibid.*: 69-72). If, then, the clauses of the constitution that purportedly support differential notions of status support no such thing, the distinct society and linguistic duality clauses of the proposed Accord *were* constitutional originals. But the competitive status phenomenon to which Cairns refers yields a funny kind of standard at which to aim, and it is hard to imagine that the authors of the clauses had it in mind.

Perhaps they did not. Perhaps they saw the clauses – certainly the distinct society clause – as another counterweight to the Charter for Québec, an addition to the legislative override that is already available to Parliament and the provincial legislatures. But they should have understood that the struggle for constitutional status observed by Cairns is a predictable response to evaluative language. Such language forces representatives of various groups to vie for similar constitutional accolades in an undignified and dangerous competition that is as far from the precepts of constitutionalism as it is possible to imagine. People looking for constitutional remedies who resort to the use of such accolades – this group is "distinct," that group is "first" – seem not to know that these claims are open invitations to group struggles, and do not belong in a constitutional order designed both to establish governments and to place limits on their powers in the name of individual freedoms. Constitutionalism is about the balance between the powers of popular governments and individual rights. It is meant to be a bulwark against claims to govern that are not based on institutions of representation.

THE CHARLOTTETOWN ACCORD

The Error of Abandoning Neutrality

When the Manitoba and Newfoundland legislatures failed to ratify the Meech Lake Accord by the deadline imposed by the amending formula, the Meech Lake round was over and a new constitutional round began almost immediately. There was a gap of some four to five months between the ratification deadline of June 23, 1990, and the establishment of the Citizens' Forum on Canada's Future in November of the same year. Called the Spicer Commission after the chairman, Keith Spicer, the Commission was a response on the part of the federal government to process criticisms. As it turned out, it was only the first of a remarkable set of consultative procedures, and therefore it is worth pausing to consider the whole process issue.

It is clear that all governments were stung by the criticism that Meech Lake was negotiated inappropriately. It was one thing to respond to doubts about the content of the Accord, quite another to defend participation in a process that was vilified as secretive, sexist, unrepresentative, and elitist. It was the same old process of executive federalism that had always been used, but the politicians were unable to defend it. They could not explain why the art of compromise – to say nothing of straightforwardness and lack of hypocrisy – requires leaders to negotiate privately with one another rather than in full sight of their respective clienteles. They could not defend their exclusive position as officially elected representatives, the only legitimate representatives of their voting jurisdictions. They could not even point out the obvious, namely, that leadership is elitist by definition, since there are always more followers than leaders (J.Smith, 1991).

Enmeshed by their own admission in the seemingly indefensible process of executive federalism, political leaders were frantic to consult with Canadians, to open up the process, to listen, or at least to appear to be doing these things. Hence the stream of commissions, legislative committees, task forces, and constitutional conferences. The premise seemed to be that the right process would generate the right result, or at least the most legitimate result. Since procedural concerns are an important part of constitutionalism, the premise would appear to have been unassailable. But it was not. No amount of fuss over process could hide the absence of a theory of constitutions, or even thought about what that might entail. It transpired that the federal and Québec governments were not about to re-consider the advisability of the main elements of the Meech Lake Accord. On the contrary, two years later most of them, in some form or other, wound up in the text of the Charlottetown Accord.

Mercifully, the linguistic duality clause was dropped, but the distinct society clause, modified, made another appearance. Thus the mistake made in the earlier constitutional round was brought forward. Worse, it was magnified. The inevitable effect of the process obsession was to broaden the number of participants involved in the negotiations, some of whom were prepared to agree to the controversial clause in return for clauses of their own. The result was the opening section of the Charlotte-town Accord, the Canada clause (Canada, 1992a: 1-2).

The high-minded Canada clause was slated to become the second clause of the Constitution Act, 1867, a rather prominent location as these things go. It was variously described as a "snapshot" or "portrait" of Canadians, or a set of principles to which Canadians subscribe. In the words of the clause itself, the sub-clauses are called statements of "fundamental characteristics" (the linguistic duality clause might have been dropped but somebody certainly liked that phrase). Incredibly, there are eight, four of which follow the unfortunate evaluative model: an expanded distinct society clause, complete with a definition of Québec's distinct society, now said to include a "French-speaking majority, a unique culture and a civil law tradition" – which is more or less what had been supposed all along; a clause on Aboriginal peoples describing them as "the first peoples to gov-ern this land"; a clause committing Canadians and their governments to the development of "official language minority communities" throughout the country; and a clause on "citizens from many lands who have contrib-uted, and continue to contribute, to the building of a strong Canada that reflects its cultural and racial diversity." Anyone who felt left out of these four categories was free to assign himself to one or other of the remaining odds and sods.[3] But the key provisions were the evaluative ones, and now there were four – in the Canada clause. The fifth appeared at the end of the Accord, and is described as a bilateral amendment between New Brunswick and Canada. It builds on the fundamental characteristic of "language minority communities."

The bilateral amendment is the one element of the Accord that is sev-erable from it, has been severed from it, and is being brought forward as an amendment on its own. Under the amending formula, an amendment applying to one or more, but not all, provinces requires the consent of

Parliament and the legislative assembly of the province(s) concerned (Reesor, 1992: 398-400). Since the New Brunswick legislature has ratified the amendment, it only remains for Parliament to do so. The amendment is fascinating because it blurs the distinction noted earlier between official languages and the communities attached to them. It refers to English and French linguistic communities in New Brunswick and declares that they "have equality of status and equal rights and privileges, including the right to distinct educational institutions and such distinct cultural institutions as are necessary for the preservation and promotion of those communities" (Canada, 1992a: 51). These clauses are to be located in the Constitution Act, 1982, immediately following section 16, which is the opening section on official languages.

Let us recall the need to prevent an official languages policy from sliding into an official cultures policy in order to maintain the idea of multiculturalism alongside the idea of official languages. The sections of the Charter on official languages and minority language educational rights deal with rights of individuals in relation to the use of official languages and corresponding responsibilities of governments. There is no mention of communities or linguistic communities. By contrast, the bilateral amendment moves from individuals to communities and asserts that they are equal in status. It is not clear what this is supposed to mean for the communities in question, or for individuals who do not regard themselves as members of these communities. Individuals can participate in official languages. It is not so easily open to them to participate in linguistic communities, especially if they were neither born nor raised in them.

The Error of Abandoning Some Old Principles

The authors of the Charlottetown Accord foundered on another shoal when they sought to change some of the oldest rules of the constitution, rules that reflect the political accommodations made at Confederation. As is well known to students of the Confederation period, the establishment of the coalition ministry in the Province of Canada in June, 1864, was the signal that the leaders of the hitherto deadlocked political forces in the province had finally reached agreement on a constitutional course of action. Obviously the agreement between the conservative factions led by John A. Macdonald and G.-E. Cartier and the Reformers led by George Brown involved some tough, basic compromises, and in the end these compromises anchored the Confederation agreement. For example,

Brown sought a federation of the two sections of the Province of Canada, not a larger federation with the Maritime provinces. However, he agreed to pursue the grand scheme on condition that the principle of representation by population, long a rallying cry of Reformers in Canada West, direct the allocation of seats in the lower house of a new national parliament (Morton, 1964: 146-47). The principle of "rep by pop" in the House of Commons has an ancient lineage, at least by Canadian standards.

The rule arrived at to govern the distribution of seats in the Senate needs to be understood in relation to the "rep by pop" issue. The Act of Union of 1841 that established the Province of Canada provided that representation in the legislative assembly be set at equal numbers for each of the two sections of the province, Canada West and Canada East. This was unfair to Canada East, the most populous of the two sections and home of the French-speaking community. But it was part and parcel of a scheme to assimilate the community to a British North American culture – a preposterous scheme that went nowhere quickly (Ormsby, 1969). By the mid-1850s, the population tables were turning. The rate of population growth in the western section was rising so rapidly that Brown began to press confidently for representation by population in the assembly, a demand to which French-speaking leaders were understandably cool. Years later, when Cartier and Etienne Taché finally made the concession to Brown, thus enabling him to enter the coalition ministry, it was in the context of a commitment to a larger project of federal union that promised to include offsetting features. One was provincial autonomy. Another was regional representation in the Senate.

At Charlottetown in September, 1864, the Canadians pitched the general idea of federation to Maritime political leaders, and it was clear that they were not contemplating an upper house, or Senate, based on equal provincial representation. Instead, they advanced the idea of equal regional representation (Browne, 1969: 45). At the conference at Québec in October of the same year, Macdonald opened the subject by proposing that the provinces be regarded in terms of regions for the purpose of Senate representation. Specifically, the two halves of the Province of Canada (destined to become Ontario and Québec) would each constitute a region, while the four east-coast provinces represented at the conference would make up the third. The outstanding revelation of the sketchy records of the debate that followed is that the Maritime leaders scarcely demurred. On the contrary, they accepted Macdonald's idea, presumably because as politicians they were alert to the compelling claim of large size, particularly when it combines geography and population. They did resist successfully the idea of the third region being composed of four provinces, instead paring it to the three Maritime provinces, with Newfoundland assigned four additional representatives. The numbers finally arrived at were twenty-four members per region, the third region consisting of ten each for Nova Scotia and New Brunswick, and four for Prince Edward Island (J.Smith, 1988: 456). Even then, Newfoundland was not envisaged as part of the regional scheme, and it is not part of it now. When the province entered Confederation in 1949, it was assigned six senators on its own.

In brief, Canadian federalism has never required the idea of the equality of the provinces (Aucoin, 1985). On the contrary, constitutional arrangements have systematically repudiated it. Senate representation is a spectacular example, but there are others, ranging from constitutional provisions in the Constitution Act, 1867, that apply to Québec alone (Milne, 1991: 289) to the general amending formula that, unlike the American formula, privileges more populous provinces at the expense of the less populous ones (Kilgour, 1983). The general amending formula is especially noteworthy in this regard because it is a recent addition to the constitution. In 1982, it seems, old habits prevailed.

Now there is nothing sacrosanct about an old constitutional arrangement in general, or even an old one rooted in formative political battles in particular. But it is not always easy to determine when the arrangement is outmoded, that is, when it is no longer a brilliant compromise of competing claims but instead a looming injustice to new parties in unforeseen circumstances. By the time of the negotiations of the Charlottetown Accord, the challenge to the old notion of the proper relationship between the provinces had been under way in the West for some years. This challenge was based on the rival idea of the equality of the provinces, and it made an initial official constitutional appearance in the form of a proposal on Senate reform. In March, 1985, the Alberta Select Special Committee on Upper House Reform issued a report entitled *Strengthening Canada: Reform of Canada's Senate*. The committee recommended an equal, elected, and effective Senate – the "Triple-E" Senate (Alberta, 1985). The report was released a second time in January, 1988, and the proposal was "affirmed in principle" a year later at the Western Premiers' Conference. Meanwhile, the western-based Reform Party, established in May, 1987, took up the Triple-E idea and championed it with considerable success, so much success that the idea eventually acquired the status of a non-negotiable constitutional demand of the West (McCormick, 1991: 343-44).

There were some other takers. For example, the government of Prince Edward Island displayed an understandable interest in equal provincial representation in a reformed Senate early on, and successive governments there remained committed to it (Prince Edward Island, 1983). Premier Frank McKenna of New Brunswick eventually supported the idea (New Brunswick, 1992: 42), and certainly Premier Clyde Wells of Newfoundland and Labrador was a vigorous exponent (Brown, 1990: 220-22). Wells emphasized the high ground of Triple-E Senate reform – the principle of the equality of the provinces. It is significant that no English-speaking political leader seemed able or willing to dispute him on the point. Perhaps they thought that would have meant defending the sticky wicket of provincial inequality. Whatever, the devotees of provincial equality had a clear field, and resistance to the application of the principle to Senate representation, which was massive, seemed nonetheless inert. When given rare expression, it was in the language of calculation. The economist T.J. Courchene (1991) was dubious about the prospects of the idea, even in a Canada without Québec, and to him the calculus of resistance was simple enough. Why would the economic "have" provinces of Ontario, British Columbia, and Alberta want a Senate dominated by the "have-not" provinces? Absent Québec, and Courchene still regarded the Triple-E proposal to be politically unrealistic. No one seriously thought the Québec government could be persuaded to accept it.

Events seemed to bear this out whenever the subject of Senate reform was inserted into constitutional negotiations. For example, during the final throes of the Meech Lake Accord in June, 1990, Prime Minister Mulroney and ten premiers reached an agreement that the three hold-out provinces, Newfoundland, New Brunswick, and Manitoba, would decide on the Accord as soon as possible. In return, commitments were made to pursue other constitutional issues, including an effective and "equitable" Senate, not an equal one (Reid, 1990: 262). The Accord died anyway, but a year and a half later, when the federal government tabled its new set of constitutional proposals in the House of Commons, it was still talking in terms of equitable representation although it was prepared to move from regional to provincial and territorial representation. In fact, in the section on Senate representation in *Shaping Canada's Future Together*, there is reference to the equitable Senate promise in the last-ditch agreement on the Meech Lake Accord, followed by the proposal that the Senate feature "much more equitable" provincial and territorial representation than it does now. Lest anyone confuse "much more equitable" with equal, the report emphasizes the need to take account of the vast inequities and special circumstances that militate against the use of a simple equality rule: linguistic duality, "the nearly 80-fold difference in provincial populations," the small number of provinces, and the need for Aboriginal representation (Canada, 1991: 18-19). There is no reference to the issue of numbers in the House of Commons, that is, to the principle underlying the allocation of seats there.

The federal government established the Special Joint Committee on a Renewed Canada (called the Dobbie-Beaudoin committee after its co-chairs, Dorothy Dobbie, MP, and Senator G. Beaudoin) to examine the proposals outlined in *Shaping Canada's Future Together*. In its report, the committee accepted the federal government's preference for an equitable over an equal distribution of Senate seats among the provinces, arguing that the issue is one of fairness and that P.E.I., with 0.5 per cent of the population, ought not to have the same number of seats as, say, Québec, with 25.5 per cent. It also offered some sample seat distributions (Canada, 1992b: 49-52). Again, there was no mention of seat allocation in the Commons. The idea of linking the distribution of Senate seats with the distribution of Commons seats was a product of the negotiations that culminated in the Charlottetown agreement.

The negotiations began in Ottawa in March, 1992. Federal, provincial, Aboriginal, and territorial leaders conducted intense discussions over the next few months to prepare a constitutional offer to the Québec government, which was poised to hold a referendum on the offer by October of the same year. According to the logic of the exercise, the Québec government was not a participant in the discussions, which may have had something to do with the fact that the outcome, a *Status Report* that summarized the multilateral meetings on the constitution through July 7, included this recommendation on Senate seats: eight per province and two per territory, plus a number of seats still to be determined (Canada, 1992c: 5). As noteworthy as the abandonment of equitable in favour of equal provincial representation was the inclusion of a section on the composition of the House of Commons. The proposal was to adjust it to "better reflect the principle of representation by population," and this turned out to mean an immediate increase in size of seventeen seats, the lion's share of ten going to Ontario, and the rest to Québec (three), B.C. (three), and Alberta (one). There was an accompanying recommendation to develop a new allocation formula, sensitive to demographic change, to redistribute seats in the future (Canada, 1992c: 9).

The political logic of the recommendations on seat distribution in the Senate and the House of Commons seemed clear enough. In return for conceding equal provincial representation in the Senate, Ontario demanded adherence to the principle of representation by population in the Commons. Over the years the various formulas devised to translate the principle into an allocation of seats among the provinces and territories have departed increasingly from it, largely by producing seat floors for the smaller provinces, and one effect has been to underrepresent Ontario, the most populous province (Sancton, 1990). While the Ontario government might have been content with the remedy arrived at, however, the same could not be said for some other political actors, notably the two who were not at the negotiations, the Prime Minister and Premier Bourassa.

Prime Minister Mulroney was in Munich when the agreement was reached, and his initial response was muted, to say the least. Certainly he showed none of the enthusiasm that might have been expected at the progress apparently made.[4] Premier Bourassa was more forthright. He expressed concern with several aspects of the agreement, including the equal Senate, which he described as a "clear loss" for Québec.[5] Negotiations resumed, with the Prime Minister in charge and the Québec Premier in attendance. August 5 was a low day for equal provincial representation in a reformed Senate. The Québec government's resistance was so strong that the federal government announced its intention to withdraw its support for the idea. The next day the chairman of the Conservative Party's Alberta caucus announced that Alberta MPs would not give up the Triple-E Senate of the Status Report. So it went. Finally, on August 20, newspapers reported that Premier Bourassa had dropped his opposition to an equal Senate, in part because the new body would have few real powers, in part because of a new agreement on representation in the House of Commons.[6]

In the final text of the Consensus Report On the Constitution, dated August 28, 1992 – the Charlottetown Accord – there was provision for a Senate composed of six senators per province and one per territory, with an unspecified number of Aboriginal senators (Canada, 1992a: 3). These numbers were somewhat lower than those in the Status Report. However, the real eye-opener was the section on representation in the House of Commons, which was more than an elaboration of the comparable section in the Status Report. There were two parts, one dealing with the size of the House, the other with the allocation rule for future redistributions.

On the size of the House, the idea was to raise it immediately from 295 members to 337 and assign Ontario and Québec an additional eighteen members each, British Columbia four, and Alberta two. On completion of an interim 1996 census, the figures would be readjusted by the addition of eight members, three each for Ontario and British Columbia, two for Alberta (Canada, 1992a: 31). More importantly, the allocation formula to be devised and used in the redistribution following the 1996 census and future redistributions was to be subject to various rules. Most amounted to protections of one kind or another for smaller provinces or provinces facing the loss of members following a redistribution. The key rule applied to Québec, guaranteeing it a minimum of 25 per cent of the membership of the House in perpetuity, irrespective of the province's population (Canada, 1992a: 12-13). Québec had been dealt into Ontario's compensation package.

As many were quick to point out, the 25 per cent guarantee nearly matches the province's share of the country's population now, which is 25.3 per cent.[7] Thus the practical effects of the rule immediately and in the foreseeable future would have been negligible. That being the case, the opposition to the idea in English-speaking Canada was almost always expressed in terms of principle – the old principle. Apparently lots of people understood that distribution of House of Commons seats is supposed to be based on the principle of representation by population, and that a guarantee to a province of a portion of the membership expressed in terms of a percentage of the whole violates the principle. Opposition was widespread. One poll conducted during the middle of the referendum campaign reported that 82 per cent of respondents outside Québec opposed the 25 per cent rule, including "*78 per cent of respondents who said they planned to vote Yes for other reasons – the so-called hold-your-nose-and-pass-it faction.*"[8] The negative view held throughout the campaign was a result in part because the Reform Party, identified closely in the public eye with promotion of the Triple-E Senate, campaigned so effectively against the Senate-House package as well as other elements of the agreement.[9]

Viewed as a compromise, the rules for the distribution of seats in the Senate and the House of Commons were a complete failure, certainly in terms of their public reception. In English-speaking Canada, hostility to the 25 per cent rule designed to govern membership in the House far outweighed any satisfaction that might have accrued from the prospect of equal provincial representation in the Senate, at least for those who supported the idea. In Québec, meanwhile, there was not much enthusiasm for the compromise at all. There, supporters of the Accord were stuck having to defend a provision widely regarded as unjust elsewhere, and it was a provision that no Québec government in memory had ever pursued before. The irony of the 25 per cent rule is that nothing remotely resembling it had been part of Québec's constitutional agenda, in the Charlottetown round or any other constitutional round.

Public reception aside, was the compromise itself so bad? The answer must begin with an admission of the overriding importance of the subject. The historical origins of the existing compromise of regional representation in the Senate and representation by population in the House, briefly adverted to earlier in the paper, surely indicate the seriousness of the issues involved. Obviously debates about numbers in representative institutions are debates about political power. And they are immensely complicated debates since there are so many other variables, not the least of which concerns the powers of the institutions in question and their relationship within a particular form of government. Given the conflicting claims of the parties involved, and assuming no one dominates the rest, a compromise is required. But what calibre of compromise? This is the second part of the answer.

An enduring compromise has to combine in some way competing claims about principles of justice. Not just any old thing will do, that is, an arbitrary arrangement that happens to suit the parties of the day. Otherwise those who think they have lost out will know that it has been for nothing. The compromise has to be shown to combine competing principles, so that the whole looks principled. The Confederation compromise passed the test with flying colours. Unfortunately for the authors of the Charlottetown Accord, the principle of representation by population that anchors the distribution of seats in the House is still regarded as a necessary principle of justice. It buttresses the idea that in a democracy the people prevail, because it ensures that minorities do not dominate majorities. It is the basis of majority rule. The other half of the compromise, representation in the Senate, was itself a compromise, albeit one that solved two problems – the huge discrepancies in size and population between a small number of provinces, and Québec – by using the neat construct of regional representation. It is neat because it retains something of the federal notion of the equality of the units of the federation, which is meant to counter national majorities. Taken together, the two halves produce a defensible whole, or at least they did until the agitation for a Triple-E Senate intensified, particularly since the demise of the Meech Lake Accord.

The presence of Québec has always meant that Canada cannot combine equal provincial representation in the Senate and representation by population in the Commons, along the lines of the American model. One or the other has to give. By acceding to the equal-provinces tenet underlying the Triple-E model, the Charlottetown authors had to find their solution in the other house, and the other principle. They had to compromise the principle of representation by population. In effect, they reversed the Confederation compromise. So how is the public hostility to the proposal to be understood? Obviously, it says that for a significant number of Canadians, "rep by pop" is a more important principle than the equal-provinces principle and therefore ought not to be tampered with. I suspect this is because "rep by pop" is understood to translate the principle of individual political equality into the premier decision-making role of the House of Commons, the national legislative body that generates and sustains the cabinet.

CONCLUSION

Following the defeat of the Charlottetown Accord in the referendum, the Prime Minister and the premiers immediately announced their intention to throw in the constitutional towel and turn their talents to the economy. People described as constitutional "experts" more or less disappeared from view, which is hardly surprising given the level of public hostility to the very mention of the word "constitution." The hostility is so profound that in the lead-up to the election of the PQ government in Québec on September 12, 1994, there was a kind of wary silence outside the province. None of the constitutional talkers had the nerve to say much – even "I told you so" – and this, despite the fact that the PQ, under leader and now Premier Jacques Parizeau, is a secessionist party that it plans to hold and win a referendum in the province on the secession question.

Of course, since the PQ won the election and is at work on the referendum campaign, there is every reason to talk about the constitution, although the experts, and the media who interview them, are still a little reluctant, sensing as they do the public's lack of enthusiasm for the subject. The hook is the referendum question that is put to Québec voters. Will it be secession versus the status quo of Canadian federalism or secession versus some other type of federalism? Or will it be something milder, like a mandate for the Québec government to negotiate constitutional change and, failing that, to secede? Should a milder question succeed with Québec voters then the project of constitutional reform might well begin again. My fear is that despite the dismal record on this score – after all, the efforts since 1982 to make constitutional amends have generated public dismay rather than acceptance – there is no evidence that the experts and the politicians are inclined to look to their own handiwork for the blame. On the contrary.

Currently fashionable is the hoax that constitutions are about people rather than governments or governmental powers. According to this view, what is needed is an "inclusive" process that brings people "into" the constitution, that enables them to see themselves in it, presumably in the form of descriptions about themselves. Consequently, the lesson of the Charlottetown debacle is the need for a more inclusive process in the next constitutional round. This line of reasoning avoids altogether the possibility that the contents of the Accord were the issue, and leads instead to the view that the unincluded voters who turned it down were either intolerant, or uninformed, or angry at the political elites for economic reasons entirely unrelated to constitutional matters and intent on avenging themselves at the first opportunity.

There are two difficulties with the people-over-power view, the first of which is the very idea of talking about people in a constitutional document. Some serious rethinking is in order about the purpose of describing people in evaluative language in the constitution, particularly if it turns out to cause nothing but misery and divisiveness, and to be an arbitrary exercise in any event – arbitrary because it depends on the play of particular political forces and their leverage at the time. The second difficulty with the people-over-power view is that it establishes a false dichotomy. There is no way around the fact that the constitutions of popular governments are most importantly about the establishment of government institutions, the allocation of power among them, and the decision-making rules that they use. The simple yet critical connection to the people is the fact that in one way or another the institutions are designed to represent them. The entire arrangement, which must be underwritten by defensible principles of justice, is meant to establish government and secure freedom, both at the same time. It is a tall order. Those who are bent on rearrangements need to understand that they are working at the level of principle and principled compromise, not just compromise.

NOTES

1   "Referendum Vote By Province," *Globe and Mail*, October 28, 1992, A4.

2   In his account of the Meech Lake saga, Andrew Cohen writes that it was "no accident" that public hearings were never held in Manitoba. The party leaders, he states, judged that public hearings would become forums for the expression of prejudice: "With the province the centre of national attention, they feared that the bigots and the crackpots, rather than the legislators, would be seen to be speaking for Manitoba" (1990: 258-59). The odd thing about Cohen's claim is that Manitoba did hold public hearings on the Accord. As Kathy Brock records, on March 3, 1989, Premier Filmon announced the establishment of an all-party Constitutional Task Force, the purpose of which was to consult the views of Manitobans on the matter (1990: 54). It did, in a series of public meetings beginning early in April and ending early in May. In her comparison of the Manitoba process with the public consultation processes of other provinces, at least the ones that had any, Brock writes flatly: "Manitoba held the most extensive public hearings on the Meech Lake Accord in Canada" (1990: 57).

3   The remaining four fundamental characteristics are: gender equality; the principle of the equality of the provinces – equal but "diverse"; individual and collective human rights and freedoms of all people; and parliamentary government, federalism, and the rule of law (Canada, 1992a: 1).

4   "PM remains cautious: Recalls failed Meech pact," *Globe and Mail*, July 9, 1992, A4.

5   "Bourassa voices concerns," *Globe and Mail*, July 10, 1992, A1, A4.

6   "Bourassa drops opposition to equal Senate: Quebec Premier insists House won't exercise any real power," *Globe and Mail*, August 20, 1992, A5.

7   "Two and a half Es, and more work ahead," *Globe and Mail*, August 21, 1992, A16.

8   "Poll gets the word from cranky electorate," *Globe and Mail*, October 9, 1992, A2; emphasis added.

9   "Reform Party a house divided," (1992, October 23). *Globe and Mail*, October 23, 1992, A6.

REFERENCES

Ajzenstat, Janet, ed. (1993). *Canadian Constitutionalism: 1791-1991*. Canadian Study of Parliament Group.

Alberta (1985). Strengthening Canada: Reform of Canada's Senate. Report of the Alberta Select Special Committee on Upper House Reform. Edmonton: Plains Publishing.

Aucoin, Peter (1985). "Regionalism, Party and National Government," Aucoin, research co-ordinator, Party Government and Regional Representation in Canada, vol. 36 in the research studies of the Royal Commission on the Economic Union and Development Prospects for Canada. Toronto: University of Toronto Press: 137-59.

Breton, Raymond (1988). "The Concepts of 'Distinct Society' and 'Identity' in the Meech Lake Accord," in Katherine E. Swinton and Carol J. Rogerson, eds., *Competing Constitutional Visions: The Meech Lake Accord*. Toronto: Carswell: 3-10.

Brock, Kathy L. (1990). *A Mandate Fulfilled: Constitutional Reform and the Manitoba Task Force on Meech Lake*. Winnipeg: University of Manitoba Outreach Fund.

Brown, Douglas M. (1990). "Sea-Change in Newfoundland: From Peckford to Wells," in Ronald L. Watts and Douglas M. Brown, eds., *Canada: The State of the Federation 1990*. Kingston: Institute of Intergovernmental Relations: 199-229.

Browne, G.P. (1969). Documents on the Confederation of British North America. Toronto: McClelland & Stewart.

Cairns, Alan (1989). "Political Science, Ethnicity and the Canadian Constitution," in David P. Shugarman and Reg Whitaker, eds., Federalism and Political Community: Essays in Honour of Donald Smiley. Peterborough, Ont.: Broadview Press: 113-40.

Cairns, Alan (1991). "Passing Judgement on Meech Lake," in Cairns *Constitutional Struggles, from the Charter to Meech Lake*, edited by Douglas E. Williams. Toronto: McClelland & Stewart: 223-63.

Cairns, Alan (1992). "Citizenship and the New Constitutional Order," *Canadian Parliamentary Review*, 15, 3 (Autumn, 1992): 2-6.

Canada (1987a). *A Guide to the Meech Lake Constitutional Accord*. Ottawa: Queen's Printer.

Canada (1987b). *The 1987 Constitutional Accord*. Report of the Special Joint Committee of the Senate and the House of Commons. Ottawa.

Canada (1991). *Shaping Canada's Future Together: Proposals*. Ottawa: Ministry of Supply and Services Canada.

Canada (1992a). *Draft Legal Text* based on the Charlottetown Accord of August 28, 1992. Ottawa, October 9, 1992.

Canada (1992b). *A Renewed Canada*. Report of the Special Joint Committee of the Senate and the House of Commons. Ottawa, February 28, 1992.

Canada (1992c). *Status Report*. The Multilateral Meetings on the Constitution. Ottawa, July 16, 1992.

Cohen, Andrew (1990). *A Deal Undone: The Making and Breaking of the Meech Lake Accord*. Vancouver: Douglas & McIntyre.

Cook, Ramsay (1989). "Alice in Meechland or The Concept of Quebec as 'A Distinct Society,'" in Michael D. Behiels, ed., *The Meech Lake Primer: Conflicting Views of the 1987 Constitutional Accord*. Ottawa: University of Ottawa Press: 147-60.

Courchene, Thomas J. (1991). *In Praise of Renewed Federalism*. Toronto: C.D. Howe Institute: 68-76.

Edelman, Murray (1967). *The Symbolic Uses of Politics*. Urbana, Ill.: University of Illinois Press.

Greschner, Donna (1988). "How Not to Drown in Meech Lake: Rules, Principles and Women's Equality Rights," in Swinton and Rogerson, eds., *Competing Constitutional Visions*. 55-63.

Kilgour, D. Marc (1983). "A Formal Analysis of the Amending Formula of Canada's *Constitution Act, 1982*," Canadian Journal of Political Science. XVI, 4: 771-77.

Knopff, Rainer (1979). "Language and Culture in the Canadian Debate: The Battle of the White Papers," Canadian Review of Studies in Nationalism. (Spring): 66-82.

Leslie, Peter M. (1987). *Rebuilding the Relationship: Quebec and Its Confederation Partners*. Conference Report. Kingston: Institute of Intergovernmental Relations, Appendix A.

McCormick, Peter (1991). "The Reform Party of Canada: New Beginning or Dead End?" in Hugh G. Thorburn, ed., *Party Politics in Canada*. 6th edition. Scarborough, Ont.: Prentice-Hall Canada: 342-52.

Milne, David (1991). "Equality or Asymmetry: Why Choose," in Ronald Watts and Douglas M. Brown, eds., *Options for a New Canada*. Toronto: University of Toronto Press: 285-307.

Morton, W.L. (1964). *The Critical Years: The Union of British North America, 1857-1873*. Toronto: McClelland & Stewart.

New Brunswick (1992). Report of the New Brunswick Commission on Canadian Federalism. Fredericton: The New Brunswick Commission on Canadian Federalism.

89

Ormsby, William (1969). The Emergence of the Federal Concept in Canada, 1839-1845. Toronto: University of Toronto Press.

Prince Edward Island (1983). The Senate in a Federal System.

Reesor, Bayard (1992). The Canadian Constitution in Historical Perspective. Scarborough, Ont.: Prentice-Hall Canada.

Reid, Darrel R. (1990). "Chronology of Events July 1989 – June 1990," in Ronald L. Watts and Douglas M. Brown, eds., Canada: The State of the Federation 1990. Kingston: Institute of Intergovernmental Affairs: 233-68.

Sancton, Andrew (1990). "Eroding Representation-by-Population in the Canadian House of Commons: The Representation Act, 1985," Canadian Journal of Political Science, XXIII, 3: 441-57.

Schwartz, Bryan (1987). Fathoming Meech Lake. Contemporary Issues Series, vol. 1. Winnipeg: Legal Research Institute, University of Manitoba.

Simeon, Richard (1990). "Why Did the Meech Lake Accord Fail?" in Watts and Brown, eds., Canada: The State of the Federation 1990: 15-40.

Smith, Jennifer (1988). "Canadian Confederation and the Influence of American Federalism," Canadian Journal of Political Science, XXI, 3: 443-63.

Smith, Jennifer (1991). "Representation and Constitutional Reform in Canada," in David E. Smith, Peter MacKinnon, and John C. Courtney, eds., After Meech Lake: Lessons for the Future. Saskatoon: Fifth House Publishers.

Smith, Lynn (1988). "The Distinct Society Clause in the Meech Lake Accord: Could it Affect Equality Rights for Women?" in Swinton and Rogerson, eds., Competing Constitutional Visions: 35-54.

Tully, James (1994). "Diversity's Gambit Declined," in Curtis Cook, ed., Constitutional Predicament: Canada after the Referendum of 1992. Montreal and Kingston: McGill-Queen's University Press: 149-98.

CHAPTER FOUR

The End of Executive Federalism?

Kathy L. Brock[1]

WHEN THE CHARLOTTETOWN ACCORD WAS DEFEATED IN THE
1992 referendum, many political analysts declared that it signalled the end
of striking political deals between the federal and provincial governments
through the process of executive federalism in Canada. The Charlottetown round of constitutional negotiations had been extolled for the extent to which it combined discussions among first ministers, high-level
government officials, and representatives of national Aboriginal organizations with the most extensive set of public hearings ever held in Canada.
Seasoned commentators observed that in contrast to the Meech Lake constitutional process, which had been viewed as closed and elitist, the Charlottetown negotiations had been open and included a significant amount
of public input. On concluding the deal, actors in the Charlottetown
process were convinced that even though the final phase of negotiations
had been conducted behind closed doors, there had been sufficient public
consultation and attentiveness of negotiators to public concerns that the
Accord would receive broad public support. As the referendum campaign
proceeded and public dissatisfaction with the Accord grew, politicians
seemed perplexed. The strength of the vote against the Charlottetown
Accord caused political actors and commentators to question the prospects of ever achieving nation-wide agreements between the federal and
provincial governments on significant matters. Some analysts observed
that the combined effect of the Meech Lake and Charlottetown processes
was to discredit First Ministers' Conferences as a vehicle for obtaining intergovernmental agreements and securing plans for constitutional or other
forms of change in the nation. Many concluded that only micro-constitu-
tional deals and bilateral negotiations between Ottawa and provincial
governments would be possible in the future.

This chapter contends that lamentations for executive federalism were premature and exaggerated. Canadians have not necessarily seen the end of executive federalism. Agreements between the first ministers and senior public officials at the federal and provincial levels of government remain an integral part of the way of doing business in Canada. First Ministers' Conferences at the apex of this structure of intergovernmental negotiations are crucial to finalizing agreements and to directing the nature of intergovernmental relations in Canada. However, what must change is the way these institutions are defined. Intergovernmental negotiations are evolving as past practices adapt to suit new expectations and demands of the Canadian public. This chapter examines the evolution of the institution of executive federalism and its viability within the current political context.

THE CONTOURS OF EXECUTIVE FEDERALISM

The term "executive federalism" gained increasing popularity during the 1970s and 1980s as a means of characterizing the nature of intergovernmental relations in Canada. Donald Smiley, who was the first political analyst to use and extensively explore this concept, defined executive federalism as "the relations between elected and appointed officials of the two levels of government" (Smiley, 1976: 54). Stefan Dupré elaborates this definition of executive federalism and explains that a distinction should be made between relations between elected and appointed officials of federal and provincial governments and relations between elected and appointed officials of provincial governments. He refers to the latter form of relations as "executive interprovincialism" and notes that it is often a response to executive federalism (Dupré, 1985: 2). This distinction is important since premiers' conferences often precede bi-level discussions and are a means of coordinating strategies among the provinces when they face Ottawa on fiscal or contentious intergovernmental issues. But also, there is increasing cooperation among the first ministers of specific regions of the country addressing common concerns, as exemplified with the western premiers' conferences and the Atlantic premiers' conferences.

The term "executive federalism' is used in a variety of ways. In a more restricted sense, it is used to contrast the period of federal-provincial relations in the 1960s and 1970s, which was one of less cooperation and more confrontation, with the preceding period of cooperative federalism, which was one of more harmonious relations and the joint expansion of state activities (Jackson and Jackson, 1994: 249). Dupré captures the breadth of the uses of the term when he explains that:

> Executive federalism has been categorized in the literature from the standpoint of outcomes, as cooperative or conflictual federalism. From the standpoint of actors, it has been called summit federalism (relations among first ministers and/or their designated ministerial or bureaucratic entourage) and functional federalism (relations among ministers and/or their officials). From the standpoint of participating governments, it has been labelled multilateral (the federal and all ten provincial governments), multilateral-regional (the federal government and the governments of some, normally contiguous, provinces), and bilateral (the federal government and a single province). These labels ... are conceptually secondary to the notion of executive federalism as embodying the relations between the elected and appointed officials of the energizing executives of our federal and provincial levels of governments. (Dupré, 1985: 3)

Thus, executive federalism refers to the arrangements used to negotiate agreements between the two levels of government for the provision of programs, services, and the coordination of policies. The results vary from agreements on fiscal arrangements and transfers from the federal government to the provincial governments to the harmonization and similar provision of health services within the provinces, to the reduction and elimination of interprovincial trade barriers, to constitutional amendments, and more.

Three key factors have led to the increasing reliance on executive federalism as a means of interaction between levels of government. First, the evolution of Canadian federalism has seen a decentralization of powers from the central government to the provinces in a manner not anticipated by the original constitutional arrangement. As Robert Vipond points out, the legacy of the provincial rights movement has been the transformation of "provincial legislatures from what Macdonald called 'nominally' responsible governments into fully self-governing and sovereign parliaments" (Vipond, 1991: 73). They negotiate as equals. This process of province-building has occurred at the same time as the expansion of the state and growing interdependence of governments. Thus, federal-provincial consultation, cooperation, and negotiation are increasingly necessary in the formulation and implementation of policy.

Second, the configuration of Canadian political institutions has encouraged the development of executive federalism. The cabinet-parlia-
mentary form of government in Canada "means that executive and legislative institutions, through the constitutional conventions of responsible
government, are fused in such a manner that what Thomas Hockin calls
the 'collective central energizing executive' (cabinet) is the 'key engine of
the state' within each of the federal and provincial levels of government"
(Dupré, 1985: 2). Within the federal and provincial legislative bodies,
power concentrates in the executive comprising the Prime Minister or
Premier and cabinet. The governments attend intergovernmental forums
as sovereign equals with the power and capacity to execute agreements
through their legislative assemblies.

The third contributing factor to the dominant influence of executive
federalism in Canadian political life is the nature of the political culture.
In a trenchant analysis of Canadian democracy, Reg Whitaker notes that
in contrast to other nations whose constitutions have been
autochthonous, "The constitution of Canada has been, from 1867 onward, an arrangement between elites.... The British North America Act of
1867 was ... almost entirely innocent of any recognition of the people as
the object of the constitutional exercise" (Whitaker, 1992: 206-07; cf.
Vipond, 1991: 73-74; Russell, 1993: 3-33, 228-35). The deference to
elites and, more especially, to political elites resulted in the emergence
and acceptance of often closed negotiations of pacts on matters of general
public concern between elected and appointed officials of the two levels
of government. It was not until the post-Charter era that this practice
faced a serious and sustained challenge (Cairns, 1991: 108-38).

These three factors combined to produce a special pattern of intergovernmental relations. Ronald Watts observes:

> This pattern has been marked in recent decades by three develop-
> ments: the proliferation of federal-provincial conferences, commit-
> tees and liaison agencies; the prominence of intergovernmental
> summitry as exemplified by the First Ministers' Conference; and the
> concentration within each government of responsibility for inter-
> governmental relations in the hands of coordinating agencies and
> specialists. (Watts, 1989: 441)

Watts further notes that the importance of this pattern of interaction has
followed not only from the frequency of contact between first ministers,

ministers, and senior officials but also from "the critical role" executive federalism has played in the provision of a wide range of programs and services to citizens, the negotiation of international trade agreements and economic policy, and the revision of the Canadian constitution (both successful and unsuccessful) (Watts, 1989: 441; Smiley, 1976: 55-57). The interactions have proliferated, resulting in an extensive and complex network of relations.

THE EVOLUTION OF EXECUTIVE FEDERALISM

Executive federalism has evolved through four main periods. The first period, from Confederation to the Second World War, was one of limited intergovernmental relations. The post-World War Two period witnessed a more harmonious and sustained level of interaction between the federal and provincial governments. By the mid-1960s, federal-provincial relations were becoming more conflictual. The 1980s to 1990s have been turbulent.

From Confederation to World War Two, the federal and provincial governments operated in relative isolation from each other. The designers of the constitution had attempted to allocate jurisdiction over local affairs to the provincial governments (section 92 of the Constitution Act, 1867) and jurisdiction over matters of national interest to the federal government (section 91 of the Constitution Act, 1867). By and large, these separate spheres of jurisdiction held. Smiley notes that while there was a Secretary of State for the Provinces in Prime Minister Macdonald's first cabinet, the position was abolished in 1873 (Smiley, 1976: 92). In "1868 there was a conference much like contemporary ones with the meetings of representatives of the Dominion, Ontario, Québec and New Brunswick governments to sort out the respective responsibilities of the two levels over immigration which had been made a subject of concurrent jurisdiction by Section 95 of the BNA Act" (*ibid.*). Although federal-provincial cooperation was possible when needed, interaction was limited.

The nature of relations is captured by Richard Simeon and Ian Robinson, who note that jurisdictional overlap and policy interdependence were limited. Federal-provincial shared-cost programs were introduced to combat venereal disease, to create employment offices and technical and agricultural programs, and to help the unemployed. Federal participation in the development of the welfare state was limited and *ad hoc*. They write that:

despite considerable expansion in the roles of the state at the provincial government level, federal government inaction left the classical model of "watertight compartments" intact. This in turn meant that complex intergovernmental machinery was unnecessary. Federal-provincial relations were confined to occasional exchanges between politicians. Before 1930, there were only nine of what we would today call "First Ministers Conferences" (FMCs). All those held before World War I were Interprovincial Conferences, with no significant federal participation. With the exception of the 1887 conference, those held before the War dealt primarily with demands for increases in fiscal transfers from Ottawa to help the provinces meet these new responsibilities. They did not serve as forums for making national decisions and federal governments did not feel much obligation to respond to them. (Simeon and Robinson, 1990: 49-50)

Still, the post-war changes in federal-provincial relations were glimpsed with the FMCs held in 1918 on taxation and federal arrangements and in 1927 and 1931 on patriation and amendment of the constitution (*ibid.*: 50). The need for cooperation and consultation was becoming evident.

The period dating from after World War Two to the mid-1960s witnessed the end of classical federalism and the development of the basis for more formalized interaction between the levels of government. The Great Depression and the world wars led to a centralization of powers within the Canadian federal state. The provinces were subordinate to the federal government. Smiley observes that:

In the period between the end of the Second World War and the establishment of the Continuing Committee on Fiscal and Economic Matters in 1955, institutionalized federal-provincial interaction was for the most part limited to two kinds of matters – the periodic renegotiation of the tax arrangements and cooperation in respect to specific services and facilities, the latter often within the framework of shared-cost programs. (Smiley, 1976: 57)

This changed with the creation of the Continuing Committee on Fiscal and Economic Matters, which proposed a more institutionalized mechanism for the exchange of information and examination of technical problems relating to economic and fiscal matters. However, "such formal consultation and coordination efforts remained primarily at the official level, seldom moving up to the political level at which policy goals, as distinct from means of implementation, were determined" (Simeon and Robinson, 1990: 151).

In the early 1960s, as the provinces began to regain their strength and demand more control and the state began to expand rapidly, the machinery of intergovernmental relations became more structured. The shift from administrative and cooperative federalism to more conflictual executive federalism occurred as federal and provincial governments vied for control of new and/or expanded areas of jurisdiction. Stevenson explains that the most compelling reason for this shift was that:

> federal-provincial conflicts were becoming too serious, too profound, and too sensitive to be safely entrusted to the diplomatic and managerial skills of subordinate officials. In particular the evident dissatisfaction of Québec during the Quiet Revolution could not be accommodated by traditional means.... At the same time or subsequently a number of other serious conflicts emerged which involved provinces other than Québec: conflicts over tax-sharing and the financing of health, education, and welfare, over economic relations with the United States, over regional development and the competitive scramble for investment, and over the division of benefits from mineral resources. All of these matters were clearly "political" rather than "administrative."... (Stevenson, 1989: 225)

The 1960s and 1970s saw an increase in tensions between the two levels of government as they became increasingly conscious of the public demands for more services and programs and the opposing need to restrain the deficits. The rise of the desire for independence in Québec and regionalism in the West exacerbated this tension in relations. The result was the development of a finely tuned mechanism for the negotiation and resolution of federal-provincial conflicts. The federal government created a Federal-Provincial Relations Office (FPRO), separate from the Prime Minister's Office but reporting to the Prime Minister, to handle intergovernmental matters. In June, 1993, Prime Minister Kim Campbell made the FPRO the responsibility of the Prime Minister. With the election of the Liberal government in October of that year, Intergovernmental Affairs was created and Marcel Massé named Minister. Québec established a Ministry of Federal-Provincial Affairs in 1961 (renamed Intergovernmental Affairs in 1967). The other provinces followed suit with Alberta

(1972), Newfoundland (1975), Ontario (1978), B.C. (1979), and Saskatchewan (1979) setting the pace (Stevenson, 1989: 226-27). The provinces also introduced regional intergovernmental forums such as the Council of Maritime Premiers and the Prairie Economic Council, which became the Western Premiers' Conference (Simeon and Robinson, 1990: 203).

The level of interaction between governments had increased exponentially. Between 1900 and 1959 there were nineteen FMCs, and between 1959 and 1984 this number had increased to thirty-nine. The number of agreements and arrangements has exploded. In 1985 alone, in addition to major fiscal transfers, there were ninety-nine cost-sharing agreements, fifty intergovernmental agreements for transfers, ninety-three joint activities, and over sixty-six other arrangements (Leslie, 1987: 71).

The nature of interactions also began to change. Relations were much more conflictual. The FMCs provided provinces with a forum to air their grievances and to press for concessions favoured by their constituents. Media coverage of the events encouraged this posturing and aggressive behaviour (Stevenson, 1989: 227). The subject matter of the conferences shifted from social policy to focus more on economic matters as deficit reduction and expenditure concerns became more pressing, and the constitution came to occupy a more central role by the 1980s.

The final period of executive federalism was presaged with the patriation and amendment of the constitution in 1982. The Constitution Act, 1982, entrenched FMCs on Aboriginal matters and to review the constitution in fifteen years. However, relations between Ottawa and the provinces were bitter (Banting and Simeon, 1983; Russell, 1993). The election of the Brian Mulroney Progressive Conservative government in 1984 and changes in provincial governments heralded a new era in intergovernmental relations and an unprecedented concentration on constitutional reform. As Simeon and Robinson pointed out,

National Reconciliation' lay at the core of the Tory's campaign message. They promised to 'bring Québec back in' to a constitutional consensus and reduce the tension and hostility between Ottawa and the provinces. The Prime Minister pledged a return to cooperative federalism, reforging the linguistic, regional and intergovernmental accommodations which had been shattered by the combination of international forces and Trudeau's New Federalism (1990: 301).

The result was a nuclear explosion of intergovernmental meetings. Simeon and Robinson document that between 1980 and 1984 there was an average of five FMCs per year, while in the first year of the Conservative government there were thirteen. However, this may include meetings with all first ministers or with the Prime Minister and one or more premiers. There were 353 ministerial meetings in 1985, compared to the average of eighty-two per year from 1980-84, and seventy-two deputy minister meetings compared to the 1980-84 annual average of forty-five (*ibid.*: 328). While the meetings encompassed a wide range of government matters – taxation, fiscal and economic matters, international trade, education, and so on – the negotiations on the constitution brought the institution of executive federalism most glaringly into the public eye. It was in this area of negotiations that the legitimacy of FMCs and executive federalism came under attack.

CONSTITUTIONAL CONSENSUS, CONFLICT, AND QUESTIONING

There have been three significant stages in the development of executive federalism in the constitutional processes of the 1980s and 1990s (see Brock, 1991; Brock, 1993). The first event that portended change for the conduct of intergovernmental relations was the patriation of the constitution and the entrenchment of the Canadian Charter of Rights and Freedoms in 1982. The second event, which challenged the past practice of negotiation through elite accommodation, was the Meech Lake process. The third stage in the evolution of intergovernmental negotiations and executive federalism occurred through the Charlottetown Accord. Each of these phases placed new pressures on the means of negotiating and achieving intergovernmental agreements, and will have lasting effects on the way business is done in Canada. Their ramifications reach beyond the constitutional sphere.

The process culminating in the patriation of the constitution and the entrenchment of the Charter signalled the beginning of the end of elite accommodation, that is, achieving political agreements between governments without public consultation and involvement. Both the process and results of the 1982 constitutional exercise encouraged this trend. In an endeavour to legitimize and to secure its constitutional amendment package, the federal government expanded the negotiations with the provincial governments by drawing societal groups into the discussions. This process as well as the substance of the Charter of Rights and Freedoms,

> bypassed governments and spoke directly to Canadians by defining
> them as bearers of rights, as well as by according specific constitu-
> tional recognition to women, aboriginals, official-language minor-
> ity populations, ethnic groups through the vehicle of multicultural-
> ism, and to those social categories explicitly listed in the equality
> rights section of the Charter. (Cairns, 1991: 109)

Incorporating these groups into the constitutional process and then giving
them a vested interest in the constitution through recognition of their
rights fundamentally altered the means of achieving constitutional change
in the future. No longer could eleven first ministers agree to changes and
then rest secure in the knowledge that they would be passed with relative
ease through their legislative bodies.

The Meech Lake process of constitutional negotiations reinforced this
change. The legacy of Meech Lake is that the constitutional process must
be open to public viewing and more inclusive of all interests in society.
Throughout the public hearings on the package of constitutional amendments achieved in a closed bargaining session between the eleven first
ministers, citizens and organizations criticized the process as hasty, un-
democratic, elitist, unrepresentative, secretive, and a violation of Canadian political norms (Canada, 1988: 2971-73; Manitoba, 1989: 69-71; Ontario, 1987: 42-45). In his review of the Meech Lake process, Andrew
Cohen concludes that the Accord was "constitution-making by stealth."
The requirement for the amendments in the Meech Lake Accord to be
passed by unanimous consent of the eleven Canadian legislatures encouraged a degree of secrecy that was inconsistent with public expectations in
"an open, pluralistic democracy." He concludes that by denying the
popular preference for openness, the first ministers created problems for
themselves. The public did not witness the concessions made by Québec,
and thus were suspicious of Québec Premier Bourassa's later claims that
he had compromised enough and could go no further. As a result,
Québec appeared unyielding (Cohen, 1990: 271-72; cf. Monahan, 1991:
7; Russell, 1993: 127-53). The emphasis on secrecy and the denial of the
necessity of a more open process undermined support for the Accord and
fuelled the opposition to it. The unravelling of Meech Lake clearly established that the process of amending the constitution through summit federalism was untenable.

The Charlottetown round of constitutional negotiations (1990–92) represented an attempt to respond to the public criticisms of the Meech Lake process. Negotiations between governments were preceded by the most extensive round of public consultations on the constitution ever held in Canada. Québec began the process with the Allaire (Liberal Party) report and the Bélanger-Campeau Commission on the Political and Constitutional Future of Québec. The federal government created the Citizen's Forum on Canada's Future, which consulted over 400,000 Canadians, the Special Joint Committee of the Senate and of the House of Commons on the Process for Amending the Constitution of Canada, which heard 200 witnesses and received over 500 briefs, and the Dobbie-Beaudoin Committee on the Renewal of Canada, which heard over 700 individuals, received over 3,000 briefs, and culminated in a series of constitutional conferences involving ordinary citizens and experts. The provinces and territories all followed suit to varying degrees of openness with their own constitutional review committees. By the end of this phase of constitutional reform, the governments had heard from a vast array of Canadians and prepared their positions for negotiation with the other governments.

The conduct of the actual negotiations between governments also differed substantially in the Charlottetown process. Although negotiations were conducted in private between elected and appointed government officials, the process appeared more deliberate and open. To the public, not privy to the pre-Meech negotiations, the Meech Lake Accord appeared to be devised in two sessions held at Meech Lake and the Langevin Block. In contrast, the Charlottetown Accord was seen to evolve through a more extensive series of meeting held between March 12 and August 28, 1992. The talks were more inclusive and representative, involving representatives from the federal, provincial, and territorial governments and the four major national Aboriginal organizations. Women's organizations were consulted during the talks as well.

The most drastic deviation from the past practice of constitutional negotiations occurred with the incorporation of a non-binding referendum into the ratification stage of negotiations. Not only did the Charlottetown Accord have to pass the scrutiny of the eleven legislative bodies, it had to pass the test of popular approval. It was at this stage that the Charlottetown Accord failed miserably. The No vote was resounding and fairly consistent throughout the country.

The Charlottetown process was a clear improvement over the Meech

Lake but it still harboured two essential weaknesses. The closed-door ne-gotiations, although more limited, rendered the process vulnerable to ac-cusations that the elites at the table were attempting to redirect the consti-tutional reforms to favour their special interests, despite the comprehen-siveness of the final package. The linkages between the early stages of public hearings and the outcome of negotiations were not clarified to the public. This raised public suspicion of the process. Further, the absence of Québec from the first stages of negotiations weakened its bargaining posi-tion and resulted in a package of proposals less responsive to its particular demands. Thus, the final package was easily subject to criticism in that province when compared to the earlier findings of its constitutional com-mittees. The attempt to blend the mechanism of executive federalism with greater public consultation failed in these two crucial respects.

The Charlottetown and Meech Lake processes have left two important legacies for the conduct of intergovernmental bargaining in Canada. First, future rounds of macro-constitutional change must necessarily be inclu-sive, open, and representative. A new threshold for public participation and influence has been set. Public hearings are a basic minimum require-ment, and a referendum for ratification of government deals is a fact of Canada's constitutional process. As Peter Russell suggests, while a refer-endum is not essential for minor changes, it is necessary for major changes (Russell, 1993: 231-35). Second, the roles and responsibilities of political leaders have been fundamentally altered. Effective leaders must listen to the public and incorporate their concerns into their negotiations, and then be prepared to defend and justify them reasonably to the public. A deal cannot appear to be a self-interested compromise between political elites but must embody a coherent vision or principle Canadians can accept that is a clear improvement from the status quo.

The experience of the constitutional process and its legacies are not just confined to that area but are seen in the operation of executive federalism in other areas of intergovernmental negotiations and policy-making gen-erally. In the past thirty years, politicians and bureaucrats have become in-creasingly conscious of the need to broaden their policy communities. In-terest groups have proliferated and become more involved in policy-mak-ing (Pross, 1986: 46-79; Cairns, 1986). This is a result of the increasing suspicion of governments since the Second World War, the expansion of the state into the lives of citizens, and the increasing reliance of govern-ments on private-sector expertise as policy becomes more complex and technically sophisticated (Pross, 1986: 66). Increasing public involvement also encourages more public involvement as groups and citizens note the successes of the lobbying efforts of others (*ibid.*: 67-68). It also means that intergovernmental negotiations are monitored more closely by the public. So, for example, federal-provincial negotiations on external and internal trade have been the subject of scrutiny by such groups as the Coalition of Concerned Canadians, business groups, and social policy advocates. Recent intergovernmental negotiations on the reduction and elimination of interprovincial trade barriers involved a series of meetings with citizens in each jurisdiction conducted by such organizations as the Canada West Foundation. Even the 1994 Western Premier's Conference was subject to a demonstration by First Nations.

The need to blend intergovernmental negotiations through the machinery of executive federalism with popular input should not be overemphasized, however. Recent interviews with two officials closely involved with intergovernmental negotiations yielded the observation that when the premiers' had agreed to open their meetings to the public, the media had declined to attend on the grounds that the content of the discussions were not sufficiently newsworthy to cover the costs of the coverage.[2] This comment was supported by members of the media covering the 1994 Western Premier's Conference.[3] Where the discussions and proposed changes are more substantive and significant, public attention and involvement increase. Still, the atmosphere and style of intergovernmental bargaining have shifted to become more attentive to public concerns and opinions, and where necessary, to direct public involvement.

THE FATE OF EXECUTIVE FEDERALISM

Executive federalism as the engine of the machinery to resolve conflicts between the federal and provincial governments in Canada has sputtered, coughed, and stalled at times, but it has generally seen Canada through turbulent periods. The ability of governments to negotiate agreements that provide for the well-being of the citizenry is essential to the preservation of Confederation. First Ministers' Conferences, ministerial meetings, and meetings of senior officials all facilitate cooperation and agreement. However, this process will continue to face mounting pressures in the 1990s.

The election of the Chrétien Liberal government in 1993 and its method of doing business with the provinces is reshaping the institution of executive federalism. On the one hand, intergovernmental negotiations remain the way of doing business, as exemplified by the extensive range of consultations Human Resources Minister Lloyd Axworthy is engaged in with the provinces over reforms to Canada's social safety net. Similarly, officials continue to meet regarding ongoing programs and services.

On the other hand, relations between Ottawa and the provincial intergovernmental offices have been more limited. In contrast to the first year of the Mulroney government, contacts in the first six months of the Liberal government between Intergovernmental Affairs and the provinces were fewer than expected by provincial officials.[4] Relations have been developing and, with the First Ministers' Conference on interprovincial trade barriers, contacts are increasing between the two levels of government. To independent observers, however, the federal focus seems to be on Québec rather than the other provinces. The federal government seems to be avoiding interactions that would detract from federal negotiations with Québec or that could adversely affect that province's view of Confederation as it stands poised on the eve of a potential sovereignty referendum (Gherson, 1994: A1).

The election of a separatist government in Québec in the fall of 1994 and the presence of a separatist party in Parliament have cast a pall over intergovernmental relations in Canada. First, the federal government is faced with the possibility that the Parti Québécois government may decline to send its representatives to meetings of elected and appointed officials of the federal and provincial governments. Instead, it might choose to negotiate bilateral agreements with the federal government. If a referendum on sovereignty yielded popular support for separation, a Québec government would press for negotiations to be bilateral with the federal government.[5] It would most likely be reluctant to cooperate in a forum of the federal and provincial governments where it would be outnumbered.[6] Memories of 1982, when Québec was left out of the constitutional deal struck between Ottawa and the other nine provinces, would only reinforce the tendency to avoid intergovernmental forums.

Second, the other provinces realize the need to prepare themselves for the prospect of either a new round of constitutional or administrative negotiations with Québec or the separation of that province. At the Western Premiers' Conference held in Gimli, Manitoba, in May, 1994, although the topic was not on the formal agenda and two premiers declined public comment, the premiers began to address the question of Québec and to discuss western strategies and positions on the separation of Québec. This form of executive interprovincialism strengthens the bargaining positions of the cooperating regions but makes the prospects for achieving agreements and compromises in the arena of executive federalism more difficult. Positions are firmer and there is less room for bargaining. This places additional stress on the forum as a means of resolving intergovernmental disputes.

Third, since the demise of the Charlottetown Accord and with the prospects of a debate over separation looming, the federal government has engaged in more bilateral negotiations and arrangements with Québec. For example, Ottawa entered bilateral negotiations with Québec on the Charlottetown provisions on labour market training almost immediately following the referendum defeat. Other provisions have been the subject of ongoing bilateral negotiations between Ottawa and the provinces. While this strategy of appeasement may be successful in allaying some of Québec's concerns with the Confederation bargain and may even serve the interests of other provinces, it weakens the sense of comity essential to the operation of a federal system of government. Rather than striving to cooperate and negotiate mutually beneficial accommodations, the provinces act in their own limited interests. In the process, the federal government is weakened and the ties of federation are attenuated. The result, asymmetrical federalism, begins to approximate a truly confederal system and weakens bonds of national unity. In this case, the prospects for executive federalism as a means of resolving disputes, containing provincial conflict, and encouraging cooperation become bleak.

The legacy of the constitutional negotiations of the 1980s and 1990s also strains the fibres of the intergovernmental network of relations. Two of the most important lessons learned at the end of Charlottetown were that the demand for greater public input into the constitutional negotiations and the future of Canada is a fact of Canadian life, and that definitions of political leadership must be revised. If the Canadian government enters into negotiations with Québec over separation or a revision to the constitution, at a minimum Aboriginal organizations will expect to be involved. Other societal groups may also demand to be included if they perceive that their rights are affected. The Canadian leadership will have to be attentive to the concerns voiced by these segments of the Canadian populace and their degree of popular support. The first ministers will have to justify their actions within this environment of heightened popular sensitivities. However, this does not place an unduly restrictive burden on the operation of executive federalism, it merely asks the governments to ensure that not only are their positions representative of their populations but that they also appear to be so. Where governments must compromise or concede on an issue of importance to the citizens, they must be able to provide a strong justification that is consistent with the principles of Confederation or would result in an improvement of the status quo. The result is a democratic check on the executive federalism.[7] However, the danger is that Québec's special position within Confederation is undermined, which could lead to an impasse.

The mixed fate of executive federalism was perhaps best captured in the July, 1994, First Ministers' Conference on interprovincial trade barriers. The Prime Minister called the provincial premiers to Ottawa to sign the agreement on the elimination of internal trade barriers. On the surface, the achievement of the agreement is a clear indication that executive federalism is alive and well. However, a look beneath the surface reveals that agreement was only secured because the more contentious and most important issues, such as agriculture and procurement policies, were not included but left subject to future negotiations. This is perhaps a portentous omen for intergovernmental negotiations on Canada's future.

Claims that executive federalism is at an end are exaggerated and premature. Its fate is not clear. It still provides the means of ensuring cooperation among governments. Yet, it is being subjected to new pressures and constraints that require modifications to its operation. Whether it will remain the way of doing business in Canada will be determined by the will or, conversely, the intransigence of Canada's elected and appointed representatives.

NOTES

1   I would like to thank the Social Sciences and Humanities Research Council of Canada for its generous support of this paper as part of a larger project on the constitutional process. The paper benefited from the suggestions of Leanne Matthes, although the faults remain mine.

2   Confidential interview with senior officials involved in intergovernmental negotiations for the Manitoba government, Winnipeg, June 27, 1994.

3   Confidential interviews with Manitoba reporters attending the conference, Winnipeg, June, 1994.

4   Private conversations with senior officials in the Manitoba government involved in intergovernmental negotiations, Winnipeg, June 27, 1994.

5   This is the line of action anticipated in the PQ policy book Des Idées Pour Mon Pays (Québec, 1994).

6   Controversy abounds on whether Québec could negotiate sovereignty with
     Ottawa or would have to negotiate with the other provincial governments
     as well. For a review of expert opinion, see Mackie (1994: A5).

7   It could be argued that this is a logical result of the creation of an institution
     for achieving intergovernmental compromises that competes with or under-
     mines the authority of Parliament.

REFERENCES

Brock, Kathy L. (1991). "The Politics of Process," in Douglas M. Brown, ed., *Can-
    ada: The State of the Federation 1991*. Kingston: Institute of Intergovernmental
    Relations: 57-87.

Brock, Kathy L. (1993). "Learning From Failure: Lessons From Charlottetown,"
    Constitutional Forum 4, 2 (Winter): 29-33.

Cairns, Alan C. (1986). "The Embedded State: State-Society Relations in Can-
    ada," in Keith Banting, ed., State and Society: Canada in a Comparative Con-
    text. Toronto: University of Toronto Press.

Cairns, Alan C. (1991). Disruptions: Constitutional Struggles from the Charter to
    Meech Lake, edited by Douglas E. Williams. Toronto: McClelland & Stewart.

Canada (1988). *Minutes of Proceedings and Evidence of the Special Joint Committee of the
    Senate and of the House of Commons on the 1987 Constitutional Accord*. No. 166: 12.

Cohen, Andrew (1990). *A Deal Undone: The Making and Breaking of the Meech Lake
    Accord*. Vancouver: Douglas & McIntyre.

Dupré, J. Stefan. (1985). "The Workability of Executive Federalism," in Richard
    Simeon, ed., *Intergovernmental Relations*. Toronto: University of Toronto Press.

Gherson, Giles (1994). "First Ministers' success solid if not dazzling." *Globe and
    Mail*, July 19: A1.

Jackson, Robert J., and Doreen Jackson (1994). *Politics in Canada: Culture, Institu-
    tions, Behaviour and Public Policy*, Third edition. Scarborough: Prentice-Hall.

Leslie, Peter (1987). *Federal State, National Economy*. Toronto: University of
    Toronto Press.

Mackie, Richard (1994). "Breakup talks must include all regions, experts say,"
    Globe and Mail, June 7: A5.

Manitoba Task Force on Meech Lake (1989). *Report on the 1987 Constitutional Ac-
    cord*. Winnipeg: Government Printer: 69-71.

Monahan, Patrick (1991). *Meech Lake: The Inside Story*. Toronto: University of
    Toronto Press.

Ontario, Select Committee on Constitutional Reform (1988). *Report on the Constitution Amendment 1987*. Toronto: Queen's Park: 42–45.

Pross, Paul (1986). Group Politics and Public Policy. Toronto: Oxford University Press.

Russell, Peter H. (1993). Constitutional Odyssey: Can Canadians Become A Sovereign People? Second edition. Toronto: University of Toronto Press.

Simeon, Richard, and Ian Robinson (1990). State, Society, and the Development of Canadian Federalism. Toronto: University of Toronto Press.

Smiley, Donald V. (1976). *Canada in Question: Federalism in the Seventies*. Second Edition. Toronto: McGraw-Hill Ryerson.

Stevenson, Garth (1989). *Unfulfilled Union*. Toronto, Gage.

Vipond, Robert (1991). *Liberty and Community: Canadian Federalism and the Failure of the Constitution*. Buffalo: State University of New York Press.

Watts, Ron (1989). "Executive Federalism: The Comparative Context," in David P. Shugarman and Reg Whitaker, eds., *Federalism and Political Community*. Peterborough, Ont.: Broadview Press.

Whitaker, Reg (1992). "Democracy and the Canadian Constitution," in Whitaker, *A Sovereign Idea: Essays on Canada as a Democratic Community*. Montreal and Kingston: McGill-Queen's University Press: 205–32.

CHAPTER FIVE

Living with Dualism and Multiculturalism

Kenneth McRoberts

THE FOCUS OF THIS CHAPTER IS HOW THE STATE DEALS WITH
cultural differences in Canadian society. The first issue to be addressed is
how the Canadian state *defines* cultural difference. Among the many forms
of cultural differentiation that might be identified within the Canadian
population, which ones does the Canadian state openly recognize? As we
shall see, the struggle over recognition of cultural difference is a major
force in the politics of contemporary Canada, as it is in most modern societies (Taylor, 1992).

A second issue is how the state seeks to *accommodate* the cultural differences it does recognize. Beyond mere recognition, groups may make a
variety of demands on the state: that public services be available in the
language and according to the mores of the group; that the group be guaranteed a presence among the personnel of the state; and that the state actively promote the survival and development of the group. Groups may
even claim that the surest way for these demands to be met is for them to
have a state of their own. This leads us to the theme of this volume. In
many settings, a major reason to adopt federalism has been to accommodate cultural difference by affording groups control over state structures
that, for certain purposes, are fully autonomous.

In this chapter we will explore the extent to which the recognition and
accommodation of cultural difference are reflected both in the fact that
Canada's political system is federal and in the way that Canadian federalism has developed and functioned. At the same time, we will see how
both the definition of cultural difference and its relationship to federalism
have become central areas of controversy in contemporary Canada. Alternative definitions of cultural difference may have radically different implications for the organization of Canadian federalism. In fact, political actors, including governments themselves, may promote particular defini-

tions of cultural difference precisely because they would justify the version of Canadian federalism they are seeking. Conversely, some individuals, including some advocates of Québec independence, may reject federalism outright from the belief that the present federal system insufficiently recognizes their preferred definition of cultural difference in Canada.

CONCEPTS OF CULTURAL DIFFERENCE:
DUALISM VS. MULTICULTURALISM

Historically, the most clearly articulated conception of cultural difference was dualist, rooted in the distinction between "English Canada" and "French Canada." The two entities were depicted alternatively as "societies," "peoples," "races," and, in some cases, even "nations." Typically, they were seen as the two founders or creators of Canada.

Not surprisingly, this notion of cultural difference was far more popular among the population designated as French-Canadian than among their English-Canadian counterparts, who would tend to deny that Canadians were fundamentally divided along cultural lines and would see Canadians as a whole as descended from British stock.[1] Clearly, this dualist conception of Canada was exclusivist in that notions of "two founding peoples" allowed no role for Aboriginal populations, despite the fact that as the first arrivals to Canada they had peopled the territory for a far longer period of time. By the same token, in focusing on the peoples presumed to have participated in Confederation, dualism seemed to deny any status to Canadians of neither British nor French origin. In effect, they were presumed to have been assimilated to one or the other community.

At the same time, this conception of the country tended to gloss over substantial cultural differentiations within each of the designated peoples. While the two entities were explicitly differentiated on the basis of language, it was usually presumed that other cultural differences closely overlapped with language. Thus, just as French Canada was Catholic and descended from France, so English Canada was Protestant and descended from Great Britain. Yet, of course, at Confederation the social reality was already more complex, and it became much more so as the years progressed.

There was a further ambiguity: how is this cultural dualism transposed onto the territory of Canada? In other words, where is French Canada located, and where is English Canada? Much of the continuing debate over the terms of Canadian federalism, and the very nature of Canada, hinges on the answer to this question.

Even if the two communities are presumed to be culturally homogeneous and are delimited on the basis of language alone, it is not at all clear where each begins and ends. How, in fact, are Canadians to be classified linguistically: on the basis of their mother tongue or on the basis of the language they are most likely to use at this point in their lives? For that matter, must people necessarily be placed in one linguistic grouping or the other? What if they have competence in both languages?

Depending on how each of the questions is answered, one can derive radically different estimates of the relative size and distribution of Canada's linguistic communities. This can be seen in 1991 census data for mother tongue and the language most often used at home. Reflecting the pressures for assimilation to English that operate in most parts of Canada, the proportion of Canadians using French at home is smaller, 23.3 per cent, than the proportion whose mother tongue is French, 24.4 per cent. The opposite is true for English: 61.7 per cent stated English as their mother tongue but 68.3 per cent used it at home (*Census of Canada, 1991,* as calculated and reproduced in Canada, 1993: 15, 17).

Furthermore, as Table One shows, if data are organized on a provincial rather than national basis, then Canada's linguistic communities appear to be concentrated in different parts of the country. Canada as whole may be dualist, but its regions are not. This is especially the case if home language is used: in all but three provinces, Québec, New Brunswick, and Ontario, the linguistic minorities are less than 3 per cent. (In Ontario the figure is just above, at 3.2 per cent). Canada's francophone population is largely contained within a single province: in 1991 Québec contained 89.5 per cent of the Canadians using French as their home language.[2] By the same token, 93.8 per cent of Canada's anglophones live in the rest of the country. As for Canadians who claim to speak both languages, they, too, are concentrated territorially: in 1991, they represented 29.5 per cent of New Brunswick's population, 35.4 per cent of Québec's, and 11.4 per cent of Ontario's, but less than 10 per cent in all the other provinces.

Thus, restrictive as the dualist conception of Canada may seem, it allows for wide differences in interpretation. Depending in part on the measure one uses and the standards one imposes, French Canada and English Canada could be seen as extending throughout Canada or French Canada could be seen as the preserve of Québec alone, with English Canada equated to the rest of the country. Obviously, these different formula-

TABLE ONE: MOTHER TONGUE AND HOME LANGUAGES FOR
OFFICIAL-LANGUAGE MINORITIES, AS PER CENT OF CANADIAN AND
PROVINCIAL POPULATIONS, 1991

	Mother Tongue	Home Language
Newfoundland	0.5	0.2
Nova Scotia	4.1	2.5
New Brunswick	33.6	31.2
Prince Edward Island	4.5	2.4
Québec	9.7	11.1
Ontario	5.0	3.2
Manitoba	4.7	2.3
Saskatchewan	2.2	0.7
Alberta	2.3	0.8
British Columbia	1.6	0.4

Source: Calculated from Census of Canada, 1991, and presented in Canada, Annual Report, 1992: Commissioner of Official Languages (Ottawa: Supply and Services, 1993), 15, 17.

tions have very different political implications.

In the late 1960s, the very legitimacy of the dualist vision of Canada was directly challenged by advocates of an alternative conception of cultural difference. Primarily within English Canada, there was growing support for a new, more open-ended definition of cultural difference in Canada based on the concept of "multiculturalism." In effect, Canada was to be composed of an infinite number of cultural entities. In fact, its cultural composition was to be seen as in constant flux, as new bases of cultural differentiation become established and are eligible for recognition.

This new conception of cultural difference has the advantage of inclusiveness. On the other hand, it denies pride of place to French Canada which becomes one of myriad cultural entities. If English Canadians had been indifferent or hostile to dualism and the status it accorded their collectivity, French Canadians had been keenly attached to their status as one of two founding peoples. Nor does multiculturalism necessarily accommodate all groups that felt excluded by the older dualist notion. In particular, Aboriginal peoples resist the notion that their distinctiveness can be equated with the contemporary differences among non-Aboriginal Canadians.

Thus, a major theme of Canadian politics in recent decades has been the conflict between two visions of Canada: dualism vs. multiculturalism. The debate over these two visions, and their respective application, is directly linked to the debate over competing visions of Canadian federalism. Each debate has, in effect, reinforced the other.

CANADIAN FEDERALISM AND DUALISM

Canadian federalism is intimately linked to the notion of a Canada fundamentally divided between two linguistic groups. The terms of Canadian federalism may not be explicit about this. The British North America Act contained only one provision about language use. Section 133 stipulates that both French and English may be used in the federal Parliament and courts as well as the provincial legislature and courts of a single province: Québec. It also states that French and English shall be used in publication of the debates and laws of the federal Parliament and the Québec legislature.

However, the fact of federalism is very much a recognition of dualism and an attempt to accommodate it. It was essentially at the insistence of French-Canadian leaders, fearful that the new central government would be dominated by the English-speaking majority, that Canada was established on a federal basis. Prevailing opinion among English-speaking leaders had favoured a unitary system. Federalism was adopted primarily to afford autonomy to French Canadians by forming a province, Québec, in which French Canadians would be in the clear majority. By the same token, the powers assigned to the provinces were primarily the powers that, in the judgment of French-Canadian leaders, were necessary to protect the cultural distinctiveness of Québec's French-speaking population: education, civil law, solemnization of marriage, hospitals and charities, etc.

To be sure, cultural dualism is not the only rationale for Canadian federalism. With time, especially as provinces were created in western Canada, Canadian federalism was increasingly seen as necessary to the protection of regional interests that were economic rather than cultural. But within Québec, the old rationale for Canadian federalism has remained predominant.

Federalism does indeed provide an important support to cultural dualism. For certain purposes, the francophones of Québec are transformed from a mere component of Canada's linguistic minority to a linguistic majority. But federalism is an imperfect support for cultural dualism: linguistic and territorial boundaries do not fully coincide. Thanks to federalism the position of some of Canada's francophones is even weaker than their minority status in Canada would suggest. Table One shows how in most provinces francophones are reduced to small minorities, far below their demographic weight in Canada as a whole. During the first century of Canadian Confederation, state recognition of cultural dualism was closely bound by this.

From Confederation on, most Québec governments saw a clear advantage in emphasizing a dualist notion of Canada in which French Canada is effectively concentrated in Québec. The defence of French Canada and protection of the status and powers of the Québec government become one and the same. As Québec Premier Maurice Duplessis declared in 1951: "the Fathers of Confederation, ignoring their differences of race, religion and political tradition, created the federal system and gave us [the province of] Québec, thus assuring the survival of the French language and culture" (cited in Bourque and Duchastel, 1988: 152, my translation). Historically, this identification of Québec and French Canada did not preclude a certain measure of dualism within the province. Until recent decades, the Québec government observed a de facto regime of linguistic equality in which government services were available in both English and French.

However, identification of Québec and French Canada did preclude recognition of dualism in the other provinces. It inhibited support by the French Canadians of Québec, and their provincial government, of the claims by French Canadians in other provinces for concessions from their provincial governments. And it reinforced the other provincial governments in their disposition to ignore these claims. Thus, by the 1920s, the elements of dualism that had been established in some provinces (most notably in the West) had disappeared. Frequently, this stemmed from explicit government policy, as with the 1890 Manitoba law that ended official use of French within provincial institutions and abolished denominational schools, thus eliminating the base for French-language education. Similarly, in 1912 the Ontario government passed Regulation 17, which established English as the sole language of instruction after the third year of schooling (Royal Commission on Bilingualism and Biculturalism, 1968: 45-51; Foucher 1991: 95, 102).

For its part, the federal government responded in only minimal terms to the claims of cultural dualism, reflecting the extent to which French Canadians were also very much in a minority within Canada as a whole. Section 133's provisions regarding Parliament and federal courts were generally respected (although simultaneous translation was not introduced to Parliament until the Diefenbaker government). But the French language was denied any coequal status in other federal institutions, such as cabinet and the bureaucracy. Here, the effective language of work was English. As for the numerical presence of French speakers, francophones normally secured a representation in federal cabinets equal to their proportion of the Canadian population but were largely absent from important economic portfolios. They were markedly underrepresented in the upper levels of the federal civil service (Gibson, 1970; Beattie, 1975).

In effect, recognition and accommodation of cultural dualism was closely defined by Canadian federalism. The province of Québec constituted a kind of "reserve." Within Québec, French-Canadian cultural distinctiveness enjoyed state support; outside Québec, it was left largely to its own resources except for token recognition in federal institutions. Yet, limited as this accommodation might have been, it seemed to be the maximum tolerable to most English Canadians. And it seemed to be provide sufficient security to the French Canadians of Québec. The French-Canadian minorities outside Québec had become politically invisible.

With the 1960s, these arrangements came under attack from a variety of directions. Within Québec, francophone leaders increasingly contended that the logic of dualism required a restructuring of Canadian federalism. Unwilling to accede to such demands, the federal government sought to undermine the logic on which they were based by reducing the linkage between dualism and federalism: dualism was redefined to exist throughout Canada and to be a preeminently federal responsibility. Yet, this new federal commitment to dualism precipitated an attack on the concept of dualism, in favour of multiculturalism. Finally, the Québec government sought to reinforce its territorially based conception of Canadian dualism by defining French alone as the official language of Québec.

QUÉBEC: RADICALIZING THE DUALISM OF FEDERALISM

With the 1960s, Québec intellectual and political elites became increasingly committed to the argument that the terms of Canadian federalism had become outmoded. A wide variety of political forces, from the separatist *Ralliement pour l'indépendance nationale* to the Québec government itself, under Liberal Premier Jean Lesage, began to demand change.

Within a new Québec-based nationalism it was argued that the set of powers afforded to the Québec provincial government at the time of Confederation was no longer sufficient to meet its responsibilities as the primary protector and promoter of the French fact in Canada. The Québec government could no longer protect Québec's cultural distinctiveness simply by precluding hostile incursions by the federal government and leaving social and economic responsibilities in private hands. The Québec government had to act itself to raise the level of well-being of francophones through expanded public services, displacing the Church from its historical position, and to carve out a role for francophones in the upper levels of the Québec economy, breaking the historical dominance of anglophones. Only in this way could francophone society develop within the urban, industrial context of modern Québec.

Underpinning this argument was the claim that, as the only government responsible to an electorate that is primarily francophone, only the Québec government could be counted on to continue the struggle to maintain and develop francophone society in Canada. Lesage declared in 1964, "Quebec has become the political expression of French Canada and for all practical purposes the homeland of all whose who speak French in our country" (cited in Balthazar, 1991: 84).

As the times had changed, so had the powers that the Québec government needed to pursue its historical role. In effect, Québec nationalists took the dualist logic embedded within Canadian federalism and modified (or "updated") it to justify a profound change in Canadian federalism. Typically, they argued that Canada's dualism now meant that Québec would have to assume powers that the other provinces did not. Québec would assume a special status or a *statut particulier*. Alternatively, some Québec nationalists argued that it meant conversion to a "confederal" Canada in which the Québec government and the federal government would have coequal status as the governments of distinct nations. By 1967, this latter vision was articulated not only by René Lévesque and his Mouvement souveraineté-association but by the Québec government, under Premier Daniel Johnson.

FEDERAL GOVERNMENT: FREEING DUALISM FROM FEDERALISM

The federal government, concerned over the evident erosion of support for the federal system among Québec francophones, responded by challenging outright the claim that Canadian dualism now necessitated a heightened role for the Québec government. Instead, Ottawa offered a new conception of Canadian dualism with radically different implications for Canadian federalism. Ottawa insisted that francophone and anglophone populations are present (or should be) throughout Canada. Accordingly, preserving dualism is not the particular responsibility of Québec or any other government. It is the common responsibility of all governments, and especially the federal government. On this basis, Québec cannot invoke dualism to advance its demands for a new federal order – at least not after the other governments have assumed their responsibilities. As Pierre Trudeau declared in 1968, if minority language rights are entrenched throughout Canada then the French-Canadian nation would stretch from Maillardville in B.C. to the Acadian community on the Atlantic coast:

> Once you have done that, Quebec cannot say it alone speaks for French Canadians.... Mr. Robarts will be speaking for French Canadians in Ontario, Mr. Robichaud will be speaking for French Canadians in New Brunswick, Mr. Thatcher will speak for French Canadians in Saskatchewan, and Mr. Pearson will be speaking for all French Canadians. Nobody will be able to say, "I need more power because I speak for the French-Canadian nation." (cited in Radwanski, 1978: 286)

In effect, the federal government sought to give dualism a base that was independent of federalism.

Accordingly, the Trudeau government embarked on a massive program to reinforce Canada's linguistic dualism. Much of the groundwork had already been laid by the Royal Commission on Bilingualism and Biculturalism (B&B Commission), created by Lester Pearson in 1963. In 1967, the Commission published its first of several volumes of recommendations for language policy. The Trudeau government adopted many of the proposed measures, although taking care that they squared with its own vision of a dualistic Canada.

In part, the task was to strengthen dualism within the federal government's own institutions so that they could project the image of a bilingual Canada. In 1966, Lester Pearson had already committed the government to the objective of public servants being able to work effectively in their own language. The Trudeau government carried on with the Pearson government's policy of designating a substantial number of positions as bilingual and providing opportunities for unilingual civil servants (primarily anglophones) to be trained in the other language. At the same time, Trudeau made a point of changing past practices and naming francophones to cabinet portfolios with major social and economic responsibilities: Finance, Industry, Trade and Commerce, Regional Economic Expansion, National Health and Welfare, and the Treasury Board (e.g., Smiley, 1983: 35).

Strengthening Canadian dualism also meant intervening directly in Canadian society. More precisely, as we have seen, the federal government had a strong interest in a dualism in which francophones and anglophones were jointly present throughout the country rather than being concentrated in different regions. Accordingly, the primary federal objective was to strengthen the francophone minorities outside Québec, so that in Trudeau's words the "French-Canadian nation" would stretch across the country.

In 1969, under Pierre Trudeau, the government passed the Official Languages Act calling for bilingual services in federal establishments, such as airports, and bilingualism in all other services within areas designated as bilingual districts. In addition, Radio-Canada's television and radio operations outside Québec were greatly expanded. By 1981, Radio-Canada could claim that its networks of AM radio and television reached 94 per cent and 92.2 per cent, respectively, of the French-speaking population outside Québec (Chevrier, 1983: 19). Ottawa sought to strengthen the position of the official-language minorities by directly supporting their organizations. By 1987 Ottawa was providing a total of close to $21 million in operational funding to 378 organizations; funds went to organizations in each of the ten provinces.[3]

Nonetheless, as it sought to assume primary responsibility for the promotion of Canadian dualism, the federal government found itself hampered by the terms of Canadian federalism. Such crucial jurisdictions as education and social services lie with the provinces. Therefore, Ottawa adopted a variety of methods to induce the provincial governments to accept its understanding of Canadian dualism within their own jurisdictions.

Personal pressure was placed on provincial premiers (most notably Ontario's) to adopt official bilingualism. In addition, funds were provided to private organizations that could be expected to lobby the provinces for "the passing and implementation of legislation recognizing the equal status of the two official languages."[4] At the same time, conditional grants were offered to the provinces under which they would provide education and other services to their official-language minorities. Ottawa also provided the provincial governments with funds to train Canadians in the other official language.

In terms of the dynamics of Canadian federalism, these various initiatives represent one of the most dramatic instances of the federal government seeking to influence directly the way in which the provincial governments act within their own jurisdictions. Nonetheless, the results of this campaign were uneven. Through its conditional grants Ottawa was able to induce most provincial governments to expand their minority-language services. Now all provincial governments have agreements with Ottawa spelling out the terms of financial assistance for minority-language education; eight provinces also have agreements regarding other minority-language services (Canada, 1993: 25).

However, Ottawa has had limited success in getting the provincial governments to adopt legislation that guarantees rights to official-language minorities. In particular, they have resisted giving the two languages official status in their institutions. New Brunswick did do so. Under the Official Languages Act of 1969 the province embraced official bilingualism. This is not surprising, given the size of its francophone minority. No other province has matched New Brunswick. Ontario has come the closest. Under *The French Language Services Act*, passed in 1986, French is recognized as "an official language in the courts and in education" (Ontario, 1986), French-language services must be provided in areas designated as bilingual districts, and as of 1991 legislation is adopted in both languages. But Ontario has steadfastly resisted Ottawa's pressures to adopt formally official bilingualism. For its part, Saskatchewan, under Bill 2, affirmed the right to use English and French in the legislature and in the courts (for criminal cases), but Bill 2 does not require that all laws be presented in both languages or that all existing laws be translated into French. Alberta's Bill 60 allows both languages to be used in the legislature but does not allow for enactment of laws in both languages.

Provinces have been more inclined to pass laws providing for the provision of services to francophone minorities. For instance, during the early

1980s the Manitoba government of Howard Pawley was unable to overcome widespread opposition to a bill that would have made French and English official languages of the province. Nonetheless, in 1990 the government of Gary Filmon passed a law providing for French-language services.

Yet, the most direct challenge to the federal government's attempts to secure the institutionalization of linguistic dualism at the provincial level came from Québec.

QUÉBEC: FROM DUALISM TO FRENCH PRIMACY

During the late 1960s Québec's long-standing policy of linguistic dualism, which the B&B Commission had seen as the model for all the provinces, came under increasing attack among Québec francophones. Nationalists contended that as long as English enjoyed a coequal status to French then the Québec government was precluded from undertaking policies needed to rectify the historical inferiority of French, and of francophones, within Québec society and economy. Pointing to demographers' projections of a decline in the francophone proportion of Québec's population, nationalists argued that the Québec government should require immigrant parents to send their children to francophone schools rather than anglophone schools as they had tended to do. By the same token, they insisted, only through the intervention of the Québec government could French assume its proper role as a language of work in the upper levels of the Québec economy. Finally, they argued that improvement in the quality of French used by Québec francophones required a concerted government effort through disseminating glossaries, staging public opinion campaigns, etc. In sum, rather than affording equal status to English and French, the Québec government needed to give a priority status to French.

As a result of these pressures, in 1974 the Liberal government of Robert Bourassa adopted Bill 22, which declared French alone to be the "official language" of Québec; required that children have a "sufficient knowledge" of English to attend English-language schools; and established a program of financial incentives to private enterprises to strengthen the role of French as a language of work. For its part, the Parti Québécois government of René Lévesque replaced Bill 22 with Bill 101, which, among other things, restricted English-language education to children whose parents were educated in English in Québec, made it an obligation for private enterprises to strengthen the role of French as a language of work, and required that commercial signs should be in French only.

Clearly, Québec's move to French primacy was a major blow to Ottawa's plans for a pan-Canadian dualism. Yet, as the Bourassa government was forced to recognize, it constituted the almost unavoidable response to linguistic conditions within Québec. Only on the basis of French primacy could the Québec state seek to reverse the historical inferiority of French within the province. It is difficult within a framework of equality between languages to legitimize state intervention on behalf of the *majority* language, even if it may be the one in an inferior situation or under assimilationist pressures. The federal government's commitment to official bilingualism led to vigorous support of the French language outside Québec but precluded it from acting to strengthen the position of French within Québec, even though that was the primary preoccupation of Québec francophones.

MULTICULTURALISM: THE ATTACK ON DUALISM

In its effort to champion a dualist vision of Canada that would deprive the Québec government of any special claims on Canadian federalism, the federal government (especially under Pierre Trudeau) was careful to define dualism in strictly linguistic terms. Yet, traditionally, Canadian dualism had been seen as more than just one of languages. Associated with each language were distinct cultures. Frequently, the linguistic communities had been portrayed as peoples or even nations.

In establishing the Royal Commission on Bilingualism and Biculturalism Lester Pearson had given it a mandate that clearly reflected this broader understanding of Canadian dualism:

> to recommend what steps should be taken to develop the Canadian Confederation on the basis of *an equal partnership between the two founding races*, taking into account the contribution made by the other ethnic groups to the cultural enrichment of Canada and the measures that should be taken to safeguard that contribution. (Royal Commission, 1965: 151; emphasis added)

Moreover, in its early deliberations, the Commission had interpreted its mandate expansively. Canadian dualism found expression in collective rather than individual terms. Treating culture as "a way of being, thinking and feeling" (Royal Commission, 1967: xxxi), the Commission saw Canada as containing "two dominant cultures ... embodied in distinct societies" (*ibid.*, xxxiii). On this basis, it was Canada as a whole, rather than individual Canadians, that was bicultural: "Culture is to the group rather what personality is to the individual; it is rare for a person to have two personalities or two styles of living at the same time" (*ibid.*, xxxi). For that matter, few Canadians could ever be truly bilingual: "complete bilingualism – the equal command of two languages – is rare and perhaps impossible" (*ibid.*, xxviii). A bilingual country is one in which institutions provide services in two languages, "not one where all inhabitants necessarily speak two languages" (*ibid.*). In short, Canada's dualism was one of two collectivities, not only speaking different languages but living according to different cultures within distinct societies.

Defined in such sweeping terms, cultural difference is bound to have implications for political institutions, including the structures of federalism. The B&B Commission had intended to draw the broad outlines of a constitutional order that would be compatible with its vision of a bicultural Canada. For a variety of reasons, this never happened.

As the concept of biculturalism became increasingly prominent, thanks to the activities of the B&B Commission, so it also came under growing attack. In part, the attack came from Canadians who felt personally excluded by the notion of a bicultural Canada. In the mandate of the Commission, the objective of an equal partnership between "the two founding races" had been followed by reference to the "contribution of Canada's other ethnic groups," but this "contribution" was clearly of a second order. For its part the Commission sought to avoid attaching "ethnic" connotations of common ancestry to Canada's two "dominant cultures," stressing the need for the francophone and anglophone societies to integrate effectively "Canadians who are of neither British nor French origin." At the same time, it contended that the two societies should aid "the other ethnic groups" to preserve their cultural heritages (*ibid.*, xxv). Yet, for the leaders of organizations representing these other groups, nothing less than formal equality among cultures would do.

Deep reservations over the concept of biculturalism also were being felt by some francophone intellectual and political elites who were strongly opposed to the claims of Québec nationalism. Pierre Trudeau and his *Cité libre* colleagues responded to the B&B Commission's *Prelimi-*

nary Report by drawing a sharp distinction between bilingualism and biculturalism. Whereas the former was to be desired, the latter could have disastrous consequences. They worried that it could legitimize the claims of Québec separatists. How, they wondered, would it be possible to construct Confederation on the basis of equality between the two cultures without "being led necessarily to propose the division of Canada into two national states?" (Comité pour une politique fonctionnelle, 1965: 14; my translation).[5]

It is primarily this second set of concerns that explains why, in 1971, the Trudeau government formally adopted a policy of multiculturalism rather than biculturalism. Trudeau was explicit as to what he was about:

> The very title of the Royal Commission whose recommendations we are now in the process of implementing seems to suggest that bilingualism and biculturalism are inseparable. But the term biculturalism does not accurately depict our society; the word multiculturalism is more precise in this respect. (Cited in *Le Devoir*, October 13, 1971; my translation.)

Within the logic of multiculturalism, Canada is composed not of two "dominant cultures," let alone founding peoples, but of many cultures all of equal status. By the same token, the province of Québec cannot claim, as the primary home of Canada's francophone culture, to have any particular status within Canadian federalism. If all of Canada's cultures are equal in status, then its provinces are assuredly of equal status. By adopting a multicultural rather than bicultural vision of Canada, the federal government was entrenching a particular conception of Canadian federalism.

Yet, however functional multiculturalism may have been in these terms it does have an uneasy relationship with the other component of the federal government's vision of Canada: bilingualism. In effect, all of Canada's cultures have official status but only two of its languages do. The adoption of multiculturalism has fuelled demands to go beyond bilingualism and give other languages official status. Indeed, the federal government has been drawn into actively supporting Canada's "non-official languages." In 1977, it established a Cultural Enrichment Program, whereby it provided funds for heritage language schools. And it has established a Canadian Heritage Languages Institute in Edmonton (Cummins and Danesi, 1990: 26).

In its rejection of older notions of Canadian dualism (in cultural if not linguistic terms), multiculturalism also has important implications for Canadian federalism. In effect, it challenges the original rationale for federalism. If Canada is composed of a multitude of cultures, why should there be a Québec provincial government? Why should francophone culture receive the favoured treatment of an autonomous state? There may well be other rationales for maintaining Canadian federalism, but within the multicultural perspective Québec's cultural distinctiveness cannot be one of them.

In sum, by the late 1970s Canadians and their governments were profoundly divided over the meaning of Canadian dualism and its implications for federalism. The federal government was actively promoting the notion that Canadian dualism existed throughout Canada and was the responsibility of all governments. The Québec government and much of French Québec opinion remained committed to the notion that Canadian dualism consisted of two largely unilingual regions, with the francophone region approximating Québec, and that Canadian federalism needed to be structured more clearly along these lines. At the same time, most other provincial governments, with the apparent support of their populations, resisted federal pressures to institutionalize dualism through official bilingualism while also resisting Québec's claims that its distinctiveness warranted a particular status. To further compound matters, a good number of Canadians rejected outright the dualist vision of Canada. In this, they found support in the federal government's adoption of multiculturalism. Within their vision, there is no clear rationale for Canadian federalism. All these divisions were played out in the constitutional debates that dominated the 1980s.

CANADA IN THE 1980S: TAKING THE STRUGGLE TO THE CONSTITUTION

Increasingly, the struggle over the meaning of Canadian dualism has been played out on the constitutional front. In part, this has centred on judicial interpretation of long-standing constitutional documents. The Canadian Supreme Court determined that the Manitoba provincial government was still constitutionally bound by provisions of the Manitoba Act, 1870, which required that laws be proclaimed in both English and French and that as a consequence all existing laws had to be translated into French. This requirement led the Pawley government into the struggle over language policy that we noted earlier. By the same token, the Supreme

Court determined that Saskatchewan and Alberta were still bound by provisions in the Northwest Territories Act of 1886 that gave French the same status as English in the legislature and courts. In this case, the Court concluded that the two legislatures could free themselves of these obligations by simply repealing them. As we have already seen, the two legislatures did so, while undertaking certain commitments.

Of course, the primary focus of debate over constitutional recognition of cultural difference has been the Constitution Act, 1982. This document clearly reflects the Trudeau government's conception of a Canadian dualism that exists throughout Canada but is purely linguistic in nature. Thus, under section 16 "English and French are the official languages of Canada and have equality of status and equal rights and privileges" in Parliament and the Canadian government. The same section also commits New Brunswick to official bilingualism, the one province to have already done so. Sections 17 through 22 outline specific procedures that flow from that. In addition, under section 23 all provincial governments are obliged to provide primary and secondary education to their official-language minorities. There are qualifications to each of these measures, but they are framed in terms not of specific provinces but of the relative demographic presence of official-language minorities (more precisely, the numbers of children with these rights). Also, reflecting the particular significance of the minority-language education provisions within the Trudeau government's vision of Canadian linguistic dualism, these sections constitute one of the few elements of the Charter not subject to the notwithstanding clause (Martel, 1991: 377-412).

As for cultural difference defined more broadly than language, there is a reference not to biculturalism but to multiculturalism. Section 27 declares that: "This Charter shall be interpreted in a manner consistent with the preservation and enhancement of the multicultural heritage of Canadians."[6]

Yet, if the Trudeau government succeeded in entrenching its own definition of cultural difference through the Charter of Rights and Freedoms, it did not put an end to debate over the matter. The Québec government's refusal to sign the Constitution Act ensured that the debate would continue.

In fact, the question of whether and on what terms to recognize Canadian dualism was central to the debate over the Meech Lake Accord, designed to secure Québec's signature to the constitution. Among the several provisions of the Accord, the ones that caused the most controversy were the clauses dealing with Canadian duality and Québec's status as a "distinct society." Section 2(1) of the Accord, an interpretative section, explicitly recognized the extent to which Canada's linguistic duality was geographically bound while also recognizing Québec's distinctiveness:

> The Constitution of Canada shall be interpreted in a manner consistent with:
> (a) the recognition that the existence of French-speaking Canadians, centred in Quebec but also present elsewhere in Canada, and English-speaking Canadians, concentrated outside Quebec but also present in Quebec, constitutes a fundamental characteristic of Canada;
> b) the recognition that Quebec constitutes within Canada a distinct society.[7]

The same section made it clear that while Parliament and all the provincial legislatures have the role "to preserve" Canada's linguistic duality, the Québec National Assembly had a specific role: "The role of the legislature and Government of Quebec to preserve and promote the distinct identity of Quebec ... is affirmed."[8]

It is probably the case that the concrete impact of these clauses, through jurisprudence, would have been minimal.[9] The fact remains that they defined Canadian linguistic dualism in a way that seemed to contradict the notion of duality in the Charter and offended a good many (mainly English-speaking) Canadians. In effect, the "distinct society" clause sought to restore the linkage between linguistic dualism and federalism that the Trudeau government had sought to deny. By the same token, in formally recognizing Québec's cultural distinctiveness, the Accord seemed to conflict with the Charter's recognition of multiculturalism.

The authors of the Charlottetown Accord, the second and equally ill-fated attempt at constitutional revision, reformulated these provisions in an effort to make them more acceptable to English-Canadian opinion. Thus, the Accord sought to limit the potential implications of any recognition of Québec's distinctiveness by defining this distinctiveness in essentially cultural terms, and quite traditional ones at that: "Quebec constitutes within Canada a distinct society, which includes a French-speaking majority, a unique culture and a civil law tradition." Similarly, the Meech Lake Accord reference to Canadian linguistic duality, which centred the two linguistic groups in different parts of the country, was replaced by a version more consistent with the Trudeau vision of a pan-Canadian dual-ity: "Canadians and their governments are committed to the vitality and development of official language minority communities throughout Can-ada." Finally, both of these statements appeared in a "Canada clause" whereby they shared pride of place with six other "fundamental charac-teristics" of Canada (Charlottetown Accord, *Draft Legal Text*, October 9, 1992: Section 2(1)(c)).

These changes apparently did render the "distinct society" clause and the duality clause more acceptable in English Canada; at least, they were not the focus of opposition that they had been with Meech Lake. Of course, this did not prevent opposition to other parts of the Charlotte-town Accord that were perceived to be too favourable to Québec, such as the guarantee to Québec in perpetuity of 25 per cent of the Commons seats. These changes may also have contributed to the perception among Québec francophones that their distinct needs were not sufficiently recog-nized (McRoberts, 1993).

THE UNRESOLVED DEBATE

There is every reason to believe that in the coming years Canadians will re-main divided over how to define Canada's cultural differences and how they bear upon Canadian federalism. The federal government has mobi-lized substantial resources to impose its definition of a dualism that is pan-Canadian, the common responsibility of all governments, rather than geo-graphically bound, equating French with Québec and English with the rest of the country. Clearly, this vision is perfectly suited to Ottawa's concern to deny Québec's claim for any particular status within Canadian federalism. However, it has yet to win the active support of most provincial govern-ments (other than New Brunswick and, to a lesser extent, Ontario) and ap-pears to have uneven support among Canadians at large. Nor has Ottawa's vision swayed the Québec government from its course of establishing the primacy of French within its territory. Some provisions of Bill 101, such as restrictions on access to English-language schools, have been pared down through application of the Charter. In June, 1993, the Québec National Assembly passed Bill 86, which allows commercial signs to be bilingual (as long as French predominates), eases slightly restrictions on access to Eng-lish-language schools, and authorizes the creation of English-language im-mersion classes. But the framework of Bill 101 remains in place, just as

French remains the sole official language of the province.

More fundamentally, the federal government has failed in its effort to create the social conditions that would make its dualist vision a reality rather than an ideal. With each census since the passage of the Official Languages Act in 1969, the demographic strength of most francophone minorities has continued to fall. Only in New Brunswick and, to a lesser extent, Ontario has the francophone minority held its own. Elsewhere, the francophone minorities have declined to the point that their survival is very much in question.

To be sure, the 1991 census reveals a different picture with respect to the federal government's effort to increase individual bilingualism by encouraging second-language instruction, most notably through immersion schools. Among people outside Québec between the ages of five and nineteen whose mother tongue is English, 11 per cent can speak French as compared with 3 per cent in 1971 (Canada, 1993: 16). Yet, this cannot be equated with the presence of Canadians whose first language is French. By and large, anglophones with a capacity in French will still be more proficient in their first language just as most francophones are more proficient in French, however familiar they may be with English. Nor does increased knowledge of French by anglophones necessarily mean a strengthening of the condition of francophones. For instance, it is commonly argued that the children of the francophone minorities are best educated in separate French-language institutions. To place anglophone immersion programs within the same institutions is to increase assimilationist pressures (Waddell, 1991: 423-32).

While most provincial governments might well have been more vigorous in collaborating with Ottawa to support the francophone minorities, it is highly unlikely that the assimilationist tide could have been turned. Even before Ottawa began its effort, the francophone populations of most provinces were already quite small. As these populations left the relative isolation of rural areas and moved to their provinces' urban centres they faced overwhelming assimilationist pressures.

In effect, despite the best efforts of the federal government to implement a vision of Canada based on the presence of francophones and anglophones throughout the country, Canadian society continued in its steady movement to a geographically defined dualism composed of two predominantly unilingual regions. Despite Ottawa's effort to establish dualism independently of Canadian federalism, dualism has become increasingly bound by it. Thanks to federalism, Québec and the rest of the country have become more and more culturally distinct.

Over the years, some experts have in fact argued that federalism, and geography more generally, might provide a sounder basis for language policy in Canada. Given the demographic reality of most provinces, it is fully appropriate that they should have a single language as their official language, just as Québec has a single official language. By the same token, within these provinces services to francophone minorities should be clearly targeted to areas where they are sufficiently concentrated. And to the extent possible they should be provided through distinct francophone institutions so as to provide the maximum support. In the last analysis, this would be of greater assistance to the francophone minorities than would official bilingualism within provincial institutions.

In 1979, a Task Force on National Unity, generally known as the Pepin-Robarts Task Force, proposed that the provinces should be allowed to determine for themselves the language regime most appropriate for their conditions:

> ... differences in perspective and in language policies between the federal and provincial levels of government, or among provincial governments themselves, need not be a major obstacle to Canadian unity.
>
> It is the very essence of federalism that each order of government is sovereign within its own sphere of jurisdiction. For good and compelling social and political reasons, each of the eleven governments must be free to respond to its unique situation. (Canada, 1979: 48)

These recommendations were summarily dismissed by the government of the day, the Trudeau Liberals, as simple heresy. Yet, relying on the structure of Canadian federalism may still be the surest basis for accommodating Canada's linguistic divisions.

At the same time, Canada's cultural difference cannot be easily reduced to differences in language alone. Thus, it raises a more profound challenge to Canadian federalism. The B&B Commission had been very clear that Canada's linguistic differences were paralleled by differences in "way[s] of being, thinking and feeling," and that these "two dominant cultures ... [were] embodied in distinct societies."

For its part, fully aware of the political implications of such an understanding of cultural difference, the Trudeau government recast cultural difference as "multiculturalism." This understanding of Canada has secured the active support of a good many Canadians, especially those of neither British nor French origin. But federal multiculturalism has been widely recognized in Québec as an attempt to negate Québec's claims to cultural distinctiveness and has been rejected on that basis. There, the older notion of two societies, if not nations, continues to have resonance. On that basis, Québec francophones remain attracted to schemes of a binational political structure, whether federal or confederal, that have been thoroughly rejected in the rest of the country, in part because they are incompatible with a multicultural vision of Canada.

In short, Canadians are now divided more than ever over the nature of cultural difference in Canada and over whether and how it should be accommodated within Canadian federalism. The federal government's formula of bilingualism and multiculturalism was clearly designed to reduce the historical linkage between cultural difference and Canadian federalism. Cultural difference was to be defined in a way that applied equally throughout the country as a whole rather than differentiated between Québec and the rest of the country. In sociological terms, the federal government has not been able to make the linguistic component of this vision a reality: the Canadian population linguistically has become more and more segregated along lines that do parallel the difference between Québec and the rest of the country. Nonetheless, Ottawa has been able to lead a good number of English Canadians to see Canada in terms of a pan-Canadian bilingualism. The federal government has been quite successful in implanting a multicultural vision of Canada, at least outside Québec.

As a consequence, as the fate of the Meech Lake Accord clearly demonstrated, it has become exceedingly difficult to restore the older notion of a territorially bound duality, linguistic or cultural, and to recognize it within the institutions of Canadian federalism. Cultural duality may have been the original rationale for Canadian federalism and may remain a powerful rationale for many Québécois, but in the rest of Canada it has lost ground to new visions of the country in which cultural duality, and even federalism, have an ambiguous status.

NOTES

1   Dr. Frank Underhill noted in 1964 that English Canadians needed to be aware of their "unconscious or subconscious assumption," born of the Conquest and of English Canada's majority status, that "Canada is fundamentally an English-speaking community and [that] our English-Canadian habits, methods, forms of social organization, and way of life generally, must in the end be accepted by the French-Canadians as their way of life also. This is a natural tendency to all comfortable majorities" (1964: 48).

2   Calculated from *Census of Canada, 1991* (93-333, 93-317, 93-318), as kindly supplied by Réjean Lachapelle, Director, Demolinguistic Division, Statistics Canada.

3   Secretary of State data as presented in Leslie A. Pal, Interests of State: The Politics of Language, Multiculturalism and Feminism in Canada (Montreal and Kingston: McGill-Queen's University Press, 1993: 163).

4   Secretary of State, Grants and Contributions Manual, 1988 (Ottawa, 1988), v. 1.4, as cited in Pal, Interests of State, 134. (The provision does not explicitly refer to the provincial governments, but Ottawa already has such a law on the books.)

5   Pierre Trudeau was reportedly the author of the document but he did not sign it since he was entering federal politics.

6   The Constitution Act, 1982, as reproduced in David Milne, *The Canadian Constitution* (Toronto: James Lorimer, 1991), Appendix 1.

7   Constitution Amendment, 1987, as reproduced in Peter W. Hogg, *Meech Lake Constitutional Accord Annotated* (Toronto: Carswell, 1988), Appendix IV.

8   Ibid.

9   To quote Peter Hogg, the distinct society clause "should probably be seen as an affirmation of sociological facts with little legal significance"(ibid., 12).

REFERENCES

Balthazar, Louis (1991). "History and Language Policy," in Schneiderman, *Language and the State: The Law of Politics and Identity*. Cowansville, Que.: Editions Yvon Blais: 83-91.

Beattie, Christopher (1975). *Minority Men in a Majority Setting*. Toronto: McClelland & Stewart.

Bourque, Gilles, and Jules Duchastel. (1988). *Restons traditionnels et progressifs*. Montréal: Boréal.

Canada, The Task Force on Canadian Unity (1979). *A Future Together*. Hull: Minister of Supply and Services.

Canada (1991). *Census of Canada, 1991.*

Canada (1993). Annual Report, 1992: Commissioner of Official Languages Ottawa: Supply and Services.

Chevrier, Richard (1983). Français au Canada: situation à l'extérieur du Québec. Montréal: Conseil de la langue française.

Comité pour une politique fonctionnelle (1965). "Bizarre algèbre," Cité libre, xx, 82 (décembre): 14.

Cummins, Jim, and Marcel Danesi (1990). *Heritage Languages: The Development and Denial of Canada's Linguistic Resources.* Toronto: Our Schools/ Our Selves Foundation.

Foucher, Pierre (1991). "Les droits linguistiques au Canada: récents développements constitutionnels," in Schneiderman, ed., *Language and the State.*

Gibson, Frederick W., ed. (1970). "Cabinet Formation and Bicultural Relations," *Studies of the Royal Commission on Bilingualism and Biculturalism,* No. 6. Ottawa: Queen's Printer.

Martel, Angéline, (1991) "Processus initié par la promulgation de l'article 23 de la Charte canadienne des droits et libertés: les revendications scolaires de la minorité de langue officielle française," in Schneiderman, ed., *Language and the State*: 377-412.

McRoberts, Kenneth (1993). "Disagreeing on Fundamentals: English Canada and Quebec," in McRoberts and Patrick Monahan, eds., *The Charlottetown Accord, The Referendum, and the Future of Canada.* Toronto: University of Toronto Press: 249-263.

Radwanski, George (1978). *Trudeau.* Scarborough: Macmillan – NAL Publishing.

Royal Commission on Bilingualism and Biculturalism (1965). *Preliminary Report.* Ottawa: Queen's Printer.

Royal Commission on Bilingualism and Biculturalism (1967). *Book I: General Introduction* (Ottawa: Queen's Printer, 1967), xxxi.

Royal Commission on Bilingualism and Biculturalism (1968). *Book II: Education.* Ottawa: Queen's Printer.

Smiley, Donald (1983). "Central Institutions," in Stanley M. Beck and Ivan Bernier, eds., *Canada and the New Constitution.* Montreal: IRPP, 1983.

Taylor, Charles (1992). *Multiculturalism and "The Politics of Recognition."* Princeton, N.J.: Princeton University Press.

Underhill, Frank (1964). *The Image of Confederation.* The Massey Lectures. Toronto: CBC Publications.

Waddell, Eric (1991). "Some Thoughts on the Implications of French Immersion for English Canada," in Schneiderman, ed., *Language and the State*: 423-32.

CHAPTER SIX

The 1982 Constitution and the Charter of Rights: A View from Québec

Robert Vandycke

THE 1982 CONSTITUTION ACT TOOK PLACE AT A PARTICU-
LAR moment in the history of Québec and Canada and reflects the power
relations between the two levels of government following the failure of
the 1980 referendum on sovereignty-association. The conception of Canada and of Québec's place in Canada that emerges explicitly and implic-
itly from the 1982 text is opposed by a large number of Québecers,
whether sovereignist or not.

One of the most important changes was the inclusion of the Charter of
Rights and Freedoms. The Charter was presented as reinforcing and protecting fundamental freedoms, while, at least in some quarters, its political
implications were underestimated. For some, the Charter appeared to be
essentially a legal document setting out norms to be applied by the courts.
Gradually, through decisions rendered by the Supreme Court and
through subsequent attempts at constitutional reform, the political significance of the Charter and the principal assumptions on which it was
based became apparent. The Charter introduced a new dynamic, as much
in the power relations between Québec or the other provinces and
Ottawa as within Québec. Québec's capacity to develop its linguistic and
cultural identity was affected as was its difficult search for a *modus vivendi*
with the anglophone community.

This analysis concentrates principally on the impact of the 1982 Constitution Act and especially the Charter of Rights on Québec. As a minority society within the Canadian federation, the centralization of powers
affects Québec in particular ways. However, although the effects of the
1982 changes are different for Québec, similar dynamics affect all the
provinces. In addition, the amount of autonomy left to a national minor-

ity is a good indicator of the evolution of a federal regime and its tolerance of competing sources of political authority.

THE CONSTITUTION ACT, 1982: THE END OF ILLUSIONS

The 1982 constitutional amendments brought to the forefront differences
between the Québec and English-Canadian visions of the country that
have been prevalent since Confederation: unitarism vs. federalism, centralization vs. decentralization, union of provinces or of peoples. In response to Québec's perennial demand for a revision of the division of
powers that brought the province to the threshold of secession in 1980,
the constitutional amendments responded by reinforcing the role of a
highly centralized institution: the Supreme Court.

In 1982, the power relations between the federal government and
Québec were very favourable to the Trudeau government. In addition to
the defeat of the sovereignist option in the referendum of May, 1980, and
the disarray that resulted in the highest echelons of the society, Québecers
were demoralized by the economic crisis and the adjustments it entailed.
Deprived of part of its intellectual and union base, particularly in the civil
service and related organizations, the PQ government searched for the cooperation of a short-lived provincialist front to resist the centralizing projects of the federal government. It was in this context that the Supreme
Court rejected the thesis, quite popular in Québec, that gave Québec the
right of veto over constitutional amendments. In fact, according to the
Court, Québec's right of veto had never existed legally or even politically
except as part of the conventional requirement for provincial consent for
constitution amendments affecting provincial powers.

Moreover, the repatriation and the modification of the constitution
were carried out without the consent of Québec; in fact, Québec was excluded from the final bargaining session between the federal government
and the other provinces, which had previously been unwilling to go along
with a deal. The political reaction in Québec was clear and unequivocal:
in the National Assembly, with a few exceptions, the members of the
government and the opposition joined forces to condemn what was
viewed as the illegitimate imposition of a new constitutional regime on
Québec without its consent. One vision of Canada had triumphed, one
that would be difficult to turn back in the future and that was widely opposed in Québec. As we will see below, the 1982 amendments meant the

triumph of the view that the status of Québec within the federation was and should remain equal to that of any other province, and, thus, the door was open to the reinforcement of the federal state.

In Québec, the reaction to the 1982 changes has been dominated by the political question of the legitimacy of a constitutional amendment that reduced the powers of the National Assembly without its consent. The rejection by political and intellectual elites has been quasi-unanimous. After winning the provincial election in 1981, the Parti Québécois government systematically attached the notwithstanding clause (section 33 of the Charter) to provincial laws as a protest and as a way of avoiding some of the political impact of the Charter. The Québec Chartre des droits et libertés de la personne (1975), which enjoys quasi-constitutional status in the province, has been considered a functional substitute for the Charter with respect to protection of rights and freedoms.

The constitutional regime after 1982 does not provide for any form of distinct status for the francophone minority other than that acquired indirectly through linguistic rights. Canada's cultural dualism has been progressively eroded by egalitarian provincialism; the federal government, therefore, serves the function of the definitive unifying agent. As in the United States, the Supreme Court is at the heart of the normative homogenization of the entire society. As well, the procedure for amending the Canadian constitution does not include any specific right of veto for Québec. Furthermore, to the central government's actual spending power in areas of exclusively provincial jurisdiction has been added the new judicial power of reviewing and invalidating provincial laws.

Before 1982 some authors, such as Rémillard (1980: 140-53), already viewed Canada as a quasi-federation rather than as a federation in the strict sense of the term: the composition of the Supreme Court and the assignment of residual powers to the federal government have been among the arguments put forward.[1] The new role of judicial review under the Charter – the provisions of which are at times very general and always open to interpretation – gives even more weight to this view. At any rate, it is clear that the constitutional amendments of 1982 go against Québec's traditional claims and reduce its room to manoeuvre, particularly as far as linguistic issues are concerned.[2]

Typical of this reaction in terms of legitimacy are the recent publications of Laforest (1992). Laforest views Canadian federalism (especially post-Meech) as incapable of sanctioning the notion of the duality of the founding peoples, and Québec's right to secede is analyzed in relation to the illegitimacy of the imposition of the Constitution Act, 1982. The centralizing and uniforming function of judicial review, as exercised by supreme courts in federal regimes and in other European countries, has been emphasized by Orban (1991) and Bzdera (1993). In sociology, the symbolic character of judicial decision-making and the creative and political role of the courts in interpreting and applying the Charter to concrete cases have been examined (Vandycke, 1986); also, other articles have been devoted to judicial activism and the power strategies of the Supreme Court, in particular concerning Québec language legislation (Vandycke, 1989), and to the individualist and anti-state ideology that prevails in the Charter and among the majority of the judges (Vandycke, 1989; 1991). Finally, the institutionalization of rights has been studied in relation to the expansion of rights conflicts and litigation (Brodeur, 1989).

In English Canada, the legitimacy of the 1982 Constitution Act has allowed for a richer and more specific debate. From the very outset, some academics discussed the political intentions behind the Charter's entrenchment. In 1983, Peter Russell argued that national unity was the primary purpose of the Charter's sponsors. For Russell, the nation-building potential of the Charter would result less from its symbolic force than from the effects of judicial review, which would involve issues that transcend regional cleavages and would involve Canada-wide ideological conflicts as well as potentially setting national standards (Russell, 1983: 40-43; Knopff and Morton, 1992: 378-81). As for the second main rationale of the Charter, the protection of rights, the new judicial decision-making includes a tendency to judicialize politics and to politicize the judiciary, a risk for democracy (Russell, 1983: 51-54). This point of view implies the rejection of the legalist ideology explicitly adopted by the Supreme Court in 1985.[3] As Monahan points out, there is no meaningful distinction between political and judicial decision-making (1984: 48). The refusal of the legalist ideology is a point of view widely shared by Charter critics, even if, in reality, many of them criticize less the document itself than its application by the courts.

One of the most prolific political analysts of the Charter is Alan Cairns. He has developed three main themes concerning the Charter and its entrenchment. If the Charter was viewed as a nation-building instrument by the federal government (1991: 30; 1992c: 167-68), it may also be considered as bringing the constitution closer to the citizenry and to the problems of their daily lives. In bringing the constitution closer to the people, the Charter has contributed to the development of what Cairns calls the citizens' constitution. The Charter also helps create a culture of "minoritarianism" by protecting and enhancing the status of different categories of citizens specifically enumerated in section 15 (equality rights), section 25 (Aboriginal peoples), section 28 (gender equality), and section 27 (multiculturalism as a rule of interpretation) (Cairns, 1990). In this "constitutional minoritarianism" and the equalizing effects of rights discourse, the Charter supports a political culture of constitutional participation (Cairns, 1992a: 4) and a Charter imperialism by its supporters (Cairns, 1992b: 616-17).

These two new constitutional characteristics make consociational accommodation between regional elites more suspect for citizens. The emergence of non-territorially concentrated ethnicities in metropolitan Canada and the evolution of English Canada into a multicultural community make federalism less instrumental (Cairns, 1992a: 112-14). For non-governmental constitutional actors, the notion of founding peoples seems anachronistic (Cairns, 1991: 178-80). Negotiations with Québec are difficult for such a community, which lacks identity and cohesion (Cairns, 1992a: 114; also Smith, 1992: 90-91), and Charter rights challenge "the historic privileging of majoritarianism by responsible government and of territorial diversity by federalism" (Cairns, 1992c: 1974).

In contrast to Cairns, some have questioned whether or not the Charter – at least in the courts' interpretation – is a democratizing instrument. With legalized politics, values such as justice and freedom are defined in an elite forum and become a matter for specialists (Monahan, 1987: 136-38; Morton, 1992: 648-49). Moreover, in addition to interest groups (Morton, 1987: 39-45), rights experts and law schools represent some of the most important constituencies of the "Court Party," notably due to the legal aid and grants provided by the state since the advent of the Charter (Morton, 1992: 637-41). From this point of view, the ascendance of the courts must be related to their capacity to satisfy the demands of newly or formerly dominant elites (*ibid.*, 651-52) as well as corporations that have been armed with an important new instrument for advancing their interests and for resisting governmental regulation (Monahan, 1987: 46). More radical analyses have criticized Charter politics as essentially authoritarian and anti-democratic in form. From this point of view, the legalization of politics means using an abstract type of discourse and obfuscating real conflicts and issues with rights discourse (Mandel, 1989: 280, 311), noticeably in the case of corporations under the Charter (Martin, 1991: 122-24).

A central object of debate has been the interpretation of section 1 of the Charter in *R. v. Oakes*.[4] The test developed by the Supreme Court in *Oakes*, to determine the validity of section 1 limits on a right, has opened the door to judicial activism (Knopff and Morton, 1992: 46) and to a view in which guaranteed rights are considered to be paramount to the numerous non-protected values (Hiebert, 1993). The Court's reasoning in *Oakes* is founded on a deep suspicion of the state; in contrast, judicial review should be aimed primarily toward policing the political process (Monahan, 1987: 248-52) and judicial restraint ought to be observed for the benefit of political debate (Monahan, 1987: 252; Hogg, 1992: 73, 88-89).

In a political system of checks and balances, the partial but valuable contribution of the courts to the political debate is not final: the other branches of government may legitimately accept or reject, after deliberation, the point of view of the judges (Knopff and Morton, 1992: 232-33). In this sense, properly using the (very unpopular) section 33 notwithstanding clause may be considered a way of enhancing dialogue between the different branches of government (Knopff and Morton, 1992: 225-32; Manfredi, 1993: 205-07).

CONSTITUTIONALISM AND THE SUPREME COURT

With some exceptions,[5] the Charter clearly privileges negative freedoms, the freedoms of individuals in relation to the state or against the state. Justice Dickson expressed this view when he stated that "the Charter was designed primarily to recognize the rights and freedoms of individuals vis-à-vis the state."[6] Undoubtedly, like any legal document, the Charter bears the imprint of its epoch and of the orientations of its creators.

In the context of our discussion, it is necessary to consider the consequences of a constitutional guarantee that grants rights primarily to individuals. First, protecting the rights of a certain individual vis-à-vis the state implies in fact that the liberties or interests of other persons are interfered with (Monahan, 1987: 46). Second, individual rights appear to enjoy a legal status superior to other kinds of rights, such as economic or social rights, which are internationally recognized as complementing an individual rights orientation. In such a manner, every time that a basic right (for example, the right to a decent standard of living or to health) or any other important objective of the government is translated into law, it may be limited by the courts if it is deemed to undermine the constitutionally enumerated rights. Therefore, the government has the burden of demonstrating that its restrictions on rights are reasonable and can be demonstrably justified in a free and democratic society (in the words of section 1). Unless, of course, the government chooses to use the notwithstanding clause, which can be applied to sections 2 and 7 to 15 of the Charter. In this case, the government must assume the resulting political consequences in invoking the clause and in renewing it every five years.

The ideology of the Charter includes the mistrust of state coercion, neglect of the power relations and constraints of civil society (Vandycke, 1991: 489), and an exaggerated confidence in the capacity of an objective judiciary to arbitrate conflicts between values and specific interests (Vandycke, 1986). A number of guaranteed freedoms have a very general sense and lead to interpretation when they are applied to concrete situations. Freedom of expression (section 2) and equality rights (section 15) are among the provisions of the Charter most susceptible to a broad interpretation.

In short, the Charter permits one federal political institution – the Supreme Court – to intervene in practically all areas that fall under provincial jurisdiction in the name of rights and freedoms: laws can be partially or completely invalidated, and the Court can indicate beacons for legislators to respect or suggest alternatives it deems acceptable.

These decisions are more political than legal in nature (*ibid.*: 1986: 145-47); they modify or strengthen power relations in society, and it is difficult to suggest that they are the strict application of pre-established norms, despite the legal rhetoric the Supreme Court uses to justify its decisions (Gold, 1988). In reality, the application of the Charter to specific situations depends largely on the values and preferences of the judges, except for clear cut violations of guaranteed rights (Heard, 1991; Morton et al., 1992: 36-37), and the same is true for decisions concerning competing values. The Supreme Court must also act to preserve its own legitimacy in society. On the whole, then, there are no easy standards or objective norms.

Judicial intervention may erode provincial power more than that of the federal government, as in the United States, and may limit the room to manoeuvre of Québec as a province representing a minority. From Ottawa, the Supreme Court dominates the whole judicial system. Now, its members are appointed in a discretionary manner, without public debate, and it would be surprising if the federal government was insensitive to the political and judicial orientations of those it selects to fulfil such important functions. The Supreme Court is not an isolated actor; it must take into account the other branches of government as well as the lawyers and the mass media. In this sense, politics shapes constitutional development more than it is constrained by constitutional law (Morton, 1992: 650). But, as long as the Court behaves in accordance with dominant interests and ideologies, it enjoys an enormous freedom; at times, the Court and its decisions replace the larger and more difficult process of political debate and bargaining through democratic means. Moreover, by subsidizing interest groups opposed to provincial legislation, the federal government exercises an influence on the number and the nature of the cases that go to court, notably concerning linguistic, cultural, and equality rights.[7]

Two major mechanisms have permitted the Supreme Court to increase the breadth of its review of the constitutionality of laws and to place maximum demands on the contents of legislation, at least when it appears to the Court to be desirable. Neither of these mechanisms are explicitly formulated in the constitution.

The judges have increased their field of intervention in their view that the rights and freedoms guaranteed in the Charter should be given a "large and liberal interpretation." Clearly, this signifies that all limitations on a right are in the jurisdiction of the courts, whether this right is infringed in its core or peripheral dimensions. For example, the legal restrictions on television commercials aimed at children were scrutinized under the argument that they encroached on freedom of expression.[8]

The second mechanism derives from a reading of section 1 by the Court.[9] According to the criteria developed by the Supreme Court, there must be a rational link between the restrictions made on a guaranteed right and the objective pursued by the legislator. In certain cases, the judges require that a link between the objective and the restrictions be demonstrated to be necessary, even though such rigour does not always appear to be appropriate[10] and may require proof almost impossible to furnish. On the other hand, according to the judges, the criterion of proportionality signifies among other things the "requirement of minimal impairment" on guaranteed freedoms by the legislature in seeking its objectives. We can see the enormous normative power the Court has given itself: it could always decide that other means would have permitted the pursuit of the legislature's goals at less cost to the guaranteed freedoms.[11] Of course, the judges affirmed that their norms were flexible and that the nature of their proportionality criterion could vary depending on the circumstances, but this decision is entirely theirs.

From the very beginning, some sections of Québec's Charter of the French Language (Bill 101) have been struck down by the Supreme Court.[12] Section 73, which restricts admission to English school to those children whose parents received their primary education in English in Québec, was invalidated under section 23 of the Canadian Charter. This opens up English-language schools to children whose parents received their primacy education in English in Canada. This so-called "Canada clause" thus prevailed over the Québec law's "Québec clause."[13] Similarly, in the *Ford* case, the Court struck down the French public advertising provisions (sections 58 and 59) of Québec's language charter.

Of course, language policy may be a matter of debate. Nevertheless, it is important to remember that unilingual territories or regions are not exceptional in democratic societies, as in Belgium or Switzerland, and have often been considered the best way of protecting a language minority (Woehrling, 1994b: 1064-66); some countries have adopted much more radical education politics than Québec's, for example.

Finally, the Oakes test and "the de facto presumption of statutory invalidity" (Morton, 1992: 629) that flows from it may be considered another form of "strict scrutiny" as the basis of interpretation of section 1 (Monahan, 1987: 248-50), or as a "tool for judicial review rather than a concession to legislative flexibility" (Manfredi, 1993: 90). In this respect, *Ford* constitutes an extreme case of judicial activism. Its reading informs us of the breadth of the review power the Supreme Court has in a favourable political context, and of the arguments, sometimes very debatable (Vandycke, 1989), by which the Court attempts to justify its interventionism. Despite that, the courts have appeared more inclined toward restraint over the last several years. For instance, the Court has made the distinction between fundamental rights and legislation that involves competing interests[14] or moral values.[15] But, according to Chief Justice Antonio Lamer, this "should not be misconstrued as providing Parliament with a licence for indifference to whatever Charter rights it deems necessary."[16]

In reality, the Court has elaborated a series of criteria to adapt the *Oakes* test according to circumstances. But the number and complexity of these criteria prevent any firm prediction about how the courts will rule in a given circumstance (Woehrling, 1993b: 406-08). In any case, even when the courts have been restrained on other issues,[17] judicial activism has been the rule with respect to Québec's language laws. Moreover, due to the powerful mechanisms of intervention in possession of the Court — the large and liberal interpretation of the Charter and the requirement of minimal impairment – future cases of judicial activism may occur, perhaps in new fields.

Quantitative data has been collected concerning the Supreme Court's first one hundred Charter decisions (Morton *et al.*, 1992: 25-30). By 1989, the Court had struck down nineteen statutes in whole or in part and upheld thirty-one. Among the nullified statutes, eleven were provincial and eight federal. From a qualitative point of view, seven of the eight nullifications of federal legislation were based on procedural grounds; in contrast, nine of the eleven invalidations of provincial statutes were made on substantive grounds. Five provincial laws struck down were Québec statutes concerning important language or education issues, while the invalidations of other provincial statutes were considered less essential by their governments. These data tend to confirm an homogenizing trend of judicial review under the Charter, and Québec as its privileged target.

In another article based on quantitative research, Heard (1991) nevertheless concludes that the Charter has both become an integral part of Québec legal culture and has involved the absorption of Canadian/Charter values by the province. The facts that lead Heard to this assertion are the wide range of Québec litigants who have launched claims based on the Charter, the willingness of Québec courts to grant Charter claims, and the use of Supreme Court and, to some extent, Ontario court precedents by Québec courts.

Heard's interpretation is debatable in some respects. First, until 1989, the success rate of challenges to laws and/or government actions (of the police, for example) is nearly equal in Québec (27 and 29), while the differences are greater in Nova Scotia (22 and 32), in Ontario (26 and 34, up to 1986), and in Canada (28 and 33). Second, only in Québec are claims against provincial laws much more frequent than against federal statutes (59 and 21 cases, respectively), although many of these involved the use of section 33 by the PQ government during its period of protest (Heard, 1991). This seems to indicate that if any value harmonization is occurring in Québec society, it certainly represents conflict within Québec, for example between the judiciary and the legislature.

It also may be somewhat dubious to infer harmonization from the professional behaviour of Québec judges: their nomination is exclusively made by the federal government, often with some partisan consideration, and, even if they wanted to, Québec judges could not systematically ignore the authority of the Supreme Court and its precedents.

The number and variety of litigants is another difficult argument. Of course, Québec society is clearly divided and its anglophone community in particular favours some kind of harmonization and political centralization (Vandycke, 1994). But, from another point of view, individuals as well as pressure groups and their counsels could be using the Canadian Charter instrumentally, as a judicial weapon, without necessarily recognizing its legitimacy. This would be the case, for example, for the overtly *indépendantiste* trade unions. In this sense, Heard's conclusions are premature or, at least, too general.

The notwithstanding clause (section 33) could have been an interesting way of counterbalancing the political power of the courts under the Charter. Not surprisingly, Chief Justice Lamer, one of the most activist of the judges (Morton *et al.*, 1992: 39-45), considers the notwithstanding clause as a "safety valve" (Lamer, 1992: 12), and in fact, the Supreme Court refused to limit the scope of its legal use in *Ford* (740). Nevertheless, its legitimacy has been denied in English Canada, in part due to the circumstances of its use by Québec governments (including the Liberal government of Premier Bourassa) (Manfredi, 1993: 202-04). The notwithstanding clause has the merit of restricting judicial supremacy and restoring parliamentary supremacy, which is more compatible with popular sovereignty. In this sense, checks on political power, whether exercised by government or by the courts, are not to be monopolized by one of these branches of the state, each of which has its own specific strengths and weaknesses (*ibid.*: 203-07; Knopff and Morton, 1992: 232-33).[18]

At the present time, both the conception of the Charter and its application lead to uniformity and centralization. This applies to every province of Canada, though with different consequences for Québec. Nor is there any counterweight in the Constitution Act, 1982, in terms of the conception and definition of a minority groups and of the rights guaranteed to them.

THE CHARTER AND LINGUISTIC MINORITIES

The way linguistic minorities are defined and the form of protection they receive in the Charter are highlighted in sections 16-23. Sections 16-22 recognize the existence of two official languages and their equal legal status within Parliament and the federal government (in the wider sense of the term), as well as the right of the public to communicate with the head office of a federal institution in either one of the official languages. Section 23 concerns minority-language education rights.

The principal traits of the vision of Canada depicted in the Charter with respect to language minorities can be sketched as follows. First of all, the Charter does not envisage language minorities at the national level (where the problem appears to be resolved due to the clauses on official languages) but only at the provincial level.[19] From this springs forth the plurality of minorities: one per province. In each province, the minority is determined by strictly numerical criteria; consequently, anglophones in Québec form a minority, and the minorities (francophones outside of Québec and anglophones in Québec) are viewed as symmetrical. This is consistent with the notion of the equality of the provinces.

Furthermore, in Canada the minorities are linguistic and not cultural, even though the International Covenant on Civil and Political Rights (1966) recognizes cultural minorities in section 27. With regard to the Charter, cultures are multiple in Canada even if, theoretically, the cultural communities do not enjoy substantive rights but rather a rule of interpretation (section 27 of the Charter), according to which the Charter should be read in accordance with the preservation and enhancement of the multicultural heritage of the country. Finally, the last characteristic trait: it is *individuals* as members of minority linguistic groups who have the right to have their children taught in their language, where numbers warrant.[20]

From Québec's point of view, the first concern with this is the legal separation of language and culture. On the contrary, the strength and longevity of a language may be assured through the values, culture, and institutions that give it impetus. Another problem is that the Charter largely reflects a distaste for collective rights, at least if we mean by that the rights attributed to a collectivity as such and not to its individual members; collective rights allow a group to define a certain number of rules that apply to its members or even to impose certain obligations on them. The liberal ideology of the Charter places collective rights in opposition to individual rights[21] or at least in a subordinate position, instead of considering that, in some ways, they are complementary and that it is at times more pertinent to establish an equilibrium between them rather than setting them against each other. In the Charter, this reconciliation takes place by the mechanism of section 1 (and its interpretation by the Court), and we know that the burden of proof is often particularly heavy for a government whose objectives conflict with a constitutionally protected freedoms.

With respect to language, the emphasis on individual rights in the Charter largely underestimates the obstacles the individual encounters in exercising linguistic rights. The questions might well be: Is there a school?

A class? Who chooses the teachers and establishes the programs? What social or economic pressures weigh on the parents demanding their rights, or on the children? Similarly, does the federal civil servant really have an interest in exercising a right that slows work down or disgruntles a superior? Internationally, there has been a tendency to recognize that judicial systems centred on individuals do not succeed in protecting the members of minority communities or the communities themselves. From this comes the need to recognize the rights of the group as such (Lerner, 1991).

Furthermore, linguistic minorities are defined exclusively by weight in a provincial population. Numerical importance is a factor that affects the power held by a group in a democracy and, often, is a practical indicator of its power. However, sociologically, a minority can only be defined in terms of domination; this exists in civil society (economic, social, linguistic, and cultural powers), and it can be more or less in contradiction with the political weight resulting from numbers.

This is even more true in a multinational state, such as Canada, where the anglophone "minority" in Québec is an extension of a clear majority at the level of the federal state (Vandycke, 1994). In this respect, the least that we can say is that a symmetry does not exist between the francophone and anglophone minorities as is depicted in the Charter. The emphasis placed on individual rights and on freedom of choice by the anglophones in Québec bears eloquent witness to their economic, social and cultural, if not political, power.

RECENT ATTEMPTS AT CONSTITUTIONAL REFORM:
MEECH AND CHARLOTTETOWN

The failed Meech Lake Accord was a compromise aimed at satisfying the Québec government's five conditions for the ratification of the 1982 Constitution Act.[22] It brought some important nuances to the earlier constitutional agreement without questioning some of its major elements, such as the Charter and its impact. Québec was recognized as a specific collective reality that must be taken into account in interpreting the constitution and the rights contained in the Charter. Indeed, a new clause of interpretation specified that Québec was a "distinct society within Canada," a specificity that the National Assembly and the provincial government have the role to promote. Furthermore, three of the Supreme Court judges were to be from the Québec bar. Other sections would have provided for provincial input into nominations to the Supreme Court and the Senate. Future changes to the powers or composition of the Senate, or to the procedure for selecting senators, would have required the unanimous consent of the provinces.

In addition, the Accord provided that provinces could opt out, with compensation, of any future shared-cost programs in areas of exclusive provincial jurisdiction. In this way, the federal spending power would no longer serve as the pretext for federal intervention in provincial jurisdiction. With the exception of the possibility of constitutionalizing certain immigration agreements, however, the Meech Lake Accord did not affect the division of powers. Rather, it aimed to modify some central institutions so as to allow greater provincial participation in their operation and federal intervention that would have been more respectful of provincial autonomy.

In other respects, the Meech vision, although more favourable to provincial autonomy and more open to the specificity of Québec, was counterbalanced by provisions that confirmed or even extended the influence of the central government. The distinct society clause also stated that the existence of francophones within English Canada and of anglophones within Québec is a fundamental characteristic of the country, and extended to the federal government the role of protecting this characteristic. The result was the legitimation of federal intervention with respect to official-language minorities, which, it will be recalled, was one of Québec's principal objections to the Charter.

The distinct society clause was ambiguous: it left open the question of reconciling the recognition of a distinct society with the protection of linguistic dualism. Of course, the institution that would be charged with reconciling this conflict would have been the Supreme Court. From this point of view, the gains made by Québec in the Meech Lake Accord were problematic. Finally, the provisions on immigration and the right to opt out of shared-cost programs involved the use of national norms and objectives to be defined by the central government. In addition, the legalization of opting out would have meant the legitimation of federal spending in areas of exclusive provincial jurisdiction, a controversial point between Québec and Ottawa.

The complex Charlottetown Accord (1992) was rejected in a referendum by Québec as well as by most of the other provinces. Generally, the guarantees offered to Québec – such as the guarantee of its existing 25 per cent of seats in the House of Commons – were added into a compromise agreement already reached by the federal government, the other provinces, and Aboriginal organizations. The Québec question was no longer at the centre of the debate or of the problematique. This may have been in part provoked by the official non-attendance of Premier Robert Bourassa, but other important factors were the role played by Aboriginal organizations, the demands of western Canada (especially on the Senate), and the evolution of Canadian public opinion.

This can be seen notably in the Canada clause, intended to be an overall clause of constitutional interpretation: the recognition of Québec as a "distinct society" – at least in some of its specific characteristics[23] – was listed along with other "fundamental characteristics" of Canada, including the commitment of governments to develop official-language minority communities throughout the country, as well as the explicit principle of the equality of the provinces. The combination of these diverse and competing principles seemed to militate against any form of asymmetry in terms of either the division of powers or the treatment of linguistic minorities in interpreting the constitution or the Charter (Pelletier, 1994: 94-99).

The equality of the provinces principle included in the Canada clause excluded any special status or exclusive right of veto for Québec. Also based on the equality principle, the elected Senate would probably have played a more important role and become a privileged forum for negotiations between the federal government and the representatives of the provinces, in spite of its formally limited powers. Elected senators would probably develop a loyalty mainly directed to their federal party, as in Australia (Woehrling, 1993a: 14).

Despite the protection Québec received in some federal institutions, such as the Supreme Court and the House of Commons, the leadership role of the federal government came out clearly. As in Meech, the spending power of the federal government in areas of provincial jurisdiction was constitutionalized, and where federal spending could be limited by intergovernmental agreement, provincial programs would still have had to be compatible with national objectives. This agreement reflected the multiplication of interests and demands in the constitutional debate and attempted to reform federal institutions by widening the influence and defining the respective places of Québec and the other provinces in the central government. From Québec's perspective, decentralization appeared to be subordinated to this aim. Finally, the comparison between these two agreements indicates an evolution in the major concerns of

English Canada and seems to indicate the difficulty of reaching any satis-factory compromise concerning the constitutional status of Québec in Canadian federalism.

CONCLUSION

The constitutionalization of a Charter guaranteeing individual rights (to the detriment of collective rights, notably); the Supreme Court's consid-erable power of normative harmonization; the tendency of the federal government to try to determine national norms in all domains and to define the rights of the anglo-Québec community; the postulate of the le-gal equality of provinces – all of these factors have profoundly modified the rules of the game in Canadian federalism and, perhaps more impor-tantly, the spirit of federalism. Distinct status or specific veto powers for Québec have been contrasted with guaranteed universal values, such as the equality of individuals and collectivities. As for the notwithstanding provision of the Charter, it hardly counterbalances this pressure toward uniformity, due to the symbolic and political costs of using it.

Some authors have criticized the divisive character of judicial review under the Charter (Morton *et al.*, 1992: 48; Manfredi, 1993: 217). As a matter of fact, the object of the conflicts is less the Charter than its impo-sition; less the entirety of the document than some particular clauses that lack universality and appear to be directed against Québec specifically; less the general values it promotes than their particular interpretation by a centralized federal institution; less the concept of constitutionalism and judicial review than judicial supremacy and activism; less section 1 than the restrictive test elaborated by the Supreme Court and the impediments put in the way of a government seeking the promotion of values, or of le-gitimate interests, not included in the Charter.

As Russell has written, if Canadians are to constitute themselves a peo-ple, they will have to elaborate a truly federal constitutional package, avoid insistence upon "agreement on fundamentals," and base proposals on the acceptance of "a diversity deep enough to accommodate different senses of national identity, different degrees of allegiance to the country as a whole, and different orderings of political values" (1992: 193). Aside from this, the only other option is Québec sovereignty in the framework of the North American economy, followed by some form of association with Canada, on the basis of common interests and the links woven by history.

NOTES

1   Rémillard (1980: 140-53) speaks of a centralized federal constitution (p. 153) and sees the Supreme Court as a strong centralizing agent (p. 152).

2   Some of the clauses in the Charter, such as section 23(1)b), are clearly destined to bring down article 73 of Bill 101, on access to school in English, as was explicitly confirmed by the courts. The same is true for section 23(1)(a), but this comes into effect in Québec only after authorization "by the legislative assembly or government of the Province" (section 59).

3   *Reference re s. 94 (2) of the B.C. Motor Vehicle Act*, [1985] 2 SCR 486. For the consequences of this legalist conception, see Monahan (1987: 7-8).

4   *R. v. Oakes*, [1986] 1 SCR 103.

5   Exceptions include the confirmation of Aboriginal rights, official-language rights, the non-prohibition of affirmative action programs for underprivileged, and an interpretation clause that refers to the multicultural heritage of Canadians. In other respects, the obligations of the state are not completely absent. See, for instance, s. 23(3)(a) and (b).

6   *Société des Acadiens v. Association of Parents*, [1986] 1 SCR 565. In opposition to that, Monahan has emphasized the communitarian values he considers embedded in the Charter and has pleaded for a positive conception of liberty, which ought to be distinguished from privacy (1987: 248-52).

7   The Court Challenges Program, created in February, 1978, and extended in 1982, was repealed by the Conservative government in 1992 but has been recently restored by the Liberals. It contributes to lawsuits notably concerning sections 16 to 23 and sections 15, 27, and 28 of the Charter.

8   *Irwin Toy Ltd. v. Quebec (A.G.)*, [1989], 1 SCR 927.

9   For a more complete picture, see *R. v. Oakes* [1986] 1 SCR at 138-40.

10   See, for example, *Ford v. Québec*, [1988] 2 SCR 712, bearing on the language of commercial signs. The Court argued that the (Liberal) government had not demonstrated this relation of necessity.

11   See, for instance, *ibid.*, 780. According to the Court, to meet the problem of promoting a French *"visage linguistique,"* requiring the exclusive use of French has not been justified by the government of Quebec; nevertheless, "requiring the predominant display of the French language, even its marked predominance," would impair freedom of expression minimally.

12   See table 8 in Morton *et al.* (1992: 27).

13   *A.G. Quebec v. Quebec Association of Protestant School Boards*, [1984] 2 SCR 66.

14   For instance, the right to bargain collectively and to strike. See *Re Public Service Relation Act*, [1987], SCR 313, at 391.

15   *Rodriguez v. British Columbia (A.G.)*, [1993] 3 SCR 519, at 564.

16   *Ibid.*, 564-65.

17   From 1984 through 1987, one of eleven section 1 defences of legislation was accepted by the Court; in 1988 and 1989, eight of fourteen section 1 defences were accepted (Morton *et al.*, 1992: 34-35).

18   On the weaknesses of the courts, notably to collect the information necessary for the application of section 1, see Manfredi (1989: 334-35).

19   Note, however, that in its evaluation of linguistic legislation in Quebec, in light of section 1 of the Charter, the Supreme Court determined that the French language was threatened in Québec (see *Ford*, 777-79). This could be interpreted to mean that there exists only one linguistic minority in Canada but that the power relations vary according to the regions.

20   However, subsequently the Supreme Court interpreted section 23 in a more collective sense and included in it the right of minorities to manage their schools.

21   In the sense of this ideology, for example, see the recent article by Deborah Coyne (1993). For a more balanced point of view, see Sanders (1991: 383-86).

22   On the Meech Lake Accord, see Swinton and Rogerson, eds. (1988).

23   The text enumerates notably a French-speaking majority, a unique culture, and a civil law tradition. Note that, if the concept of society appears generally to carry the idea of universality, the enumeration of some characteristics, even when not restrictive, seems to go against this and to limit the general meaning.

REFERENCES

Brodeur, Jean-Paul (1989). "La manufacture des droits," *Cahiers de recherche sociologique*, 13 (automne): 53-72.

Brun, Henri, and Guy Tremblay (1990). *Droit constitutionnel*, Second edition. Montréal: Yvon Blais.

Bzdera, André (1992). "Perspectives québécoises sur la Cour suprême du Canada," *Canadian Journal of Law and Society*. 7, 2 (Fall): 1-21.

Bzdera, André (1993). "Comparative Analysis of Federal High Courts: A Political Theory of Judicial Review," *Canadian Journal of Political Science*. 26: 3-29.

Cairns, Alan C. (1988). *Constitution, Government, and Society in Canada. Selected Essays by Alan C. Cairns*, edited by Douglas E. Williams. Toronto: McClelland & Stewart.

Cairns, Alan C. (1990). "Constitutional Minoritarianism in Canada," in Ronald L. Watts and Douglas M. Brown, eds., *Canada: The State of Federation, 1990*. Kingston: Institute of Intergovernmental Affairs: 71-95.

Cairns, Alan C. (1991). "Political Science, Ethnicity, and the Canadian Constitution," in Disruptions: Constitutional Struggles, from the Charter to Meech Lake, edited by Douglas E. Williams. Toronto: McClelland & Stewart: 161-80.

Cairns, Alan C. (1992a). *Charter versus Federalism: The Dilemmas of Constitutional Reform*. Montreal and Kingston: McGill-Queen's University Press.

Cairns, Alan C. (1992b). "The Charter: A Political Science Perspective," *Osgoode Hall Law Journal*, 30, 3: 615-25.

Cairns, Alan C. (1992c). "Reflections on the Political Purposes of the Charter: The First Decade," in Gérald-A. Beaudoin, ed., *La Charte: dix ans après / The Charter: Ten Years Later*. Cowansville, Que.: Editions Yvon Blais: 161-91.

Coyne, Deborah (1993). "Le mirage collectif du Nouveau-Brunswick," *Le Devoir*, September 14: A8.

Dahl, Robert A. (1957). "Decision-Making in a Democracy: The Supreme Court as a National Policy-Maker," *Journal of Public Law*, 6: 279-95.

Foster, Elizabeth (1989). "La Charte canadienne des droits et libertés: pour la protection des droits de la personne humaine ou instrument d'évolution de la société?" *Les Cahiers de Droit*, 30, 1 (mars): 237-55.

Gold, Marc (1988). "La rhétorique des droits constitutionnels," *Revue juridique Thémis*, 22, 2: 2-35.

Heard, Andrew D. (1991). "The Charter in the Supreme Court of Canada: The Importance of Which Judges Hear an Appeal," *Canadian Journal of Political Science*, XXIV: 2 (June): 289-307.

Heard, Andrew D. (1993). "Quebec Courts and the Canadian Charter of Rights," *International Journal of Canadian Studies*. 7-8 (Spring-Fall): 153-66.

Helly, Denise (1994). "Politiques à l'égard des minorités immigrées," *Sociologie et sociétés*, XXVI, 2 (automne): 127-44.

Hiebert, Janet (1993). "Rights and Public Debate: The Limitations of a 'Rights Must Be Paramount' Perspective," *International Journal of Canadian Studies*, 7-8 (Spring-Fall): 117-35.

Hogg, Peter W. (1992). "Judicial Reform of Criminal Law under Section 7 of the Charter," in Beaudoin, ed., *La Charte: dix ans après / The Charter: Ten Years Later*. 71-89.

Knopff, Rainer, and F.L. Morton (1992). *Charter Politics*. Scarborough: Nelson.

Laforest, Guy (1992). "La Charte canadienne des droits et libertés au Québec: nationaliste, injuste et illégitime," in François Rocher, dir., *Bilan québécois du fédéralisme canadien*. Montréal: VLB: 124-51.

Lamer, Antonio (1992). "Énoncé d'ouverture/Opening Remarks," in Beaudoin, ed., *La Charte: dix ans après/The Charter: Ten Years Later.* 9-16.

LaSelva, Samuel V. (1993). "Re-imagining Confederation: Moving Beyond the Trudeau-Lévesque Debate," *Canadian Journal of Political Science.* XXVI, 4 (December): 699-720.

Lerner, Nathan (1991). *Group Rights and Discrimination in International Law.* Doordrecht, Boston, London: Martinus Nijhoff Publications.

Mandel, Michael (1985). "The Rule of Law and the Legalisation of Politics in Canada," *International Journal of the Sociology of Law*, 13: 273-87.

Mandel, Michael (1989). *The Charter of Rights and the Legalization of Politics in Canada.* Toronto: Wall and Thompson.

Manfredi, Christopher P. (1989). "Adjudication, Policy-Making and the Supreme Court of Canada: Lessons From the Experience of the United States," *Canadian Journal of Political Science.* XXII, 2 (June): 313-35.

Manfredi, Christopher P. (1993). *Canada and the Paradox of Liberal Constitutionalism.* Toronto: McClelland & Stewart.

Martin, Robert (1991). "The Charter and the Crisis in Canada," in D.E. Smith *et al.*, eds., *After Meech Lake. Lessons for the Future.* Saskatoon: Fifth House Publishers: 121-37.

Milne, David A. (1988). "Much Ado About Meech," in Peter M. Leslie and R.L. Watts, eds., *Canada: The State of the Federation 1987-88.* Kingston: Institute of Intergovernmental Relations: 97-116.

Monahan, Patrick J. (1984). "At Doctrine's Twilight: The Structure of Canadian Federalism," University of Toronto Law Journal, 34, 1: 47-99.

Monahan, Patrick J. (1987). *Politics and the Constitution: The Charter, Federalism and the Supreme Court of Canada.* Toronto: Carswell/Methuen.

Morton, F.L. (1985). *Law, Politics and the Judicial Process in Canada.* Calgary: University of Calgary Press.

Morton, F.L. (1987). "The Political Impact of the Canadian Charter of Rights and Freedoms," *Canadian Journal of Political Science*, XX, 1 (March): 31-56.

Morton, F.L. (1992). "The Charter Revolution and the Court Party," *Osgoode Hall Law Journal*, 30, 3: 627-52.

Morton, F.L., *et al.* (1992). "The Supreme Court's First One Hundred Charter Decisions: A Statistical Analysis," *Osgoode Hall Law Journal*, 30, 1: 1-56.

Orban, Edmond, *et al.* (1991). *Fédéralisme et cours suprêmes/Federalism and Supreme Courts.* Bruxelles/Montréal: Établissements Émile Bruylant/Les Presses de l'Université de Montréal.

Pelletier, Benoît (1994). "La clause Canada dans la défunte entente de Charlottetown," *Les Cahiers de Droit*, 35, 1 (mars): 51-111.

Rémillard, Gil (1980). *Le fédéralisme canadien*. Montréal: Québec/Amérique.

Robert, Denis (1988). "La signification de l'Accord du lac Meech au Canada anglais et au Québec francophone: un tour d'horizon du débat public," in Leslie and Watts, eds., *Canada: the State of the Federation 1987-88*: 177-56.

Rocher, François, and Daniel Salée (1991). "Charte et société: vers un nouvel ordre politique canadien?" Revue québécoise de science politique, No. 20 (automne): 35-64.

Rocher, François, and Daniel Salée (1993). "Démocratie et réforme constitutionnelle: discours et pratique," *International Journal of Canadian Studies*, 7-8 (Spring-Fall): 167-85.

Roy, Nicole (1993). "Les intérêts économiques corporatifs et la Charte canadienne des droits et libertés: impact sur la protection de l'environnement," *Les Cahiers de Droit*, 34, 2 (juin): 395-516.

Russell, Peter H. (1983). "The Political Purposes of the Canadian Charter of Rights and Freedoms," *Canadian Bar Review*, 61: 30-54.

Russell, Peter H. (1986). "Overcoming Legal Formalism: The Treatment of the Constitution, the Courts and Judicial Behaviour in Canadian Political Science," *Canadian Journal of Law and Society*, 1: 5-33.

Russell, Peter H. (1988). "The Supreme Court and Federal-Provincial Relations: The Political Use of Legal Resources," in R.D. Olling and M.W. Westmacott, eds., *Perspectives on Canadian Federalism*. Scarborough: Prentice-Hall: 90-100.

Russell, Peter H. (1992). *Constitutional Odyssey: Can Canadians Be a Sovereign People?* Toronto: University of Toronto Press.

Sanders, Douglas (1991). "Collective Rights," *Human Rights Quarterly*, 13: 368-86.

Schnapper, Dominique (1993). "Ethnies et nations," *Cahiers de recherche sociologique*, 20: 157-67.

Sigurdson, Richard (1993). "Left- and Right-Wing Charterphobia in Canada: A Critique of the Critics," *International Journal of Canadian Studies*, Nos. 7-8 (Spring-Fall): 95-116.

Smith, Miriam (1992). "Le choc des identités au Canada: du rejet de la dualité à la quête d'une identité plurielle," in Rocher, dir., *Bilan québécois du fédéralisme canadien*: 79-92.

Swinton, Katherine E., and Carl J. Rogerson, eds. (1988). *Competing Constitutional Visions: The Meech Lake Accord*. Toronto: Carswell.

Thériault, Yvon J. (1994). "Entre la nation et l'ethnie. Sociologie, société et communautés francophones," *Sociologie et sociétés*, XXVI, 1 (avril): 15-32.

Tuohy, Carolyn J. (1992). *Policy and Politics in Canada: Institutionalized Ambivalence*. Philadelphia: Temple University Press.

Vandycke, Robert (1986). "Les droits de l'homme et leur mode d'emploi. A propos de la Charte constitutionnelle de 1982," *Sociologie et sociétés*. XVIII, 1 (avril): 139-52.

Vandycke, Robert (1989). "L'activisme judiciaire et les droits de la personne," *Les Cahiers de Droit*, 30, 4 (décembre): 927-51.

Vandycke, Robert (1991). "La Charte canadienne des droits de l'homme et le contrôle de la constitutionnalité. A propos de quelques enjeux sociaux," *Revue trimestrielle des droits de l'homme*, 8 (octobre): 473-90.

Vandycke, Robert (1994). "Le statut de minorité en sociologie du droit. Avec quelques considérations sur le cas québécois," *Sociologie et sociétés*, XXVI, 1 (avril): 87-99.

Woehrling, José (1986). "La constitution canadienne et la protection des minorités ethniques," *Les Cahiers de Droit*, 27, 1 (mars): 171-88.

Woehrling, José (1988). "La modification constitutionnelle de 1982, la reconnaissance du Québec comme société distincte et la dualité linguistique du Canada," *Les Cahiers de Droit*, 29, 1: 3-64.

Woehrling, José (1993a). "La crise constitutionnelle et le réaménagement des rapports entre le Québec et la Canada anglais," *International Journal of Canadian Studies*, 7-8 (Spring-Fall): 9-40.

Woehrling, José (1993b). "La Cour suprême du Canada et la problématique de la limitation des droits et libertés," *Revue trimestrielle des droits de l'homme*, 15 (juillet): 379-410.

Woehrling, José (1993c). "La Constitution canadienne et l'évolution des rapports entre le Québec et le Canada anglais, de 1867 à nos jours," *Points de vue*. Centre of Constitutional Studies: University of Alberta.

Woehrling, José (1994a). "La justice constitutionnelle, l'État de droit et la démocratie libérale au Canada," in Chantal Millon-Delsol and Jean Roy, dirs., *Démocraties, l'identité incertaine*. Bourg-en-Bresse: Musnier-Gilbert Éditions: 165-80.

Woehrling, José (1994b). "Les droits des minorités linguistiques et culturelles en cas d'éventuelle accession du Québec à la souveraineté," *Revue juridique Thémis*, 28: 1037-90.

CHAPTER SEVEN

The Federal-Provincial Power-grid and Aboriginal Self-Government

Radha Jhappan

OVER THE LAST FEW DECADES, THE CANADIAN FEDERAL SYSTEM has been besieged by a range of political, economic, social, and legal pressures that have threatened to upset the traditional balance of power between the two tiers of government. These include: the political pressures emanating from Québec nationalists, who have been both demanding and assuming greater provincial autonomy since the 1960s; the world-wide recession and escalating deficits, which have led the federal government to off-load some of its traditional responsibilities to the provinces or to vacate provincial policy turf it had invaded via its spending power; free trade with the United States and Mexico, which affects the powers of the federal and provincial governments over economic, fiscal, trade, labour, social, and environmental policies; and social and legal pressures arising from the Charter of Rights and Freedoms, which has to some extent manacled both levels of government.

The new trends in Canadian federalism engendered by the political, economic, and social pressures sketched above have undoubtedly complicated the practical operation of the federation. Yet, with the exception of the Charter, these changes have occurred without any formal amendment to the constitutional division of powers. They amount to minor modifications to the system; no matter how politically contentious, they nevertheless leave the formal structure of power divided between two tiers of government untouched.

Aboriginal self-government, however, represents the newest and most far-reaching trend in Canadian federalism. Although the right has not yet been explicitly enshrined in the constitution, several forms of self-government are already operating in some Aboriginal communities, while others are in the process of negotiating agreements with the federal and provincial governments. Notwithstanding these non-constitutional initiatives, however, the national Aboriginal organizations are committed to having the right recognized in the fundamental law of the land. This objective was almost achieved in the Charlottetown Accord of 1992, which included an extensive package of constitutional reforms premised on the recognition of Aboriginal peoples' inherent right to self-government. The Accord was ultimately defeated in a national referendum. However, it seems more than likely that such a right will eventually be entrenched in the constitution in the future (Jhappan, 1993). If and when this happens, it will mean a fundamental restructuring of the federation to accommodate an entirely new order of government.

This new order, however, will not be found in one location but in hundreds of small territories within larger provincial and northern territorial boundaries. Nor will it be represented politically by a single collection of individuals, such as a cabinet; rather, it will comprise hundreds of local governments with discrete leaderships. Moreover, no section of the constitution will provide an exhaustive list of the jurisdictions and powers to be exercised by each of these governments. Self-government models will vary considerably between Aboriginal communities: some will assume a wide range of powers currently exercised by the federal and provincial governments; others will tackle a more limited sheaf of responsibilities. There will be bilateral and multilateral agreements between the various levels of government so that each Aboriginal government will manage a unique package of shared and separate jurisdictions. The design of each package will depend on the circumstances of the particular Aboriginal community, including (among other things) whether it currently has a land base under the reserve system and the Indian Act, whether it is urban or rural, and whether it has a substantial population and resource base.

Furthermore, this third order of government is to be based essentially on ethnicity. Although federalism was in part a compromise to allow the descendants of the French colonizers in Canada to maintain their distinctive culture and language through a provincial government, ethnicity is not the explicit basis of provincehood in the constitution. All residents of Québec, regardless of their ancestry, are members of the provincial political community and are subject to the laws under the Québec government's jurisdiction. Moreover, under section 92 of the British North America Act (1867), Québec received the same powers over the same subject matters as the other provinces.

Aboriginal self-government, however, entails a significant departure from historical constitutional practice. Only in the Northwest Territories and the Yukon is Aboriginal government likely to be public, meaning that everyone resident in a given territory would be subject to the authority of a government dominated by Aboriginal people. However, it is generally assumed that Native governments in the provinces will only exercise law-making authority over Aboriginal people and lands (Boisvert, 1985). Thus, self-government promises to introduce fresh intricacies into what is already a complex federal system.

The purpose of this chapter is to survey the current roles and responsibilities of the federal and provincial governments with regard to Aboriginal peoples and lands, and to assess how these roles have changed over the past two decades. This discussion will provide some clues as to why many Aboriginal peoples are dissatisfied with the current constitutional and practical situation such that they have demanded constitutional recognition of their right to govern themselves.

FEDERAL POWERS AND RESPONSIBILITIES

It is widely believed that the federal government bears sole legislative responsibility for Aboriginal peoples. Certainly, anyone perusing section 91 of the Constitution Act, 1867, would be left with that impression. Tucked between "Copyrights" and "Naturalization and Aliens," we find in s. 91(24) "Indians, and Lands reserved for the Indians." Indians are in fact the only people defined directly as a "class of subjects" among the various objects, institutions and practices falling under federal jurisdiction. Hence, they are to be regulated, acted upon, or otherwise treated as impassive subjects, but only, of course, by the federal government. The following discussion examines first, how and why Indians were so classified and, second, the practical meaning of s. 91(24).

Although the colonial history of Canada is beyond the scope of this chapter, it must be noted that from the beginning, the Europeans who colonized North America proceeded on the assumption that the continent was *terra nullius* (uninhabited). This was despite the fact that estimates of the Aboriginal population north of the cities of Mexico in the early sixteenth century range from 4.5 million to 18 million people (Wilson and Urion, 1995: 51) who governed themselves according to their various cultural and political traditions. However, the European colonizers consid-

157

ered Christianity the essential prerequisite of the ability to hold rights to lands and political autonomy (Dickason, 1992: 108-09). In fact, the doctrine of discovery in international law treated as vacant any non-European lands not colonized by a European power. It presumed that sovereign power went to the nation discovering the area, which then had the sole right of acquiring the land from the Natives and of settling it (see *Johnson v. Macintosh*, 1823; Henderson, 1985; and Slattery, 1991). Hence, British settlement of the lands that became Canada was deemed sufficient to assert British sovereignty.

This presumption was underlined by the Royal Proclamation of 1763, the first constitutional enactment governing the territories later to become Canada, which is still in force today. Among other things, the Proclamation set out the rules by which Indian title could be ceded or purchased, thus establishing a constitutional foundation for the treaty-making process followed with indigenous peoples in about half of the territories that became Canada. Although the precise meaning of the Proclamation has been debated (Slattery, 1985, 1987; Elliott, 1985; Jackson, 1984), it did acknowledge that the indigenous inhabitants had a legal right to their lands, though this right was seen only as a burden on the underlying and ultimate title of the Crown. Hence, with blanket assertions of political sovereignty and land ownership, by Confederation in 1867, it was assumed that the Crown, newly incarnated as the government of Canada, would naturally exercise law-making authority over indigenous peoples and their lands.

The question of indigenous peoples' consent to these arrangements, like the question of whether the Crown's assumption of sovereignty had any moral basis, did not even arise in the minds of the Fathers of Confederation. Their consent was either merely assumed or considered irrelevant (Macklem, 1991: 415-16). Under the Royal Proclamation, King George III had simply declared "the several Nations or Tribes of Indians with whom We are connected" to be under the "protection" of the Crown. The Proclamation referred to the fact that "Great Frauds and Abuses have been committed in purchasing lands of the Indians ... to the Great Dissatisfaction of the said Indians." The Proclamation therefore decreed that Indian lands could only be alienated to the Crown, according to a particular procedure. It established the legal requirement that treaties be concluded with Indians, through which the Crown would obtain legal surrenders of land. As Sanders (1988: 152) has argued, the protection of the Crown was warranted by the political necessities of colonialism:

Early Indian resistance was a response to exploitation at the hands of the local settler populations. To secure peaceful relations with the tribes, the British took control of Indian policy away from local colonial governments in the late eighteenth century. The goal was to protect Indian interests from local settler populations in order to ensure peaceful colonial expansion.

During the nineteenth century, it was felt that the Indian tribes still needed the special protection of the federal Crown, a policy "plainly based upon a fear that the provincial administrations would have too local a focus and too short-term an interest to honour the Crown's duties of protection" (Pratt, 1991: 24). In light of the federal Crown's subsequent dereliction in its duty of protection in the treaty-making process and in various Indian policies, this appears to have been a rather grand assumption. Nevertheless, "Indians, and Lands reserved for the Indians" were included among the federal powers in s. 91.

Thus fortified with constitutional authority, the federal government proceeded to administer its charges under the Indian Act (1876). Though amended in 1951 and 1985, the Act has remained the primary federal statute under s. 91(24). The long arms of the Indian Act have reached almost every facet of the lives of status Indians (those who are registered under the Act and qualify for certain benefits provided by it). It vests power over registered Indians on reserves in the cabinet, and regulates such matters as the establishment of band councils, elections, education, health, management and spending of Indian moneys, disposition of lands, agriculture, law enforcement, wildlife management, traffic, and labour relations (see Woodward, 1990; Imai, Logan, and Stein, 1993). The imposition of government controls over these and other matters, regardless of Aboriginal traditions, cultures, and wishes, was crucial to a policy of forced assimilation. What was enforced was not only the colonizers' views of governance and law in the Western tradition, but also an ideology of racism that sought systematically to invalidate all things Aboriginal. As Morse (1991: 55-56) has summarized, so confident was the government of Canada in its powers to do as it pleased regarding Indians that:

Ancient governmental systems could be abolished by the stroke of the lawmaker's pen and replaced by an allegedly democratic model in which women and young men were disenfranchised and non-Indians could be elected chief. Traditional religious practices were outlawed while Christian denominations received frequently exclusive domain over particular Indian communities. A pass system was established whereby the approval of the local Indian agent was necessary to obtain permission to leave a reserve for employment, food gathering or any other purpose. A scheme was created through which children would be forcibly sent to residential schools far away from their homes. Aboriginal languages were suppressed, customary laws ignored and long-standing cultural practices undermined. Even membership in the community ... was regulated by statute.... All of these restraints and impositions were debated and selected by Parliamentarians for whom the people directly affected had no electoral voice. Indian people were treated as if they were children or mentally incompetent wards who required a guardian to make all decisions.

In many ways, the Indian Act simply carried on the colonial tradition of treating Indians differently from the settler populations, a tradition exemplified by the Royal Proclamation, the treaty-making process, the common law, and the BNA Act itself. However, the scope of the Act is quite narrow, since it applies only to registered Indians, some 573,657 individuals according to the Indian Register as of December 31, 1994. Based on the 1991 census, Statistics Canada has estimated that for 1994, the non-status Indian population stood at 405,962 persons, while there were 195,642 Metis (Nault and Jenkins, 1993). The latter are not registered under the Indian Act, either because they or their ancestors were omitted from the census, were of mixed race, became enfranchised, or were Indian women (and their children) who lost their status after marrying non-Indian men (prior to 1985). Nor has the Indian Act been fully extended to the 52,077 Inuit of northern Canada (see *Re Eskimo*, 1939; Dickason, 1992: 366-82). Non-status, landless Aboriginal people, together with registered Indians who reside in urban areas, now constitute the majority of the Native population. Hence, Parliament's exclusive legislative authority has only been directed at approximately 46 per cent of the 1.2 million Aboriginal people in Canada; the remainder are "left in constitutional limbo" (George, 1992: 2). Their situation gives rise to complex issues regarding the portability of rights and the establishment of urban governments that will have to be dealt with in the future (see Wherrett and Brown, 1992).

In fact, the narrow application of the Indian Act has been a matter of parliamentary choice. It has been a mixed blessing for those not under the Act, for while they have not been tightly regulated by the Department of Indian Affairs, they have also not enjoyed the benefits of the Act. Lacking reserve bases, they have not enjoyed land, hunting and fishing, and other Aboriginal rights. Nor have they been insulated from certain federal and provincial laws, as have reserve-based status Indians. In addition, the latter have also had certain advantages in maintaining their languages and cultures, particularly as many Indian bands have taken control of education, health and welfare, and other services.

Inevitably, there are conflicting views of the meaning of s. 91(24). While governments have interpreted it as a grant of exclusive legislative power over Indians and their lands, the First Nations have seen it rather differently. They point out that they never surrendered their inherent sovereignty via treaty or any other mechanism, nor could it be extinguished without their explicit consent (Mercredi and Turpel, 1993). To them, s. 91(24) signified the historic and continuing nation-to-nation relationship with the Crown, and "simply granted to the federal government the exclusive jurisdiction to administer the responsibilities assumed by Britain in the treaties, and [to] enter into further negotiations and agreements with the First Nations on behalf of the Crown" (Ryder, 1991: 315).

Canadian courts have not been guided by the Aboriginal view. Traditionally, they have understood Indians to be wards of the state with limited civil rights, although their "care and welfare are a political trust of the highest obligation" (Woodward, 1990: 110). Since the 1980s, however, higher courts have characterized the federal role less as a power and more as a responsibility, specifically a fiduciary or trust-like responsibility. In the *Guerin* case of 1984, the Supreme Court of Canada found that the federal government had not discharged its fiduciary obligation to the Musqueam band when it leased reserve lands to a Vancouver golf club at far below market rates. Writing the leading decision in the case, Chief Justice Dickson found that the Indian interest in lands is "a pre-existing legal right not created by the Royal Proclamation, by ... the Indian Act, or by any other executive order or legislative provision" (*Guerin v. the Queen*, 1984: 336). However, because Indian lands can only be surrendered or otherwise alienated to the Crown, the latter has an obligation to deal with the land for the benefit of the Indians surrendering it. Any breach of this fiduciary relationship by the Crown would oblige it to make good any losses suffered.

Following *Guerin*, the 1990 *Sparrow* decision expanded on the fiduciary obligation in an analysis of s. 35(1) of the Constitution Act, 1982, which recognizes and affirms "existing aboriginal and treaty rights." Although the Court did not question the federal government's assertion of law-making power over First Nations, it did find limits to that power. Holding that "the relationship between the Government and aboriginals is trust-like," the Court required that any government regulation that infringes on or denies Aboriginal rights had to be justified (*R. v. Sparrow*, 1990: 1108-09).

The two principles of a fiduciary relationship and of limits on the exercise of sovereign power signal that the federal government does not have unrestricted latitude to do whatever it pleases in respect of Aboriginal peoples or their lands. Rather, it must act for their benefit or at least avoid impairing their interests. Yet neither *Guerin* nor post-*Guerin* cases have cleared up the matter of whether the fiduciary duty applies only to the taking of Indian lands without compensation, or whether it is a general duty toward all Aboriginal peoples.

Nor is it clear whether the fiduciary duty also binds provincial governments, though some have argued that it must, because "insofar as provincial Crowns have the power to affect native peoples, they also share in the trust" (Slattery, 1987: 755). Although to date no higher court has made an explicit ruling on this point, the Supreme Court decision in *Sparrow* seems to suggest that s. 35, which has been held to incorporate fiduciary obligations, applies equally to the provinces (*R. v. Sparrow*, 1990: 1112). Further, in a case decided shortly before *Sparrow*, Chief Justice Dickson remarked that:

> One can over-emphasize the extent to which aboriginal peoples are affected only by the decisions and actions of the federal Crown. Part and parcel of the division of powers is the incidental effects doctrine, according to which a law in relation to a matter within the competence of one level of government may validly affect a matter within the competence of the other.... This fluidity of responsibility across lines of jurisdiction accords well with the fact that the newly entrenched s. 35 ... applies to all levels of government in Canada. (*Mitchell v. Peguis Indian Band*, 1990: 58)

If s. 35 incorporates a fiduciary duty on the part of the provincial governments, then they must act for the benefit of all Aboriginal peoples. In reality, however, the provinces have not been particularly sympathetic toward their Aboriginal citizens. Historically, they have been very interested in assuming ownership over Aboriginal lands and resources but far less interested in assuming responsibility for providing services to those populations.

PROVINCIAL ROLES

In practice, the jurisdictional profile is not as simple as s. 91(24) of the Constitution Act, 1867, would indicate. Far from exhausting the matter of Aboriginal peoples' position vis-à-vis the two levels of government, the section is fraught with ambiguities and, in fact, the provinces exercise a wide range of roles with respect to Aboriginal peoples.

In the first place, as the federal government has chosen to exercise its legislative power over Indians registered under the Indian Act but not over the majority of the Aboriginal population, non-status Indians and Metis have come under provincial jurisdiction. Hence, they have been subjected to all federal and provincial laws without buffers to protect their distinctive ethnic, cultural, economic, and political interests.

Second, s. 91(24) does not imply that reserve-based status Indians enjoy immunity from provincial laws. Although it would seem to preclude any assertion of provincial jurisdiction, in reality a large number of provincial laws apply to Native people whether they are residents of reserves or not. The jurisdictional picture is clouded by constitutional ambiguities: the federal government's selection of those portions of the Aboriginal population over which it chooses to exercise jurisdiction; the Indian Act's legal monopoly over the definition of an Indian and subsequent entitlements; provincial ownership of Crown lands; and statutory provisions, such as s. 88 of the Indian Act, that authorize the application of provincial laws to Indians and their lands subject to certain constraints.

Section 88 of the Indian Act

Despite the grant of exclusive legislative authority to the federal government in s. 91(24), that government has in fact chosen to open the field to provincial governments through a statutory empowerment in s. 88 of the federal Indian Act. Certainly, as Lyon points out, it would have been impossible for the federal government to enact a comprehensive code of distinct laws for Aboriginal peoples that would protect them from all provincial laws. "Separate traffic laws for Indians on provincial roads," he argues, "would make no constitutional sense" (Lyon, 1985: 431). Section 88, then, explicitly authorizes the application of provincial laws to all Indians, whether they reside on reserves or not, as long as they do not conflict with treaty provisions, any other Act of Parliament, or matters for which the Indian Act makes provision.

Unfortunately, the case law regarding application of provincial laws to Indians under various circumstances is quite inconsistent and often confusing. With regard to treaties, two important Supreme Court decisions in the 1980s have affirmed the principle that they provide a shield against provincial encroachments. The 1985 case of *Simon v. the Queen* involved a Micmac Indian who had been convicted for offences under Nova Scotia's Lands and Forests Act. Simon claimed that he was exercising his right to hunt under a Treaty of 1752 and that he was exempted from the provincial legislation by s. 88 of the Indian Act. The Supreme Court held that the treaty offered "a positive source of protection against infringements on hunting rights," that it was "an enforceable obligation between the Indians and the Crown," and that it had not been demonstrated that the hunting rights protected by the treaty had been extinguished (*Simon v. the Queen*, 1985: 387). The decision therefore affirmed the paramountcy of treaty rights over provincial legislation that would abrogate them.

Although earlier cases had held that provincial game laws applied because they did not relate to Indians *qua* Indians, in the 1985 case, *Dick v. R.*, Justice Beetz of the Supreme Court drew a distinction between "provincial laws which can be applied to Indians without touching their Indianness, like traffic regulation" and "provincial laws which cannot apply to Indians without regulating them *qua* Indians." Laws of the first kind, that is, laws that did not somehow affect the core of Indianness, applied independently of s. 88. However, Dick's conviction for hunting deer out of season was to be overturned since the application of the B.C. Wildlife Act "did impair the Indianness of the Alkali Lake Band" (*Dick v. R.*, 1985: 320-21); see also *R. v. Sioui*, 1990). This line of reasoning is constitutionally supported by s. 35 of the Constitution Act, 1982, which protects "existing aboriginal and treaty rights." Because those rights are entrenched in the fundamental law of the land, a strong argument can be made that they supersede ordinary legislation.

On the other hand, whereas some treaty rights have been held to invalidate some provincial wildlife laws, it must be noted that approximately half of the First Nations of Canada have never signed treaties. Their hunting, fishing, trapping, and other Aboriginal rights are subject to provincial laws (see *Kruger and Manuel v. R.*, 1978). This means that non-treaty Indians and Metis do not enjoy the same insulation from provincial statutes as treaty Indians, and hence, some Indians effectively have more rights than others under Canadian laws.

Since Indian reserves are not considered enclaves beyond provincial jurisdiction, even reserve-based status Indians have been subject to a wide range of provincial laws of general application. Courts in various decisions have taken the position that s. 88 makes provincial law applicable as part of federal law by referential incorporation (see Little Bear, 1988: 178-80). For example, in 1975 the Supreme Court of Canada found that although a provincial adoption law did affect Indians as Indians, the law had been incorporated by federal legislation via s. 88 and so it did apply to a status Indian child (*Natural Parents v. Superintendent of Child Welfare*, 1975; Sanders, 1985: 456-61). Four years later, in *Four B Manufacturing*, the Court held that provincial labour legislation applied to a manufacturing business owned and staffed by Indians on a reserve because there was nothing inherently Indian about the business. Similarly, in 1993 the Saskatchewan Queen's Bench overturned a lower court decision, holding that an Indian charged with starting a fire on a reserve had failed to take the precautions required by the Prairie and Forest Fires Act of 1982. The Act was viewed as a safety law of general application and applied under "the general rule … that provincial laws apply to Indians and lands reserved for Indians" (*R. v. Fiddler*, 1993).

The problem with the Indianness test is whether it is to be based on Indians' legal status under the Indian Act, or whether it refers to the unique aspects of Indian cultures or ways of life. Aboriginal people are understandably angry at the prospect of having court interpretations decide which provincial laws apply to them on the basis of non-Aboriginal judges' perceptions of what constitutes Indianness. In 1985, for example, the Supreme Court, in *Jack and Charlie v. R.*, found against two Salish Indians who had been hunting deer for a religious ceremony without a licence and out of season. Justice Beetz ignored evidence given at trial that raw deer meat was required for the ceremony on the grounds that there was no evidence that "the use of defrosted deer meat was sacrilegious" (1985: 344). Hence the non-Aboriginal court presumed to amend a Native religious rite in light of modern technologies such as freezers, an act of cultural definition clearly unacceptable to Native people.

Through court interpretations of constitutional and legislative provisions, many seemingly innocuous provincial statutes have been applied to Aboriginal people. Yet many of them have had detrimental effects on indigenous peoples' cultural, political, social, economic, and religious practices. The practice of Native medicine, for example, is effectively illegal, since the *Hill* decision applied a provincial Medical Act's licensing requirement to Indians (*R. v. Hill*, 1907). As Native medicine is not endorsed by the federal and provincial medical associations, Native practitioners cannot expect to be licensed by them. Child welfare legislation that allows for the apprehension of Native children or their adoption by non-Natives is obviously problematic in terms of the cultural integrity of Aboriginal communities. In fact, almost all provincial laws can be argued to affect the cultural integrity of Native peoples, but they are subject to judicial assessments of whether or not Indianness is impaired. Native people themselves are never asked for their assessments.

The Indian Act, then, means that provincial economic and social legislation will apply to reserve communities, including laws regulating hunting and fishing, child welfare, workers' compensation, labour standards, labour relations, marital property, family maintenance, minimum wages, rent control, automobile insurance, the taxation of non-Indian residents or businesses, and building standards. In fact, so extensive is the provincial role in Native affairs that every province has a separate department responsible for coordinating the various policies concerned (see Exell, 1988; Spiegel, 1988; Gourdeau, 1988). Hence, as Sanders points out, "the only real legislative powers of ... Indian band councils are over land use and motor vehicles" (Sanders, 1988: 153). Moreover, wherever there has been uncertainty, courts have accepted overlapping federal and provincial jurisdictions, so that "The outcome of this judicial course has been that authority exercised by Indian bands is always subject to either federal or provincial jurisdiction. The courts have left no room for Indians to exercise inherent jurisdiction" (Boldt and Long, 1988: 7).

Social Services

Apart from the application of provincial laws regulating various social and economic matters, provinces have belatedly taken on a fairly large role regarding the provision of services to Aboriginal peoples. In fact, before the middle of the twentieth century, the provinces had tended to respect the exclusive federal legislative role vis-à-vis registered Indians, although they

166

were the beneficiaries of federal policies that had extracted lands from the Indians via treaty, "voluntary" cession and surrenders, and similar instruments. Moreover, in direct violation of the Royal Proclamation, the provinces both expropriated and leased to third parties Indian lands not formally ceded to the federal government (see Tennant, 1990; Frideres, 1993: 34-128). Hence, the provinces were happy to let responsibility for Aboriginal peoples rest in federal hands, while they enjoyed the economic and other benefits of the lands and resources appropriated from them. Meanwhile, their only real formal roles were related to law enforcement activities and regulation of Native hunting and fishing on Crown lands.

It was not until the 1950s that the provinces began to take on expanded roles. At the same time as social welfare programs were being developed in Canada, a substantial migration of reserve Indians to the cities was under way. Whereas on-reserve Indians were excluded from provincial programs, off-reserve Indians were excluded from federal programs. Many fell through the cracks of both systems. As the provinces have jurisdiction over health and social welfare, exclusion from those services meant that Native people did not enjoy services equal to other Canadian citizens.

As Boldt and Long note, the 1960s saw the development of co-operative federal-provincial programs, such as technical, vocational, and agricultural training, that were open to Natives. The provinces began to include Native people in provincial programs such as old age assistance, and as the residential schools were abandoned, Natives were integrated into provincial school systems. Finally, under various cost-sharing agreements provincial welfare services were extended to Natives (Boldt and Long, 1988: 4). Therefore, today, although there is considerable variation between provinces, provincial services and programs to Aboriginal people include child care, social welfare, health care, education, community and economic development, law enforcement, and the administration of justice.

The federal government was in fact keen to slough off its responsibility for Indians, which, through the Indian Act and the corpulent bureaucratic machine that administered it (the Department of Indian Affairs and Northern Development, or DIAND), had proved both expensive and inconvenient. This desire was expressed with vigour after the election of Pierre Trudeau's Liberal government in 1968, which lost no time in formulating a plan to evacuate the s. 91(24) policy field. Trudeau's concept of the Just Society gloried in liberal individualism and promised formal equality for all, regardless of race or other characteristics. Hence, the famous White Paper of 1969 proposed to terminate special status for Indians, dismantle the Indian Act and the Indian Affairs bureaucracy, and treat Indians as ordinary citizens (Weaver, 1980).

Unfortunately for the government, First Nations people did not wish to lose their communities, cultures, languages, Aboriginal rights, Aboriginal title, treaties, and special status. Nor did they care to be bequeathed to the provinces, which had not in the past been devoted to their welfare and for whom they would constitute a low priority. Thus, the policy was not only vehemently rejected by status Indians across the country (see, e.g., Cardinal, 1969), but it also led to the unprecedented politicization of Aboriginal peoples. After 1969, national Aboriginal organizations were developed with the assistance of funding from the federal government, and Aboriginal political discourse around the issues of Aboriginal title, Aboriginal rights, and self-determination became increasingly sophisticated. These events were complemented by political activities ranging from protest actions to legal challenges, to lobbying strategies in the international arena (Jhappan, 1990, 1992). In addition, the federal government was forced to retract the White Paper and to develop a new comprehensive land claims policy and different approaches to Aboriginal policy.

These events notwithstanding, the provinces have still managed to assume certain responsibilities regarding Aboriginal peoples within the terms of the current division of powers. The provision of services is constitutionally valid since the provinces are spending but not legislating for or regulating Aboriginal peoples *per se*. Nevertheless, this situation is not optimal from many Aboriginal peoples' perspectives. Various provinces have taken the view that because those covered under the Indian Act are exempted from income tax if they reside and earn their incomes on reserves, they should not be incorporated into the same distributional system as non-Aboriginal citizens who are fully subject to the wealth collection system (see Woodward, 1990: 299-316).

Moreover, since the provinces are not constitutionally compelled to provide social and other services to reserve-based First Nations, funding levels are precarious. Although the federal government currently funds the provision of services to on-reserve Indians through cost-sharing agreements, transfers, and block payments to the provinces, it is not constitutionally compelled to reimburse provinces for any services they provide to Native people. Thus, in recessionary periods, spending cuts in the federal budget result in a direct reduction of service levels to these populations. In the meantime, health, education, welfare, and other services to urban Aboriginal populations cost the provinces almost double the per capita costs of those services to non-Aboriginal citizens. So, while the federal government would prefer to transfer all services to the provinces, the latter are not particularly anxious to assume the costs, especially if they cannot rely on compensation from the federal government. In addition, Aboriginal people have little or no representation or control over the design and operation of provincial programs in areas such as child welfare and education. Hence, Aboriginal leaders have demanded that their historic special relationship with the federal Crown be respected, the better to protect their communities from the assimilationist pressures associated with provincial laws and programs of general application. As Boldt and Long (1988: 6) note, "Indians are genuinely worried that the gradual assumption of services and programs by the provinces will be used as a pretext for asserting provincial control over Indian lands, resources, and affairs."

Land

With the exception of the territories, a few small pockets of federal Crown lands, and reserve lands, Canadian law recognizes the provinces as the owners of all lands and resources within provincial boundaries. Thus, a literal reading of s. 91(24) is misleading to the extent that it grants law-making authority over "lands reserved for the Indians" to the federal government. Because reserve lands account for only a very small proportion of the lands that traditionally supported Native subsistence economies, s. 91(24) does not give the federal government legislative authority over very much land. The provinces in fact exercise authority over traditional tribal territories not formally defined as reserve lands.

While the provinces have resisted being burdened with responsibility for Aboriginal peoples, they are keen to increase their jurisdiction over Aboriginal lands and resources. In fact, many conflicts have arisen over hunting, fishing, and gathering rights. These rights are subject to provincial game and wildlife laws unless explicitly protected by treaty or constitutional provisions. The situation is complicated by the fact that treaties were concluded with only approximately half of the indigenous peoples of Canada, leaving First Nations in most of British Columbia, Québec, and the Maritimes without treaty-based hunting and fishing rights. This means that the rights of non-treaty indigenous peoples to hunt, fish, and gather are not distinguished from those of other non-Aboriginal citizens and are regulated in their entirety by provincial governments under general legislation. Hence, non-treaty Aboriginal people have had to make broader rights claims in litigation. Such claims are much more difficult to win in court, especially where judges take the position that Aboriginal rights ought to be settled via negotiation because of their large economic and political implications.

Claims to unextinguished Aboriginal rights have not in fact fared well before the courts. Indeed, the 1990 *Sparrow* decision was an important exception to the general trend. In that case, the Supreme Court of Canada found that a Musqueam Indian was exercising an unextinguished Aboriginal right to fish in British Columbia, a right that gave Indians top priority over the sports and commercial fisheries. In spite of the Supreme Court decision, however, conflicts continue between the parties, and further litigation regarding Aboriginal peoples' right to sell their catches is expected in the near future. The ongoing problems in the fisheries illustrate that governments can ignore even Supreme Court of Canada decisions, and the costs of returning to court for fresh judgments can be prohibitive for the Aboriginal people concerned.

Apart from harvesting rights on traditional tribal territories, claims to land ownership have been even more difficult to settle. In fact, the federal government only drafted a land claims policy twenty-two years ago after the Supreme Court split on the Nisga'a claim to unextinguished Aboriginal title in northern B.C. in the famous *Calder* decision. However, the 1981 document, *In All Fairness*, insisted that Aboriginal rights be extinguished in exchange for limited ownership and resource rights, and held that only six claims would be negotiated at any particular time (Canada, 1981). Within such restraints, it is not surprising that few agreements have been concluded to date.

These problems aside, perhaps the chief difficulty in settling land claims is the need for provincial agreement. Because Crown lands are held by the provinces, when First Nations claim lands outside reserves they are making claims against the provincial governments, as well as any third parties that have been granted ownership, harvesting or other rights by those governments (Sanders, 1988: 159). Thus, no matter what its land claims policy, the federal government is not in a position to return lands it does not own to their original Aboriginal holders. The conclusion of claims to both unceded traditional territories (comprehensive claims) and reserve and other entitlements (specific claims) requires that the provincial governments be willing to cede lands back to Aboriginal peoples (see

Frideres, 1993: 66-125). The provinces have generally not been willing to do so, however. For example, although the Québec Boundaries Extension Act of 1912 obliged that province to negotiate treaties in northern Québec, it was not until 1974 that an agreement was concluded, following Native protests and a Québec Superior Court injunction against the James Bay hydroelectric project (Diamond, 1985).

Meanwhile, although there are more than twenty outstanding comprehensive claims in British Columbia, successive provincial governments have refused even to acknowledge the concept of Aboriginal title, let alone participate in negotiations. This refusal has led Aboriginal groups in B.C. to initiate litigation to gain legal recognition of their claims, the largest and most important of which to date is the claim of forty-eight hereditary Gitksan-Wet'su'wet'en chiefs to land and self-government rights over some 22,000 square miles of land in British Columbia. The case was lost at the B.C. Supreme Court and the B.C. Court of Appeals levels, and is now on appeal to the Supreme Court of Canada (see Jhappan, 1991). However, since August, 1990, the B.C. government has agreed to negotiate land claims and has established a Treaty Commission and a process for negotiating treaties. The province's resistance to land claims has been grounded in fears of loss of jurisdiction and access to natural resources, particularly where competing third-party interests and economic development prospects are affected. These pressures have not abated just because British Columbia has decided to recognize claims. However, they have been softened considerably by an agreement signed by the governments of Canada and British Columbia in June, 1993. The federal government has undertaken to cover between 75 and 90 per cent of the cash costs of settling outstanding land claims in the province (including the buying out of third-party interests), if B.C. provides the Crown land and some of the cash costs (Wilson, 1993). Although no agreements have yet been concluded in B.C., there is now a greater possibility that outstanding land claims can be settled.

RECENT CHANGES IN FEDERAL-PROVINCIAL ROLES

The preceding discussion has given some indication of the extent to which Aboriginal peoples' lives are controlled by the federal and provincial governments. This situation is the inescapable outcome of a constitutional system that divides law-making power and authority between two levels of government and that denies the right of indigenous people to govern themselves. Since the late 1960s, therefore, Canada's Aboriginal peoples have tied their cultural and political rejuvenation to the need for self-government. Moreover, the national organizations have insisted on a constitutional accommodation of Aboriginal peoples' unique rights and needs, rather than changes at the non-constitutional level via legislation or other instruments that would be amenable to alteration by the federal and provincial governments.

Constitutional rights, however, have not been easily won. The following discussion analyzes briefly the constitutional changes won in 1982 and, more recently, the near miss on a constitutional right to self-government in the 1992 Charlottetown Agreement. It also traces changes at the non-constitutional level in the form of the delegated authority model of the Department of Indian Affairs' community-based self-government program and recent land claims settlements such as Nunavut.

Constitutional Changes: 1982 to 1992

When the Trudeau government decided to repatriate the Canadian constitution in the late 1970s and add to it a Charter of Rights, none of the political actors subsequently involved contemplated any changes to the constitutional status of Aboriginal peoples. There was no thought that the colonial system that had deprived Aboriginal peoples of their rights and titles and made registered Indians wards of the state ought to be overhauled to meet their needs and aspirations. The constitution was largely viewed as the power map setting the boundaries of the relationship between the federal and provincial governments.

Aboriginal organizations, however, saw constitutional reform as an opportunity to restructure their relationship to the Canadian state. The National Indian Brotherhood (forerunner to the Assembly of First Nations), together with various provincial organizations, lobbied the Queen and the British Parliament to halt the patriation process unless the reform package guaranteed Native rights. Although the constitution was repatriated anyway, the campaign opened a space for Aboriginal issues, and the national organizations succeeded in lobbying for the inclusion of several clauses in the final agreement (Sanders, 1983: 301-32). Through sections 25 and 35 of the Constitution Act, 1982, Aboriginal organizations secured for the first time in Canadian history constitutional entrenchment of Aboriginal and treaty rights. Section 25 provides that Aboriginal and treaty rights (including those recognized by the Royal Proclamation or by land claims agreements) should not be derogated by rights and freedoms guaranteed in the Charter. Section 35 recognizes and affirms the "existing aboriginal and treaty rights" of the Indian, Inuit, and Metis peoples, and guarantees those rights equally to male and female persons.

Although the exact nature and content of the Aboriginal and treaty rights so recognized and affirmed have not been interpreted by the courts, Aboriginal people see the clauses as a full box of rights, while governments have tended to see them as an empty box to be filled via negotiation. Nevertheless, although Aboriginal organizations insist that self-government is one of the Aboriginal rights recognized and affirmed by s. 35, the lack of specificity in the wording led to unsuccessful attempts to secure an amendment on self-government during the three First Ministers' Conferences on Aboriginal Matters held between 1983 and 1987 (see Schwartz, 1986). In fact, within a month of the failure of the last conference, the federal and provincial governments were able to sign the Meech Lake Accord, which met Québec's demands for a restructured federation but ignored Aboriginal demands. As a result of their exclusion from the Accord, Aboriginal organizations were to play a leading role in its ultimate defeat.

By the 1991-92 round of constitutional talks, Aboriginal organizations were determined that their inherent right to self-government would at long last be explicitly recognized in the constitution. After a year of curious twists and turns in the public and elite debates, the final text of the Charlottetown Accord of August 28, 1992, proposed to entrench Aboriginal peoples' "inherent right of self-government within Canada." For the first time in Canadian history, Aboriginal governments would have been recognized as a third order of government. Although the inherent right was to be limited by the application of the Charter of Rights, and federal and provincial laws of general application would continue to apply until self-government agreements were concluded, the Accord would have greatly expanded s. 25 and s. 35 rights. It would have given Aboriginal peoples constitutional security, even as it acknowledged that their pre-existing rights could not be erased at will by other levels of government. Had it been passed in the national referendum of October 26, 1992, the Charlottetown Accord would have transformed the relationship between Aboriginal communities and the federal and provincial governments radically: it would have freed self-governing communities from federal and provincial jurisdictions for which they assumed responsibility themselves (Jhappan, 1993).

The ultimate failure of the Charlottetown Accord was a significant blow and an enormous disappointment for the national Aboriginal organizations that had participated in its design. Several leaders predicted that Aboriginal peoples' strategies would become more localized and more militant in the domestic sphere. First Nations would take direct action to protect their lands and resources, as well as to assert their authority in a number of areas now under federal or provincial jurisdiction. At the same time, strategies would become more internationalized as Aboriginal peoples forged more linkages and support networks with groups in other countries and stepped up their appeals to international organizations such as the United Nations to pressure Canadian governments to implement at the non-constitutional level the promises they had been willing to make in Charlottetown (see York, 1992). In the meantime, however, two existing federal policies (community-based self-government and comprehensive land claims) will take on a renewed importance, having been overshadowed somewhat by the constitutional process.

Community-Based Self-Government

Given the absence of an explicit constitutional right to self-government, one of the options available to status Indian bands is the community-based self-government policy announced by the federal government in 1986. The policy illustrates that government's continued preference for the municipal model, which does not alter the current division of powers. Although agreements should not prejudice Aboriginal rights, existing or future land claims, or future constitutional reforms, Aboriginal governments must be fashioned within the existing constitutional framework (Frideres, 1993: 453-62).

The policy sets out a complicated four-stage process involving development of an initial proposal by a band, a framework proposal, substantive negotiations, and final implementation. It is important to note that although more than 200 bands have at least expressed an interest in the policy, many have dropped out and few agreements have been concluded to date. Currently, some twenty groups representing forty or so bands are in negotiations (Platiel, 1992). While a full analysis of this process is beyond the scope of this chapter, the policy suffers from several major problems.

In the first place, the community-based self-government program is only available to status Indian bands under the Indian Act. Hence, it offers no opportunities to the majority of the Aboriginal population. Yet, even if it did apply to non-reserve constituencies, it is still a model of delegated authority, a model that has been rejected by the vast majority of Aboriginal organizations. Delegated authority would leave so-called self-governing communities subject to the governments that granted the authority and that could therefore alter it unilaterally.

In the second place, the federal government determines which items are negotiable. This means that if the federal government wishes to retain control over items such as labour relations, band membership, third-party harvesting rights, or disposition of lands or monies, the band concerned cannot insist that they be placed on the agenda. Third, about two-thirds of the twenty-five areas of jurisdiction typically implicated are within provincial jurisdiction, so that each agreement will depend on provincial willingness to vacate certain fields. Finally, other problems surrounding funding regimes and the complicated process required by the policy make it unlikely that Aboriginal self-government can be achieved through this instrument.

RECENT LAND CLAIMS AND SELF-GOVERNMENT AGREEMENTS

Despite the lack of progress toward a constitutional amendment, self-government for land-based status Indians has been an emerging reality as more bands take over the administration and sometimes design of services such as education, health care, resource management, economic development, child welfare, and policing. In two notable but very different cases, special legislation has authorized the Inuit, Cree, and Naskapi of James Bay and the Sechelt Indian band of British Columbia to exercise various powers.

In the former case, the agreements reached in 1975 and 1978 were prompted by Aboriginal peoples' resistance to Québec's grand hydroelectric schemes. They were basically land claim agreements. However, as well as providing for compensation, ownership of certain lands, and a range of special hunting and other rights, the James Bay and Northern Québec Agreement and the Northeastern Québec Agreement were later supplemented by the Cree-Naskapi (of Québec) Act, 1984. Under these modern treaties and statutes, some measure of local self-government has been restored: the Indian Act no longer applies; and provincial laws of general application are of no force if they are inconsistent with the Cree-Naskapi Act.

The Cree-Naskapi governments so established, however, are basically municipal-style governments, although they do enjoy some wider powers over harvesting rights and the environment. Nevertheless, due to a number of implementation problems and broken promises on the part of governments, the James Bay model has not been widely lauded by other Aboriginal groups; it is unlikely to be emulated in the future (see Moss, 1985: 684-94).

A more controversial model is that of the Sechelt band of British Columbia. In that case, the band was anxious to benefit from its valuable real estate holdings on the coast close to Vancouver, and sought to release itself from the constraints of the Indian Act and various provincial powers (Taylor and Paget, 1988). The Sechelt Indian Band Self-Government Act was passed by the federal Parliament in 1986, followed by a provincial enabling Act nine months later. The legislation establishes the band as a legal entity that can hold and acquire property, enter into contracts, spend, borrow, or invest money, and sue and be sued. The band holds all of its reserve lands under fee simple title (that is, outright private ownership not held in trust by the Crown, as are other reserve lands). It can dispose of them as it wishes, subject to the band constitution and a referendum among the membership.

The Sechelt Act is not only a real estate deal, however. It is also a self-government agreement. The band is responsible for matters such as education, health, social and welfare services, child custody, and public order. It has assumed a range of powers formerly exercised by the federal and provincial governments, though the Indian Act still formally applies in some matters. However, the Sechelt band council exercises much wider powers than Indian Act bands, and its jurisdiction applies equally to non-Indians on Sechelt lands (see Cassidy and Bish, 1989: 135-55).

The Sechelt model, like the James Bay model before it, has been widely criticized by other Indian bands and organizations because of its municipal-style government. It does not recognize the Sechelt people as an Aboriginal people with historic and unextinguished rights to land and self-government. Rather, senior governments have granted delegated powers to the very junior Sechelt government. Moreover, it is the preferred model of the federal and provincial governments, who have resisted the idea of recognizing self-government in the constitution as a pre-existing, independent, exclusive right.

Despite government preferences, however, Aboriginal communities have become increasingly insistent that their Aboriginal rights be recognized and respected in land claims and self-government agreements. In fact, some have succeeded in having the items of land and self-government tied together in settlements. For example, two agreements were signed in the Yukon in 1992 between the government of Canada and the Vuntut Gwich'in and the Champagne and Aishihik First Nations. The first is a land claim agreement that includes provisions for self-government, although the latter is an exclusive self-government agreement (Canada, 1992a; Canada 1992b). Once implemented, each of these agreements will be fully protected under sections 25 and 35 of the Constitution Act, 1982; they will not be susceptible to unilateral amendment by the federal government.

The most far-reaching agreement to date, however, is that to create a third territory in the eastern Arctic in 1999. The federal government passed the necessary legislation in July, 1993, in the final days of the Mulroney administration. In the most significant change to the map of Canada since Newfoundland entered the federation in 1949, the new territory of Nunavut ("the people's land" in Inuktitut) will cover one-fifth of Canada's land mass. The agreement, which took fifteen years to negotiate, gives the Inuit title to 350,000 square kilometres of land, including 36,000 square kilometres of subsurface mineral rights; a cash settlement of $1.15 billion over fourteen years; and the right to hunt, fish, and trap in the whole territory. A number of management boards will oversee Nunavut, and the Inuit will share power with the federal government on boards regulating wildlife, the environment, land-use planning, and offshore resources. These rights, however, come at the expense of extinguishment of general Aboriginal rights, which are exchanged for specified, limited rights (Canada, 1993).

In addition to the land and economic provisions, a political accord creates a new territorial government that is to assume its full powers by 2008. Through it, the Inuit will have *de facto* self-government: they will effectively control the legislature since they comprise 85 per cent of the population of the territory (Cernetig, 1992). It must be noted, however, that this form of public rather than ethnically exclusive government is vulnerable to population shifts; it is possible that if resource development projects lead to an influx of non-Aboriginal residents, Inuit may lose control of the territorial government. In addition, the government of Nunavut will be part of the parliamentary system of Canada and will in no way represent either traditional Inuit government or a third level of (Aboriginal) government.

Nunavut will not be a particularly useful model for other Aboriginal peoples, who do not live in territories or provinces in which they comprise the majority. In fact, it is obvious that the Nunavut deal could only have come about in a northern territory under the direct control of the federal government, where no provincial governments were required to relinquish powers and resources. Also, although the agreement will be protected as a modern treaty under s. 35 of the Constitution Act, 1982, Nunavut has not been established by a constitutional amendment recognizing an inherent right to self-government on the part of Inuit. Hence, for some Aboriginal groups, any model that stops short of constitutional recognition of the pre-existing right to self-government is inadequate because it implies Aboriginal peoples' subordination to other governments.

Finally, the Liberal government elected in 1993 has recently embarked on an ambitious experiment in Manitoba, its chosen test site for a new approach to self-government. Preliminary negotiations with the provincial Native organizations are aimed at devolving authority over federal programs to local chiefs, with the intention ultimately of dismantling the Department of Indian Affairs within the province. Although at the time of writing very little information on the initiative has been made public, it is likely that the federal government intends to pursue a similar approach in other provinces, if not at the national level. In the absence of progress on the constitutional front, it is possible that amendments to the Indian Act will proceed incrementally on various items until many federal powers have devolved onto band governments. Alternatively, it is to be hoped that the Royal Commission on Aboriginal Peoples, appointed by the Mulroney government and due to issue its final report in the spring of 1995, will propose fresh, less piecemeal approaches to Aboriginal self-government.

CONCLUSION

This chapter has surveyed the various and complex roles played by the federal and provincial governments in Aboriginal peoples' lives. Certain constitutional anomalies have contributed to the complexity. Although s. 91(24) of the Constitution Act, 1867, confers legislative power over Indians and lands reserved for the Indians on the federal government, it does not compel that government to legislate, spend money on, or provide services to Indians or their lands. Nor does it insist that the federal government assume responsibilities for all Aboriginal people. Instead, that government has been able to define "Indians" through an Act of Parliament in narrow terms that have nothing to do with Aboriginal peoples' self-definitions. It has thus created a class of so-called non-status Indians and Metis peoples who are subject to all federal and provincial laws and who have been stripped of their Aboriginal rights and titles.

In the meantime, status Indians on reserves have been subjected to the almost absolute control of the Indian Act and the federal department that administers it. However, they are not insulated from provincial laws either. On the contrary, provincial laws of general application apply to all Indians, either by referential incorporation or by s. 88 of the Indian Act (as long as they do not regulate Indians *qua* Indians or conflict with federal legislation or treaty rights). The two-tiered federal system thus permits no power vacuums: provincial laws are automatically sucked into any void neglected by the federal government. This system leaves no space for Indian communities to exercise self-government, except for those powers delegated to them by the other two all-powerful levels of government.

In recent decades, the provinces have also taken on greater roles and responsibilities in the provision of social and other services to both on- and off-reserve Aboriginal peoples. Further, the provinces ostensibly own Crown lands outside reserves so that the settlement of land claims to unsurrendered traditional territories depends on their willingness to relinquish control of valuable lands and resources. To date, provincial governments have tended to ignore Aboriginal interests when granting resource licences and other rights to third parties. With the provinces so deeply implicated in Aboriginal peoples' lives, the call for self-government has arisen in part because federalism has created an air-tight system that gives law-making privileges to all but Aboriginal governments.

Although the Constitution Act, 1982, recognized and affirmed Aboriginal and treaty rights, the latter have not really been spelled out. Nor did that Act change the division of powers to accommodate Aboriginal governments. That was precisely what the 1992 Charlottetown Accord would have done, had it been passed in the national referendum of October, 1992.

The re-entrenchment of the constitutional status quo has different consequences for different constituencies of Aboriginal peoples, however. Status Indians may choose to participate in the federal government's community-based self-government process, even though it provides only for delegated, municipal-style government, a far cry from the inherent right that Charlottetown would have constitutionalized. Status Indians also have an advantage in pressing land claims, both specific and comprehensive, as they already have limited land bases – reserves – on which they still form discrete communities. Further, as land claims and self-government come to be seen as virtually senseless one without the other, status Indians are also reasonably well-placed to pursue dual agreements.

On the other hand, landless Aboriginal groups such as non-status, off-reserve Indians and Metis have not been able to avail themselves of similar institutional strategies to forward their political agendas. While self-government can proceed at the non-constitutional level for land-based status Indians and Inuit, it is simply not a reality for non-status, landless and off-reserve Indians and Metis, even though they were included among those enjoying an inherent right to self-government under the Charlottetown Accord. Without a constitutional compulsion, there is little if any incentive for the federal and provincial governments to negotiate a giveaway of their powers to Aboriginal people who do not already have a land base.

It seems unlikely that a constitutional amendment on self-government can be achieved in the near future. The new Liberal government's attention is on economic regeneration rather than constitutional reform, and for a variety of reasons a repetition of the unique configuration of political forces that allowed for the Charlottetown compromises seems a remote possibility. Nevertheless, the 1991-92 process at last impressed upon governments Aboriginal peoples' dissatisfaction with current arrangements. Some provincial governments have expressed a willingness at least to negotiate the transfer of some powers to existing Aboriginal governments. Non-constitutional initiatives can vary considerably in scope and approach, from devolutionary models of self-government to land claims/self-government settlements, to specific legislation that displaces Indian Act provisions by increments. Thus, although the formal division of powers between the federal and provincial governments probably will not change, new arrangements (at least for land-based status Indians) will certainly evolve as we approach the millennium.

REFERENCES

Boisvert, David (1985). *Forms of Self-Government*. Kingston: Institute for Intergovernmental Relations.

Boldt, M., and J.A. Long (1988). "Introduction," in Boldt and Long, eds., *Governments in Conflict?: Provinces and Indian Nations in Canada*. Toronto: University of Toronto Press.

Canada, Indian Affairs and Northern Development (1981). *In All Fairness: A Native Claims Policy, Comprehensive Policy*.

Canada, Indian Affairs and Northern Development (1992a). *Champagne and Aishihik First Nations Self-Government Agreement*.

Canada, Indian Affairs and Northern Development (1992b). *Vuntut Gwich'in First Nation Final Agreement*.

Canada, Indian and Northern Affairs Canada (1993). *Agreement Between the Inuit of the Nunavut Settlement Area and Her Majesty the Queen in Right of Canada*.

Cardinal, Harold (1969). *The Unjust Society: the Tragedy of Canada's Indians*. Edmonton: Hurtig.

Cassidy, F., and R.L. Bish (1989). *Indian Government: Its Meaning in Practice*. Halifax: Institute for Research on Public Policy.

Cernetig, Miro (1992). "Accord sets up Inuit territory called Nunavut," *Globe and Mail*. October 31: A4.

Chartier, Clem (1985). "Aboriginal Rights and Land Issues: the Metis Perspective," in M. Boldt and J.A. Long, eds., *The Quest for Justice: Aboriginal Peoples and Aboriginal Rights*. Toronto: University of Toronto Press.

Chartrand, Paul (1993). "Aboriginal Self-Government: the Two Sides of Legitimacy," in Susan D. Phillips, ed., *How Ottawa Spends: A More Democratic Canada?... 1993-94*. Ottawa: Carleton University Press.

Davies, Maureen (1985). "Aspects of Aboriginal Rights in International Law," in B. Morse, ed., Aboriginal Peoples and the Law: Indian, Inuit and Metis Rights in Canada. Ottawa: Carleton University Press.

Diamond, Billy (1985). "The James Bay Experience," in Boldt and Long, eds., *The Quest for Justice*.

Dickason, Olive Patricia (1992). *Canada's First Nations: A History of Founding Peoples from Earliest Times*. Toronto: McClelland & Stewart.

Elliott, D.W. (1985). "Aboriginal Title," in Morse, ed., *Aboriginal Peoples and the Law*

Exell, Robert (1988). "British Columbia and the Native Community," in Boldt and Long, eds., *Governments in Conflict?*

Frideres, James (1993). *Native Peoples in Canada: Contemporary Conflicts*. 4th edition. Scarborough: Prentice-Hall.

George, Ron (1992). *Becoming Visible: Urban Self-Government in the 1990s*. Ottawa: Native Council of Canada.

Gourdeau, Eric (1988). "Quebec and Aboriginal Peoples," in Boldt and Long, eds., *Governments in Conflict?*

Henderson, James Youngblood (1985). "The Doctrine of Aboriginal Rights in Western Legal Tradition," in Boldt and Long, eds., *The Quest for Justice*

Imai, S., K. Logan, and G. Stein (1993). *Aboriginal Law Handbook*. Scarborough: Carswell.

Jackson, Michael (1984). "The Articulation of Native Rights in Canadian Law," *U.B.C. Law Review*, 18, 2: 255-87.

Jhappan, R. (1990). "Indian Symbolic Politics: the Double-Edged Sword of Publicity," *Canadian Ethnic Studies*, XXII, 3: 19-39.

Jhappan, R. (1991). "Natural Rights vs. Legal Positivism: Indians, the Courts, and the New Discourse of Aboriginal Rights in Canada," *British Journal of Canadian Studies*, 6, 1: 60-100.

Jhappan, R. (1992). "A Global Community?: Supranational Strategies of Canada's Aboriginal Peoples," *Journal of Indigenous Studies*, 3, 1: 59-97.

Jhappan, R. (1993). "Inherency, Three Nations and Collective Rights: the Evolution of Aboriginal Constitutional Discourse from 1982 to the Charlottetown Accord," *International Journal of Canadian Studies*, 7-8 (Spring-Fall): 225-60.

Little Bear, Leroy (1988). "Section 88 of the Indian Act and the Application of Provincial Laws to Indians," in Boldt and Long, eds., *Governments in Conflict?*

Lyon, Noel (1985). "Constitutional Issues in Native Law," in Morse, ed., *Aboriginal Peoples and the Law*.

Macklem, Patrick (1991). "First Nations Self-Government and the Borders of the Canadian Legal Imagination," *McGill Law Journal*, 36, 2: 384-456.

Mercredi, Ovide, and Mary Ellen Turpel (1993). *In the Rapids: Navigating the Future of First Nations*. Toronto: Penguin.

Morse, B. (1985). "Aboriginal Peoples and the Law," in Morse, ed., *Aboriginal Peoples and the Law*.

Morse, B. (1991). "Government Obligations, Aboriginal Peoples and Section 91(24) of the Constitution Act, 1867," in David C. Hawkes, ed., *Aboriginal Peoples and Government Responsibility: Exploring Federal and Provincial Roles*. Ottawa: Carleton University Press.

Moss, Wendy (1985). "The Implementation of the James Bay and Northern Quebec Agreement," in Morse, ed., *Aboriginal Peoples and the Law*.

Nault, F., and E. Jenkins (1993). "Projections of Canada's Population with Aboriginal Ancestry, 1991-2016," Statistics Canada, Population Projects Section, Demography Division.

Platiel, Rudy (1992). "Powers shift to aboriginals, government says," *Globe and Mail.* November 20: A7.

Pratt, Alan (1991). "Federalism in the Era of Aboriginal Self-Government," in Hawkes, ed., *Aboriginal Peoples and Government Responsibility.*

Ryder, Bruce (1991). "The Demise and Rise of the Classical Paradigm in Canadian Federalism: Promoting Autonomy for the Provinces and First Nations," *McGill Law Journal*, 36, 2: 309-81.

Sanders, D.E. (1983). "The Indian Lobby," in K. Banting and R. Simeon, eds., *And No-one Cheered: Federalism, Democracy and the Constitution Act.* Toronto: Methuen.

Sanders, D.E. (1985). "The Application of Provincial Laws," in Morse, ed., *Aboriginal Peoples and the Law.*

Sanders, D.E. (1988). "The Constitution, the Provinces, and Aboriginal Peoples," in Boldt and Long, eds., *Governments in Conflict?*

Schwartz, Brian (1986). *First Principles, Second Thoughts: Aboriginal Peoples, Constitutional Reform, and Canadian Statecraft.* Montreal: Institute for Research on Public Policy.

Slattery, Brian (1985). "The Hidden Constitution: Aboriginal Rights in Canada," in Boldt and Long, eds., *The Quest for Justice.*

Slattery, Brian (1987). "Understanding Aboriginal Rights," *Canadian Bar Review*, 66: 727-83.

Slattery, Brian (1991). "Aboriginal Sovereignty and Imperial Claims: Reconstructing North American History," *Osgoode Hall Law Journal*, 29: 682-703.

Spiegel, Shelley (1988). "Ontario Provincial Native Policy and Directions," in Boldt and Long, eds., *Governments in Conflict?*

Taylor, J.P., and G. Paget (1991). "Federal/Provincial Responsibility and the Sechelt," in Hawkes, ed., *Aboriginal Peoples and Government Responsibility.*

Tennant, Paul (1990). *Aboriginal Peoples and Politics: the Indian Land Question in British Columbia, 1849-1989.* Vancouver: University of British Columbia Press.

Weaver, Sally (1980). Making Canadian Indian Policy: the Hidden Agenda, 1968-70. Toronto: University of Toronto Press.

Wherrett, J., and D. Brown (1992). Self-Government for Aboriginal Peoples Living in Urban Areas. Ottawa: Native Council of Canada.

Wilson, Bill (1985). "Aboriginal Rights: the Non-status Indian Perspective," in Boldt and Long, eds., *The Quest for Justice.*

Wilson, C. Roderick, and Carl Urion (1995). "First Nations Prehistory and Cana-
    dian History," in R. Bruce Morrison and C. Roderick Wilson, eds., *Native Peo-
    ples: The Canadian Experience*, Second edition. Toronto: McClelland & Stewart:
    22-66.

Wilson, Deborah (1993). "Siddon to cover cash end for B.C.," *Globe and Mail*.
    June 22: A1-A2.

Woodward, Jack (1990). *Native Law*. Toronto: Carswell.

York, G. (1992). "For Aboriginals: New arena in fight for rights," *Globe and Mail*,
    October 27: A1; "Natives set to move ahead with own laws," November 20:
    A5.

LEGAL CASES CITED

Calder et al. v. Attorney General of British Columbia [1973] SCR 313.

Delgamuukw v. British Columbia [1993] 5 WWR 97 (BCCA).

Dick v. R. [1985] 2 SCR 309.

Four B Manufacturing Ltd. v. United Garment Workers [1979] 102 DLR (3d) 385.

Guerin v. the Queen [1984] 2 SCR 335.

Jack and Charlie v. R. [1985] 2 SCR 332.

Johnson v. Macintosh (1823) 21 US (8 Wheat) 543.

Kruger and Manuel v. R. [1978] 1 SCR 104.

Mitchell v. Peguis Indian Band [1990] 3 CNLR 46 (SCC).

Natural Parents v. Superintendent of Child Welfare [1975] 60 DLR (3d) 148.

Re Eskimo [1939] SCR 104.

R. v. Fiddler [1993] 3 WWR 594.

R. v. Hill [1907] 15 OLR 406 (CA).

R. v. Sioui [1990] 1 SCR 1025.

R. v. Sparrow [1990] 1 SCR 1075.

Simon v. R. [1985] 2 SCR 387.

Part Two:
Public Policy and the Division of Powers

CHAPTER EIGHT

Federalism and Economic Policy

Robert M. Campbell

A CENTRAL FEATURE OF THE MODERN STATE HAS BEEN THE notion that governments have the responsibility to manage their economies to attain high levels of employment, economic stability, and growth. The origins of this responsibility lie mainly in the devastating social and political impact of the Great Depression. Mammoth levels of unemployment, collapsing income, and incalculable human dislocation shook the liberal economic system and political democracy to their very roots (Campbell, 1987).

The notion of political responsibility for economic conditions evolved in a particular way in Canada, given its federal system of overlapping economic and social authority. This chapter explores the shifts in the relationship between federalism and economic management in Canada, with particular respect to employment and price stability (other goals such as regional balance, trade, etc. are considered in other chapters). The depression undermined the laissez-faire ideas that had perpetuated the notion of the self-regulating market, which insisted on a limited government role in the economy. Thus, our discussion can be limited temporally to the postwar Keynesian period, the era in which governments committed themselves to using their fiscal and monetary tools to smooth out the business cycle. Despite its apparently far-reaching consequences, the coming of the Keynesian era did not require complex institutional or constitutional changes. As a result, federalism and economic management in Canada will be discussed mainly in political terms.

Central to the discussion is the Keynesian idea that governments can determine economic stability. More recently, the Reagan and Thatcher revolutions challenged the Keynesian idea, weakening to a considerable extent the notion that governments can be a positive force, for example, in maintaining high levels of employment. Thus, faith in market mecha-

nisms has been reborn. This, in turn, has changed the relationship between federalism and economic management.

THE DIVISION OF POWERS

Keynesian management comprises the manipulation of tax and interest
rates and government spending in a countercyclical way. When the economy is weak, the government might cut interest and tax rates or increase
its spending to get the economy moving via cheaper money and a budget
deficit. When inflation threatens, higher interest rates and a budgetary
surplus constrain economic activity. Which government initiates these actions? In a federation, sub-national units give up two economic levers:
control over tariffs (see Chapter 10) and monetary/exchange policy.
While the central government pursues monetary policy, fiscal policy is a
shared responsibility and tends to be the greatest source of intergovernmental friction (Bird, 1989: 126).

Canada's monetary policy is centralized. Section 91 of the Constitution
Act, 1867, established exclusive federal jurisdiction over currency and
coinage, banking, the incorporation of banks, the issue of paper money,
and interest and legal tender. The main instruments of control, including
printing money, rest exclusively in federal hands (Courchene, 1986: 52-
54). Provinces influence the exchange rate when they borrow and exert
political pressure when unhappy about monetary policy. This pressure is
limited, as monetary policy is managed by the Bank of Canada, which is
insulated from day-to-day political pressures. The courts have defended
federal claims and federal authority has been largely unchallenged since
World War Two (Howlett, 1992: 213-16). Monetary policy has played
the lead role in economic management since 1975, partially as a result of
the federal government's unencumbered line of authority in this area. The
federal government raised the idea of regional representation on the board
of the Bank of Canada in its 1991 constitutional proposals, in response to
long-standing concerns that monetary policy has harmed the various regions (for example, high interest rates to contain inflation in Ontario
might inhibit economic growth in less prosperous regions).

Fiscal policy is decentralized in Canada. The federal and provincial
governments share authority and capacity for taxing and spending. Section 91 allows the federal government to raise money "by any mode or
system of taxation," that is, it has unlimited taxing power. Section 92

gives the provinces powers for direct taxation. Both the federal and provincial governments have jurisdiction in important areas of expenditure – for example, the federal government in military matters and the provinces in education. Prior to the advent of Keynesian economic management, there were few jurisdictional conflicts over tax and spending powers. But there have since been regular disputes.

Constitutional amendments gave the federal government authority for unemployment insurance (1940) and old age security (1952), but differences over tax and spending authority have been played out politically rather than constitutionally (see Chapter 11), as have overlapping jurisdictions in economic management. The Meech Lake Accord included a clause limiting the federal spending power, but this issue was only indirectly related to economic management and was a political as much as a constitutional gesture. A similar political gesture, as will be seen below, was the federal government's presentation of a number of proposals related to shared economic responsibilities in the 1991-92 Charlottetown constitutional phase (Canada, 1991). But these political hot potatoes were among the first to be dropped once serious negotiations began. As a broad generalization, tax and fiscal matters have not been central in recent constitutional dramas although they will continue to be so in political terms.

THE ORIGINS AND THEORY OF KEYNESIANISM

Keynesian management theory suggests that governments lower taxes and interest rates and increase spending in bad economic times and do the reverse in good times. Keynesianism first developed in the United Kingdom, a unitary system, and the government referred to was the central government. There were theoretical reasons to suggest that the federal government in Canada be predominant in economic management.

The case for a centralized monetary policy was persuasive and persistent. Capital's mobility makes it easily relocatable, disallowing significant interregional variation in interest rates (Rabeau, 1986: 178; Norrie, 1986: 303). The provinces have no authority in this area and there are no examples of sub-national entities having their own currency (Courchene, 1986: 52-54).

The case for a centralized fiscal policy was also persuasive, but it is less compelling today. Provinces, it was argued, are badly positioned to manage their economies. Their openness allows an enormous amount of interprovincial trade. This limits their management capacity, as the benefits of any initiative are likely to "leak" into other provinces. Similarly, there are spillover effects from other provinces' actions. Why should a province undergo the costs and risks of a particular policy if other provinces will be the substantial, if not the major, beneficiaries of its initiative? Thus, provincial governments are likely to "under-produce" stabilization policies (Maslove et al., 1986: 32; Maslove, 1989: 2; Shepherd, 1986: 171; Norrie, 1986: 79). It was also argued that provinces were unlikely to pursue countercyclical policies for two practical reasons. Their lack of access to central bank borrowing would limit deficit financing (Jamieson and Amirkhalkhai, 1988: 82), and the inflation rate does not vary regionally, so there would be no provincial interest in controlling inflation (Rabeau, 1986: 174). Indeed, a "perversity hypothesis" was formulated, suggesting that provinces would undermine federal countercyclical initiatives: "as a result of provincial pre-occupation with creditworthiness and fiscal prudence, the provinces may seek an annually balanced budget, prompting them to lower expenditures as revenues decline during periods of recession and to increase expenditures as revenues swell during boom times" (Jamieson and Amirkhalkhai, 1988: 84). There was a sense that the federal government should play the predominant management role, like the central government in a unitary system, and that its fiscal capacity should approximate its monetary capacity. Tax powers should be centralized and the federal government should have some aggregate influence over spending powers. It was argued also that Ottawa's tax and spending powers had to be substantial if their manipulation was to impact on economic conditions.

These ideas did not influence the Confederation settlement, the terms of which overdetermined by nation-building goals that gave disproportionate economic authority to the federal government (Simeon and Robinson, 1990: 19-30). Moreover, economic policy required little coordination between levels of government and constitutional arrangements reflected this (Stevenson, 1989: 177-78). However, by the time John Maynard Keynes had developed his ideas in Britain in the 1930s, the Canadian federal government had lost much of its economic authority. Court decisions limited the impact of the "peace, order, and good government" and trade and regulation clauses, while expanding the meaning of the "property and civil rights" clause (ibid.). When the depression drove economic management and the division of powers onto the policy agenda, coordinative and collaborative mechanisms were not in place; both governments attempted to protect their revenue bases, and a tax jungle developed (Simeon and Robinson, 1990: 86-87; Strick, 1985: 112).

Tax powers were centralized during World War Two when the federal government "rented" the provinces' tax powers. By war's end, the federal government was responsible for 83 per cent of all public expenditures. This was a state of affairs that Keynesian advocates wished to perpetuate. The federal government attempted to overcome the "federal" constraint on Keynesian economic management by extending its exclusivity over corporate and personal income taxes (Smiley, 1980: 186-93). Federal Finance Minister Ilsley insisted that "unless the Dominion retains exclusive control in the present income and corporate tax fields ... we will find it quite impossible to solve Canada's post-war economic and financial problems.... [The federal government] is the only government which, because it can budget for the whole business cycle, is able to set [tax] rates in such a way as to contribute to a high and stable level of employment" (Department of Reconstruction, 1945: 21; Granatstein, 1973: 273).

At the Dominion-Provincial Conference on Reconstruction in 1945, the federal government proposed to restructure federal fiscal arrangements to allow it to manage the economy. The provinces were unlikely to accept a constitutional re-arrangement of powers, so the federal government pursued its goal through political arrangements. Over the early post-war period, it negotiated new tax rental agreements whereby it dominated income and corporate and secession taxes in return for grants to the provinces. Similarly, the provinces were drawn into a number of social security programs through shared-cost financing. These tactics centralized tax and spending powers – without any constitutional changes (Simeon and Robinson, 1990: 86-146). This approach was designed to mimic a unitary state, to centralize a large enough share of taxes and spending to make federal economic management effective (Stevenson, 1989: 182-87).

The provinces subsequently played a minor role in economic management. Their management capacity at war's end was limited: their bureaucracies were small, with more pressing matters to consider, and their revenue and spending base was too insubstantial to consider in demand management terms. Lacking authority to print or raise their own significant sources of finance, they felt little choice but to opt into the national programs. This had the subsequent effect of constraining their policy flexibility, as they were locked into a network of national programs (Maslove et al., 1986: 5-6; Rabeau, 1986: 155ff.). This was rationalized as desirable by Keynesian reasoning up through the late 1950s: "If the power and influence of the federal authority should be seriously weakened ... as a result of voluntary abdication of responsibility by the Federal Govern-

191

ment the results in the long run might prove to be very serious indeed. Responsibility for preventing any substantial unemployment and for controlling inflation cannot successfully be distributed among ten provinces" (Royal Commission on Canada's Economic Prospects, 1957: 434).

THE DECLINE OF CENTRALIZED ECONOMIC MANAGEMENT

Economic management was pursued almost exclusively by the federal government after the war. However, the optimistic post-war assurances about Keynesianism dissipated slowly but steadily (Campbell, 1987: 117ff.). This was particularly the case with regard to the idea that Keynesian management had to be centrally driven.

First, the *de facto* reality of fiscal centralization was replaced by *de facto* decentralization. This developed as a result of political, not constitutional, developments. Fiscal arrangements evolved away from tax rental agreements to various systems of tax abatement and tax sharing (see Chapter 11). The provinces evolved to have a greater share of revenues and expenditures than the federal government (Courchene, 1986: 71). They demanded more tax and spending power to pursue their responsibilities, particularly in the health, education, and welfare areas. Starting with the Diefenbaker administration in the late 1950s, federal governments re-allocated more tax room and gave the provinces more flexibility to set their own tax rates. This happened in a piecemeal way, but with significant results. By the mid-1960s the provincial share of total income from tax revenues had more than doubled since the 1950s (Simeon and Robinson, 1990: 196). Ottawa's share of revenues declined from 71.4 per cent in 1945 to 58 per cent in 1960 to 47 per cent in 1982. Federal spending in 1955 had been almost twice the combined spending of the provinces and municipalities ($4.6 billion vs. $2.7 billion); by 1975, the latter were spending more than Ottawa ($40 billion vs. $34 billion) (Campbell, 1987).

Moreover, it became widely appreciated that federal spending was less flexible than that of the provinces. The high proportion of federal spending on statutory outlays and transfers was less easy to alter or manipulate for management purposes than provincial spending on roads, social services, and so on. The Royal Commission on Banking noted that the provinces' capital spending was five times as much as federal capital spending and that their expenditures on goods and services were one and a half times as great (1964: 519-20). The Economic Council of Canada found that only 4 per cent of federal spending was suitable for stabilization purposes, compared to 10 per cent of provincial spending; the provinces were responsible for 75 per cent of public investment in the federal-provincial sector (Economic Council of Canada, 1977; Economic Council of Canada, 1982: 82). The federal government's 1991 constitutional presentation noted that the provinces spent 70 per cent more on programs than the federal government and 3.5 times as much as on goods and services (Canada, 1991: 29).

What were the implications of these developments? Critics concluded that "the central government in Canada has less effective power to make economic policy than that of any other industrialized power" (Stevenson, 1989: 178). On the other hand, while its proportion of the total government account declined, Ottawa's share of GDP remained stable (Courchene, 1986: 71). This led others to conclude that the federal government's stabilization capacity had not been compromised (Norrie, 1986: 306).

These fiscal changes contributed to the view that the provincial governments should play a role in managing the economy. Various provinces had been sceptical of arguments that Keynesian management required economic centralization. But they had little strength or capacity to resist the federal government in 1945. Provinces like Québec never accepted the need for centralized economic management (Tremblay Commission) and, along with Ontario, always felt capable of economic management (Maslove et al., 1986: 114). There was also a loss of faith in federal managerial competence beginning in the late 1950s. The federal government seemed unable to initiate policies to deal with the weak economic conditions of the time (Campbell, 1987: 117ff.). This prodded the provinces into taking initiatives on their own, particularly as they had by now built up bureaucratic expertise and fiscal capacity (Fortin, 1982: 19; Smiley, 1980: 190). Moreover, their publics came to see them as responsible for economic conditions. This placed the provincial governments in the political position of having at a minimum to criticize federal economic policy if not developing policies themselves (Maslove, 1989: 4).

The idea of a provincial role was encouraged by the sense that "a single unified stabilization thrust may not be appropriate for all regions" (Courchene, 1986: 78). Uneven regional unemployment rates indicated provincial variations in the business cycle. When Ottawa initiated restraint measures as the central Canadian economy heated up, these policies appeared to be premature in regions where the expansion was still unfolding and unemployment remained high. Different budget timetables required provincial participation in managing the business cycle (Rabeau, 1986: 152–55; Jamieson and Amirkhalkhai, 1988: 82; Economic Council of Canada, 1982: 82; Fortin, 1982: 31).

In addition, various studies demonstrated that the provinces could manage their economies, that the argument that the potential benefits would "leak" out of the provincial economy through interprovincial trade had been exaggerated and were less substantial than thought (Jamieson and Amirkhalkhai, 1988: 83; Fortin, 1982; Courchene, 1986: 79). In particular, this seemed to be the case where provinces concentrated economic stimulus on capital spending or on specific measures to assist particular sectors and industries within their borders (Strick, 1985: 193; Maslove, 1989: 2–3). Ontario, Québec, Alberta, and British Columbia acted countercyclically in the 1970s and after, albeit unevenly (Fortin, 1982: 5; Maslove et al., 1986; Strick, 1985: 188).

The scale of their taxation and spending suggested that provincial actions impacted on economic conditions and should be considered in stabilization terms. There was concern that this might undermine federal management efforts. The Royal Commission on Taxation found "no inherent barrier to a strong federal stabilization policy resulting from the growth of provincial and municipal expenditures," but warned that "unless each province took into account what all the other provinces and the federal government were doing, and were going to do, the individual provincial efforts could be offsetting, too extreme or ill-timed" (Royal Commission on Taxation, 1966: 93, 102). Numerous studies covering the years 1952 to 1984 did not confirm the perversity thesis (Rabeau, 1986; Jamieson and Amirkhalkhai, 1988). This was attributed to various factors, including the provinces' reliance on commodity taxes (relatively uninfluenced by the business cycle), "the automatic adjustment mechanisms built into the federal fiscal system [that] have served to increase economic stability," and the harmonization of tax bases and federal influence on the structure and level of taxation (Economic Council of Canada, 1982: 85; Royal Commission on the Economic Union, 1985: 160). By the late 1960s, there was no unanimity on the need for a federal monopoly in economic management (Rabeau, 1986: 152). Economists maintained that the provinces should participate in economic management to stabilize their economies (Shepherd, 1986: 171). Indeed, it was argued that "if federal and provincial actions could be more formally coordinated, the scope for innovative fiscal policy could be that much better" (Norrie, 1986: 305). The Macdonald Commission concluded that "the very scale of provincial taxing and spending, along with the interdependence of federal and provincial fiscal systems, means that they must be involved in stabilization policy" (Royal Commission on the Economic Union, 1985: 149). But how was this to be done?

INSTITUTIONAL AND COLLABORATIVE MECHANISMS

Despite acceptance that the provinces should be involved in economic management, there were few effective mechanisms for federal-provincial collaboration. As Smiley points out, "The 1945 plans contained a very limited recognition of the need for intergovernmental collaboration in sustaining full employment and price stability" (Smiley, 1980: 188). As a result, the adoption of the Keynesian strategy in 1945 did not lead to new institutional arrangements or mechanisms: "The federal government's focus on macro-economic policy, given the control secured by the tax collection agreements, meant that there was little policy interdependence in that sphere" (Simeon and Robinson, 1990: 150). Similarly, given the lethargic pace in the development of the welfare state (Campbell, 1991), "the pressure for extensive policy rationalizations within governments, and for increased coordination between them, was correspondingly weak" (Simeon and Robinson, 1990: 150-51).

A certain degree of systemic coordination developed. Federal and provincial budgets were coordinated to the extent that each jurisdiction has defined responsibilities and revenue sources. Interprovincial spending patterns and outputs were similar, given similar pressures for services and the constraints imposed on all provinces by the transfer and tax arrangements (Maslove et al., 1986: 32, 160). Tax equalization, the sharing of the basic fiscal capacity, and tax agreements generate coordination as well. Canada's tax collection arrangements "represent an ingenious compromise that has permitted the development of a decentralized yet very harmonized approach to direct taxation" (Courchene, 1986: 92). This has been realized indirectly by transfer arrangements and the use of the spending power, not by constitutional arrangements.

Some institutional arrangements developed: the Continuing Committee of Officials on Fiscal and Economic Matters (1955), *ad hoc* liaisons like the Tax Structure Committee and the Tri-Level Task Force on Public Finance (1973), the annual pre-budget consultations among finance ministers, and periodic First Ministers' Conferences (FMCS) on the economy (the Meech Lake Accord proposed to constitutionalize annual FMCs). These institutions and processes are neither substantial nor effective.

For example, continuous information flow among the various finance ministers does not create effective collaboration (Smiley, 1980: 193). The Macdonald Commission recommended more formal consultation among governments, with designated and closer budget times to reduce uncertainty (Royal Commission on the Economic Union, 1985: 160). Ottawa argued in 1991 that institutions are "not currently structured to address what a coordinated fiscal policy approach would mean and what it could achieve"; budgets are poorly timed, with provincial budgets following the federal budget, which is "typically prepared with little information about forthcoming provincial fiscal policies.... While there are federal-provincial discussions before federal budgets are brought down, factors such as budget secrecy, the absence of a more formal collaborative mechanism, and the lack of clearly and publicly specified macroeconomic objectives have tended to limit the extent of intergovernmental fiscal deliberations" (Canada, 1991: 33).

The Continuing Committee of Officials on Fiscal and Economic Matters has comprised a bureaucratic and non-political process, which has not moved beyond policy implementation to policy formulation. There have been informal and *ad hoc* processes, but "permanent administrative machinery for this purpose remains relatively underdeveloped and inadequate.... There are ... no formally organized units or agencies with the specific responsibility for coordinating federal and provincial policies and programs" (Strick, 1985: 144-45).

FMCs give the appearance of collaborative action but have been ineffective. Provincial governments call for them because they remain powerless in setting national economic policy. FMCs give them an opportunity to gang up and criticize the federal government, but not to design policy collaboratively. They are typically disastrous. The 1978 FMC collapsed under its heavy agenda and governments' efforts to jockey for advantage (Thorburn, 1984: 169-76). The provinces ganged up and grandstanded against the federal government's high interest rate policy at the 1982 FMC; this meeting "revealed deep differences between the two levels of government on how economic policy ought to be determined and ultimately failed ... [demonstrating] an intractable deadlock on questions of short run economic policy" (Canadian Annual Review, 1982; Savoie, 1990: 175, 274; Simeon and Robinson, 1990: 291). The 1985 conference saw the provinces attack the federal government over cuts in transfer payments;

the 1986 conference saw regional attacks on the government's decision to award the CF-18 maintenance contract to a Québec firm; the March, 1992, FMC saw a vicious and futile battle between Ottawa and Ontario. In sum, "The Conferences undermine the legitimacy of the federal government, lessen the accountability of all governments to their respective legislatures, and provide premiers with an irresistible temptation to indulge in irresponsible criticism" (Stevenson, 1989: 186).

There were a few demonstrations of federal-provincial cooperation in economic management. The federal government initiated a system of wage and price controls in 1975, even though it had no "normal" authority to control wages and profits in the private sector. All provinces except Québec agreed to put their workers under the jurisdiction of the Anti-Inflation Board (Québec set up its own board and cooperated). This incident demonstrated successful bilateral consultation and negotiation within federal-provincial executive and bureaucratic forums (Burns, 1986: 230). On the other hand, Ottawa's six-and-five anti-inflation program was announced in the 1982 federal budget without prior consultation with the provinces. It tried to lever provincial cooperation by making transfers to the provinces (and to businesses) contingent on compliance with these guidelines. The provinces did not endorse Ottawa's restraint program and called, predictably, for a conference on the economy instead.

Another example of collaboration in economic management occurred in 1978. Finance Minister Chrétien proposed that the provinces reduce their sales taxes by 3 per cent for a six-month period in order to stimulate the economy. Ottawa would compensate the provinces for two-thirds of their revenue loss (or compensate for a 2 per cent reduction if this were extended for a further six months). Ottawa claimed that the provinces had been widely consulted. However, the four western provinces criticized its unilateralism and the Québec government called the proposal an intrusion in its jurisdiction. Québec eliminated its sales tax on items whose production was predominantly Québec-based (clothing, textiles, shoes, furniture) and demanded compensation. Ottawa declined, paying a direct rebate to Québec taxpayers instead (Smiley, 1980: 192-93). A promising federal collaboration ended in conflict.

Federal and provincial economic policies have been in direct conflict, as in the mid-1950s when the federal government tried to restrain inflation when provincial spending was high. This has been most noticeable in Ontario. In the early 1970s, Ottawa's anti-inflation curbs on spending were deliberately offset by the Ontario government (Leslie, 1987: 6), as they were in 1991 when Ontario's NDP government introduced a $9 billion budgetary deficit. In its 1991 constitutional presentation the federal government argued for collaboration, citing two examples where governments worked against each other: the rapid increase in federal fiscal deficits during the eighties when the provinces were containing deficit pressure and Ontario's expansionary fiscal policy during the 1986-89 boom (Canada, 1991: 28).

In sum, the provinces grew in stature to take on joint responsibility for economic management. While governments' broad goals have been similar, they have differed on how to proceed to ensure economic stability. As a result, efforts at coordination have been weak and half-hearted (Leslie, 1987: 6).

FEDERALISM, ECONOMIC MANAGEMENT, AND NEO-CONSERVATISM

The perception of Ottawa's declining managerial efficacy had a double effect. It encouraged the provinces to manage their economies and weakened the case for centralized management. It also saw Keynesianism dethroned as the policy paradigm around which economic management revolved. Two post-Keynesian phases ensued, each producing new scenarios for Canadian federalism.

First, Ottawa presented three non-Keynesian initiatives in the mid-1970s. The Bank of Canada announced a policy of "monetary gradualism" (monetarism) to limit monetary expansion to the rate of economic growth. Second, the 1976 budget limited federal spending to the rate of growth of the economy. These policies constrained the creative uses of monetary and fiscal policy to influence economic conditions. Third, the federal government imposed wage and price controls in October, 1975.

This last action marked the beginning of a phase of economic interventionism by both levels of government. Ottawa pursued what Peter Leslie characterized as a "nationalist-interventionist" development policy centred on supply-side and micro concerns. While the Keynesian focus on macro and demand management had had limited implications for federal-provincial relations, this new orientation caused jurisdictional conflicts, as micro and supply-side policies and tools lay primarily in provincial jurisdiction. Other chapters rehearse these conflicts (energy, regional policy, and training). We note here how the federal and provincial governments pursued statist, industrial policies, producing rival and conflicting nation-building vs. province-building strategies. The National Energy Program was a metaphor for the first post-Keynesian phase, which intensified federal-provincial conflicts (Simeon and Robinson, 1990; Leslie, 1987: 102).

The second (and current) post-Keynesian stage of economic management de-emphasized state economic intervention. Ottawa's new strategy has been characterized by Leslie as "liberal internationalism." It is informed by the conclusion of the Macdonald Commission: "A central theme of this report is that relative to current practice, governments should rely more on market forces and less on intervention designed either to frustrate or anticipate these forces" (Royal Commission on the Economic Union, 1985: 157). Ottawa rejected both Keynesian economic management and post-Keynesian economic planning in favour of neo-conservatism, a by now generic term referring to a market-oriented strategy. A metaphor for this approach is the Free Trade Agreement (and, subsequently, NAFTA), which symbolized the federal government's acceptance of the logic of globalization and the market. The implications of this trade strategy for Canadian federalism are examined elsewhere (see Chapter 10). Here, we focus on the implications for federalism of the two central domestic policies that comprise Ottawa's post-Keynesian market orientation to economic management: deficit-cutting and anti-inflation policy.

Deficit-Cutting

Deficit-cutting symbolized Ottawa's objective of rolling back the state presence in the economy. However, this could not be realized unilaterally by the federal government, particularly given its reduced share of revenue and spending. It was not clear how to coordinate the withdrawal of the state from the economy (Simeon and Robinson, 1990: 285). As early as the 1978 FMC there was a sense that deficits and spending had to be restrained, but no agreement was reached on how to proceed. Ottawa attempted to redraw its fiscal arrangements with the provinces in 1982 and to make transfers conditional on deficit reduction. Efforts in the Trudeau era to grapple with the deficit exacerbated already tense federal-provincial relations.

The Mulroney government made deficit reduction a policy priority but tried to envelop it in its broader policy of national reconciliation. A more collaborative process was designed to cushion the provinces from federal budget cuts, and the provinces were widely consulted. Three FMCs were held in 1985 alone. The first saw the federal government seduce the provinces with more revenue for training programs. However, by the end of 1985 and through 1986, the honeymoon ended (*Canadian Annual Review*, 1984-86). In 1985 Ottawa limited transfers to the provinces to the rate of economic growth minus 2 per cent (for an annual savings of $2 billion). Through the remainder of the 1980s, federal-provincial discourse took a predictable and divisive shape. Provinces complained that cuts in transfers cost them enormous revenues for the rapidly growing costs of post-secondary education and health care. Ottawa replied that transfers were too big a budgetary item to ignore and asserted that the provinces were the problem: their program spending was accelerating faster than the federal government (by an average of 6.5 per cent over the last five years, compared to 3.5 per cent for the federal government) (*Globe and Mail*, November 9, 10, 1989; see Chapters 11, 12, 13).

Ottawa introduced even more dramatic transfer limits in 1990. "The deficit is a national problem. It demands a national solution," the budget declared; "therefore the provinces must do their share." It froze transfers for health and education spending to $755 per capita and tied the growth of Canada Assistance Plan (CAP) transfers to the rate of growth of the population (equalization payments were exempted). This would save Ottawa $1.5 billion in 1990-91 and $7.4 billion over five years. The provinces would receive $2.6 billion less over the next two years. The 1991 federal budget extended for three years the restrictions on health and post-secondary education transfers and CAP transfers to the three richest provinces. These policies did not actually cut transfers but rather limited (halved) their past rate of increase. Major transfers would continue to grow by 3.7 per cent through 1995-96. However, these transfers were directed to program spending in labour- and service-intensive areas, whose costs increased rapidly and inexorably, particularly at a time of recession. The provinces accused the federal government of offloading its fiscal problems; claimed that the federal government was turning into an unreliable fiscal partner; and argued that Ottawa should better control its own spending. Three provinces fought the CAP cuts in court; some mooted collecting their own taxes and called for a new fiscal federalism; intergovernmental fiscal coordination fell into disuse; and federal-provincial fiscal relations deteriorated (*Globe and Mail*, April 25, May 8, June 11, July 28, September 18, 1990).

Provincial criticism of transfer cuts was followed by exactly what Ottawa had intended: draconian deficit-cutting budgets at the provincial level. There was frenzied panic about provincial deficits in 1993. The media reported that Ottawa had talked to financial institutions about what would happen if provinces were not able to sell bonds to pay their deficits, that the federal government had a contingency plan to take provinces into trusteeship and to provide emergency borrowings through the Bank of Canada. These rumours were denied on all sides (*Globe and Mail*, March 12-13, 1993). Speculation was prompted by growing market doubts about the provinces' capacity to service their swollen debts – half the federal debt and growing far faster. This reflected a combination of federal transfer cuts, which the C.D. Howe Institute claimed offloaded $4 billion of debt to the provinces (*Globe and Mail*, March 15, 1993), and the impact of the recession, which diminished tax revenues and increased social security expenditures. As a percentage of GDP, provincial debt ranged from 15 per cent in B.C. to 55 per cent in Saskatchewan; factoring in municipal and Crown corporation debts increased the range from 30 per cent in B.C. to 78 per cent in Newfoundland (*Globe and Mail*, March 8, 1993). The credit ratings of four provinces were downgraded in 1992, and the Dominion Bond Rating Service assigned a negative rating to all ten provinces (*Globe and Mail*, March 23, 1993). The number of institutions willing to lend to Saskatchewan had fallen from 150 to twenty-five. Along with Newfoundland, its bond ratings were at Double-B level. If dropped lower, its bonds would require enormous interest rate returns like in the infamous junk bond market of the speculative 1980s.

There was some provincial talk – for example, among the NDP governments – that a national debt-management strategy was required (*Globe and Mail*, March 2, 1993). In the absence of collaborative mechanisms or processes, each government initiated its own draconian actions to reduce deficits and placate the bond markets. The Newfoundland budget announced $30 million in cuts to limit its projected deficit to $51 million, after having raised taxes in December. Saskatchewan cut spending by $100 million and increased taxes by $200 million to cut its current deficit from $592 million to $296 million. Manitoba and New Brunswick also presented tough tax-increasing, spending-decreasing budgets. Prompted by a blue-ribbon panel's report of an alarming deficit situation, the Alberta government promised tough measures. The Nova Scotia government introduced the idea of a balanced budget law. Even prosperous British Columbia increased its sales tax, the personal income tax surtax, and the corporate tax; closed some government agencies; and froze salaries and cut management to reduce its deficit by $500 million (*Globe and Mail*, March 30, 31, 1993). Ontario – at $1 billion a month the world's largest borrower outside of national governments – looked to cut its spending by

14 per cent and entered into "social contract" negotiations with its pub-
lic-sector unions in an attempt to lower its projected $17 billion deficit to
below $10 billion.

The federal government has effectively determined provincial fiscal
and budgetary policy by its economic management initiatives. In conjunction with its anti-inflation policy, its policy of cutting transfer payments encouraged the provinces to cut their spending and deficits. Aided
by outside credit agencies, the federal government re-emerged in the economic management driver's seat – without legislative or constitutional
changes or an elaborate institutional process.

Anti-Inflation Policy

The second element of Ottawa's post-Keynesian economic management
strategy has been a relentless program to eliminate inflation. Deficit reduction played a role to this end, but monetary policy has been the predominant tool, and a tight money, high interest rate policy has been pursued even during the recession. There has been an institutional and policy
bias in Canada toward controlling inflation rather than minimizing unemployment, and the Keynesian commitment in 1945 and afterwards was
modest (Campbell, 1991). Countercyclical policy was constrained by political, regional, supply-side, and international factors, and its resulting
inefficacy led to its loss of legitimacy in the 1970s. Deficits and the internationalization of economic life (globalization) further limited the weak
capacity of fiscal policy in the 1980s. Furthermore, tax reform aimed to
make the tax system neutral in its impact on economic conditions. This
was accomplished by de-emphasizing progressive income taxes (which
had a countercyclical economic effect) in favour of commodity taxes. The
goal of tax neutrality inhibited the tax system's use for stabilization purposes. The federal government has chosen to concentrate on monetary
policy – precisely because this is the area in which it has policy capacity
(Coleman, 1993: 207-09). It is also a policy area in which it has exclusive
jurisdiction.

Ottawa's shift from Keynesianism to neo-conservative policy – from
fiscal policy to monetary policy – has had a double effect on the provinces.
First, the economic impact of anti-inflation policy is far less obliging for the
provinces than a focus on unemployment. Second, an exclusive focus on
monetary policy puts Ottawa in the economic management driver's seat.

This has been frustrating for the provinces and divisive for federal-provincial relations, especially during the early 1990s recession. As unemployment rose, Ottawa pursued a tight monetary policy and waited out the recession. The provinces called for a First Ministers' Conference and for more federal economic leadership. The Prime Minister refused, saying that the opportunity for this died with Meech Lake; a proposed fall conference in Calgary was then cancelled (*Globe and Mail*, October 22, 1990). Instead, Ottawa reconfirmed its anti-inflation determination and its disinclination to influence economic circumstances. The 1991 budget legislatively capped future federal spending increases and proposed formal inflation targets with the Bank of Canada.

Ontario's NDP government tried to confront the recession on its own through a Keynesian budget that, despite a $1 billion tax hike, produced a $9.7 billion deficit. Ottawa attacked this budget viciously, Finance Minister Mazankowski claiming it was "out of step with the collective wisdom" and an "economic disaster." The Prime Minister accused the Ontario government of creating "a burden ... on our children and grandchildren" and caused a controversy on an Asian trip by declaring that Japanese businessmen were more concerned about the Ontario deficit than about Québec separatism (*Globe and Mail*, April 3, May 1, May 28, 29, 1991). Ontario-Ottawa relations have not recovered since.

The provinces continued to demand that Ottawa take the lead in dealing with the economic recession, which had pushed the unemployment rate over 11 per cent. Their call for an FMC on the economy was looked upon suspiciously by Ottawa, which feared a barrage of complaints. After criticizing provincial spending, the federal government finally agreed and three FMCs were held between December, 1991, and March, 1992. At the first meeting, the provinces presented an eclectic expansionary wish list, including tax changes, infrastructure investments, the use of RRSPs for house purchases, and so on. No action was taken, as there was no consensus on how to compromise on all the various approaches ("they're all over the map," declared a provincial official). At the February FMC, the provinces complained about the lack of consultations about the various proposals since the December meeting. No consensus for a plan of action was set. Instead, eight working groups were to look at tax coordination, agriculture, fisheries, infrastructure, social programs, manpower training, and international and interprovincial trade. In the interim, the provinces again looked to the federal budget for economic stimulus. But the February, 1992, budget comprised but a small cut in income tax and the RRSP withdrawal house-purchase strategy. Another wave of provincial attacks on

Ottawa ensued, particularly for the lack of federal infrastructure action that provinces claimed had been agreed to at the February FMC. Ontario declared that Ottawa's refusal to help Ontario get through the recession showed that "Confederation isn't working" (*Globe and Mail*, November 3, December 4, 11, 13, 14, 16, 19, 20, 1991; January 31, February 10, 11, 26, 27, 28, 1992).

This process of federal-provincial "collaboration" culminated in the third FMC in March, 1992. Ottawa faced relentless pressure to set up a national public works strategy to kick-start the economy. Two agreements were reached, to develop a code of conduct to avoid "destructive competition" and to reduce interprovincial trade barriers over the long run. The federal government made a modest commitment to help build some roads, bridges and airport runways. These actions went unnoticed, as Ottawa and Ontario insulted each over throughout the meeting. Premier Rae accused Ottawa of being an "absconding debtor" by refusing to help Ontario pay the costs of the recession. Mazankowski in turn accused Rae of being juvenile and irresponsible (*Globe and Mail*, March 24, 25, 26, 1992).

The federal infrastructure plan was modest indeed, involving few new resources. Ottawa agreed to match normal provincial spending on highways, about $750 million a year. In his December, 1992, financial statement, Mazankowski outlined that federal spending for this program would comprise but $2 billion over five years, the remainder coming from the private sector (*Globe and Mail*, December 3, 1992). Ottawa had intended to announce this policy during the Charlottetown referendum campaign, but it was held up by Ontario. It claimed that Ottawa had made a more substantial promise ($12 billion of federal money over ten years); that Ottawa's focus on roads, bridges, and runways ignored Ontario's agenda of treatment plants and rail transportation; and that it would not get its fair share, receiving but 15 per cent of the program's benefits (per capita $64 compared to New Brunswick's $779) (*Globe and Mail*, September 25, October 15, 29, December 3, 1992).

Ontario did benefit from the rarely used Federal Stabilization Program, which provides federal money to provinces that suffer a sudden recession-induced drop in revenues. Ontario asked for $585 million (the maximum allowable, given a $60 a head limit) and a $355 million interest-free loan. The program had been used only twice before, when British Columbia received $174 million in 1982-83 and when Alberta received $419 million in 1986-87. Ontario received $300 million (*Globe and Mail*, January 8,

March 18, 1993).

Ottawa played the dominant economic management role during the 1990s recession. Despite relentless provincial criticism, it maintained a tight money policy in the face of 1.5 million unemployed. The provinces exercised no influence in setting this monetary policy. Moreover, Ottawa resisted provincial entreaties to stimulate the economy. The provinces enjoyed little influence at the various federal-provincial conferences; collaboration in economic management was negligible. The provincial governments themselves adopted spending and deficit-cutting fiscal policies, more or less in harmony with Ottawa's economic orientation. Ironically, after years of building up their fiscal capacity and the case for collaborative policy involvement, the provinces reverted to a junior partner role in economic management. They accepted, and participated in, an economic policy largely set and driven by Ottawa. This has been attained by the federal government without constitutional change or formal political arrangements, and suggests the extent to which the federal government – even with its diminished fiscal capacity – can set the economic management agenda.

SYNOPSIS AND PROGNOSIS

In sum, there have been five stages of economic management under Canadian federalism:

- There was no state responsibility for economic management for stabilization purposes prior to World War Two, so federalism was not a factor.

- After the war, the state was given responsibility for maintaining economic stability. This was pursued in a relatively centralized way, tax rental agreements and shared-cost programs mimicking the design of a unitary state (monetary policy was a federal jurisdiction). Despite shared fiscal jurisdiction, no institutional arrangements were put in place to create a collaborative federal approach.

- Over the course of the post-war period, the provinces gained fiscal capacity, substantial tax and spending powers reverting to them. They were encouraged to manage their economies and enter into collaborative processes with Ottawa. However, institutional mechanisms to this end were not in place and collaborative efforts were halting and ineffective.

- When the Keynesian design lost its legitimacy in the mid-1970s, Ottawa and the provinces pursued statist strategies that increased federal-provincial conflict.

- Since the mid-1980s, the neo-conservative agenda has privileged Ottawa's role in economic management. Deficit reduction required cuts in federal transfer payments, which forced corresponding "harmonized" provincial debt reduction measures. The predominance of price stability over full employment elevated the stature of monetary policy, an exclusive federal jurisdiction. This fifth or present stage sees a high degree of federal-provincial aggravation over Ottawa's predominant strategy. But this aggravation is tempered by widespread acceptance of the substantial challenges posed by the national deficit and an appreciation of the policy limits and constraints of the international political economy.

Canadian federalism's flexibility has been demonstrated by experience in the economic management area. The evolution through these five stages has been effected without constitutional change and without extensive or formal political agreements.

As to the future, the politics of federal cuts in transfer payments to the provinces will continue to affect federal-provincial relations. Two other issues will likely dominate the federal-provincial agenda with regard to economic management: the development of collaborative processes in setting fiscal policy and provincial input into monetary policy (trade, training, and the economic union are discussed elsewhere).

Increased federal-provincial collaboration on fiscal policy has been a long-standing goal. The Royal Commission on Banking (1964: 519-20) insisted that "some coordination of federal with provincial and municipal expenditures" was necessary to "achieve substantial [stabilization] results." The Royal Commission on Taxation (1966: 103) recommended collaborative sharing of projections and information, and consensus on short-run policies: "it would be prudent to work gradually toward a system in which the provinces could play an active role in coordination with federal stabilization policy and under the guidance of the federal government." The Task Force on Canadian Unity (1979: 71-72) concluded that "one area where coordination is essential is economic stabilization." It recommended that the Conference of Finance Ministers develop a consensus on the economic outlook, devise shared forecasts, and establish consolidated information about planned expenditures and anticipated revenues and borrowings. The Macdonald Commission, while emphasizing a market approach to economic management, recommended more formal consultation among finance ministers and closer coordination and timing of budgets (Royal Commission on the Economic Union, 1985: III, 160). The Meech Lake Accord proposed to constitutionalize FMCs, including an annual conference on the economy. In its constitutional document *Canadian Federalism and Economic Union* (1991), Ottawa proposed to rectify the fact that "no authority has responsibility for the aggregate fiscal policy of the country." It suggested a fixed annual budget cycle; a fixed annual schedule of finance ministers' meetings to articulate economic and fiscal outlooks, pressures, and objectives; an independent agency to assess macro issues, including pre-budget assessments, the soundness of fiscal policies, and their consistency with monetary policy; guidelines to harmonize fiscal and monetary policies; and balancing budgets over the course of the business cycle. This was to be set in federal legislation under the proposed economic union power and operationalized by the Council of the Federation (1991: 27-41). Finance Minister Mazankowski's April, 1993, budget announced a May meeting with the provincial finance ministers to "develop practical approaches and solutions" to the national debt and deficit problem. Conservative leadership candidates Campbell and Edwards also proposed a coordinated, cooperative federal-provincial approach to debt management (*Globe and Mail*, April 27, 1993).

While the idea of increased federal-provincial collaboration in devising fiscal policy has been well-rehearsed, it has not come close to being implemented. None of the federal proposals in 1991 made it to the Charlottetown Accord (many provinces, including Québec, saw them as comprising a centralizing strategy). Collaboration has some legitimacy and theoretical appeal, but there remain real practical limits to its adoption. For example, could the fiscal policies of the three NDP provincial governments (particularly Ontario's) have been harmonized in a collaborative way with federal approaches in the early 1990s? Moreover, the federal government has managed to harmonize provincial with federal policies without formal collaboration. At most, First Ministers' Conferences on the economy will likely be the collaborative policy instrument of choice, but without much impact. Provincial finance ministers welcomed Mazankowski's proposed May, 1993, meeting on national debt management. Its impact will be constrained by provincial insistence that the agenda move beyond debt reduction to lowering unemployment (Ontario) and that the process "preserves the government's freedom of action" (Québec) (*Toronto Star*, April 27, 1993). Weak fiscal policy capacity, itself a partial reflection of divided jurisdiction, will likely ensure the predominance of monetary policy. Indeed, given the prevalence of a neoconservative approach to economic management, the goal of federal-provincial fiscal collaboration has become a relatively abstract ideal.

Second, federal-provincial discussions on economic management will be affected by provincial demands for input into monetary policy. Provinces have longed complained that a single, central monetary policy harms regional economies, whose economic cycles lag behind the central provinces; a tight money policy to stem national inflationary pressures may prematurely curtail regional economic expansion. This view has taken on greater urgency, given the increased prominence of monetary policy. Indeed, the federal government proposed in 1991 to formalize national anti-inflation targets and to limit the Bank of Canada's mandate to pursuing this goal. Ottawa rejected a regionally differentiated monetary policy, insisting that "in an economic union monetary policy can only be Canada-wide in scope." It made a number of symbolic recommendations that a panel give regional advice and that there be regional representation on the board of the Bank of Canada (via consultation with the provinces and a reformed Senate role in ratifying the appointment of the its governor) (1991: 37-40).

Only the last idea remained in the *Consensus Report on the Constitution* (although most of the recommendations could be pursued legislatively). There will likely be continuing demands to increase regional input into the policies of the Bank of Canada. But the prospects for federal-provincial collaboration on monetary policy are negligible. The provinces have no constitutional leverage. Mainstream economic theory rejects the idea, and practical politics is suspicious of the idea because there is little provincial interest in controlling inflation that does not vary regionally (Rabeau, 1986: 174-75). Most importantly, there is no incentive for the federal government to diminish its authority in this area, where it has some economic policy efficacy.

In conclusion, Courchene's assessment seems apt: "The optimal assessment of powers ... depends on the overall economic goals pursued by the federation. A change in the nature of their economic policy objectives will probably call for a corresponding change in the division of powers (either de facto or de jure)" (1986: 232). If a neo-conservative orientation to economic policy persists – with market goals, inflation control, and deficit spending in the forefront – then the federal government will remain in the economic management driver's seat.

REFERENCES

Bird, Richard (1989). "Federal–Provincial Fiscal Arrangements: Is There an Agenda for the 1990s?" in R.L. Watts and Douglas M. Brown, eds., *Canada: The State of the Federation*. Kingston: Institute of Intergovernmental Relations.

Campbell, Robert (1987). *Grand Illusions: The Politics of The Keynesian Experience in Canada 1945-1975*. Peterborough, Ont.: Broadview Press.

Campbell, Robert (1991). *The Full Employment Objective in Canada: Historical, Conceptual and Comparative Perspectives*. Ottawa: Economic Council of Canada.

Canada (1991). *Canadian Federalism and Economic Union: Partnership for Prosperity*.

Canadian Annual Review of Politics and Public Affairs. (Various years). Toronto: University of Toronto Press.

Coleman, William (1993). "Macroeconomic Policy: Dwindling Options," in Michael Atkinson, ed., *Governing Canada: Institutions and Public Policy*. Toronto: Harcourt Brace Jovanovich.

Courchene, Thomas J. (1986). *Economic Management and the Division of Powers*. Toronto: University of Toronto Press.

Department of Reconstruction (1945). *Employment and Income with Special Reference to the Initial Period of Reconstruction*.

Doern, G. Bruce *et al.* (1988). *Budgeting in Canada: Politics, Economics and Management*. Ottawa: Carleton University Press.

Dominion Provincial Conference on Reconstruction (1945). *Proposals of the Government of Canada*.

Economic Council of Canada (1982). *Financing Confederation*.

Fortin, Pierre (1982). *Provincial Involvement in Regulating the Business Cycle: Justification, Scope and Terms*. Ottawa: Economic Council of Canada.

Granatstein, Jack (1973). *Canada's War: The Politics of the Mackenzie King Government, 1939-45*. Toronto: Oxford University Press.

Howlett, Michael and M. Ramesh (1992). The Political Economy of Canada: An Introduction. Toronto: McClelland & Stewart.

Howlett, Michael and M. Ramesh (1992). The Political Economy of Canada: An Introduction. Toronto: McClelland & Stewart.

Jamieson, Barbara, and Saleh Amirkhalkhai (1988). "Evaluating Provincial Budgetary Policy," Canadian Public Administration, 33, 1 (Spring).

Leslie, Peter (1987). Federal State, National Economy. Toronto: University of Toronto Press.

Maslove, Allan, et al. (1986). Federal and Provincial Budgeting. Toronto: University of Toronto Press.

Maslove, Allan, ed. (1989) Budgeting in the Provinces: Leadership and the Premiers. Ottawa: The Institute of Public Administration of Canada.

McRoberts, Kenneth (1993). "Federal Structures and the Policy Process," in Michael Atkinson, ed., Governing Canada.

Norrie, Kenneth, et al. (1986). Federalism and the Economic Union in Canada. Toronto: University of Toronto Press.

Rabeau, Yves (1986). "Regional Stabilization in Canada," in John Sargent, ed., Fiscal and Monetary Policy. Toronto: University of Toronto Press.

Royal Commission on Banking and Finance (1964). Report.

Royal Commission on Canada's Economic Prospects (1957). Report.

Royal Commission on Taxation (1966). Report. Vol. II.

Royal Commission on the Economic Union and Development Prospects for Canada (1985). Report.

Savoie, Donald (1990). The Politics of Public Spending in Canada. Toronto: University of Toronto Press.

Shepherd, Anthony (1986). "Taxation Policy and the Canadian Economic Union," in Mark Krasnick, ed., Fiscal Federalism. Toronto: University of Toronto Press.

Simeon, Richard (1980). "Intergovernmental Relations and the Challenge to Canadian Federalism," Canadian Public Administration, 23, 1 (Spring).

Simeon, Richard, and Ian Robinson (1990). State, Society and the Development of Canadian Federalism. Toronto: University of Toronto Press.

Smiley, Donald (1980). Canada in Question, Third edition. Toronto: McGraw-Hill Ryerson.

Stevenson, Garth (1989). Unfulfilled Union, Third edition. Toronto: Gage.

Strick, J.C. (1985). Canadian Public Finance, Third edition. Toronto: Holt, Rinehart and Winston.

Task Force on Canadian Unity (1979). A Future Together.

Thorburn, Hugh (1984). Planning and the Economy: Building Federal-Provincial Consensus. Ottawa: Canadian Institute for Economic Policy.

CHAPTER NINE

Global Economic Restructuring
and the Evolution of Canadian Federalism
and Constitutionalism

François Rocher and Richard Nimijean[1]

IN 1989, DONALD SMILEY ARGUED THAT TRADITIONAL approaches to the study of Canadian federalism tended to focus on three axes: the relationships between anglophones and francophones, Canada and the United States, and central and provincial governments. This, he suggested, meant that contemporary matters of prime importance relating to ideological cleavages and to the roles of governmental and non-governmental actors in the political process are often ignored (Smiley, 1989).

In pointing to the oft-overlooked relationship of the economy, the federal system, and the constitution, Smiley reminds us of the utility in studying Canadian federalism at a conjuncture marked by significant upheavals, both nationally and internationally, in the political, social, and economic spheres. International concerns with competitiveness and democratization remind us that these debates are also taking place in Canada. On the economic front, there is a desire to develop and implement an appropriate set of policies to allow the Canadian economy to be restructured so that it can remain competitive with other national economies. On the political and social fronts, two concerns are visible: on the one hand, there is a desire to "democratize" a constitutional process that has been called elitist and exclusionary; on the other hand, there is a desire to rework Canadian federalism so that the policy goals and programs of the central and provincial governments work together rather than at cross purposes to achieve economic goals.

This chapter explores the impact that new concerns about globalization and competitiveness have had on Canada, particularly in terms of the dis-

course on federalism and constitutionalism. The first section offers an overview of changing conditions in the international political economy (globalization and competitiveness) and suggests some of the key policy considerations emerging as a result of them. The second section sets out the parameters by which issues pertaining to globalization, competitiveness, and
restructuring can be related to Canada. This involves two tasks: examining
the relationship between the economy and the Canadian constitution and
examining the relationship between federalism and globalization. Both
tasks address the relationship between political and economic structures
and as such can help us understand how each has evolved in Canada.

This analysis will help us to understand if the economic pressures associated with globalization, competitiveness, and restructuring have altered
the discourse and practice of Canadian constitutionalism and federalism. It
can also shed light on the issue of which order of government might assume responsibility for assuring economic restructuring in Canada and on
the means through which this authority is to be delegated.

THE NATURE OF THE NEW ECONOMIC CONDITIONS

"Competitiveness" and "globalization" are now common words in economic policy debates. They have essentially become political slogans for
politicians, bureaucrats, business people, academics, and even organized
labour, all of whom have been stressing the need for structural reform of
the economy to maintain current standards of living and to increase rates
of economic growth.

But what are the new economic conditions everyone is talking about?
A useful summary of the conditions that mark the changing international
political economy is provided by Richard Morris:

- emergence of the city-state

- globalization of markets

- globalization of business, including start-ups

- acceleration of technological innovation

- internationalization of research and development

- concern with intellectual property (sovereignty of nations)

- burgeoning of the international service sector

- increased and fluctuating demand for skilled labour

- changing role of governmental intervention. (Morris, 1992: 181)

The impetus behind the desire to make national economies more competitive (in other words, to help them adapt to the new economic conditions) is rooted in a variety of factors. These include the inability of the economies of many advanced industrialized countries to sustain high levels of growth and employment with low inflation rates; the inability of monetarist economic policies to achieve better results than the more interventionist policies of the Keynesian era; the changing nature of production, including not only the introduction of new technologies into the production process but also the reorganization of work and production, both within the workplace and across national boundaries; and, finally, the economic pressures emanating from newly industrializing countries (NICs), whose increased use of new technologies and low-wage advantage relative to the industrialized North have challenged traditional economic growth strategies.

These factors have led countries to encourage the transition to knowledge-based, high value-added economies premised on technological and organizational innovation. The promotion of research and development and the implementation of new labour market policies have been key components in this strategy. Together, these policies are intended to make labour and firms, and therefore the national economies in which they are located, more flexible and competitive so that they can adapt to the changing conditions of the international political economy.

The call for economic restructuring stems from a recognition that significant changes are occurring in the production system. Kaplinsky, for example, speaks of the "epochal" transition from Fordism to post-Fordism. In the Fordist system, firms produced standardized goods for mass markets using dedicated machinery operated by semi-skilled labour. Now, however, flexibility is emphasized in all facets of production. Flexible or smart machines, made possible through advances in microelectronics, are increasingly employed. The organization of labour has emphasized flexibility, in terms of both skills (multi-task-oriented; the employment of autonomous work teams) and the organization of production, featuring greater inter-firm cooperation, horizontal sub-contracting, and just-in-time production. Competitiveness and productivity are no longer based solely on price but on continuous innovation, the quality of the product, and the search for specialized product niches. Moreover, instead of being seen as a cost, labour is increasingly seen as a resource whose contribution is important for a firm's success.[2]

POLICY IMPLICATIONS OF RESTRUCTURING

There is increasing recognition that the state will have to adapt its methods of promoting economic reorganization and growth in light of the changes associated with the transition to post-Fordism. While there does not as yet exist a consensus on the exact nature of the policy implications of restructuring, some issues can be raised.

Clearly, the restructuring of production has had spatial consequences. The most visible outcome, the decentralization of production, has had both supranational and subnational effects. The supranational effects are illustrated by the increasing number of international trade and economic integration agreements (such as "Europe 1992" and the North American Free Trade Agreement) and the transfer of production to countries with net lower wages (such as Mexico). Subnational effects are seen in the appearance of regional clusterings or agglomerations (such as Silicon Valley) and in the continuing evolution of the city.[3]

Changes in the international political economy, Jessop argues, have led to the "hollowing out" of the nation-state: its ability to effect change given the new conditions of production is limited. The national state's ability to manage the economy is constrained by the internationalization of financial and industrial flows, the transition to post-Fordism, and the emergence of regional trading blocs (Jessop, 1993).

The state's role in promoting economic growth in the transition period to post-Fordism is thus quite different from that of the Fordist regime. Not only must it promote industrial reorganization according to the nature of the new production processes, but it also must reorganize itself. It must adopt the new principles of organization, namely flexible management structures, decentralization, and greater two-way flows of information. The state can no longer act in a *dirigiste* fashion, as in the days of industrial policy; rather, it must promote industrial strategy, which is a "participative process setting out the broad areas of restructuring, the principles on which this will occur and identifying an institutional framework within which it can occur" (Kaplinsky, 1993: 45).

National governments must thus come to grips with the new conditions of governance: they must recognize that they no longer dispose of the same degree of political sovereignty. Their power to act is constrained by the nature of the new international political economy. Power flows outward, in that new economic arrangements directly limit national sovereignty. Corporations, in this environment, are less susceptible to national control because of these arrangements as well as factors related to changes in production. Power also flows inward, due to an emphasis on regional economic linkages, the clustering of economic activities and the subsequent desire to have more direct local control over the shape and direction of economic activity.

With the advent of regional trading blocs based on formalized agreements, it is clear that power is flowing outward from the national state. While national governments remain legally recognized actors in the international political economy, their power to effect economic changes is limited due to the presence of trade agreements that provide new constraints to national sovereignty. Linge and Riche, for example, state that:

> Many governments, while retaining sovereignty within their national borders, are none the less being forced to abnegate important decision-making and regulatory powers and defer to various kinds of supranational bodies to facilitate the formation and operation of more globally competitive and political blocs. In effect, then, the management of change is becoming a cause by groupings of sovereign states acting in concert rather than as adversaries. (1991: 20)

Drache argues that the emergence of regional trading blocs has altered the nature of the nation-state. The "post-national" state differs from the traditional nation-state because of lost national identities and the loss of traditional boundaries. The post-national state has two significant characteristics: a weakened national economy, with economic performance and well-being increasingly determined by external factors; and a loss of internal economic and political power to act, as traditional power levers are surrendered with these new arrangements (Drache, 1993: 265).

Rostow picks up on the point made by Linge and Riche, namely that countries are acting more in concert. Rather than focusing on regional trading blocs, however, he explores changes in technology. He argues that the "fourth technological revolution," based on microelectronics, genetic engineering, new industrial materials, and lasers, is so profound and diversified that, unlike the previous technological revolutions, no one country will establish world-wide economic leadership. He suggests this is the key factor that has allowed for previously unthought of alliances between more and less developed nations, a change that reinforces what he calls the "macrofederal" tendency. This can be seen with the movement toward regional economic integration marked by multinational agreements in Europe, North America, and the Pacific Rim (Rostow, 1992: 11–17).

The spatial implications of the changes occurring in the international political economy do not only relate to nation-states and their relationships with each other: there are varying impacts on subnational regions as well. For example, the impact of economic policy varies from city to city and region to region, as do responses to significant changes in economic conditions. Thus, when reflecting on the evolution of the international political economy, it is important to bring cities and regions into the analysis (Kresl, 1992).

The rise and development of regional development analysis as a significant academic field, especially in Europe, is testimony to this fact (Benko and Dunford, 1991; Albrechts et al., 1989; Camagni, 1991). This trend has been inspired by the recognition that economic development and growth have been spatially uneven over time, that changes in the production system make cities and regions more significant economic and political actors, and that national economies alone are not the exclusive site of economic activity.

Kresl, for example, notes that economic impact analyses are usually restricted to national units. This, however, ignores the fact that past economic performance and contemporary adaptations to new economic conditions have and will continue to vary across cities and regions. While some prosper, others stagnate. It is often forgotten, he notes, that prosperity and stagnation are linked, as they are consequences of the same economic conditions (Kresl, 1992: chs. 1, 2).

This phenomenon has been compounded by changes in governance in the 1980s. Kresl argues that one of the consequences of the supply-side economic strategies adopted in many nations in the 1980s was that many national governments downloaded responsibilities to lower levels of government. There was, of course, an ideological component to this, as seen in the rise of neo-conservatism in many industrialized countries. There was also, however, a decrease in the ability of national governments to intervene. As Kresl notes, in an important point often overlooked in the literature, this not only increasingly exposes cities and regions to the fallout of restructuring, but it also forces them to develop their own strategies for adjustment.

Thus there is a greater recognition that governments must develop endogenous strategies to overcome regional inequities and promote regional development. Cappellin, for example, argues that regional policy should focus on the local nature of regions. In particular, he notes that "the major factors of regional development (physical infrastructures, local labour force skills, local sectoral and institutional structures, etc.) are rather immobile." The key, therefore, is to maximize the development and use of local resources, structures, and institutions. With this approach, "regional development may be interpreted not as the result of separate location decisions by the various national firms, but as the result of the changes in the local environment determined by the choice by local entrepreneurs of those new productions which are most appropriate with respect to the local available resources" (Cappellin, 1991).

It is one thing, however, to develop new strategies; a mechanism that allows regional policy to be developed and implemented is still required. Roberts argues that the resources and legal powers available to cities and regions for implementing policy are important considerations, for they vary across nations. Nevertheless, he notes that changes in policy have occurred, from a more passive and *ad hoc* approach to the development of economic development strategies to deal with restructuring (Roberts, 1989, 170-79). This can be seen as an explicit recognition that in the process of globalization and integration, cities and regions are now crucial actors in determining the success of such policies. The strategies they adopt to promote economic development are therefore of prime importance, not only within the context of national economic development, but increasingly because they now operate in an economic environment marked by competition with other cities. Moreover, there is a more direct relationship between regions and the international economy (Kresl, 1992; Cappellin, 1991).

Politics and Policy in the New International Political Economy

The preceding suggests that governance in the new international political economy will be radically different from previous forms. Despite the changes noted, it is important to remember that national governments will remain important in the formulation of public policy aimed at coping with globalization and restructuring. As Jessop (1993) indicates, institutional legacies, the balance of political forces, the process of policy learning, and the fact that the nation-state still embodies national economic space mean that national governments remain important. As well, they allow for the possibility of different paths being adopted, in response to changing economic conditions, in different countries.

Hence, it would appear that the development and implementation of public policies geared at adapting to the new economic conditions must reconcile the supranational and subnational effects of the new economic conditions and how they play out over national economic space. Jenkins (1992), however, reminds us of the important role states can potentially play, even in an environment marked by (in the case of North America) an emphasis on market forces and continental integration. The complex relationship between markets and states and the important pressures of domestic politics do not mean that states only react to market forces; they also have a proactive role in changing economic conditions. Thus she suggests that there is a "paradox" at play: states have willingly relinquished control over key policy tools, but strong political forces nevertheless affect trade and investment relationships. This creates space for national and subnational state policies.

CANADA'S RESPONSE TO THE NEW ECONOMIC CONDITIONS

Despite the dramatic changes now occurring in the international political economy, the policy responses in any one country are likely to be unique given the presence of, among other factors, institutional legacies and the balance of political factors. Thus in Canada it is not surprising to discover that Canadian policy responses to the new economic conditions are influenced by the dynamics that have significantly affected Canadian politics: the spatial dynamic, which involves our federal system of governance, and the constitutional dynamic, which governs the division of powers between governments. These issues reflect some of the consequences and policy implications of the new economic conditions: how they play out over space, and who is to assume responsibility for developing and implementing restructuring policies.

The spatial dimension of Canada has historically overshadowed other political cleavages in Canadian politics. Brodie notes that the process of capital accumulation has produced uneven spatial development over time. In Canada, this created "spatially based political conflict," a phenomenon driven by the mediating role of the state. Economic strategies, presented under the label of "national development," still embody class and spatial biases. State elites "grope" to discover new strategies in a world of uncertainty, keeping in mind the goals and interests of various social, political, and economic actors. The state often produces policies supportive of capital because it is in its own interest to do so: a booming economy endears a government to supporters and capital produces revenues for the state, helping it to finance its activities. This produces spatial conflict because, invariably, economic resources and opportunities are not only distributed unevenly across social groups but across geographic areas as well (Brodie, 1990).

Spatial conflict has been at the core of Canadian federalism and constitutionalism. This has tended to play out in terms of struggles between the federal and provincial governments over power and the constitutional right to perform activities. The balance of power has tended to ebb and flow between the provinces and the federal government over time. Initially, disputes tended to revolve around the issue of government jurisdictions. As time went by, however, this focus changed somewhat. The rise of the welfare state took on a particular dynamic in Canada, as many of the key responsibilities involved were under provincial jurisdiction. As well, in an era of increasing nationalism, pressures from Québec for increased powers of self-determination and the subsequent rise of the dynamic of province-building have put the constitution and federal-provincial relations in the forefront of political and public policy debates (Rocher, 1992, 1993).

There has, however, tended to be an inward-looking bias in many analyses of the subject, as if politics occurred in a vacuum. Many studies of federalism, as Smiley indicated, focus on three dominant themes: anglophone-francophone relations, centre-periphery relations, and Canadian-American relations. But just as it is argued that national economic policy can no longer be conceived of within a closed national economy, so it is also important to extend analyses of federalism beyond the institutional realm. This has recently begun in Canada, as studies have examined the link between constitutional change and the economy (Leslie, 1987); the impact of substantial changes in the international economic order (Milne, 1986; Simeon, 1989); and the changing nature of political actors and activity, such as the growing importance of new social movements (Cairns, 1991; Smiley, 1987).

While the traditional themes of Canadian federalism obviously remain significant, it is important to extend that approach to understand the current environment of the Canadian political economy. As was noted above, the policy implications of globalization and competitiveness have altered the conditions of governance in national states. Indeed, in examining the recent history of Canadian constitutionalism and federal-provincial relations in the context of globalization, it is possible to see the awkward transition of Canadian federalism, constitutionalism, and policy-making, as well as analyses of them, from the more traditional themes to the new approaches.

This transition is awkward because the constitutional terrain has been altered. Traditional issues like centralization, decentralization, and institutional modification (such as Senate reform and the Supreme Court) remain on the agenda. However, the complex relationship of the economy, federalism, and the constitution, driven in part by the public's dissatisfaction with political elites focusing on the constitution instead of the economy, has forced itself to the top of the public policy agenda.[4]

This has occurred in an environment marked not only by unsettled economic times but also by an assault on the welfare state. As well, there has been a downloading of federal responsibilities to the provinces, without the accompanying financial resources to fulfil many of the obligations. Thus it is difficult to disentangle the pressures that affect the evolution of Canadian constitutionalism. While the new economic issues clearly have altered the discourse of constitutionalism, the very nature of the latter complicates the issue because of the extensive bargaining and give and take involved in constitutional negotiations and federal-provincial relations.[5]

The broader political and economic environment in which recent Canadian constitutional negotiations took place was one of neo-conservatism, simply defined here as a challenge to the post-war economic and political order marked by (admittedly sporadic) state intervention in both the economic and social spheres. Fiscal restraint and reduced state activism were among the major policy thrusts of the late 1970s up to the present. In Canada, this began with the Bank of Canada's conversion to the principles of monetarism in 1975. The movement truly gained force, however, with the election of Brian Mulroney's Conservative government in 1984.

In the past decade, economic policy and federal-provincial relations have been significantly affected by two seemingly contradictory tendencies: fiscal decentralization within the Canadian federation, on the one hand, and the movement toward North American economic integration, on the other. The federal government's desire to reduce the role of government in the economy and to reduce the amount of government debt, as its preferred way of meeting the challenges of globalization and competitiveness, has been critical in the evolution of Canadian federalism.

Courchene argues that a "deficit and debt burden" has produced fiscally driven decentralization. This can be seen in changes to Established Programs Financing (EPF) and the Canada Assistance Plan (CAP). Cash transfers under EPF, he notes, are predicted to fall to zero by 2010, which will have a decentralizing effect. Increased provincial taxes to maintain services would reduce the federal ratio of taxes. Redesigned programs (or cutbacks) would mean that "national" programs would increasingly be designed by provincial governments. Finally, declining cash transfers effectively reduce Ottawa's clout in maintaining or upholding national standards (Courchene, 1991a: 42).

Courchene also notes that the Free Trade Agreement enhances decentralization, not only because it effectively reduces the scope of government intervention but because it increases North-South economic integration to the detriment of East-West integration. It is likely that there will be increased agitation by the provinces if federal policies deter provinces from effectively acting in their own interests with corresponding regional economies south of the border. Another consequence might be that provinces will demand more say in national economic policy (*ibid.*: 43).

A contrary view is offered by Scott Sinclair, who argues that FTA and NAFTA effectively curtail provincial powers. He states that "the federal government has traded away significant provincial powers and usurped authority to police this surrender" (Sinclair, 1993: 229; also Rocher and Salée, 1992: 105-10). Because the federal government is the party to these agreements, it is responsible to ensure that provincial actions do not contravene the agreements in the event of complaints from the U.S.A. or Mexico. He points out that while the courts have ruled that the federal government is limited in its ability to implement treaties (an unquestioned federal right) in provincial jurisdictions, it still retains the lever of the spending power and the power of disallowance (even though it has been decades since it has been used) to ensure provincial compliance.[6]

RECENT CONSTITUTIONAL HISTORY

An examination of recent Canadian constitutional history reveals how, over time, issues relating to the new economic conditions have unevenly influenced the constitutional agenda. The new economic conditions appeared to serve as a strategic bargaining chip for the federal government in the patriation debates of the early 1980s, although the final constitutional package did not really reflect this. The debates surrounding the Meech Lake Accord, while acknowledging more explicitly a changing economic environment, did not really address this either. Only in the debates leading up to the Charlottetown Accord of 1992 can we see an explicit recognition of the relationship between the constitution and strategies aimed at restructuring the national economy in light of globalization and competitiveness.

The Constitution Act, 1982

McWhinney has argued that the impetus behind constitutional activities changed from the 1960s to the 1980s. In the 1960s and 1970s, it was essentially driven by demands from Québec, but by the 1980s this dualist approach had been eclipsed. He argues that:

> regionally based political and economic special interests had begun to challenge the post-Keynesian conceptions that had dominated Canadian political thinking and political practice since the Great Depression of the 1930s and the Second World War – a strong federal government and strong federal direction and leadership to political, social, and economic planning throughout Canada. (1982: 7)

As well, Milne notes that regional resentment against central Canadian dominance and the new political and economic clout of the regions, particularly the West, changed the constitutional agenda: a new division of powers that would increase provincial economic and political strength and a federalization of central government institutions were now part of the agenda (Milne, 1982).

Despite the *de facto* recognition of the need for institutional rearrangement and new power arrangements so that the Canadian political economy recognized and better reflected the changing economic and political environment, the activities leading up to the new Constitution Act of

1982 did not reflect this state. There seemed to be little recognition of a world outside of Canada. The driving force was a contest of wills reflecting internal power struggles: Trudeau's nationalist vision versus the more regional vision of most of the provinces. Indeed, most debate about the final product, the Constitution Act, 1982, centred on this theme: Québec's refusal to sign the final document, the impact of the Charter of Rights and Freedoms, and the nature of the new amending formula.

As Hudon notes, however, the division of economic powers was on the agenda (although it was late in getting on). The federal government in 1980 made proposals for "securing the economic union." This measure would have enhanced mobility rights and strengthened central powers to ensure economic integration and uniformization of laws and regulations, a thrust that was clearly centralizing. Interestingly enough, changing international economic conditions were cited as the reason why this approach was necessary (Hudon, 1983: 138-41; Rocher and Salée, 1992: 100-05).

This position was rejected by the provinces (except for Ontario). Hudon suggests that the federal government's economic proposals were a major reason why Québec rejected the entire constitutional package and why the initial package was indeed smaller in scope at the end of negotiations. Nevertheless, as Rocher and Salée argue, the Constitution Act effectively served as a brake on provincial initiatives. For example, the Charter of Rights primarily addresses individual rights, an orientation they believe makes it more difficult for provincial governments to act on behalf of a collectivity of interests. They also believe that Charter decisions will more often strike down provincial legislation than they will federal legislation. Entrenched mobility rights, despite certain limitations, will also allow the courts to strike down some provincial economic development strategies. At the same time, however, the federal government, through the provision of equalization payments, will be able to respond to particular needs of the regions. Finally, while recognizing exclusive provincial jurisdiction in the fields of non-renewable resources, forestry, and electrical energy, under the guise of the economic union the Constitution Act still forbids discriminatory pricing by provincial governments and, in disputed cases, the federal government's position would prevail over that of the provinces.

The final package was less than what the federal government wanted, but some of the issues pertaining to the economic union did get included. However, these important issues, which revolved around the strength and roles of the federal and provincial governments, were overshadowed by

the domestic political concerns and spatial dynamics that drove the constitutional agenda. The intense and very public spectacle of a power struggle
between the federal and provincial governments, inspired largely by competing visions of the country both politically and economically, relegated
important economic questions to the sidelines. There appears to have
been some recognition that constitutional and institutional changes would
be necessary in light of changing international economic conditions;
however, these were cast aside because of the greater resonance of internal
political struggles.

The Meech Lake Accord

Patriation of the constitution in 1982 did not end the Canadian constitutional debate. The Québec government's lack of consent to the package,
the decision of the Trudeau government and the remaining nine premiers
to go ahead and pass the agreement despite Québec's dissent, and the
promise of "renewed federalism" following the 1980 referendum in effect
ensured that debate would continue.

With the arrival of Canadian Prime Minister Mulroney and Québec
Premier Bourassa on the federal-provincial scene, a new debate was
launched. In 1986, the Québec government established five conditions for
any future constitutional agreement: recognizing Québec as a distinct society, more powers over immigration, curbing the federal spending
power, a revised amending formula, and provincial participation in the
appointment of Supreme Court judges. These demands formed the basis
of the subsequent series of constitutional negotiations as well as the Meech
Lake Accord of 1987.

This round of negotiations, however, was internally driven, seeking to
resolve long-standing tensions within the Canadian federation. The content of the Accord did not explicitly address issues pertaining to the
changing international economy. If the Accord was decentralizing, as
many people claim, it would have perhaps indirectly reflected some of the
policy implications noted above, namely allowing for more local control
over economic and political levers. This is particularly true of the clauses
on immigration, financial compensation when opting out of new national
programs, and the spending power. The provision for annual First Ministers' Conferences on the economy might also have ensured increased economic policy coordination.

All in all, however, the dynamic involved was not centralization or decentralization *per se*, in the legal sense. Rather, the issue was which order of government would have an increased ability to act independently. Looked at this way, the Accord would have had a "deconcentrating" effect. In terms of new national shared-cost programs in areas of exclusive provincial jurisdiction, it would have been Ottawa and not the provinces that would set national goals. If a province chose not to participate, it would have received financial compensation only if it put in place its own program that conformed to national objectives. In this sense, contrary to popular opinion, the Accord was not decentralizing at all. Rather, it proposed to establish a new legal mechanism allowing the federal government to intervene in provincial jurisdictions.

The Charlottetown Accord

The failure of the Meech Lake Accord did not end constitutional negotiations. The anger and bitterness experienced in Québec and in much of English Canada, which led many to expect that the constitutional issue would be put to rest for a long time, nevertheless re-emerged. The Québec government's decision to hold a referendum on sovereignty unless it received an adequate constitutional proposal agreed to by the federal government and the other nine provinces was the driving factor. The reports of the Québec Liberal Party (the Allaire Report) and the Bélanger-Campeau Commission, which both proposed massive alterations to Canadian federalism, ensured that the label of the ensuing round of negotiations as the "Canada round" was a bit of a misnomer.

In September, 1991, the federal government released its proposals for constitutional reform. While many of the proposals dealt with traditional issues of Canadian constitutionalism, this document was significant because it placed on the agenda the Conservative government's economic agenda as well. It cited the twin global pressures of global economic activity and the desire for decentralized political decision-making as reasons to ensure that Canada have "an economic union that is both modern and truly functional" (Canada, 1991: vii).

Thus the government bluntly emphasized that "to prosper we must change." (*ibid.*: 29). In its view this meant giving the federal Parliament new powers to manage the economic union and to ensure that the economic policies of the federal and provincial governments were harmonized. The result was an awkward balance between centralization and decentralization. On the one hand, there was a decentralizing orientation to the document, as seen in granting labour market policy to the provinces, recognizing exclusive provincial jurisdiction in several key policy areas (forestry, mining, housing, and municipal affairs, for example), and eliminating the federal declaratory power.

On the other hand, centralizing elements were much more significant. New powers for managing the economic union granted to the federal government and the entrenchment of the federal spending power were the key elements here. The document attempted to constitutionalize free market principles through the securement of the Canadian common market (McBride, 1993; Schneiderman, 1992). Enhanced mobility rights and the reduction of interprovincial trade and economic barriers in a new section 121 were the primary means to do so. Proposals to harmonize federal and provincial economic policies, to subject them to the evaluation of an independent agency, and to alter the Bank of Canada Act to ensure that price stability was its mandate would all have the effect of diminishing the role of government's ability to intervene in the economy.

In a most intriguing way, therefore, these proposals explicitly acknowledged the compelling forces of changing economic conditions as reasons for constitutional and institutional change. The federal government, however, used this opportunity to attempt to ensure that its political agenda (a diminished economic role for government, fiscal and monetary austerity) was also constitutionally entrenched.

The 1992 *Consensus Report on the Constitution* (the Charlottetown Accord) carried over many of these points. While the negotiations subsequent to the 1991 federal proposals were subject to a variety of political dynamics that changed their content, many of those proposals remained. These included the common market proposals and the division of powers. The mandate of the Bank of Canada, however, was dropped.

Constitutional Overview

As we know, both the Meech Lake and Charlottetown Accords were not ratified. Nevertheless, constitutional negotiations from 1982 onward serve as an interesting illustration of the problems and dilemmas governments face in responding to the new economic challenges. Governments everywhere are constrained, but in Canada this takes on a special dynamic. Over the past decade, there has clearly not been a consensus on how Canada should respond to the new economic conditions. In part this has to do with the controversial nature of the Conservative economic agenda, both intra- and extra-constitutionally. In suggesting that Meech Lake and Charlottetown were attempts to constitutionalize the principles of liberal political economy, McBride perhaps leads us astray. By linking decentralization and increased economic coordination to liberal political economy, we are then faced with a new dilemma: is a return to a strong central government the solution, or is it simply a nostalgic look back to an era when centralization worked by ensuring sustained economic growth?

Institutional and constitutional paralysis is again the result because of the traditional way in which the constitution is evaluated in Canada: ethnicity, regionalism, and centralization or decentralization. In a sense this is not surprising: democratization movements promoting human rights and the equality of citizens have influenced, to a certain degree, resentment against the Québécois and the Aboriginals, portraying them as seeking special constitutional status. On the other hand, the nature of the new economic conditions as outlined above appears to privilege diversity and decentralization. They seem to suggest that new social and institutional arrangements are necessary for any one country to meet the new challenges.

This is not meant to suggest that any particular constitutional package should or should not have been accepted. Rather, it illustrates the major institutional obstacle Canadian governments face in adapting the institutions and mechanisms of economic governance in light of changing economic conditions. In essence, it is first necessary to determine how governments should respond to the new economic conditions and which order of government should perform what tasks. In Canada, the difficulty exists in determining this through the traditional prism of centralization and decentralization (Rocher and Salée, 1992: 93-5), which raises emotions, angst, and ire in many people. As well, as was seen in both the patriation and Charlottetown rounds of negotiations, bargaining and negotiating mean that final constitutional packages do not usually reflect the variety of issues and interests on the table.

CONCLUSION

Is it necessary to reconcile the effective centralization of power with a formally acknowledged decentralization of power (i.e., constitutionally)? As Courchene and McDougall note, there are non-constitutional means by which governments can act, as the existing constitution has proven to be flexible (Courchene, 1991a; McDougall, 1991). This is a particularly important message given the analysis provided above, which suggests that constitutional paralysis could become a significant factor in Canada's response to the new economic conditions.

Recent developments also send a mixed message. The former Conservative government had reached agreements with Québec and New Brunswick over the transfer of labour market policy to the respective provincial governments, but with the election of the Chrétien Liberals the fate of these deals is unknown. On the other hand, there are now ongoing negotiations to remove interprovincial barriers, a move that could weaken the ability of provincial governments to act.[7] As well, the new Liberal infrastructure plan involves federal-provincial-municipal cooperation without resorting to constitutional negotiation. Marcel Massé, the new Minister for Public Service Renewal, is seeking to reduce inefficient overlaps in the administration and delivery of government services. Whether this can be achieved, particularly given the precarious financial state of most provincial and municipal governments, is unclear.

What is clear, however, is that increased North-South economic integration is making it more difficult to sustain the East-West axis upon which the Canadian political economy was originally based (Courchene, 1991a). For some, contemporary political and economic dynamics will likely lead to a reworking of the constitutional foundations of the country, granting the federal government responsibility for areas traditionally the domain of provincial governments (education, health, and welfare, for example), while the provincial governments assume more economic responsibilities (Courchene, 1991b). For others, these dynamics point to the need for a strengthening of the central government. In this view, securing the economic union to enhance prosperity and unity is a desirable goal, but to do so requires a strengthening of the economic powers of the central government. This is necessary to maintain a politically sovereign Canada in light of greater economic integration. Increased fragmentation and regionalization, it is believed, could lead to a harmonization of Canadian and U.S. policy (Harris and Purvis, 1991; Purvis and Raynauld, 1992).

The latter approach, however, could very well continue rather than halt the regionalization of the country. The first section of this paper illustrated how power is flowing both outward and inward from national governments in response to the new economic conditions. It is not only necessary to rethink traditional state economic development strategies; it is also necessary to devise new mechanisms for their implementation. A failure to do so could stall the process of economic restructuring. Continued poor economic performance, in this case, would then probably serve to increase, not decrease, regional political pressures, thus contributing to political disintegration.

Attempts over the past fifteen years to secure the economic union, both constitutionally and through the FTA, and appeals to national unity have essentially been an effort to maintain the powers of the central government. This clearly differs from the nature of changes in the new international political economy. In going against the tide on these issues, the federal government's attempts to maintain its ability to intervene despite an apparent devolution of powers (as in the Meech Lake and Charlottetown Accords) can be better understood. Both centralization and deconcentration were seen by the federal government as the best way to secure its position in light of the new economic conditions. It was the best way for it to deal with and minimize the loss of power, both outward and inward, in the new economic environment. Whether such a political gambit is beneficial, however, remains to be seen.

NOTES

1   Thanks to Dan Cohn for his comments on an earlier draft of this paper, which was delivered at the biennial meeting of the Association for Canadian Studies in the United States (New Orleans, Louisiana, November 17-21, 1993). This research was supported by a research grant from the Social Sciences and Humanities Research Council.

2   See Kaplinsky (1993). It is recognized that this description of the changes in production are not applicable to all countries and more particularly to specific sectors of any national economy. Rather, it is intended to highlight the variety of changes that have occurred and that do influence public policy and firm strategy. For a thorough overview of the nature of the transition to post-Fordism, see Kaplinsky. For a discussion of competing theories of flexible specialization, see Wood (1989).

3   The "continuing evolution of the city" refers to changes occurring in major cities. Up to the 1950s, the foundations of cities were heavy industry and low value-added activities in centralized cities. Successful cities then became marked by increased technology exploitation and suburbanization. Tatsuno suggests that we are now witnessing the rise of "global network" and "intelligent" cities based on high value-added services, information swapping, and power-sharing. Instead of focusing on technology exploitation, the emphasis

is increasingly on "linkages and networking" (Tatsuno, 1992). While he does not explicitly address the issue, there is a strong similarity to the changes in the production system associated with the move away from Fordism.

4   The Chrétien government's desire to modernize the entire network of social programs and to tie them in more closely to the new economy is a prime example of this phenomenon.

5   Richard Simeon nicely describes the increasingly complex nature of Canadian constitutionalism. Writing after the collapse of the Meech Lake Accord, he notes that politically it will be difficult to achieve a national consensus on constitutional goals as well as a constitutional deal (a view since borne out by the defeat of the Charlottetown Accord in the 1992 national referendum). He also notes that globalization will have "important implications" for constitutionalism – while its effects are unknown as of yet (that is, whether it promotes centralization or decentralization), it still raises important questions for policy-makers and constitution-makers, especially whether the constitution should accommodate decentralizing pressures or counter them so that Canada has "one voice" in the international political economy (Simeon, 1991: 3).

6   The irony, as Sinclair points out, is that provinces would be able to implement discriminatory policies directed at other provinces to achieve social and economic goals, but not at international trading partners. The favoured solution, it seems, is to negotiate the removal of interprovincial trade barriers rather than to restore the power of governments to act. The recent ceasefire in the Ontario-Québec trade dispute is but one notable example.

7   On November 3, 1993, Québec and New Brunswick signed a deal to open bidding on government procurement contracts, thus opening up markets of $450 million and $70 million respectively to businesses in the two provinces. This is seen as a first step toward fewer barriers between the two provinces. Indeed, on March 30, 1994, the two governments signed an agreement lifting most interprovincial trade barriers, meaning that firms can bid on up to $12 billion worth of contracts. The two agreements are seen as a step toward deals with other provinces. For example, Québec and Ontario are currently negotiating a procurement agreement. (Globe and Mail, November 4, 1993: B-3; March 31, 1994: A-7).

REFERENCES

Albrechts, L., *et al.*, eds. (1989). *Regional Policy at the Crossroads: European Perspectives*. London: Jessica Kingsley Publishers.

Benko, Georges, and Mick Dunford, eds. (1991). *Industrial Change and Regional Development: The Transformation of New Industrial Spaces*. London: Belhaven Press.

Brodie, Janine (1990). *The Political Economy of Canadian Regionalism*. Toronto: Harcourt Brace Jovanovich.

Cairns, Alan C. (1991). *Disruptions: Constitutional Struggles, from the Charter to Meech Lake*, edited by Douglas E. Williams. Toronto: McClelland & Stewart.

Camagni, Roberto, ed. (1991). *Innovation Networks: Spatial Perspectives*. London: Belhaven Press.

Canada (1991). *Shaping Canada's Future Together: Proposals*.

Cappellin, Ricardo (1991). "International Networks of Cities," in Camagni, ed., *Innovation Networks*. London: Belhaven.

Courchene, Thomas J. (1991a). "Forever Amber," in David E. Smith, Peter MacKinnon, and John C. Courtney. eds., *After Meech Lake: Lessons for the Future*. Saskatoon: Fifth House Publishers.

Courchene, Thomas J. (1991b). "Mons Pays, C'est l'Hiver," *Canadian Public Policy*, XVII, 4.

Drache, Daniel (1993). "The Future of Trading Blocs," in Duncan Cameron and Mel Watkins, eds., *Canada Under Free Trade*. Toronto: James Lorimer.

Harris, Richard G., and Douglas D. Purvis (1991). "Constitutional Change and Canada's Economic Prospects," *Canadian Public Policy*, XVII, 4: 379-94.

Hudon, Raymond (1993). "Quebec, the Economy and the Constitution," in Keith Banting and Richard Simeon, eds., *And No One Cheered: Federalism, Democracy and the Constitution Act*. Toronto: Methuen.

Jenkins, Barbara (1992). *The Paradox of Continental Production: National Investment Policies in North America*. Ithaca, N.Y.: Cornell University Press.

Jessop, Bob (1993). "Towards a Schumpeterian Workfare State? Preliminary Remarks on Post-Fordist Political Economy," *Studies in Political Economy*, 40 (Spring): 7-39.

Kaplinsky, Raphael (1993). "Post-Fordist Industrial Restructuring: Some Policy Implications," in Jane Jenson, Rianne Mahon, and Manfred Bienefeld, eds., *Production, Space Identity: Political Economy Faces the 21st Century*. Toronto: Canadian Scholars' Press: 25-51.

Kresl, Peter Karl (1992). *The Urban Economy and Regional Trade Liberalization*. New York: Praeger.

Leslie, Peter (1987). *Federal State, National Economy*. Toronto: University of Toronto Press.

Linge, G.J.R., and D.C. Rich (1991). "The State and Industrial Change," in Rich and Linge, eds. *The State and the Spatial Management of Industrial Change*. London: Routledge.

McBride, Stephen (1993). "Renewed Federalism as an Instrument of Competitiveness: Liberal Political Economy and the Canadian Constitution," *International Journal of Canadian Studies*, 7-8 (Spring-Fall): 189-205.

McDougall, John (1991). "North American Integration and Canadian Disunity," *Canadian Public Policy*. XVII, 4: 395-408.

McWhinney, Edward (1982). *Canada and the Constitution 1979-1982: Patriation and the Charter of Rights*. Toronto: University of Toronto Press.

Milne, David (1982). *The New Canadian Constitution*. Toronto: James Lorimer.

Milne, David (1986). *Tug of War: Ottawa and the Provinces Under Trudeau and Mulroney*. Toronto: James Lorimer.

Morris, Richard W. (1992). "Economic Development, Technology Transfer, and Venture Financing in the Global Economy," in David V. Gibson, George Kozmetsky, and Raymond W. Smilor, eds., *The Technopolis Phenomenon: Smart Cities, Fast Systems, Global Networks*. New York: Lanham, Rowman & Littlefield.

Purvis, Douglas D., and André Raynauld (1992). "LAO," in Douglas Brown and Robert Young, eds., *Canada: The State of the Federation 1992*. Kingston: Queen's University, Institute of Intergovernmental Relations: 129-43.

Roberts, Peter (1989). "Local Economic Development: Alternative Forms of Local and Regional Policy for the 1990s," in Albrechts et al., eds., Regional Policy at the Crossroads.

Rocher, François (1992). "Quebec's Historical Agenda," in Duncan Cameron and Miriam Smith, eds., Constitutional Politics. Toronto: James Lorimer: 23-36.

Rocher, François (1993). "Dividing the Spoils: American and Canadian Federalism," in David Thomas, ed., *Canada and the United States: Differences That Count*. Peterborough, Ont.: Broadview Press: 127-47.

Rocher, François, and Daniel Salée (1992). "Logique d'État et fédéralisme canadien: l'improbable décentralisation," in Rocher, ed., *Bilan québécois du fédéralisme canadien*. Montréal: VLB Éditeur.

Rostow, W.W. (1992). "Technology in the Coming Era of Federalism," in Gibson, Kozmetsky, and Smilor, eds., *The Technopolis Phenomenon*.

Schneiderman, David (1992). "The Market and the Constitution," in Cameron and Smith, eds., *Constitutional Politics*: 59-69.

Simeon, Richard (1989). "We Are All Smiley's People: Some Observations on Donald Smiley and the Study of Federalism," in David P. Shugarman and Reg Whitaker, eds., *Federalism and Political Community: Essays in Honour of Donald Smiley*. Peterborough, Ont.: Broadview Press: 409-21.

Simeon, Richard (1991). "Setting Out the Framework," in Richard Simeon and Mary Janigan, eds., *Toolkits and Building Blocks: Constructing a New Canada*. Toronto: C.D. Howe Institute.

Sinclair, Scott (1993). "Provincial Powers," in Cameron and Mel Watkins, eds., *Canada Under Free Trade*.

Smiley, Donald V. (1987). *The Federal Condition in Canada*. Toronto: McGraw-Hill Ryerson.

Smiley, Donald V. (1989). "Meech Lake and Free Trade: Studies in Canadian Federalism," *Canadian Public Administration*. 32, 3 (Fall): 470-81.

Tatsuno, Sheridan M. (1992). "The Multimedia City of the Future," in Gibson, Kozmetsky, and Smilor, eds., *The Technopolis Phenomenon*: 197-207.

Wood Stephen (1989). "The Transformation of Work?" in Wood, ed., *The Transformation of Work? Skill, Flexibility and the Labour Process*. London: Unwin Hyman: 1-43.

CHAPTER TEN

Trade Policy, Globalization, and the Future of Canadian Federalism

Ian Robinson

SINCE 1982, STUDENTS OF CANADIAN FEDERALISM HAVE BEEN fascinated by two Herculean efforts to amend the constitution. Both efforts failed. Meanwhile, three important international (so-called) trade agreements were negotiated and signed. The Canada-U.S. Free Trade Agreement (FTA) was signed in 1988 and implementation began the following year. The North American Free Trade Agreement NAFTA and its labour and environmental side-deals were signed in 1993). NAFTA and its side deals began to be implemented in 1994. Formal negotiations on the Uruguay Round of GATT were completed in December, 1993, and the first countries began implementation in January, 1995.

It could be argued that these trade agreements amount to a series of amendments to Canada's economic constitution, with implications for Canadian federalism at least as profound as those entailed by the ill-fated Meech Lake and Charlottetown Accords. This paper explores three clusters of questions related to this claim and is, accordingly, divided into three sections.

The first cluster recognizes that Canada has been reducing its tariff barriers to trade in goods since the apex of twentieth-century North American protectionism in the early 1930s. Why, then, will the agreements of the 1980s and early 1990s have a greater impact on the character of Canadian federalism than their predecessors? What is new and different about these more recent agreements that warrants the use of the constitutional metaphor? How will Canadian federalism be altered by the trade deals? Will they shift the balance of political power and policy initiative toward the federal government or provincial governments? Will they increase or decrease levels of federal-provincial conflict?

These agreements are fundamentally different from their predecessors because their most important innovations increase capital mobility rather than reducing tariff barriers. Their proponents minimize this difference by describing them as trade agreements, but this paper will refer to them as free capital agreements or FCAS, in recognition of their very different focus. The FCAS are likely to centralize economic and political power. They are also likely to intensify levels of federal-provincial conflict, as the crises of the 1930s and the early 1940s did. The new form of Canadian federalism ushered in by these agreements is labelled residual federalism.

The second cluster of questions flows from these conclusions. How is it that the government of Québec – long Canada's strongest defender of provincial government jurisdiction and power – became the federal government's staunchest ally in promoting the FCAS? Why did it react so defensively to the labour and environmental side deals to NAFTA, when the main text of the agreement had much greater implications for provincial jurisdiction and policy capacity than the side deals? When neo-liberal ideology and the economic interests it serves came into direct conflict with the goal of preserving and enhancing Québec state power, the latter was sacrificed to the former. Such is the character of the "nationalism" of Québec's current political élites, on both sides of the aisle. This, in itself, is a sea change in the dynamics of Canadian federalism.

The third cluster of questions deals with how the FCAS and Canadian federalism interact with the processes commonly labelled "globalization." Would a more "communitarian" form of globalization, characterized by a strong international social dimension, be any more compatible with the kind of Canadian federalism that emerged in the post-war period? Or must we conclude that all plausible versions of globalization lead to residual federalism? Both forms of globalization probably imply further centralization of the federation with respect to the diverse policy fields affected by the FCAS. However, a communitarian form would likely be more compatible with the spirit of Canadian federalism. It would also be less likely to generate the intense levels of federal-provincial conflict predicted to flow from neo-liberal globalization.[1]

All of the arguments advanced in this chapter are speculative. Analysis of the legal provisions of the FCAS depends to some degree on how key terms will be interpreted by courts and panels of trade law experts. Analysis of market constraints involves predictions of how firms will react to the new legal regime they face. Predicting the impacts of the economic and political power shifts associated with these agreements – even if we had perfect information as to how their terms would be interpreted – is even more difficult. Some are inclined to dismiss such speculation as unscientific. Still, policy decisions are made by estimating as best we can the probable consequences of alternative courses of action. The greater the scale of the policy changes considered, the more extensive and complex the consequences are likely to be, and so, the more difficult the analyst's task.

FIGURE ONE: TWO PATHS FROM FCAS TO RESIDUAL FEDEALISM

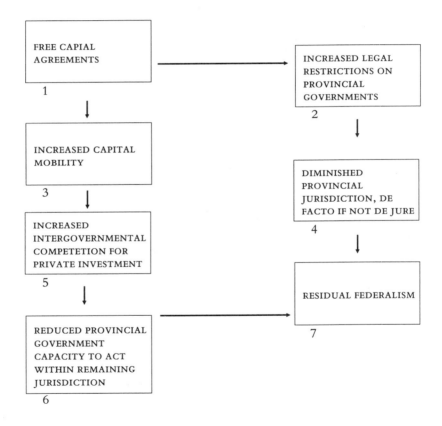

THE FCAS AND THE CHARACTER OF CANADIAN FEDERALISM

How the FCAs Erode Provincial Government Powers

The FCAS erode provincial government powers in two basic ways: first, by imposing unprecedented legal restrictions on the actions that provincial governments may take; and second, by increasing the market constraints faced by provincial governments. These two routes to "residual federalism" are set out schematically in Figure One. The first route generally receives the most attention, particularly from constitutional lawyers. But the second is probably more important.[2]

Legal Restrictions

Prior to the Tokyo Round, the GATT focused primarily on the reduction of tariffs on imported goods.[3] Tariffs fall unambiguously under exclusive federal jurisdiction. This is illustrated in Table One. The third column, labelled "Pre-Tokyo GATT," has an X only in the cell that designates non-agricultural tariffs and quotas. A single X indicates that these policies fall exclusively within federal jurisdiction. A double X indicates that the rules in this area affect provincial jurisdiction as well – sometimes matters hitherto considered to fall under exclusive provincial jurisdiction.

With the Tokyo Round, signed in 1979, non-tariff barriers (NTBs) to trade became a major focus of all trade agreements. This is evident in column four of the same table. The best known forms of NTBs are subsidies and government purchasing (or procurement) policies. But virtually any government policy that has the effect of placing foreign producers at a competitive disadvantage vis-a-vis domestic producers can be construed as an NTB under what is known as the "national treatment" principle.[4]

By targeting NTBs, the Tokyo GATT had the potential to reach deep into provincial jurisdiction. As it turned out, the impact of the cases was quite limited because subnational governments were expressly exempted from some rules that would otherwise have applied to them (e.g., the government procurement code), while the code with the greatest potential reach into provincial jurisdiction – the subsidies code – proved weaker than its signatories had initially imagined.[5] However, the FCAS of the 1980s and early 1990s go well beyond the Tokyo Round in these respects and many more.

The Canada-U.S. Free Trade Agreement

The most important new areas of provincial jurisdiction affected by the FTA are identified in column five of Table One. They include (i) restrictions on provincial government rights to control levels of exports of natural resources, including hydroelectric power; and (ii) a panoply of new American investor rights, some of the most important of which are listed in the table.

Most of these restrictions were "grandfathered," meaning that non-complying measures existing prior to the implementation of the FTA were exempted, provided they were listed in annexes to the agreement prior to its implementation. However, new non-complying measures cannot be introduced, and grandfathered measures cannot be modified in ways deemed to increase their restrictiveness.

If a grandfathered trade restrictive measure is eliminated or made less trade restrictive, no subsequent government can go back to the prior level of restrictiveness, much less increase it. Thus, the grandfathering provisions function like handcuffs that can be tightened but not loosened. These handcuffs allow relatively laissez-faire (or neo-liberal) governments to bind future, more interventionist governments, but not the other way around. Thus, most of the FTA's deregulatory impact is imposed on future rather than existing governments and on more interventionist rather than more market-oriented governments.

Finally, article 103 of the FTA states that "[t]he Parties to this agreement [i.e., the two federal governments] shall ensure that all necessary measures are taken in order to give effect to its provisions ... by state, provincial and local governments." It is widely agreed that this language is stronger than the GATT's "reasonable measures" standard.[6] The federal obligation in Article 103 applies not only to all of the areas in which the FTA goes beyond the GATT, but also to those where it incorporates GATT obligations. In the latter case, the FTA effectively attaches a stronger federal obligation to enforce prior restrictions on provincial measures.

The North American Free Trade Agreement

The most important new restrictions found in NAFTA can be seen in column six of Table One. They include:

- prohibitions on two new kinds of foreign investor "performance requirements": technology transfer and product mandating;[7]

- a much broader definition of who will count as a NAFTA investor for purposes of claiming the new investor property rights created by the FTA and NAFTA;

- a new investor-state dispute process, permitting NAFTA investors to go to an international tribunal with binding arbitration powers, or to the domestic courts;[8]

- a plethora of restrictions flowing from the entirely new Intellectual Property Rights chapter; and

- the tightening of restrictions on technical standards; and the application of those restrictions to provincial measures for the first time.[9]

Uruguay GATT[10]

As column seven of Table One indicates, the Uruguay GATT resembles NAFTA in many respects. But there are at least two areas in which the new GATT will impose legal restrictions on provincial government measures that go beyond those already found in the FTA and NAFTA.

The first important innovation is the inclusion of agricultural tariffs and quotas, hitherto exempted from coverage in trade agreements. The battles over agricultural subsidies were the single most important sticking point between the United States and the European Union in the Uruguay Round. But the new GATT will also gradually eliminate provincial supply management systems, first by transforming into tariffs the import quotas essential to controlling overall supply levels and then by reducing those tariffs by an average of 36 per cent over six years, beginning January 1, 1995. Further reductions beyond this are likely.

The Uruguay GATT subsidies code also goes beyond the Tokyo Round by defining subsidies. The FTA and NAFTA, as indicated in Table One, had no subsidies code at all. The new GATT code divides all subsidies into "general" and "specific." Specific subsidies (i.e., those targeted on particular firms, sectors, or regions) are trade restrictive by definition. If the nation is the unit of analysis, all provincial and local government subsidies are regionally specific, whatever their specific content and focus, since

TABLE ONE: TRADE AGREEMENTS AND PROVINCIAL JURISDICTION

POLICY AREAS COVERED	SUB-FIELDS	PRE-TOKYO GATT	TOKYO GATT	FTA	NAFTA	URUGUAY GATT
TARIFFS & QUOTAS ON GOODS	NON-AGRICULTURAL GOODS	X	X	X	X	X
	AGRICULTURAL GOODS			XX	X	XX
NON-TARIFF BARRIERS (NTBS)	SUBSIDIES & COUNTERVAILING DUTIES (CVDS)		XX	XX		XX
	ANTI-DUMPING DUTIES (AD)		X		X	X
	GOVERNMENT PROCUREMENT		X	X	X	X
	TECHNICAL STANDARDS		X	X	XX	XX
NATURAL RESOURCES	SUPPLY GUARANTEES			XX	XX	
FOREIGN INVESTOR PROPERTY RIGHTS (TRIMS)	LIMITS ON GOVERNMENT-IMPOSED PERFORMANCE REQUIREMENTS			XX	XX	XX
	LIMITS ON GOVERNMENT-IMPOSED RESTRICTIONS ON THE REPATRIATION OF FOREIGN INVESTOR PROFITS			XX	XX	
	LIMITS ON OPERATION OF PUBLIC & PRIVATE MONOPOLIES			XX	XX	
	LIMITS ON OPERATION OF PUBLIC CORPORATIONS			X	XX	
	BINDING ARBITRATION ENFORCEMENT PROCESS AVAILABLE TO FOREIGN INVESTORS				XX	
TRIPS	INTELLECTUAL PROPERTY RIGHTS				XX	XX
SERVICES	FINANCIAL & OTHER SERVICES			XX	XX	XX

X — EXCLUSIVE FEDERAL JURISDICTION
XX — RULES AFFECT FEDERAL AND PROVINCIAL JURISDICTION

they apply to only a portion of the nation's territory.

The Dunkel draft of the Uruguay GATT seemed to endorse this view.[11] Article 2.2 of its subsidy code stated that a "subsidy which is available to all enterprises located within a designated geographical region shall be specific irrespective of the nature of the granting authority." Understood in this fashion, all subnational government subsidies are necessarily specific. One implication of this rule is that a Québec government subsidy that would be considered general and non-trade distorting if Québec were a sovereign nation-state becomes specific and subject to challenge as a distortion of trade should Québec remain a province of Canada.

The final Uruguay text is less clear on this important point. It states that a "subsidy which is limited to certain enterprises located within a designated geographical region within the jurisdiction of the granting authority will be specific." The code does not indicate whether sub-national governments can be "granting authorities." If they can be, this new formulation appears to treat general provincial subsidies in the same way that it would treat general federal subsidies – i.e., as non-trade restrictive and hence non-countervailable. If not, the problem with the Dunkel draft remains. Either way, provincial (and federal) subsidies appear to be "specific" if they do not apply to all enterprises in a particular region. For example, an economic development policy that seeks to promote particular industries or types of business – such as the development of mining and forestry machinery or Aboriginal-owned enterprises – would appear to be "specific" under this definition.

Under articles 3 and 5 of the final Uruguay text, all specific subsidies are either prohibited or "actionable." Actionable means that if a World Trade Organization member can convince the WTO Subsidies Committee that a specific measure adopted by another WTO member has resulted in "serious adverse effects" to one of its industries, and the offending government does not remedy this problem in accordance with the Committee's recommendations, then the complaining member is authorized to take "countervailing" action, subject to the usual WTO guidelines.[12] Existing nonconforming measures must be rendered consistent with the code within three years.[13]

Article 8 contemplates three possible exceptions to the rule that specific subsidies are countervailable: (1) assistance for a range of research activities, (2) assistance to disadvantaged regions, and (3) assistance to promote the adaptation of existing facilities to new environmental requirements imposed by law or regulation, where they impose an additional

TABLE TWO: FEDERAL STRATEGIES TO ENCOURAGE
PROVINCIAL COMPLIANCE

1. Legislative

    a. *Treaty Power.* requires overturning or narrowing of Labour Conventions (1937) decision.

    b. *POGG Power.* use or extend the Crown Zellerbach (1988) decision, which developed three criteria that must be met in order to uphold the federal regulatory scheme trenching on what would otherwise be considered exclusive provincial jurisdiction:

        i. it must have a singleness and distinctiveness of purpose that distinguishes it from provincial legislation;

        ii. it must have a limited scale of impact so as not to cut a devastating path through provincial jurisdictions; and

        iii. it must have been shown that the failure of a province or provinces to deal effectively with the problem would have significant extra-provincial impacts.

    c. *Trade and Commerce Power.* use or extend the CN Leasing (1989) decision, which also developed three criteria that must be met by any federal regulatory scheme trenching on what would otherwise be considered exclusive provincial jurisdiction:

        i. it must be national in scope, rather than local, and pertain to trade in general, rather than a particular business;

        ii. provinces must be constitutionally incapable of implementing the type of regulation in question; and

        iii. failure to include one or more provinces must jeopardize the successful operation of the regulatory scheme in other parts of the country.

2. Non-Legislative

    a. *Federal "Bluff":* Threaten to introduce legislation if provincial compliance is not forthcoming.

    b. *Federal Spending Power.* Provide resources to assist in structural adjustments only if compliance is secured ("carrots"), and/or reduce federal transfers to provincial governments that do not comply (perhaps based on any fines that the federal government is forced to pay for provincial non-compliance).

Source: Whyte (1991).

financial burden on firms.[14] Would the second exception cover provincial government regional economic development policies? Only if a WTO panel finds them to be "pursuant to a general framework of regional development." It is not clear whether subnational governments can develop a "general framework," or whether that is something that only a national government can do.[15] Suppose that the WTO Subsidies Committee decides to interpret the agreement in the latter way. In that case, provincial governments seeking to protect their regional policies against WTO challenges would presumably have to gain federal approval of any aspect of their programs that could be construed as involving subsidies.

The WTO focus extends some of the most important NAFTA provisions, and the new ones just discussed, to all WTO signatories. At this global level, it is much more costly for any country to abrogate the agreement, and it is also more difficult to amend, given the complexity of multilateral negotiations. The new rules thus more closely resemble an entrenched economic constitution than is the case with bilateral or trilateral agreements such as the FTA or NAFTA.

Federal Compliance Strategies

In the FCAS, the federal government undertakes to employ "all necessary measures" to ensure subnational government compliance with the new restrictions summarized above. As summarized in Table Two, Ottawa could pursue a legislative or a non-legislative compliance strategy.

It has long been understood that the federal government's exclusive power to make international treaties has the potential to undermine the federal principle. If the federal government could acquire the right to legislate in an area that would otherwise fall under exclusive provincial jurisdiction simply by signing a treaty, it could unilaterally make profound changes in the division of powers without formally amending the constitution or even consulting with the provinces.

This potential end-run around the federal principle was foreclosed with the *Labour Conventions* case of 1937, in which it was determined that the federal government had the power to make an international treaty on any matter but it could only introduce implementing legislation on matters falling within federal jurisdiction. In areas of exclusive provincial jurisdiction, the federal government would have to convince provincial governments to introduce the required laws or to refrain from actions contravening the treaty. This decision still stands.[16]

Nothing in the *Labour Conventions* case prevents the federal government from expanding its jurisdiction by convincing the courts to increase the scope of one of its existing heads of power. In the case of a trade deal, the most promising avenues for federal expansion are probably the "peace, order and good government" (POGG) clause and the trade and commerce clause (sections 91 and 91(2), respectively, of the Constitution Act, 1867). Broadly defined, either power could be used to justify federal legislation in almost any economic area otherwise falling under exclusive provincial jurisdiction.

In the United States, the commerce power was dramatically expanded, with just this effect, in a series of landmark cases that decided the constitutionality of President Roosevelt's New Deal legislation.[17] In Canada, the Judicial Committee of the Privy Council (JCPC)[18] defined the trade and commerce and the POGG powers more narrowly. The Supreme Court of Canada initially followed the JCPC's lead on this point.[19] However, decisions handed down in the latter half of the 1980s – particularly *Crown Zellerbach* (1988)[20] and *City National Leasing* (1989)[21] – appear to have expanded both federal powers significantly, while stopping well short of the position taken by the U.S. Supreme Court.

It is impossible here to assess the likelihood that federal implementing legislation related to, say, NAFTA's investment chapter will meet the tests, summarized in Table Two, necessary to justify it as *intra vires* the trade and commerce or pogg powers. If the Ontario government follows through on its plan to launch a reference case on NAFTA, the Ontario Court of Appeal (and, no doubt, the Supreme Court of Canada on appeal) will have to undertake such a detailed analysis for whatever elements of NAFTA are identified in the Ontario Attorney General's reference. Meanwhile, the only certainty is that there is great uncertainty here as to the legal status of federal efforts to legislate in all of the areas covered by the FCAs.

Ottawa's international obligation to ensure compliance with FCA restrictions on subnational governments does not imply that it must legislate. It is enough if provincial governments bring their actions into conformity with the agreement. The threat of federal implementing legislation might achieve this end. If challenged and upheld by the courts, such legislation might have more serious ramifications for provincial jurisdiction than compliance with a particular GATT provision. Risk averse provincial governments might consider discretion the better part of valour. The federal spending power is another potential weapon (see Chapter 11). The threat to reduce federal transfers – commensurate, perhaps, with the estimated costs of trade sanctions levied against Canada for FCA violations by the non-complying provincial government – cannot be dismissed lightly, particularly in the case of poorer provinces.

Market Constraints

Provincial jurisdiction matters insofar as it enables provincial governments to act effectively on behalf of their electorates. But the capacity to act can be reduced by market constraints as well as legal restrictions, as Figure One (route 1-3-5-6) indicates. In a recent discussion of the character of the European Union, *The Economist* made this point clearly:

> two ideas have long struggled for the control of Western Europe's economic destiny. One is that the economic power of the state must be kept in check. Liberal trade, by forcing national policies into competition with one another, does this: in an open economy a government cannot, as it were, take too many liberties. Against this is the idea that governments need to protect their sovereignty. (1993: 60)

Governments are constrained because they must compete with one another to maintain existing private investment and attract new private investment (Lindblom, 1984). The FCAs would increase such market constraints even if the legal restrictions sketched above applied only to the federal government. Indeed, in the cases of NAFTA and the WTO, they would do so even if Canada refused to sign the agreement, provided that the United States and other countries signed. The FCAs increase the constraints on governments primarily by increasing the freedom of transnational corporations (TNCs) to invest profitably outside of Canada.

Corporate capital mobility is increased by all of the treaty provisions that reduce barriers to trade, so that market access can be assured as long as production facilities are located in one of the signatory nations. It is also increased by the new investor and intellectual property rights that reassure TNCs that their profits will be well protected against regulations, competing state enterprises or monopolies, and expropriation in the countries where they locate production.

The new market constraints are more comprehensive than the legal restrictions just summarized. For example, they limit the level of corporate taxes that governments can impose – a power that is not legally restricted by the FCAS. Moreover, these market constraints require no complex and expensive enforcement process to make them effective. Capital flight by past or potential investors – or the mere threat of it – is generally adequate to the task, if sufficient in magnitude. For these reasons, the market constraints intensified by the FCAS are probably more important than the legal restrictions summarized above.

Increased capital mobility reduces the bargaining power of both orders of government vis-a-vis TNCs. However, it is much easier for TNCs to play off ten Canadian provinces, fifty U.S. states, and thirty-one Mexican states against one another than it is to play three national governments off against each other. Ninety-one state and provincial governments, as *The Economist* notes, amount to a competitive market in which governments compete with one another to meet the conditions set by prospective corporate investors (e.g., tax breaks or weak labour and environmental regulations). Three national governments as large as those of North America are an oligopoly, retaining the power to impose some conditions on TNC investors. Thus, market constraints have a much greater impact on subnational governments than on national governments, even when the legal restrictions on national governments are broader (as they are in the FCAS). This point holds all the more for local governments (Peterson, 1981).

A shift of manufacturing away from Canada will also have an important impact on the economic and political power of the labour movement (Robinson, 1994). Where a strong labour movement exists, governments are constrained not to bend too far in the direction of TNC interests. A degree of countervailing power exists at the level of civil society, and this is reflected in public policy. In the 1970s and 1980s, countries with highly unionized work forces and strong labour or social democratic parties tended to have larger and more activist governments (Cameron, 1986; Stephens, 1986: 89-176), more egalitarian distributions of the benefits of economic growth (Stephens, 1986: 163-76; Green *et al.*, 1992), and lower levels of inflation and unemployment (Cameron, 1984; Golden, 1993).

Thus, governments lose bargaining power that used to flow from instruments either no longer legally at their disposal or no longer used for fear of scaring off private investment. At the same time, labour movement countervailing power is weakened. These shifts in the balance of economic and political power increase the tension that has always existed between trade policies that increase nations' exposure and vulnerability to international market forces, on the one hand, and social policies intended to reduce the costs of economic restructuring for those who lose their jobs and to distribute benefits more equitably (Keohane, 1984; Helleiner, 1994).

In the absence of a "social dimension"[22] (Robinson, 1993b; Stanford et al., 1993) designed to redress this power imbalance, calls by the Macdonald Commission (1985) and others for freer trade and capital flows and increased state economic intervention (i.e., more active labour market policies and increased redistribution of the gains from liberalization) are politically naïve. The social movements and collective actors necessary to maintain the political pressure for such market intervention are weakened by the increased capital mobility that these agreements promote, other things being equal.[23] Moreover, the state's capacity to tax and transfer the resources necessary to make these programs work is also reduced.

Only an economic analysis that systematically averts its gaze from the power relations that shape national and international political economies could imagine that both aspects of Macdonald Commission-type policy prescriptions are politically realizable. But mainstream economists, and the policy-makers who rely on their theories, are exceedingly reluctant to acknowledge, much less make, the "hard choice" that follows from this: either neo-liberal globalization that carries Canada down the road of class polarization travelled by Latin America in the 1980s, or an alternative approach to globalization that regulates the global market economy we have created.

Centralization of the Federation

That the FCAS erode provincial government powers does not, in itself, imply the centralization of the federation. Indeed, if the agreements eroded federal government powers even more, they might contribute to its decentralization. Three arguments to the effect that the FCAS are decentralizing could be made. The first points to the fact that all of the FCAS' legal restrictions apply to federal governments, while only some apply to subnational governments. Second, most of the policy areas that will be critical to global competitive success in the kind of world market economy promoted by the FCAS — such as education and labour market policy — fall under exclusive provincial jurisdiction. Finally, since increased economic integration in the European Union has been accompanied by increasingly assertive regional governments, the same is likely to happen in North America.[24]

The chief problem with the first argument is that it focuses exclusively on the legal restrictions imposed by the FCAS. It has already been argued that the market constraints intensified by these agreements are more important for both orders of government than the new legal restrictions. This holds all the more for subnational governments, which are subject to fewer legal restrictions but are much more vulnerable to increased market constraints.

As to the second argument, in the kind of global and regional market economies constructed by the FCAS, governments will be scrambling to adapt their programs – indeed, their entire societies – to the presumed requirements of successful competition. Education and labour market policies will be among the most important policy instruments for responding to these pressures, not only because they are important in their own right but also because the FCAS deny governments access to many of the other policies that might otherwise be employed. It is also true that provincial governments have primary responsibility for these policy areas. However, what provincial governments do in these fields will be driven – more than ever before – by international market pressures. Both the intensity and the direction of these pressures are, to a great degree, a function of the content of the FCAS and other rules of the global market economy, all of which are negotiated exclusively by the federal government with other national governments.

Provincial governments, like other "interest groups," are encouraged to submit their views as to what the federal government should pursue in these agreements. Provincial governments have been kept better informed of how negotiations are proceeding than most such groups. But such consultations should not be confused with a genuine codetermination of policy. Indeed, the level and quality of provincial government participation in the FCAS were much lower than in the Tokyo Round of the GATT, despite the fact that the FCAS will have a much greater impact on provincial government powers.[25] Provincial governments may choose their steps, and those steps matter, but more than ever before, they must dance to the tune determined by the federal government. To call this decentralization seems odd.

The third, "Europe of Regions" argument rests on the assumption that the integration processes on the two continents are broadly analogous. This assumption is false. The European Union (EU) has a powerful Commission, to which (limited) powers to regulate labour and environmental standards at the Union level have been transferred. *The Economist* (1993) argues that the Maastricht Treaty greatly strengthened the idea that state

power should be transferred to the supranational level, rather than devolved to the private corporations that collectively constitute what are
euphemistically called "market forces." Unlike earlier EU treaties, "it does
virtually nothing to increase individual economic freedom, but much to
centralize the exercise of political power. Its ruling ideas are common policy-making and harmonization. The results are dispiriting. It follows logically from what has been done within Western Europe that either har-
monisation or protection are the right responses to unbridled competition."

There is some exaggeration here, informed by *The Economist*'s laissez-
faire economic agenda, but the essential point is valid. The national and
subnational governments of the EU receive some protection from intra-EU
"social dumping" pressures through supranational regulation, but this is
still very weak and underdeveloped. The Commission also has a budget
that includes substantial structural funds for transfer to poorer regions.
Subnational governments thus have strong financial incentives to form alliances with the Commission on a range of issues where it may be more
helpful than their national government (e.g., Scotland and northern England). For its part, the Commission needs political allies in its struggles to
wrest powers from national governments and TNCs. The result is the sub-
supranational alliance known as the Europe of the Regions.[26] International economic integration of the sort promoted by the FCAs does have a
supranational regulatory dimension. But it is confined to protecting the
private property rights of investors and intellectual innovators, and minimizing national and subnational government impediments to the movement of goods, services, capital, and professional labour. North American
economic integration is not governed by a permanent, supranational bureaucracy accountable (at least to some degree) to the member nations in
council and a parliament comprised of member-state representatives.
There are only government-appointed, quasi-judicial panels that will
function much like politically unaccountable courts. Neither is there a serious anti-social dumping component to supranational regulation or an
equivalent to the EU's structural funds.[27]

In this context, policy instruments and regulatory powers given up by
national governments are not transferred to supranational agencies or to
subnational governments. They are instead devolved to the market. With
no equivalent to the European Commission or the European Parliament,
there is no supranational level of government with which provincial or
municipal governments can build links and from which they can get ma-

terial resources or relief from downward market pressures on their regulations and standards. Thus there is no space for the emergence of a "North America of the Regions."

To sum up, the net impact of the FCAS is likely to be centralizing. This does not mean that other forces might not override the impact of the FCAS. Courchene (1992) has argued that the federal government will be forced to retreat from a wide range of policy areas in which it had previously deployed its spending power to considerable effect. Ottawa's intractable budget difficulties, he argues, mean that it can no longer make the same levels of transfers to provincial governments. The spending power worked by attaching conditions that provinces had to meet in order to qualify for those transfers. As the federal spending power is eroded, provincial governments will be left in "unconditional" possession of more and more policy fields. This, Courchene argues, will result in substantial decentralization.

The argument developed here suggests that the FCAS will exacerbate federal government budget deficit problems, other things equal. But provincial governments also suffer from deficit difficulties, and the FCAS' negative impact on revenue raising capacities will be greater for subnational than for national governments. So it is not as though monies that once went to Ottawa and were then transferred to provincial governments (with federal strings attached) will now go to provincial governments without conditions. Rather, they will get less money from Ottawa, and they are not likely to be able to make up the difference by raising their own taxes.

With a weakened federal spending power, provincial governments will be able to respond to mounting deficit problems by cutting costs in ways that would earlier have been denied to them by federal conditions (e.g., by imposing user fees and premiums in the health care system forbidden under the Canada Health Act). However, provincial governments are not freer to set their own priorities and pursue their policy objectives than when the federal spending power was greater. To continue with the health care example, provincial governments – or most of the people that elect them – do not want to see cuts in health care coverage or user fees or premiums. If they move in this direction, it is because they feel forced to implement such cuts in response to the fiscal consequences of the economic restructuring that has characterized the last twenty years.

National governments (acting collectively) set the international rules that determine the pace and direction of this restructuring process. To suggest that this process enhances provincial government power vis-a-vis the federal government – a reasonable working definition of "decentralization" – seems odd indeed. Reasoning by analogy, unemployed workers must also be freer and more powerful vis-a-vis the federal government when their unemployment benefits – which also have conditions attached (e.g., the obligation to look for work) – are cut or terminated.

Intensified Federal-Provincial Conflict

Under the regime created by the FCAS, the federal government will act as the domestic enforcer of an international system that reduces the scope and effectiveness of provincial policy instruments. At the same time, Ottawa will be seeking to cut its transfers to the provinces in order to cope with deficit problems that the FCAS exacerbate. Meanwhile, provincial and local governments will be experiencing an even more severe erosion of their tax bases owing to the same global market dynamics. In such a world, should we expect intergovernmental harmony or conflict?

Provincial governments will not support such a system because it enhances their power and resources – it does just the opposite. Public choice and "realist" analysts postulate that politicians and officials seek to maximize the power and resources of their states and departments, independent of the public will. Were this assumption essentially correct, we should expect extensive federal-provincial conflict, particularly from the most powerful provincial governments as they resist the federal policies that weaken them: the FCAS themselves, and the cuts in federal transfers that further undermine their fiscal capacity to sustain their programs.[28] The implausibility of public choice premises is illustrated by the case of Québec, considered in the next section, and more generally by neo-liberal governments throughout the world that did their best in the 1980s to reduce the economic powers of their states.

Developments of the 1980s suggest that government support for the diminution of state power depends on two factors: political ideology and economic results. Applied to Canadian federalism, some provincial governments have embraced neo-liberal economic dogmas and are thus ideologically predisposed to transfer many of their economic powers to the courts, expert panels, and private corporations. These governments particularly favour measures – such as the FCAS – that will help to impose neo-liberal policy prescriptions on future governments that might not share their ideological commitments. Other things being equal, these provincial governments will support the centralization of power in the federation, provided that it continues to advance their economic agenda.

Other things are not equal. Even neo-liberal governments must respond to the majority of their voting population in democratic political systems. Hence the importance of the economic results of the FCAS. If the economy booms and most citizens benefit from "trickle-down" effects, neo-liberal policy prescriptions will be vindicated. In that happy world, federal-provincial relations may resemble those of the era of "classical" federalism (1896-1929) more than any period before or since.[29] The two orders of government will do much less in the fields of industrial, regional and social policy. As a result, the extent of jurisdictional overlap and policy interdependence will decrease. This will reduce one important source of intergovernmental conflict. At the same time, *ex hypothesi*, the kind of economic crisis that generated federal-provincial conflict in the 1930s will not exist.

This scenario, while not impossible, seems most improbable. It is unlikely that all provincial governments will embrace neo-liberal premises for the foreseeable future. Indeed, the political pressure to reject this ideology appears to be building among the electorate in Canada (Robinson, 1994b). These pressures will be greater in some provinces than in others, and hence, some provincial governments will become champions of an alternative conception of economic and social organization before others. Their proximate target will be the federal government that enforces the neo-liberal regime through its trade, tax, and intergovernmental transfers policies. Nor is it likely, on the experience of the 1980s and early 1990s, that neo-liberalism will result in increased prosperity or economic security or leisure time for the majority of Canadians. Quite the contrary (Robinson, 1993a).

Consequently, the more likely prospect is federal-provincial relations more akin to Ottawa's battles with the Social Credit government of Alberta in the late 1930s and the CCF government of Saskatchewan in the early 1940s (Mallory, 1954, 1976; Simeon and Robinson, 1990: 59-116). Arguably, relations between the NDP governments of Ontario and British Columbia and the federal Tories that signed the FCAS were approaching this point before the Tories' near-destruction in the 1993 federal election. It is unclear whether Jean Chrétien's Liberals can establish a significantly different tone while implementing the FCA. Federal-provincial conflict escalated from the late 1980s not because Prime Minister Mulroney was an abrasive character or because he cared little about intergovernmental harmony. On the contrary, he put great stress on improving these relations, particularly in his first term (Simeon and Robinson, 1990: 301-03). Conflict intensified in spite of this because of the actual and anticipated consequences of his government's economic policies.[30]

To conclude, the FCAs seem likely to generate a form of federalism that is more centralized and more conflictual than any we have seen since the last great crisis of national and global capitalism – the Great Depression. We may dub this the era of "residual federalism" in recognition of the fact that what will remain of provincial jurisdiction and policy capacity in the context of neo-liberal globalization will be only that which is tolerated by hyper-mobile private investors, as (de)regulated by the federal government under the auspices of trade policy.

THE QUÉBEC PARADOX

Canadians have grown accustomed to the stalwart defence of provincial government power and jurisdiction by Québec governments, regardless of political stripe. If the arguments advanced in the previous section are valid, why did both the Liberal government of Québec and the Parti Québecois (PQ) opposition strongly support the FTA and NAFTA? Have these parties become less concerned with protecting provincial sovereignty than they once were? If so, why?

One response is that the analysis of the FCA's impact on provincial powers is exaggerated. A problem with this response is that the government of Ontario – not usually regarded as obsessive about provincial powers – takes a view of the FTA and NAFTA similar to the one outlined here (Ontario, 1993: 30-35). In its assessment of the FTA, tabled in the Ontario legislature in April, 1988, the Ontario Ministry of the Attorney General argued that:

> the Agreement will permanently alter the capacity [of provincial governments] to make economic and social policy in Canada, sometimes shifting it to the federal government, sometimes abandoning it for all governments. This dramatic change in the ability of governments to respond to the legitimate expectations of their populations amounts to a constitutional change.... In addition, the federal government will be obliged to assert interpretations of the Constitution that go beyond what the courts have allowed to fed-

eral authority in the past. Success in such assertions would change the formal division of powers as well. (Ontario, 1988: 4-5)

As to NAFTA, as already noted, the Ontario NDP government announced plans in the fall of 1993 to launch a constitutional challenge – in the form of a reference to the Ontario Court of Appeal – to a number of its (unspecified) provisions.

At the very least, then, there is room for disagreement on the FCAS' implications for provincial jurisdiction. It was once the case that where it seemed possible that Québec government powers might be significantly reduced by federal actions, Québec vigorously resisted such moves. This still appears to be the governing norm with respect to the federal spending power (notwithstanding Courchene's arguments that it is a spent force) and NAFTA side deals.

So the question can be restated: Why is the Québec government so risk averse when it comes to the possible impact on provincial jurisdiction of the federal spending power – witness the importance attached to this issue in the Meech Lake and Charlottetown Rounds – and yet so cavalier about the risks associated with the amendments to the economic constitution embodied in the FCAS? Three types of responses might be made: first, that the FCAS increase provincial autonomy; second, that they are inevitable – beyond the control of either order of government in Canada and therefore not worth fighting about; and third, that the FCA are what Québec voters want and the parties are merely responding to this demand.

Provincial Autonomy

There are two distinct versions of this argument, one advanced by the Liberal Party of Québec and the other by the PQ. The provincial Liberals, some have argued, wish to stand the PQ's "sovereignty-association" formula on its head. They hold that national sovereignty becomes irrelevant in a world governed by supranational agreements such as the FCAS. Seen in this light, Canadian federalism is less of a sacrifice of Québec's political sovereignty than it once was. The focus then shifts to enhancing the economic sovereignty of Québec businesses vis-a-vis federal bureaucrats.[31] The FCAS, it is argued, promote this latter objective by depriving the federal government of many of its economic powers.

The Liberal argument does not address the central contention of this chapter – that the FCAS constrain provincial economic powers more than federal economic powers. It thus makes sense only if it is assumed that Québec businesses (and Quebecers as a whole) are better off with greater freedom from the regulations (and support) of both orders of government – the central claim of neo-liberals.

The PQ argument is that the less Québec relies on the Canadian market, the less scope there will be for economic retaliation by Canada outside Québec should the majority of the people of Québec vote for political independence. Fear of such retaliation appears to be a major obstacle to public support for Québec independence. So, it is argued, the FCAS promote the cause of sovereignty by reducing the risks associated with such retaliation.

The premise here is that the FCAS will improve access to the American market for internationally competitive Québec firms. The problem is that the FTA and NAFTA are quite marginal as devices for securing access to the U.S. market (Clark, 1993). U.S. tariffs were not high in most sectors to begin with. Where they were (as in the clothing and apparel sectors), American industry protected itself in NAFTA through manipulations of the rules of origin.

The real problem with access to the U.S. market in the 1980s was expanded American use of duties to countervail the alleged subsidies and dumping practices of its trade partners, including Canada (Destler, 1992). Canada failed to secure a subsidies and countervailing duties code in either agreement, despite the fact that Prime Minister Mulroney claimed that this was his government's principal objective in pursuing the FTA (Doern and Tomlin, 1991). Canada did get a right to challenge U.S. administration of its own laws in these areas, but Congress can change those laws at will (Sinclair, 1993). The Uruguay WTO looks better on this score, at least on paper, because it has stronger subsidies and anti-dumping codes than the Tokyo GATT. Still, this does not explain the strong support of Québec's two major provincial political parties for the FTA or NAFTA.

Perhaps the best indicator that the pursuit of an independent Québec does not clearly or directly lead to support for the FTA or NAFTA is the fact that no important element of the Québec labour movement – still the core of the sovereignist movement at the grassroots level – supported either agreement. They did not support them because they would render Québec less capable of pursuing the kind of economic and social policies that the Québec labour movement has long argued sovereignty will help to realize. That the PQ took a pro-FTA and pro-NAFTA line, in spite of the rejection of these agreements by the entire Québec labour movement, is testimony to the minimal influence this labour movement has on the economic policy platform of a PQ led by their old friend from 1983, Jacques Parizeau.

Economic Necessity

Even marginal gains in access to the U.S. market may be better than nothing, but they need to be weighed against what was given up in order to achieve them. The answer, this chapter has suggested, is a great deal of provincial government power. The loss of this power might be judged a mere formality if global market forces meant that Québec's citizens no longer have a real choice about what kinds of economic and social policies they would like. This is the argument from economic necessity. It was articulated with greater clarity and candour than usual by Reed Scowen, Québec's delegate-general to New York, in a 1993 speech to the Canadian Club of Montreal. Proclaimed Scowen (1993):

> From now on, when we examine such fundamental social issues as the benefits and costs of our educational system, workmens' compensation, our health care system, and our tax structure, we had better see that we are comparable with those in North Carolina, or accept the consequences in lost job opportunities for Québec workers. To put it bluntly, the logic of a single North American market is leading us to a major harmonization of provincial public policy in a whole range of areas which up to now were considered as the exclusive jurisdiction of our own "distinct society." Nothing will be sacred, not even our health-care program.

We are a long way from Premier Daniel Johnson when he laid out his rationale for Québec's constitutional agenda in 1966: "As a basis for its [Quebec's] nationhood, it wants to be master of its own decision-making in what concerns the human growth of its citizens – that is to say education, social security, and health in all their aspects ..." (cited in Balthazar, 1993: 12).

Setting aside questions of the relative moral and political appeal of the two visions, there are at least two basic problems with the economic necessity argument. First, it assumes that other countries will sign FCAS even if Canada does not and that it is better to be part of such an agreement than outside of it. But NAFTA was very nearly defeated in the U.S. Had President Bush been re-elected, or had the Liberal government of Canada lived up to its election promise to either substantially renegotiate or abrogate NAFTA, or had the Chiapas revolt in Mexico broken out two months earlier, the congressional balance might well have tipped against the agreement. Moreover, if the agreement is sufficiently bad, it may be best to remain outside of it, even if it is implemented by the other parties. Canada would still have the protections afforded by the GATT (Clark, 1993).

In any case, it is disingenuous to pull out all the political stops to push through the FCAS and then claim that the very continental market pressures that these policies intensify are inevitable. This is like campaigning to convince citizens to eliminate all forms of gun control and then telling them that they have no choice but to cut spending on schools and health care in order to increase spending on police and prisons. Too bad, but we live in an increasingly violent and dangerous world!

Québec Public Opinion

Between 1988 and 1993, the population of Québec has usually exhibited stronger support for the FTA and NAFTA than the populations of other regions of Canada. But the differences among regions − aside from Ontario's consistent and intense antipathy − were neither large nor stable. For example, in October, 1988, a month before the federal election in which the FTA figured as the central issue, 37 per cent of the Québec population supported the FTA, as opposed to 44 per cent in the Atlantic provinces, 27 per cent in Ontario, 39 per cent in the Prairies, and 32 per cent in British Columbia. In March, 1991, in the midst of NAFTA negotiations, Québec support for a NAFTA stood at 45 per cent, as opposed to 30 per cent in the Atlantic provinces, 26 per cent in Ontario, 36 per cent in the Prairies, and 46 per cent in British Columbia.[32]

More important for our purposes is the fact that within Québec, support for and opposition to the FTA and NAFTA were highly volatile while these agreements were being negotiated and debated. The same October, 1988, poll showed 37 per cent in favour and 31 per cent opposed to the FTA in Québec. A month later, another poll found that only 26 per cent of Quebecers favoured the deal, while 41 per cent opposed it. The March, 1991, poll suggested that 33 per cent of Quebecers opposed NAFTA, compared to the 45 per cent who favoured it. Under these conditions a poll-driven government would have found it difficult to know whether to support or oppose the FTA or NAFTA.

In any case, it is a mistake to treat public opinion on matters such as this as an independent variable driving political élites. To a considerable degree, the political parties – and the debates among them – shape public opinion (Jenson and Brodie, 1980). With both major provincial parties supporting the FCAS in Québec, that electorate was less exposed to anti-FCA arguments than its counterparts in other parts of the country. It is impossible to gauge the importance of this difference. It should not be exaggerated, given the existence of real debates among the federal parties operating in Québec and the vocal opposition to the deals emanating from Québec's "popular sector," including but by no means confined to its labour movement (Simard, 1991; Roy, 1992; Murray, 1992; Clarke, 1994).

Thus, it is difficult to argue convincingly that Québec governments and opposition parties were driven by Québec public opinion to support the FCAS. Nor does the pursuit of greater Québec autonomy from federal government economic policy or a politically sovereign Québec lead logically to support for the FTA or NAFTA. To get from either political objective to this policy prescription another premise must be added to the syllogism: one must be indifferent to the reduction of the Québec state's economic power, or more strongly, one must positively desire to see that power curtailed. Neo-liberal ideas supply the rationale for the stronger version of this additional premise. On this view, Québec's political élites supported the FCAS because they placed neo-liberal policy goals above traditional nationalist concerns when the two objectives came into direct conflict.

Perhaps the most telling evidence in favour of this interpretation is the way the Québec government responded to President Clinton's call for labour and environmental side deals to NAFTA. While sanguine about the constraints that NAFTA itself imposed on the provincial state, the Québec government strongly urged federal trade negotiators to fight Washington on the side deals, in spite of the fact that the side deals would do no more (and quite possibly much less) than hold national and subnational governments to their own laws and regulations, while much in NAFTA itself requires provincial governments to alter or forego policies they could otherwise pursue.[33]

The concern to preserve provincial jurisdiction *per se* cannot account for the striking difference in response to NAFTA and its side deals. What can? NAFTA erodes provincial jurisdiction in ways compatible with neo-liberal prescriptions. The side deals run counter to them by shoring up provincial government capacity to resist the kind of downward harmonization pressures that Scowen claims are inexorable and beyond political control. So the side deals had to be weakened as much as possible, while still leaving President Clinton with the fig leaf he needed to squeak the deal through Congress.

To conclude, that successive Québec governments support the FCAS should not be taken as evidence against the claim that the FCAS will substantially reduce provincial government powers. The élites of both major Québec parties routinely invoke the shibboleth of provincial rights when it is consistent with the economic agenda they now share. But when provincial rights conflict with this ideology, they are sacrificed on the altar of neo-liberalism. In effect, there was a second Quiet Revolution in the Québec of the 1980s, in which its political élites fought as vigorously to subordinate Québec state power to the global marketplace as the generation of the first Quiet Revolution had fought to protect and expand that power. More than any other single factor, the vigorous defence of Québec government rights has kept Canadian federalism on a more decentralized course than the federalism of our neighbour to the South. The implications of this second Quiet Revolution for the character of Canadian federalism are thus profound.

GLOBALIZATION AND CANADIAN FEDERALISM

Suppose that the FCAS were either abrogated or "tamed" by the addition of strong international social dimensions that would mitigate or eliminate many of the negative social and political consequences expected to flow from neo-liberal globalization. Would the resulting communitarian globalization be more compatible with the kind of Canadian federalism that emerged in the post-war period? Or do all plausible forms of globalization lead to what was earlier dubbed residual federalism? The answer depends in part on whether we adopt a formal or a pragmatic viewpoint.

In principle, federalism is a system of divided sovereignty in which the powers assigned exclusively to each order of government cannot be unilaterally altered by either order of government. The new federalism violates this requirement under either scenario, because both entail the unilateral imposition of (very different kinds of) obligations on provincial governments by the federal government through the medium of trade and other international agreements. Provincial governments may respond by demanding a more substantial and institutionalized role in formulating federal negotiating positions and responses to treaty-based challenges, as have the *Länder* in Germany (Hrbek, 1991). While this may be the best available response to their concerns, it is likely to further blur traditional notions of exclusive federal and provincial jurisdictions. Moreover, the federal government is bound to maintain its leadership role, even if it ceases to act as unilaterally as was the case with the FCAS.

Considered pragmatically, however, the two forms of globalization have very different implications for what we might call the spirit of Canadian federalism. By "spirit" is meant the substantive constitutional objective behind the federal principle. This ideal may be crudely put as follows: to permit territorially concentrated subnational political communities to define their own priorities and policies in economic and cultural matters of vital interest to their flourishing as communities, insofar as this is consistent with the flourishing of the national political community.

Neo-liberal globalization, because it intensifies market constraints on all governments, but especially subnational ones, makes it more and more difficult for provincial governments to make effective use of their powers, even where these are not restricted by new federally enforced international legal obligations. The international social dimension that is the institutional heart of communitarian globalization will also entail new restrictions on traditional provincial jurisdiction. However, a strong international social dimension should reduce global market constraints on provincial policy options by controlling social dumping and conditioning capital mobility in various ways that reduce TNCs' political leverage (Robinson, 1993b: Section D).

Consequently, communitarian globalization is more consistent with the spirit of Canadian federalism. This conclusion is reinforced if there are few cases in which provincial governments have to modify existing regulations to comply with minimum international labour and environmental standards and basic worker rights. This seems likely, as regards labour rights, in most Canadian provinces, though Newfoundland may soon become an exception here.[34] It is less clear whether Canadian environmental standards and practices would pass international muster for countries with similar levels of per capita GDP.[35]

Paradoxically, then, the intrusions into both federal and provincial government sovereignty associated with an enforceable international social dimension are likely to increase the capacity of federal and provincial governments to make effective use of their constitutional powers. Put another way, while state sovereignty would be reduced for the life of the international agreements, popular sovereignty would be increased, since governments would once again be better able to realize the policy outcomes desired by most of the electorate.[36]

CONCLUSIONS

The Supreme Court of Canada may never reinterpret the constitution to give the federal government of Canada formal economic powers parallel to those possessed by its American counterpart. But if Ottawa is able to increase substantially the market constraints on how provincial governments may use their constitutional powers, and to threaten or entice most provincial governments into complying with the many legal restrictions set out in the FCAS, it will have achieved a similar result by less direct and formal means. In that case, Canada will move a large step toward the residual federalism that has prevailed in the United States since 1937.

It is worth remembering that the first great expansion of central government power in Canada after World War II was also achieved by informal means – the expanded use of the federal spending power. No constitutional amendment or Supreme Court decision caused or sanctioned this expansion of *de facto* federal power. Instead, it was driven by a shift in the balance of economic and political power in Canada associated with the dramatic expansion of the labour movement. This shift was reflected in and reinforced by a new Keynesian conception of the appropriate economic role of the state and by the conviction that only the federal government could effectively play that role (Simeon and Robinson, 1990: 59-211).

The 1980s witnessed parallel, if antithetical, changes in the balance of societal forces and the prevailing ideology regarding the appropriate economic role of the state. These changes have undoubtedly weakened the federal spending power, but they were made possible by – and have helped to greatly expand – what we might call the *de facto* federal treaty power. Even if rising unemployment and income polarization produce a political realignment that shifts us toward a more communitarian version of globalization, this new form of central government power will remain a key component of Canadian federalism in the era of globalization.

It therefore appears that Canadian federalism will gradually but inexorably be centralized in this important respect no matter which form of globalization prevails. Nonetheless, the form of globalization that prevails will profoundly affect the degree to which the new *de facto* constitutional order is consistent with the spirit of federalism. In this light, there is no little irony in the fact that the government of Québec is today in the forefront of support for FCAS that effectively violate the spirit of Canadian federalism.

NOTES

I The terms "neo-liberal and "neo-conservative" are often used interchangeably, but the former term refers to a type of economic policy, while the latter refers to the political elites espousing it. Economic policies in favour of privatizing public enterprises, deregulating markets, abandoning efforts to use macro-economic instruments to maintain low levels of unemployment, weakening organized labour, and severely cutting the welfare state are "neo-liberal" because their theoretical underpinnings are to be found in the economic theories of nineteenth-century British liberalism. Discredited by the economic disaster of the Great Depression and its political repercussions, these ideas were revived by economists and philosophers such as Milton Friedman and Friedrich Hayek. Conservative political elites had traditionally opposed the kind of untrammelled free markets espoused by the classical liberals. But a new generation of conservative elites – led by Thatcher in the U.K., Reagan in the U.S., and Mulroney in Canada – rejected the essentially Burkean ideas of their precursors in favour of the neo-liberalism of Friedman, Hayek, and others. This new right was thus called "neo-conservative" to distinguish it from earlier forms of conservatism that had rejected liberal economic assumptions and ideals.

2 Readers wishing more details on the provisions of the FTA and NAFTA relevant to provincial jurisdiction will find them in Robinson (1993a).

3 For a brief history of the evolution of the GATT negotiations, see Winham (1992).

4 The "national treatment" principle requires that governments treat the goods (and under the FCAs, services and investments) of foreign businesses no less favourably than they treat the goods, services, or investments of nationally owned or controlled businesses.

5 The subsidies code contained a "commitment" by the parties not to employ export subsidies (except for certain primary products). But it did not define

an "export subsidy" or distinguish countervailable from acceptable subsidies, leaving this judgment to national governments. The code's principal impact was on countervailing duties. National governments wishing to impose such a duty had to hold prior consultations and demonstrate that some of their producers had suffered material injury. The scale of any duty levied was to be commensurate with the scale of the subsidy it was supposed to neutralize. Provincial governments provide subsidies, but they do not levy countervailing duties, so the code did not restrict them in this respect.

6   See Anonymous (1988) and Brown (1993:115) for additional analysis and references.

7   NAFTA's investment chapter is the only one that American negotiators sought to protect with a clause guaranteeing that its provisions would continue to apply for a full decade after abrogation, should any party exercise its right to abrogate the agreement. This provision was cut in the final round of negotiations and does not appear in the final text, but it indicates the unique importance attached to investment by American negotiators. For an examination of the rules governing foreign investment in Canada, the United States, and Mexico and analysis of why provisions such as those forbidden by the FCAS are important, see Jenkins (1992).

8   Article 2021 of NAFTA makes it clear that mere citizens will have no such standing in their courts to enforce NAFTA provisions.

9   "Technical standards" encompass most forms of government regulation, including environmental, agricultural, consumer protection, and occupational health and safety laws and regulations. All of these areas fall partially or primarily under exclusive provincial jurisdiction.

10   The Uruguay GATT created the World Trade Organization to interpret and administer its provisions, and the agreement is sometimes referred to as the WTO. This chapter will use the two terms interchangeably.

11   The Dunkel draft was the penultimate draft of the Uruguay GATT, brokered by the GATT's chairman of the time, Arthur Dunkel. It served as the basis from which the final round of bargaining, officially concluded in December, 1993, began.

12   Article 9 of the Agreement on Subsidies and Countervailing Measures.

13   Article 28 of the Agreement on Subsidies and Countervailing Measures.

14   This last exception, which presumably applies to provincial policies designed to facilitate the introduction of tougher environmental protections, is festooned with qualifiers. The assistance must be a one-time, non-recurring measure and limited to 20 per cent of the cost of adaptation, among other things.

15   A footnote to this clause in article 8.2(b) of the Agreement on Subsidies and

Countervailing Measures states only that "A 'general framework of regional development' means that regional subsidy programs are part of an internally consistent and generally applicable regional development policy and that regional development subsidies are not granted in isolated geographical points having no, or virtually no influence on the development of the region."

16   See Hogg (1985: 251-54) and Anonymous (1988:42 n,7).

17   The leading cases from this period are *NLRB v. Jones and Laughlin Steel* 301 U.S. 1(1937) and *U.S. v. Darby* 312 U.S. 100 (1941). For a succinct discussion of these cases and subsequent developments that further extended the scope of the commerce clause, see Kincaid (1993). For more details, see Gunther (1985: 157-76).

18   The JCPC, lodged in the British House of Lords, was the highest court of appeal in Canada until 1949.

19   See Hogg (1985: ch. 17, 19, and 20), Whyte (1991).

20   In *Zellerbach*, the Supreme Court of Canada upheld federal legislation prohibiting the dumping of any substance at sea, even though the definition of "sea" included provincial internal waters, and some kinds of dumping might have no direct effect on an expressly conferred federal jurisdiction such as the fisheries. The Court upheld the federal law not on the ground that it was necessary to implement an international convention, but on the ground that it was necessary to realize an objective of "national concern" (Whyte, 1991). For the three conditions set out by the court, see Table Two.

21   In *General Motors v. City National Leasing*, all six of the Supreme Court of Canada judges participating in the decision upheld the federal Combines investigation Act on the ground that it fell within the scope of the federal trade and commerce power. In so doing, the Court affirmed the criteria developed by Dickson, J. (as he then was) in the *C.N. Transportation* case (Whyte, 1991). These criteria are outlined in Table Two.

22   For a discussion of what such a social dimension might look like in the North American case, see Office of Technology Assessment (1992), Robinson (1993b) and Stanford *et al* (1993); for a simple model of a global social dimension, see Robinson (1995).

23   Other things may not be equal. It is possible that the social and political costs of neo-liberal globalization will catalyze the further evolution of the alliance of social movements and progressive non-governmental organizations (NGOs represented in the Action Canada Network. Such an alliance could actually increase the political power of these groups over the medium to long term. See Robinson (1994a).

24   The author is not aware of anyone who has actually made the first argument, but it seems an obvious point. The second argument was popularized by

Courchene (1992). The third was suggested to me by Ron Watts in comments on an earlier draft of this paper.

25 For an account of the role of provincial governments in the Tokyo Round, see Brown (1993). No parallel analysis of the provincial role in NAFTA and the Uruguay GATT has yet been published. The conclusion that provincial participation – with the important but purely *ad hoc* and behind-the-scenes exception of the Quebec and Alberta governments – was weaker in NAFTA and the Uruguay GATT is based on the author's observations of the process while an employee of the Ontario government.

26 The EU's structural funds (not counting the Common Agricultural Policy) are not trivial. The Congressional Office of Technology Assessment (OTA) estimates that if Mexico received regional fund transfers according to the EU's pre-Maastricht formula, it would be eligible for U.S. $10 billion, or about 4 per cent of its GDP – roughly the amount that Mexico has been paying annually in debt service. The Maastricht Treaty promises to double the size of the structural funds between 1994 and 1997 (OTA, 1992: 52, n. 40).

27 A labour side-deal was attached to the NAFTA implementing legislation, a symbolic measure that went beyond anything in the FTA or the Uruguay GATT. Still, it seems unlikely that its provisions are strong enough to reduce social dumping pressures. For a detailed assessment, see Robinson (1993b).

28 Alan Cairns (1977, 1979) popularized the application of basic public choice ideas to the dynamics of "province-building" and intensifying federal-provincial conflict in the 1970s and early 1980s.

29 See Simeon and Robinson (1990) for a more extended discussion of the stages in the evolution of Canadian federalism.

30 This includes the sado-monetarism of the Bank of Canada. See Barber (1992).

31 The inverted sovereignty-association formulation is advanced by Fraser (1989: 354).

32 All poll figures in this and the next paragraph are from Survey Research Consultants International (various years).

33 The NAFTA side deals are analyzed in more detail from a federalist perspective in Robinson (1993a).

34 A June, 1994, Newfoundland White Paper proposes to deny the right to strike to workers in new businesses for a period, in most cases, of at least five years. Where an employer and a union are unable to arrive at a collective agreement, a government-appointed panel with binding arbitration powers would determine the content of the first contract, subject to the constraint that wage increases may not exceed "the percentage rise in the consumer price index as reported by Statistics Canada for that area" (Newfoundland,

1994: 7-9).

35   For an instructive comparison of environmental standards enforcement in
      the forestry industries of Canada and the United States, see Harrison (1993).
      She finds that, while Canadian standards look good on paper, compliance is
      considerably lower in Canada than in the United States.

36   This distinction between state and popular sovereignty is developed in more
      detail in Section III of Robinson (1995).

REFERENCES

Anonymous (1988). "Issues of Constitutional Jurisdiction," in Peter M. Leslie and
    Ronald L. Watts, eds., *Canada: The State of the Federation, 1987-88*. Kingston: In-
    stitute of Intergovernmental Relations: 39-55.

Balthazar, Louis (1993). "The Faces of Quebec Nationalism," in Alain-G. Gagnon,
    ed., *Québec: State and Society*. Scarborough: Nelson Canada: 2-17.

Barber, Clarence (1992) "Monetary and Fiscal Policy in the 1980s," in Robert C.
    Allen and Gideon Rosenbluth, eds., *False Promises: The Failure of Conservative
    Economics*. Vancouver: New Star Books: 101-20.

Brown, Douglas M. (1993). "The Evolving Role of the Provinces in Canada-U.S.
    Trade Relations," in Douglas M. Brown and Earl H. Fry, eds., *States and Prov-
    inces in the International Economy*. Berkeley, Cal.: Institute of Governmental
    Studies Press: 93-144.

Cairns, Alan (1977). "The Governments and Societies of Canadian Federalism,"
    Canadian Journal of Political Science, 10: 695-725.

Cairns, Alan (1979). "The Other Crisis in Canadian Federalism," *Canadian Public
    Administration*, 22: 175-95.

Cameron, David R. (1984). "Social Democracy, Corporatism, Labour Quiescence,
    and the Representation of Economic Interest in Advanced Capitalist Society,"
    in Goldthorpe, ed.(1984). *Order and Conflict in Contemporary Capitalism: Studies
    in the Political Economy of Western European Nations*. Oxford: Clarendon Press.:
    143-78.

Cameron, David R. (1986). "The Growth of Government Spending: The Cana-
    dian Experience in Comparative Perspective," in Keith Banting, ed., *State and
    Society: Canada in Comparative Perspective*. Toronto: University of Toronto Press:
    21-51.

Courchene, Thomas (1992). "Global Competitiveness and the Canadian Federa-
    tion," in Courchene, ed., *Rearrangements: The Courchene Papers*. Oakville, Ont.:
    Mosaic Press: 110-46.

Clark, Mel (1993). *Restoring the Balance: Why Canada Should Reject the North American Free Trade Agreement, Terminate the   and Return to   . Ottawa: Council of Canadians.

Clarke, Tony (1994). Interview in Ottawa (July 23).

Destler, I.M. (1992). American Trade Politics, Second Edition. Washington, D.C.: Institute for International Economics and the Twentieth Century Fund.

Doern, G. Bruce, and Brian W. Tomlin (1991). Faith and Fear: The Free Trade Story. Toronto: Stoddart.

Economist, *The* (1993). "Fortress Europe: Poor Men at the Gate," April 16: 60.

Fraser, Graham (1989). *Playing for Keeps: The Making of the Prime Minister, 1988.* Toronto: McClelland & Stewart.

Golden, Miriam (1993). "The Dynamics of Trade Unionism and National Economic Performance," American Political Science Review, 87, 2 (June): 439-54.

Green, Francis, Andrew Henley, and Euclid Tsakalotos (1992). Income Inequality in Corporatist and Liberal Economies: A Comparison of Trends within OECD Countries. Working Paper 92/13. Leicester: Centre for Labour Market Studies, University of Leicester.

Gunther, Gunther (1985). *Constitutional Law*, Eleventh Edition. Mineola, N.Y.: The Foundation Press.

Harrison, Kathryn (1993). "Is Cooperation the Answer: A Comparison of Canadian and U.S. Enforcement of Environmental Regulations," paper presented to the annual meeting of the American Political Science Association, Washington, D.C..

Helleiner, Eric (1994). *States and the Resurgence of Global Finance.* Ithaca, N.Y.: Cornell University Press.

Hogg, Peter W. (1985). *The Constitutional Law of Canada*, Second Edition. Toronto: Carswell.

Hrbek, Rudolf (1991). "German Federalism and the Challenge of European Integration," in Charlie Jeffrey and Peter Savigear, eds., *German Federalism Today*. Leicester and London: University of Leicester Press: 84-102.

Jenkins, Barbara (1992). *The Paradox of Continental Production: National Investment Policies in North America.* Ithaca, N.Y.: Cornell University Press.

Jenson, Jane, and M. Janine Brodie (1980). *Crisis, Challenge and Change: Party and Class in Canada.* Toronto: Methuen.

Keohane, Robert (1984). "The World Political Economy and the Crisis of Embedded Liberalism," in Goldthorpe, ed.: 15-38.

Kincaid, John (1993). "Constitutional Federalism: Labor's Role in Displacing Place to Benefit Persons," *Political Science and Politics*, 26, 2 (June): 172-77.

Lindblom, C.E. (1984). "The Market as Prison," in Thomas Ferguson and Joel Rogers, eds., *The Political Economy: Readings in the Politics and Economics of American Public Policy.* Armonk, N.Y.: M.E. Sharpe: 3-11.

Mallory, James (1954, 1976). *Social Credit and the Federal Power in Canada.* Toronto: University of Toronto Press.

Macdonald Commission (Royal Commission on the Economic Union and Development Prospects for Canada) (1985). *Final Report.* Parts I and V. Ottawa: Supply and Services.

Murray, Gregor (1992). "Union Culture and Organizational Change in Ontario and Québec," in Colin Leys and Marguerite Mendell, eds., *Culture and Social Change: Social Movements in Québec and Ontario.* Montreal: Black Rose Books: 39-61.

Newfoundland (1994). *Attracting New Business Investment: A White Paper on Proposed New Legislation to Promote Economic Diversification and Growth Enterprises in the Province.*

Office of Technology Assessment (OTA) (1992). *U.S.-Mexico Free Trade: Pulling Together or Pulling Apart?* Washington, D.C.: U.S. Government Printing Office.

Ontario Attorney General. (1988). *The Constitutional Impact of the Free Trade Agreement.*

Ontario (1993). *Final Report of the Cabinet Committee on the North American Free Trade Agreement.*

Peterson, Paul E. (1981). *City Limits.* Chicago: University of Chicago Press.

Polanyi, Karl (1944, 1957). *The Great Transformation: The Political and Economic Origins of Our Time.* Boston: Beacon Press.

Robinson, Ian (1993a). "The NAFTA, the Side-Deals, and Canadian Federalism: Constitutional Reform by Other Means?" in Douglas Brown and Ron Watts, eds., *The State of the Federation,* 1993. Kingston: Institute for Intergovernmental Relations: 193-227.

Robinson, Ian (1993b). *North American Trade As If Democracy Mattered: What's Wrong with NAFTA and What are the Alternatives?* Ottawa and Washington: Canadian Centre for Policy Alternatives and International Labor Rights and Education and Research Fund.

Robinson, Ian (1994a). "NAFTA, Social Unionism, and Labour Movement Power," *Relations industrielles/Industrial Relations* (Fall).

Robinson, Ian (1994b). "The Canadian Labour Movement Against 'Free Trade': An Assessment of Strategies and Outcomes," paper presented to the Conference on Labor, Free Trade and Economic Integration in the Americas, National Labor Union Responses to a Transnational World, Durham, N.C., August 25-28.

Roy, Marianne (1992). "Solidarity in Quebec: SPQ's Roots." *Action Canada Network Dossier Special: Inside Coalition Politics*, 37 (May-June): 4.

Scowen, Reed (1993). "We Are All Americans Now: Free Trade Deal Has Created a Single Market," *Montreal Gazette*. February 2: B3.

Simeon, Richard, and Ian Robinson (1990). *State, Society and the Development of Canadian Federalism*. Toronto: University of Toronto Press.

Simard, Monique (1991). "Whose Interests Does Free Trade Serve?" *The Pro-Canada Dossier: Inside Fortress America*, 29 (January-February): 7.

Sinclair, Scott (1993). "NAFTA and U.S. Trade Policy: Implications for Canada and Mexico," in Ricardo Grinspun and Maxwell A. Cameron, eds., *The Political Economy of North American Free Trade*. Montreal and Kingston: McGill-Queen's University Press: 219-33.

Stanford, Jim, Christine Elwell, and Scott Sinclair (1993). *Social Dumping Under North American Free Trade*. Ottawa: Canadian Centre for Policy Alternatives.

Stephens, John D. (1986). *The Transition from Capitalism to Socialism*. Chicago: University of Illinois Press.

Survey Research Consultants International (Various years). *Index to International Public Opinion*. Westport, Conn.: Greenwood Press.

Whyte, John D. (1991). "The Impact of Internationalization on the Constitutional Setting," *Think Globally: Proceedings of the 42nd Annual Conference*. Toronto: Institute of Public Administration of Canada.

Winham, Gilbert. (1992). *The Evolution of International Trade Agreements*. Toronto: University of Toronto Press.

CHAPTER ELEVEN

Fiscal Federalism: The Politics of Intergovernmental Transfers

Gérald Bernier and David Irwin[1]

THIS CHAPTER DEALS WITH INTERGOVERNMENTAL TRANSFERS. First, the origins of the current system of intergovernmental transfers in Canada will be described. Second, differences and similarities between the three main intergovernmental transfer programs – equalization, Established Programs Financing (EPF), and the Canada Assistance Plan (CAP) – will be discussed. Third, the relevance of using specific criteria to compare the effects of intergovernmental transfers will be highlighted. Finally, in order to assess the extent to which some provinces depend on federal resources more than others, a ratio of their degree of financial dependence on transfers will be proposed.

HISTORICAL BACKGROUND

The federal system of transfers to the provinces can be seen as a consequence of the sharing of legislative powers provided for in the 1867 British North America Act (by virtue of which each level of government, in principle, has exclusive jurisdiction in certain fields), as a means to compensate for economic inequality between provinces, as well as a manifestation of the spending power of the federal government. Three categories of beneficiaries can be identified within the transfer system: individuals, enterprises, and provincial governments.

In 1867, the federal government committed itself to make statutory payments to the provinces of the new federation.[2] This mechanism of vertical redistribution of resources has expanded constantly since Confederation,[3] to the extent that, in 1991, federal transfers to individuals, enterprises, and other levels of government represented more than 55 per cent of federal program expenditures.

The federal transfer system attempts to promote two distinct objectives. The first is to meet the needs of individuals directly through programs such as unemployment insurance (1940) and family allowances (1945). The second, which will be dealt with in more detail, relates to transfers to provincial governments. The objective is to mitigate the impact of regional economic disparity by ensuring a relative interprovincial equality in terms of the provinces' financial ability to meet the needs of citizens.

The first attempts at implementing a social security system to meet individual needs go back to the thirties (Armitage, 1988). As early as 1920, federal programs to compensate World War One veterans were created. In 1927, the federal Parliament passed the Old Age Pension Bill. During the Great Depression, the number of unemployed rose drastically so that local private aid organizations and municipalities could no longer meet growing needs. In this context, intervention by provincial governments was desirable, even necessary. However, they could not all equally afford it. Federal intervention was required, although this initiative did create some tensions (Reesor, 1992). For example, a 1935 federal law to implement an unemployment insurance system was declared *ultra vires* in 1937 after a legal challenge from Ontario.[4]

Following the publication of the Rowell-Sirois Commission report in 1940, relations between the two levels of government changed markedly. Although its recommendations were not all adopted, it inspired the equalization principle as well as the unemployment insurance and universal old age pension programs, which gave rise to constitutional amendments.

In 1947, Saskatchewan took the uncommon initiative of implementing a public insurance system covering hospitalization fees. Following a federal law, similar programs were introduced in other provinces in the late fifties. The central government agreed to meet 50 per cent of the cost of these programs in all provinces. Federal government expenditures in fields of provincial jurisdiction set a precedent that was to be followed with the implementation of national programs in selected spheres: post-secondary education (1977), health (1977), and public assistance (1966). Federal initiatives in these fields were justified by the reports and recommendations of various committees of the House and Senate or royal commissions: Heagerty (1942), Marsh (1943), Green (1945), and Hall (1961).

Conflicts arising from this federal activism forced federal and provincial governments to re-examine the power-sharing and revenue-sharing system, with debate centred on the issue of the provinces' fiscal capacity. In fact, their revenue did not allow them to meet their constitutional obligations. Thus, a shift occurred from a classical federalism framework with clearly identified constitutional jurisdictions to an era of compromise federalism dictated by the requirements of redistribution that resulted from the disparities in the fiscal capacities of provincial governments. The implementation of federal programs came within this framework. The election of the Liberal government led by Pierre Elliott Trudeau in 1968 not only consolidated the transfer system to individuals and provinces but also institutionalized a system of intergovernmental relations based on Parliament's spending power.

INTERGOVERNMENTAL TRANSFERS

Payments made by the federal government to the provinces in accordance with intergovernmental transfer programs are of two kinds: cash and tax room (Canadian Tax Foundation, 1991: ch. 15). In addition, transfers can be accompanied with conditions or granted unconditionally.

Equalization

Since they consist of unconditional grants, fiscal equalization payments, implemented in their current form in 1957, can be seen as a guaranteed income supplement for poorer provincial governments. Through this redistribution mechanism, these provinces receive payments with no federal control on their use. Entrenched in the 1982 Constitution Act, the equalization principle, by giving provincial legislatures access to sufficient income, enables them to provide public services of comparable quality at a relatively similar tax rate (Stevenson, 1990: 384). If the principle stated in section 36(2) of the Constitution Act has its political justification in the equal rights of all citizens regardless of their place of residence, it is not necessarily justified in economic terms (Leslie, 1988). In fact, fiscal equalization increases the resources of beneficiary governments without increasing their citizens' fiscal effort. Equalization payments[5] to the have-not provinces totalled $8.1 billion in 1990, compared to $5.4 billion in 1984 and $2.6 billion in 1978. By its very nature, equalization generates enormous interprovincial differences in redistributed funds.

Differences in the amounts received, as shown in Table One, indicate

TABLE ONE: EQUALIZATION TRANSFERS, 1978-1990 ($ PER CAPITA)

	1978	1980	1982	1984	1986	1988	1990
NFLD	562	664	837	1,002	1,226	1,510	1,687
P.E.I.	553	715	967	1,032	1,135	1,333	1,571
N.S.	442	531	675	718	741	907	1,051
N. B.	448	545	700	766	895	1,100	1,268
QUE.	221	269	431	474	432	494	566
ONT.	0	0	0	0	0	0	0
MAN.	213	335	425	455	419	664	800
SASK.	20	42	0	0	167	342	436
ALTA.	0	0	0	0	0	0	0
B.C.	0	0	0	0	0	0	0
YUKON	0	0	0	0	0	0	0
N.W.T.	0	0	0	0	0	0	0

Source: Canada, Federal-Provincial Relations Office, *Federal-Provincial Programs and Activities, 1979-1991* (Ottawa, 1991).

TABLE TWO: PROVINCIAL AND TERRITORIAL GOVERNMENT
IN-PROVINCE REVENUE, 1978-1988 ($ PER CAPITA)

	1978	1980	1982	1984	1986	1988
NFLD	1,049	1,261	1,501	1,873	2,191	2,576
P.E.I.	860	1,148	1,454	1,918	2,062	2,607
N.S.	903	1,142	1,396	1,779	2,164	2,567
N.B.	997	1,251	1,522	2,020	2,421	2,941
QUE.	1,522	1,899	2,537	2,897	3,434	4,207
ONT.	1,235	1,537	1,920	2,421	2,942	3,639
MAN.	967	1,240	1,696	2,210	2,648	3,755
SASK.	1,694	2,281	2,431	3,084	2,724	3,689
ALTA.	2,960	3,884	4,650	5,413	4,155	4,615
B.C.	1,628	1,969	2,509	2,795	3,004	3,609
YUKON	844	1,928	2,134	2,078	2,851	2,817
N.W.T.	986	1,365	1,667	2,335	2,165	2,395

Source: Statistics Canada, Provincial Economic Accounts, *Annual Estimates* (Ottawa, March 1990).

TABLE THREE: TOTAL PROVINCIAL AND TERRITORIAL INCOME PER
CAPITA, 1978-1988

	1978	1980	1982	1984	1986	1988
NFLD	2,078	2,456	3,001	3,461	4,140	4,836
P.E.I.	2,041	2,573	3,162	3,853	3,886	4,739
N.S.	1,735	2,150	2,584	3,136	3,487	4,198
N.B.	1,883	2,268	2,825	3,443	3,992	4,795
QUE.	2,053	2,506	3,369	3,879	4,357	5,208
ONT.	1,523	1,874	2,254	2,897	3,448	4,191
MAN.	1,560	2,038	2,653	3,257	3,664	5,188
SASK.	2,128	2,781	3,043	3,781	3,523	4,756
ALTA.	3,286	4,206	5,149	6,024	4,829	5,425
B.C.	1,945	2,348	2,942	3,382	3,668	4,326
YUKON	3,200	5,247	5,565	7,835	12,298	13,135
N.W.T.	5,573	7,830	8,059	10,798	14,943	19,904

Source: Statistics Canada, *Provincial Economic Accounts* (Ottawa, March, 1990).

TABLE FOUR: PROVINCIAL GROSS NATIONAL PRODUCT, 1986-1990
($ PER CAPITA)

	1986	1987	1988	1989	1990
NFLD	11,940	12,998	13,986	14,844	15,335
P.E.I.	11,795	12,512	13,806	14,592	15,198
N.S.	14,927	15,897	17,083	18,096	19,013
N.B.	14,196	15,281	16,478	17,613	18,414
QUE.	17,965	19,682	21,372	22,343	22,764
ONT.	22,244	24,162	26,758	28,380	28,419
MAN.	17,200	18,065	19,898	21,141	21,770
SASK.	16,984	16,951	17,937	19,321	20,335
ALTA	24,133	25,048	26,056	27,058	28,534
B.C.	19,848	21,496	23,327	25,237	25,760

Sources: Statistics Canada, *Provincial Economic Accounts*, (Ottawa, March, 1990); *Postcensus Annual Estimates of Population*.

significant disparities in the ability of each province to generate comparable autonomous revenue on a per capita basis (see Table Two). At first glance, equalization seems to bear comparison with an interfinancing system between provinces. However, as Boadway (1986) noted, fiscal equalization that benefits some provinces is not translated into a corresponding increase in tax effort for citizens of richer provinces.

Clearly, fiscal equalization does not constitute an interfinancing system; it tends, moreover, to embody an imperfect form of vertical redistribution (Boadway and Flatters, 1991). As the average income from the sources used to calculate equalization rights does not include all provinces but only those so-called representative, total equalization rights paid to poorer provinces do not allow them to meet the Canadian average with respect to fiscal capacity (see Table Three).

Equalization guarantees that citizens from all provinces have access to relatively comparable public services at a relatively similar taxation rate. However, this redistribution mechanism is likely to perpetuate an institutionalized form of provincial financial dependence on the federal government. Thus, despite the implementation of such a system and of other programs designed to guarantee some economic equality between provincial administrations, permanent regional economic disparities persist (see Table Four).[6]

Established Programs Financing

Established Programs Financing, implemented by the federal government in 1977, is an umbrella program through which the central government participates in the financing of provincial health services and post-secondary education.[7] In creating EPF, which derived from the consolidation of cost-sharing programs created during the 1950s and 1960s, the federal government had two objectives. On one hand, it intended to limit the growth of its financial obligations in cost-sharing programs since, under this method of sharing costs, federal contributions were determined by provincial expenditures. On the other hand, the consolidation was designed to ease federal constraints and standards dictated by cost-sharing programs through a system comparable to the American block grants (Aronson and Hilley, 1986) by which the American federal government transfers resources to states and communities to allow them to finance projects in specific fields. The main characteristic of EPF is that funds are transferred to provinces on a uniform, per capita basis. Transfers are made through cash payments as well as tax room granted to provincial administrations in the form of tax points.

At the time of EPF implementation in 1977, federal financial contributions to post-secondary education and health care were intended to grow at the same rate as the gross national product (GNP). However, from 1984 on, the federal government unilaterally undertook to limit the growth of its contribution. In addition, the 1984 Canada Health Act imposed restrictions on overbilling and on other measures that had been considered by provincial administrations to reduce health expenditures.

Bill C-96 adopted by the House of Commons in 1986 held that the growth of federal contributions to EPF would be capped at the GNP growth rate minus 2 per cent starting in 1986-87. In 1989, the Minister of Finance stated that federal contributions would be decreased by another percentage point. Finally, a two-year freeze on EPF payments at their 1989-1990

TABLE FIVE: ESTABLISHED PROGRAMS FINANCING TRANSFERS, 1978–1990
($ MILLIONS)

	1978	1980	1982	1984	1986	1988	1990
NFLD.	191.0	228.4	286.2	333.8	374.6	410.3	434.6
P.E.I.	40.4	49.6	61.8	73.0	83.5	92.7	98.8
N.S.	286.7	341.2	428.7	504.1	575.5	636.1	677.8
N.B.	233.8	280.8	351.8	412.9	468.2	544.1	548.4
QUE.	2,222.0	2,578.6	3,261.6	3,786.2	4,310.5	4,789.9	5,130.7
ONT.	2,924.4	3,460.3	4,387.2	5,191.6	6,006.4	6,802.5	7,385.1
MAN.	353.8	413.8	520.7	615.4	706.0	781.9	827.4
SASK.	321.6	387.4	492.8	583.5	655.8	731.0	757.6
ALTA.	676.5	944.3	1,167.0	1,363.9	1,565.5	1,722.9	1,873.4
B.C.	853.4	1,090.6	1,404.9	1,560.8	1,904.2	2,149.6	2,369.9
N.W.T.	15.1	18.0	23.8	29.2	34.4	37.7	40.8
YUKON	7.8	9.9	11.9	13.5	15.5	18.2	19.8
TOTAL	8,126.5	9,802.9	12,398.4	14,467.9	16,700.1	18,716.9	20,164.3

*Including cash transfers for the purpose of this program and 5.0 federal income tax points in accordance with non-participation agreements.

Source: Canada, Finance, Direction of federal-provincial relations and social policy, *Special Compilation*, June 5, 1992.

level was announced in the federal Finance Minister's budget speech in February, 1990.

The federal government's unilateral decision to reduce its EPF expenditures was expressed in restrictions on the growth of these transfers. Furthermore, standards and rules relating to these programs were not relaxed to allow provinces to deal with the adverse effects of the EPF freeze. Until now, the Canada Health Act remains untouched, preventing provinces from compensating for loss of income through different forms of patient contribution (see chapter 13).

Despite restrictions made to the program, EPF funds collected by the provinces grew from $9.8 billion in 1980-81 to $20.8 billion in 1992-93 (see Table Five).[8] In Québec, for instance, restrictions on the growth of federal EPF expenditures resulted in decreased federal contributions to health and post-secondary education. In 1977-78, the federal share of these programs in Québec represented 47.9 per cent of total expenditures; it dropped to 40.7 per cent in 1990-91 (Québec, 1991: annexe E).

Canada Assistance Plan

The Canada Assistance Plan, created in 1966, is the only remaining cost-sharing program in social services.[9] Through the CAP, the federal government pays back to the provinces 50 per cent of eligible expenditures. The following expenditures are recognized:

1. welfare payments to individuals in need;

2. social services to individuals in need or to individuals likely to be in need in the absence of such services;

3. training projects authorized by Health and Welfare Canada. (Canada, 1991: 26, 13)

Unlike EPF, CAP transfers are not determined on a per capita basis; they are proportional to provincial expenditures on social assistance. And since richer provinces can choose to spend more than poorer provinces in this sphere of activity, the federal government decided unilaterally, in 1991, to cap the growth of its annual contribution at 5 per cent for Alberta, British Columbia, and Ontario.[10] This decision resulted in the federal government acknowledging two categories of provinces for CAP purposes: the haves and the have-nots. It is believed that the federal government at-tempted to decrease its budgetary deficit by limiting its contributions to richer provinces (Mimoto and Cross, 1991: 3.1-3.17).

THE EFFECTS OF INTERGOVERNMENTAL TRANSFERS

In comparative analysis, both differences and similarities are examined ac-cording to explicitly stated criteria. When comparing, an identical basis of analysis is required. The interpretation of differences and similarities must be based on a thorough understanding of the transfer programs. In a com-parison of the economic impact of intergovernmental transfers, the three types of transfers must be considered separately, especially since they do not have the same objectives. The following comparison of the three transfer programs described previously will be based on two criteria: eq-uity and need.

The *equity criterion* determines to what extent transfer funds are more or less similar on a per capita basis. A transfer program that fails to meet this

TABLE SIX: ESTABLISHED PROGRAMS FINANCING TRANSFERS, ($ PER CAPITA)

	1978	1980	1982	1984	1986	1988	1990
NFLD.	340	404	506	584	660	721	758
P.E.I.	334	403	507	584	657	719	754
N.S.	342	404	504	583	659	721	757
N.B.	340	404	505	583	659	762	760
QUE.	353	404	505	583	659	721	758
ONT.	346	404	504	583	659	721	757
MAN.	343	404	504	583	659	721	760
SASK.	341	404	504	583	649	721	760
ALTA.	341	441	504	583	659	721	758
B.C.	336	409	504	548	659	721	756
N.W.T.	343	400	506	584	662	725	756
YUKON	339	450	496	587	646	728	762

Source: Canada, Finance, Direction of federal-provincial relations and social policy, *Special Compilation*, June 5, 1992.

criterion would challenge the complementary and compensatory function of the intergovernmental transfer system in Canada. The *need criterion* determines to what extent the transfer system cuts purposely against the equity criterion to compensate for differences in the fiscal capacity of provincial administrations. Of all three intergovernmental transfer programs, only EPF meets the equity criterion requirements. Payments made to the provinces are basically identical on a per capita basis. However, EPF does not meet the specific needs of some provinces with less fiscal capacity (see Table Six).

The equity criterion, when applied to equalization payments, shows significant per capita variations in funds collected by the provinces (see Table One). In this case, the need criterion prevails. Thus, the equalization program runs completely counter to the equity criterion since its explicit purpose is to remedy disparities in fiscal capacity among provincial governments. This could in no way be accomplished through equal transfers – on a per capita basis – to the provinces. As shown in Table One, on a per capita basis, the Atlantic provinces received more funds than other provinces under this program. Comparison between equalization payments collected by Québec and Ontario shows an imbalance in favour of Québec simply because, under the method used to calculate equalization entitlements,[11] Ontario has never received such payments. Québec collects the largest amount in equalization payments and ranks first in percentage terms (Table Seven). However, when these figures are compared on an identical basis, i.e., on a per capita basis, Newfoundland is favoured. Under this method, Québec ranks seventh among beneficiary provinces. This is an example of three different readings of a single phenomenon. The basis of comparison varies according to interests and ideological biases.

There is no reason to envy provinces benefiting from equalization payments. The less a province collects under this program, the higher its fiscal capacity to generate autonomous income. In this perspective, the less Québec benefits from this program, the more its fiscal capacity will compare favourably to that of richer provinces. As a consequence, equalization transfers that meet the need criterion do not allow references in terms of winners and losers since, by definition, equalization only benefits losers.

Obviously, the Canada Assistance Plan does not meet the equity criterion any more than it can respond to the needs of provinces with a fiscal capacity lower than the national average. To the contrary, the CAP is likely to generate more intergovernmental disparities because federal contributions are determined by the level of provincial expenditures. For instance,

TABLE SEVEN: EQUALIZATION TRANSFERS, 1978-1990 ($ MILLIONS)

	1978	1980	1982	1984	1986	1988	1990
NFLD.	316	376	474	573	696	859	967
P.E.I.	67	88	118	129	144	172	206
N.S.	371	449	574	620	647	800	941
N.B.	309	379	88	542	636	786	916
QUE.	1,332	1,721	2,782	3,074	2,828	3,281	3,828
ONT.	0	0	0	0	0	0	0
MAN.	220	343	439	480	449	720	872
SASK.	19	40	0	0	169	347	435
ALTA.	0	0	0	0	0	0	0
B.C.	0	0	0	0	0	0	0
N.W.T.	0	0	0	0	0	0	0
YUKON	0	0	0	0	0	0	0
TOTAL	2,632	3,396	4,875	5,418	5,567	6,965	8,163

Source: Canada, Federal-Provincial Relations Office, Federal-Provincial Programs and Activities, 1978-1991 (Ottawa, 1991).

in 1978, Québec collected $105 per capita under the CAP compared to $49 for Ontario (Table Eight).

Since funds collected are not determined on a per capita basis, differences are due to a higher level of social expenditures in some provinces. In peripheral areas, differences in the level of expenditures can be explained by higher costs; elsewhere, they can be attributable to a more generous attitude from some provincial governments with regard to the poor, as eligibility criteria for federal funds are strictly identical across Canada.

LEVEL OF PROVINCIAL FINANCIAL DEPENDENCE ON INTERGOVERNMENTAL TRANSFERS: A TOOL FOR COMPARISON

The intergovernmental transfer system is likely to have several effects on beneficiary authorities. One can state *a priori* that the first effect of transfers is to increase financial resources of provincial administrations. From

TABLE EIGHT: CANADA ASSISTANCE PLAN PAYMENTS TO PROVINCES AND TERRITORIES, 1978–1990 ($ PER CAPITA)

	1978	1980	1982	1984	1986	1988	1990
NFLD.	70	93	117	129	151	160	202
P.E.I.	83	102	150	141	156	175	186
N.S.	56	72	102	121	142	173	198
N.B.	89	113	155	178	204	210	234
QUE.	105	133	180	233	236	249	264
ONT.	49	62	85	106	124	160	232
MAN.	56	68	89	125	144	182	197
SASK.	61	75	123	143	159	153	170
ALTA.	58	72	132	143	180	204	217
B.C.	80	118	170	210	219	223	226
N.W.T.	175	147	215	204	231	288	337
YUKON	52	23	108	104	0	324	215

Source: See Table Seven.

this standpoint, all provincial governments have access to additional financial resources without having to further tax their citizens.

From a comparative perspective, some issues can be raised to identify the effects particular to each province or region. For instance: Do some provinces depend on transfers more than others? Do some benefit more from the transfer system? A comparison tool is required to answer these questions. The ratio of financial dependence proposed below constitutes such a tool.

$$\text{Ratio of financial dependence} = Ir/Te$$
$$\text{Where}$$
Ir = In-province revenue [total provincial income (Ti) minus intergovernmental transfers (It)]
Te = Total provincial expenditures

The ratio allows a comparison of the degree of financial self-sufficiency of provincial administrations and consequently shows the degree of dependence on federal transfers. Three kinds of comparison are possible

TABLE NINE: IN-PROVINCE REVENUE (IR) & INTERGOVERNMENTAL
TRANSFERS (IT) AS PERCENTAGES OF TOTAL PROVINCIAL
EXPENDITURES (TE)

	1989		1990		1991	
	IR/TE	IT/TE	IR/TE	IT/TE	IR/TE	IT/TE
NFLD	51.9	45.4	50.7	48.0	53.4	44.8
P.E.I.	54.8	44.4	53.8	46.8	55.9	43.4
N.S.	55.4	35.9	56.5	35.9	61.2	35.3
N.B.	57.6	39.9	58.4	40.5	58.0	38.3
QUE. *	75.8	18.7	77.2	19.8	78.2	18.2
ONT.	86.0	12.7	90.1	12.2	91.6	11.5
MAN.	73.9	25.8	72.8	27.9	69.5	26.9
SASK.	67.7	20.7	73.7	23.0	70.0	21.2
ALTA	72.5	14.5	74.0	13.1	81.3	14.2
B.C.	88.7	16.0	90.3	14.3	87.7	12.3
N.W.T.	18.3	80.3	18.5	76.8	21.3	78.2
YUKON	21.1	75.6	22.2	72.1	22.5	79.4
AVERAGE	60.3	35.8	61.5	35.9	62.5	35.3
EXCLUDING N.W.T. AND YUKON	68.0	27.0	70.0	28.0	71.0	27.0

*Includes EPF, equalization, and CAP transfers.
Source: Canadian Tax Foundation, *Provincial and Municipal Finances 1991*. (Toronto, 1992).

with this ratio: (1) comparing the level of dependence/self-sufficiency of a single province on a long-term basis; (2) comparing provinces among themselves in the same time frame; (3) comparing a province or a number of provinces to the national average. In addition, such a ratio allows us to make comparisons among provinces on an identical basis.

The types of comparison made possible with this ratio differ from the dependence analysis suggested by Kabir and Hackett (1989). For them, the level of provincial dependence is based on the difference between sums transferred to the federal government in the form of taxes and funds collected in the form of intergovernmental transfers.

Table Nine shows that, in the last three years, Québec's in-province revenue represented an increasing share of total expenditures. However, it would be wrong to assume that this tendency results essentially from a decrease in intergovernmental transfers (It). In fact, the share of intergovernmental transfers represented 18.7 per cent of Québec expenditures in 1989, 19.8 per cent in 1990, and 18.2 per cent in 1991 while in the same period the province's own income increased from 75.8 per cent of its total expenditures in 1989 to 77.2 per cent in 1990, and 78.2 per cent in 1991.

On the other hand, financial self-sufficiency is best exemplified by British Columbia and Ontario where, in 1991, federal transfers represented only 12.3 per cent and 11.5 per cent of provincial expenditures compared to 44.8 per cent in Newfoundland.

Table Nine can serve several purposes. With the Ir/Te ratio, provinces and territories can be classified according to criteria other than strict geographic distribution. On the basis of the 1991 data, the ratio makes it possible to distinguish four groups of provinces based on different dimensions.

Two groups – the Maritimes and the Yukon and Northwest Territories – are determined on a geographical basis. These are the main beneficiaries of the intergovernmental transfer system. In 1991, 40.45 per cent of the Maritimes provincial administration's income derived from intergovernmental transfers. In the case of Yukon and the Northwest Territories, intergovernmental transfers, at 78.8 per cent, made up the main part of their income. The marginal situation of Yukon and the Northwest Territories requires that they be excluded from some analysis to avoid biased interpretations. A third group relates more to the economic and financial dimension. It includes Ontario, Alberta, and British Columbia. With the exception of Alberta, whose financial situation varies depending on the reference time period, this group is that of the "rich provinces" – the haves. Finally, there remains an outlier group that changes from year to year. In 1991, this group included Québec, Manitoba, and Saskatchewan. No economic or socio-political factor seems to account for this grouping of provinces on the basis of the relative similarity of their Ir/Te ratio. Using 1989 as a reference, Alberta replaced Saskatchewan in this group whereas Québec and Manitoba remained in it.

The financial dependence ratio indicates significant variations in the extent to which provinces benefit from federal transfers. This does not suggest, however, that some provinces win while others lose. The fact that the three programs have different, if not contradictory, objectives explains this. In fact, it would be an improper generalization to state simply that a province benefits from fiscal federalism without referring to specific criteria or programs. A province where federal transfers represent a more significant share of its income is not necessarily a winner insofar as surplus transfers collected may be considered as the result of a deficient fiscal capacity. Furthermore, what is meant with references to winners and losers? Provincial administrations, individuals, enterprises? It is a gross exaggeration to state that the citizens of the Atlantic provinces benefit from the federal government's generosity since their per capita income is lower than the national average, even taking federal transfers into account. In the last analysis, such a logic amounts to saying that welfare recipients benefit from the government generosity more than high income earners simply because they receive government benefits.

CONCLUSION

The current transfer system in Canada can be seen as a response to constitutional constraints inherent in the federal structure of the Canadian state. It can also be seen as an instrument designed to mitigate centrifugal effects that could flow from significant disparities in provincial governments' fiscal capacity.

The crisis in public finances experienced by Canada since the 1970s resulted in recurrent budgetary deficits and in a significant increase in debt-servicing costs, which led the federal government to limit the growth of its contributions to the three main intergovernmental transfer programs analyzed in this chapter.

As mentioned, comparative analysis of intergovernmental transfers requires a uniform basis of comparison. Explicit criteria must be used in order to interpret the effects of transfers. The proposed criteria indicated that the objectives underlying the three main types of transfers differ more than they converge; each follows its own distinct rationale.

Finally, the analysis of the provincial governments' financial dependence suggests that the degree of their reliance on federal transfers varies significantly. In the long term, the current Canadian intergovernmental transfer system is likely to exacerbate political and economic disintegration (Phillips, 1986: 38-39) rather than mitigate it (Cannon, 1989). The citizens of rich provinces, suffering from the effects of the crisis in public finances, will believe they have contributed too much to the welfare of other provinces. Inversely, citizens of poor provinces will judge that they do not receive their fair share from a federal system that is supposed to remedy regional disparity.

Furthermore, the current situation of public finances no longer allows the federal government to initiate new "national" social programs to reduce interprovincial disparities. Interest payments on Canada's public debt, the threat of tax revolt in some regions, and the necessity for the Canadian economy to equalize its cost structure in the context of economic globalization may limit the federal government's will and capacity to intervene in spheres of provincial jurisdiction. Hence, in the long run, voters will decide whether or not they wish their government to use its spending power to pursue the goal of reducing fiscal disparities among provincial administrations in Canada.

NOTES

1   This research has benefited from funds provided by the Social Sciences and Humanities Research Council of Canada and the Fonds pour la formation de chercheurs et l'aide à la recherche (Québec). The authors wish to thank David Rolland for his contribution to their research. This chapter was translated from the original French by Maya Berbery.

2   It was agreed that provinces could not impose indirect taxes likely to exceed their boundaries. As this source of revenue, then the most important one, was entrusted to the federal government, provinces were unable to fulfil the responsibilities granted to them. A transfer system had to be implemented. (Ip and Mintz, 1992: 14). From 1867, "la Constitution prévoit le versement annuel par le gouvernement central d'une somme de 70 000 $ et d'un subside de 80 cents par habitant recensé en 1861" (Hamelin and Provencher, 1987: 72).

3   In Québec, for instance, transfer payments were the main source of revenue until 1901 (Gow, 1980: 20).

4   Until 1949, the Judicial Committee of the Privy Council (London) acted as final appeal court with regard to Canadian constitutional law.

5   Payments made in accordance with the equalization principle in Canada were established for the 1987-92 period from thirty-seven sources of provincial income to which an average rate of taxation was applied. To receive payments, the income a province was likely to generate from these thirty-seven sources had to be lower than a national average determined by the method prescribed in Part 1 of the Federal-Provincial Fiscal Arrangements

and Federal Post-Secondary Education and Health Contributions Act.

6   For a chronology of different programs and the evolution of federal struc-
     tures relating to regional development, see Bernier (1992).

7   Prior to 1977, federal contributions to health services and post-secondary
     education cost-sharing programs were based on a combination of condi-
     tional money transfers and tax allowances.

8   Federal Ministry of Finance, Special Tabulations, June, 1992.

9   However, this form of financing tends to characterize other fields of govern-
     mental intervention such as regional economic development.

10   Despite a British Columbia legal appeal of this decision, the Supreme Court
     stated that the federal government could reduce the growth of its financial
     contributions to richer provinces for the purpose of this program.

11   See note 4.

REFERENCES

Armitage, Andrew (1988). *Social Welfare in Canada*. Toronto: McClelland & Ste-
     wart.

Aronson, J. Richard, and John L. Hilley (1986). *Financing State and Local Govern-
     ment*. 4th edition. Washington: Brookings Institution.

Bernier, Gérald (1992). "Les politiques fédérales de développement régional au
     Québec: 1969-1992," in François Rocher, dir., *Bilan québécois du fédéralisme ca-
     nadien*. Montréal: VLB éditeur: 268-302.

Boadway, Robin (1986). "Les transferts fédéraux-provinciaux au Canada: un ex-
     amen critique des structures existantes," in Mark Krasnick, ed., *Le fédéralisme
     fiscal*. Ottawa: Approvisionnements et Services Canada: 1-54.

Boadway, Robin, and Frank Flatters (1991). "Federal-Provincial Fiscal Relations
     Revisited: Some Consequences of Recent Constitutional and Policy Develop-
     ments," in Melville McMillan, ed., *Provincial Public Finances: Provincial Surveys*.
     Toronto: Canadian Tax Foundation.

Canada, Office of Federal-Provincial Relations (1991). *Répertoire des programmes et
     activités fédéraux-provinciaux, 1990-1991*. Ottawa: Décembre.

Canadian Tax Foundation (1991). The National Finances 1990. Toronto: Cana-
     dian Tax Foundation.

Cannon, James B. (1989). "Directions in Canadian Regional Policy," The Cana-
     dian Geographer, 33, 3: 230-39.

Gow, James Iain (1980) Histoire de l'administration québécoise. Chronologie des
     programmes de l'État du Québec (1867-1970). Montréal: Département de sci-
     ence politique, Université de Montréal.

Hackett, D.W., and M. Kabir (1989). "Is Atlantic Canada Becoming More Dependent on Federal Transfers?" *Canadian Public Policy*, 15, 1 (March): 43-48.

Hamelin, Jean, and Jean Provencher (1987). *Brève histoire du Québec*, Nouvelle édition. Montréal: Boréal.

Ip, Irene K., and Jack M. Mintz (1992). *Dividing the Spoils: The Federal-Provincial Allocation of Taxing Powers*. Toronto: C.D. Howe Institute.

Leslie, Peter M. (1988). *National Citizenship and Provincial Communities: A Review of Canadian Fiscal Federalism*. Kingston: Institute of Intergovernmental Relations.

Mimoto, H., and P. Cross (1991). "La croissance de la dette fédérale," *L'observateur économique canadien* (juin).

Phillips, Paul (1986). "National Policy: Continental Economics and National Disintegration," in David J. Bercuson, ed., *Canada and Beyond: The Burden of Unity*. Toronto: Copp Clark Pitman.

Québec (1991). *Budget 1991-1992 : discours sur le budget et renseignements supplémentaires* (2 mai).

Reesor, Bayard (1992). *The Canadian Constitution in Historical Perspective*. Scarborough: Prentice-Hall.

Stevenson, Garth (1990). "Federalism and Intergovernmental Relations," in Michael S. Whittington and Glen Williams, eds., *Canadian Politics in the 1990s*, 3rd Edition. Toronto: Nelson.

CHAPTER TWELVE

Social Policy and Canadian Federalism: What Are the Pressures for Change?

Leon Muszynski

IT IS EASY TO BECOME DESPONDENT ABOUT THE PROSPECTS for Canadian social policy. The burden of the debt and deficits has put pressure on governments to restrict spending of all kinds. Economic growth and tax revenues have been sluggish compared to the period when Canada's major social programs were adopted. And conservative ideology has influenced public perceptions of the value of government and of social spending. From 1984 to 1993 the federal Progressive Conservative government made a concerted effort to restrict significantly the growth of social spending as a percentage of Canadian gross domestic product (GDP) (National Council of Welfare, 1989; Canada, Department of Finance, 1992: 109). Provincial governments have also been forced to restrict social program improvements in the face of burgeoning provincial deficits and reductions in federal transfers.

To many observers the prospects for improvements in Canadian social policy hinge on the ability of the federal government to lead in the development and financing of social programs even if they are delivered by the provinces and territories. In Canada outside Québec there is a pervasive belief in the historically progressive nature of the federal government in the evolution of social policy. Many critics of the ill-fated Meech Lake and Charlottetown Accords argued that if they had been adopted the federal government would have had considerably less power to implement new social programs and to maintain national standards. In Québec there was and is a different perception. For Québec, federal commitments to national social policy have always been viewed negatively. They are often interpreted as initiatives of a dominant federal government too willing to intervene in the constitutionally assigned affairs of Québec. For political and cultural reasons Québec has always been most vociferous in its opposition to federal activity in its jurisdiction, especially in social policy.

Criticism of the constitutional accords, especially Charlottetown, vastly overstated the actual redistribution of power that would have occurred if they had passed. There would have been some decentralization of spending and administration to the provinces from the federal government and a transfer of program responsibility for some labour market programs. These would have contributed to the resolution of long-standing demands by the provinces for more effective control of areas in which the federal and provincial governments operate concurrently. But these proposed shifts in responsibility were minimal in the final Charlottetown Accord, which in any case was defeated by the Canadian electorate.

Canadians are certainly familiar with constitutional debate. Over the past decade constitutional issues have dominated Canadian political discourse in a way that would be quite foreign to people in the United States. What we might call "the constitutional perspective" was widespread in the social policy community. This is the belief that the division of powers between the provinces and the federal government determines the level and nature of social policy commitments. Many advocates of social programs have shared the belief that the federal government has been a singular force for advances in social policy. The provinces have always had constitutional authority for much of what we consider social policy. The federal government has led some of the time, and it has followed much of the time. However, this spending power has significantly eroded as a result of economic conditions, the deficit and debt, and the emergence of more conservative attitudes toward social policy.

Concerns about the constitutional division of powers also reflect deeply felt ideals and fears about the role of government in people's lives and about the willingness of particular governments to commit to greater levels of equality and security. In this way constitutional debates are at root about how much should be done by government to protect Canadians against market forces that create inequality and insecurity. Nevertheless, debates about the constitution have also tended to obscure the deeper problems influencing social policy in the 1990s.

Much of what we call social policy in Canada is relatively enlightened in comparison to the United States. Canada has a tradition of universal non-means-tested social programs non-existent south of the border (Blank and Hanratty, 1993). Canada's system of national health insurance in particular is a symbol Canada's commitment to social justice. Québec was unique in developing its own, and in many ways superior, systems of social provision. The reorganization of health and social services in Québec in the early 1970s still stands as a model for the other Canadian provinces attempting to rationalize and integrate health and social services at the local level. Québec's struggle to establish its own social policy framework in the 1960s and early 1970s consistently upstaged Ottawa and pushed the federal government to move in areas that it might not have otherwise. More recently, in the context of demands for sovereignty, Québec has renewed its desire to control key social programs such as unemployment insurance.

But the welfare state in Canada, both inside and outside Québec, is not a model of social progress or social justice. If the welfare state is about creating a fairer and more equitable society, then the Canadian welfare state and its Québec variant have been at best marginally successful. More to the point, what progress has been made is being substantially undone as governments are forced to react to changed economic circumstances. For at least the past decade the federal government has been the chief architect of a leaner and meaner welfare state. Administrative and constitutional relationships are important issues in the development of social policy. But debates about constitutional renewal, administrative decentralization, and even the potential sovereignty of Québec obscure the fact that what makes social policy progressive is not how much of it we have, or even who funds it, but what it does.

THE WELFARE STATE AND CANADIAN FEDERALISM

Since Confederation, provincial jurisdiction over the health, education, and welfare field was inferred from their constitutional authority granted in the British North America Act over "hospitals, asylums, charities, and eleemosynary institutions," "municipal institutions," "property and civil rights," and "all matters of a merely local or private nature in the province."[1] However, the constitution also granted residual powers to both the federal and provincial governments and imposed no constraints on either level to spend on activities "important to Canadians." Until the 1930s the federal government was content to let the provinces handle social policy. It had almost grudgingly agreed to provide *ad hoc* relief of unemployment to the provinces and a means-tested old age pension (Banting, 1982: 48).

The depression of the 1930s changed this traditional pattern. High unemployment and burgeoning municipal welfare roles led to increased pressure on the federal government, often by provinces, to enter the field of income security through the introduction of a national unemployment insurance program. Prime Minister R.B. Bennett introduced the Employment and Social Insurance Act in 1935 as part of his New Deal. It was struck down by the Judicial Committee of the Privy Council (JCPC) as *ultra vires* or unconstitutional after several provinces challenged the law. The JCPC determined that constitutional authority for social insurance fell squarely within provincial jurisdiction and that the proposed unemployment insurance program was an intrusion into a field reserved by the constitution for the provinces. However, the pressures of high unemployment on provincial and municipal treasuries were too great and by 1940 the provinces were willing to give up their exclusive responsibility for social insurance. In the first modification of constitutional responsibility for social policy, the BNA Act was amended to allow the federal government exclusive authority over unemployment insurance because of its importance for the national economy.

Constitutional uncertainties regarding other contributory programs, such as pension plans, survivors' benefits, and disability benefits, were resolved in constitutional changes, although it is not clear they were necessary, and by administrative accommodation with the provinces. The result is that unemployment insurance is exclusively of federal jurisdiction, workers' compensation is exclusively provincial, and contributory pension plans are under concurrent jurisdiction with the provinces having "paramountcy" in law over pensions. In this way the social insurance field is by tradition and constitutional accommodation a relatively well-defined area of social policy.

By contrast, the responsibilities for other areas of social policy are much less well defined and constitute a hodge-podge that has evolved for a wide variety of reasons. The provinces have clear responsibility for health and education, but the idea of welfare as we know it today did not exist when the BNA Act was forged in 1867.[2] What was to emerge was an exceedingly complex system of shared taxes, transfers, and authority for a wide variety of health, education, income security, labour market, and social service programs. As Banting argues, "when it comes to welfare, Canada manifests a decidedly schizophrenic character" (Banting, 1982: 58).

The devastating effects of the Great Depression of the 1930s had signalled a need for strong federal leadership, especially to finance the costs of unemployment. In order to finance the war and the costs of national reconstruction it had also become evident even to the provinces that the federal government would have to take control of the personal income and corporate tax fields if it was to achieve a policy of high employment and economic stability. Initially the provinces were to receive compensating grants, and in 1941 they entered into "tax rental agreements" with the federal government whereby the federal government would occupy tax fields and collect taxes for the provinces. This led to the development of what has been called the "federal spending power." The formidable federal spending power that emerged from these agreements represented a significant shift in the locus of power in the development of social security from the provinces to the federal government (Guest, 1980: 179).

These changes heralded a major shift in the Canadian political economy. The post-World War Two era witnessed the adoption of a Keynesian macro-economic framework among most advanced industrial nations, with the expansion of social spending pursued as much for reasons of economic efficiency, growth, and stabilization as it was for social equity. In this framework, the state was to play a central role in the management of economic affairs. Although favoured by labour and resisted by business, this commitment to intervention in markets was part of an implicit bargain that saw labour and business each securing significant benefits. For labour a key achievement was social programs that provided income security; for business the key achievement was a stable industrial relations system and the maintenance of high levels of consumer demand (Wolfe, 1984). An important element of the framework was the need and ability of governments to maintain, if not full employment, then at least high levels of employment (Muszynski, 1985). The critically important idea contained in this, which has been treated with increasing scepticism in the framework guiding current political economic development, is that a high degree of compatibility existed between economic efficiency and social goals such as equity, equalization, and citizenship.

The period between 1945 and 1962 was characterized by the emergence of shared federal-provincial decision-making and financial responsibility for the growth of social programs. The chief mechanisms of shared responsibility were the federal conditional grant and the cost-shared program. In this era the federal government appeared as the leader in the development of programs even within health and education, the traditional and clearly defined provincial responsibilities. However, Ottawa's primary involvement was to fund provincially run programs. The shift to federal leadership in the financing of social policy actually predated federal

economic commitments with a 1941 agreement on tax-sharing that secured federal control of the income tax and the corporate tax. The result
was the evolution of a complex and often poorly integrated system of
health, education, income security, and social services over the 1940s,
1950s and 1960s.

This history of shared decision-making and joint financial responsibility for social policy was not as cooperative as one might think. The
Québec view was that conditional grants and cost-sharing were an invasion of provincial jurisdiction and rights. Québec refused to participate in
the tax agreements from 1945 to 1961. Criticisms of cost-sharing were
also shared by other provinces who objected to the way in which it transferred provincial policy-making from provincial capitals to Ottawa: it
forced a uniformity across provinces that was not always desirable, and it
increased the distance between the recipient of social security and the ad-
ministrator, thus increasing the cost (Guest, 1980: 180). Tensions arose
between levels of government on this issue, but they were minor compared to those before 1940. By the 1960s these tensions had mounted as
provincial governments outside Québec started to develop their own
plans for social and economic development. But the most important development was the emergence of Québec from the Duplessis era through
the Quiet Revolution of the early sixties.

In the 1960s Québec emerged as considerably more self-assured and
stepped up pressure on the federal government to hand over more tax
room and to end cost-sharing entirely. This position, which was supported by some of the other provinces, was viewed not altogether unsym-
pathetically by the federal government. Ottawa suggested that it should
withdraw from mature programs where the provinces could take over responsibility for administration and financing but that it should not be restricted from establishing new cost-shared programs (ibid.: 182). There
followed a great flurry of federal activity in the 1960s that included: the
establishment of the Canada/Québec Pension Plan, the adoption of a federally funded national health insurance system, federal funding of provincial post-secondary education, and the adoption of the Canada Assistance
Plan, federal legislation requiring the federal government to pay 50 per
cent of the costs of provincial social assistance (welfare) and services to the
needy. Of these, only the Canada Pension Plan was an exclusive federal
program.[3]

The provinces were ambivalent about these developments. They were
both irritated by these incursions and pleased to be the beneficiaries of

new program expenditures. Québec's position, as always, was much stronger. It felt that Ottawa should withdraw entirely from the field of social policy, including unemployment insurance. Québec maintained that although Ottawa had the right to make laws in relation to social policy, if a provincial statute existed or was created for the same purpose that it should have primacy and the federal government should withdraw. Québec was doubly frustrated because it was consistently committed to a more progressive and integrated approach to social policy than was the federal government.[4] Major concessions were made to allow for special funding arrangements for Québec.

The constitutional issue took on a different tone with the election of the fiercely federalist Pierre Elliott Trudeau as Prime Minister in 1968. Opposition to the vision of a radically decentralized federalism constituted Pierre Trudeau's "magnificent obsession" (Clarkson and McCall, 1991). Trudeau's and Ottawa's view was that a strong federal role in social policy was essential for reasons of equality, opportunity, and the need to foster a sense of shared community. A strong federal government in Ottawa would have the ability to redistribute among individuals, families, regions, and generations. In addition, a strong federal role was essential to maintain consistent national standards or similar standards of service regardless of a province's ability to raise revenue. Ottawa also argued that national economic stabilization was directly associated with the provision of social transfers and was, therefore, an essential tool of national economic policy (Guest, 1980: 182). These two visions clashed at the Victoria Constitutional Conference in 1971. Premier Bourassa of Québec demanded control of social policy and the federal government, supported by the other provinces, rejected this position. The conference broke down without agreement on a formula for repatriation of the BNA Act, which remained under the authority of the British Parliament.

Despite this, from the early 1970s on the tide shifted back from the federal government to the provinces. The provinces continued to demand and received many administrative concessions from the federal government for the operation of programs within their jurisdiction. Québec was allowed to opt out of certain federally funded programs with compensation to set up its own programs. It was also permitted to modify certain federal programs to conform to its own priorities. A new Family Allowances Act in 1974 dramatically increased benefits and allowed the provinces to vary family allowance payments according to age and number of children in the family, an option taken up by Québec and Alberta at the time.

The early 1970s saw numerous proposals for significant income security reform based on the discovery of significant levels of poverty in Canada despite the massive reforms of the 1960s.[5] The federal government's response was a proposal for a Family Income Security Plan in 1970, which was to do away with universality and restrict payment of family allowance benefits to people in need.[6] The vision of reform put forward by Québec and all other reports was considerably more extensive. The federal proposal, which was greeted with considerable opposition, actually passed third reading in the House of Commons. It failed to be proclaimed, however, because an election was called in 1972. After the 1972 election in which the Liberals were re-elected with a minority of seats, the federal government remained under pressure to come up with some major social policy reform effort. The NDP held the balance of power and this political reality influenced the subsequent direction of income security reform. Ultimately, the Liberal government chose to pursue a radical expansion of its unemployment insurance program as an alternative to other income security reform (Muszynski, 1985).

Massive income security reform was proposed by the federal Minister of Health and Welfare in his 1973 Working Paper on Social Security in Canada (the Orange Paper). This report initiated the federal-provincial Social Security Review, which was known primarily for its work over three years on the design of an income supplement program for the working poor, or as it is more popularly known, a guaranteed annual income. It was also concerned with the introduction of a new Social Services Act that would provide a broader range of services to Canadians than could be provided under the Canada Assistance Plan. All these efforts failed, doomed in large measure because the mid-1970s was the start of a dramatic turnaround in Canada's economic fortunes and the emergence of the period of restraint that has lasted to the present.

The development of the Canadian welfare state from the 1940s up to this point had represented an important shift in the relation between state and citizen. It symbolized a shift from social provision based on benevolence to one based on justice. Government spending on health, welfare, and education increased from 6.5 per cent of GNP in 1951 to 11.6 per cent in 1961 and 19.4 per cent in 1971 (Vaillancourt, 1985: 34). The expansion of government was motivated by the desire initially to prevent the recurrence of the devastating experience of the Great Depression. The framework embodied a belief that governments played a positive role in assuring well-being. Politically, the expansion of the welfare state was based on the strengthening of left/labour social forces and their ability to influence policy. In addition, the welfare state bureaucracy itself played an important role in expanding social policy commitments (Haddow, 1993).

THE FEDERAL GOVERNMENT AND WELFARE EROSION

The 1970s saw the beginning of the unravelling of the Keynesian formula for economic and social development that had been so successful for close to thirty years. During the seventies the long post-war period of almost uninterrupted growth came to a halt. Wages grew faster than productivity, and other factors, such as oil price shocks and increased international competition from newly industrialized countries, helped to cause stagflation (there was inflation without growth). Government spending continued to grow and deficits emerged as a central economic issue. In this context the federal government started to turn from traditional Keynesianism to more conservative alternatives. In 1975 the federal government introduced wage and price controls, cut $1.5 billion in expenditures, and committed the Bank of Canada to a policy of monetary gradualism to contain inflation (Wolfe, 1984). These had a decisive impact on the development of federal social policy in Canada. The changes that were introduced to unemployment insurance in 1972 were significantly curtailed in 1978, job creation programs were drastically reduced, and family allowances were temporarily deindexed. The national plan for income supplementation that was emerging from the Social Security Review was scuttled.

The election of the Parti Québécois in 1976 sharpened the differences between Ottawa and Québec on social policy issues. The last remnant of the Social Security Review, the Social Services Act, was denounced by Québec as "a massive and unacceptable federal invasion of provincial jurisdiction" (Guest, 1980: 197). Ottawa was forced to withdraw the Social Services Act for the expansion of cost-shared services and replace it with a new plan for block funding of provincial social services with only very limited conditions attached to the funding. Block funding was attractive to the provinces because it would allow them to design and administer services as they saw fit. Although the federal government bowed to the provinces on this, block funding was also a way for Ottawa to curb its burgeoning costs associated with cost-sharing arrangements where provincial spending automatically triggered federal contributions. Social policy advocates by and large opposed block funding at the time because they believed it would lead to significant reductions in actual services and considerable variation in the scope and quality of services across the country. However, as part of the expenditure restraint effort in 1978 the proposal for block funding was withdrawn.

In 1981 Canada was thrown into a deep recession and the Canadian economy underwent dramatic restructuring in response to changes in the global economy and technological change. Inflation, rather than unemployment, had become the central preoccupation of governments. The federal government abandoned the historic national policy commitment to full employment (or high levels of employment). In its place was the idea that the state has the responsibility to assure that the rate of unemployment did not exceed its so-called "natural rate," which is the non-accelerating inflation rate of unemployment (Campbell, 1991: xiii). The drive for government expenditure restraint intensified particularly from business as deficits and government social expenditure were increasingly perceived to be the root cause of Canada's economic difficulties (Social Planning Council of Metropolitan Toronto, 1985).

In 1984 the Progressive Conservatives were elected to federal office and soon after the Department of Finance released a statement entitled *A New Direction for Canada: An Agenda for Economic Renewal*. The principles elaborated in the statement were to constitute the plan for the Tory government for the next decade: deficit and debt containment, privatization, a reduction in the size and scope of government, and modified income security programs to assure they are provided only to people "who really need it."

Although government spending on social programs and indeed all government spending increased in real terms over the decade of the 1980s, there was a reduction in the amount spent by government on programs relative to the gross domestic product (GDP). Nationally all government spending in Canada as a proportion of GDP dropped from 46.5 to 44.3 per cent. Federal expenditures on programs (excluding interest payments on the debt) have declined in real terms from 19.6 per cent of GDP in 1984 to 16.6 per cent in 1991–92 (Canada, Department of Finance, 1992: 118). The most notable declines on the social policy side have been in federal child benefits, federal funding of provincial health and education, and federal income tax. Many of the changes since 1984 have relied on technical amendments to taxes and transfers that are difficult for most people to understand and have largely escaped media scrutiny. This strategy, according to one seasoned observer, "camouflages regressive changes in the rhetoric of equity in an attempt to convince Canadians that tax increases are tax cuts and that benefit cuts are benefit increases; it is a social policy by stealth" (Gray, 1990: 17).[7]

Starting in the 1960s with the Canada/Québec Pension Plan, many major income security programs were indexed to increases in the cost of living. This provision was critical to maintain the purchasing value of benefits in a period when inflation was consistently high, and it was considered by most Canadians to be an essential requirement for income security. One of the most important ways in which the federal government has cut back on its social spending recently is through a device called "partial indexation," which means that benefits rise not by the full amount of increase in the cost of living but only by the amount over 3 per cent each year. Partial indexation was applied to family allowances in 1986, and to tax brackets and tax credits in the personal income tax system. This is a devious mechanism by which the federal government is slowly cutting benefits and, because it also applies to elements of the tax system, raising taxes. Federal spending through the Established Programs Financing Act, which provides for federal payments to the provinces for health and education, has also been seriously eroded through a series of small freezes on the escalator formula (Maslove, 1992). Between 1986 and 1991 these three forms of partial indexation resulted in federal benefit cuts to Canadian individuals, families, and the provinces estimated to be $26.5 billion (National Council of Welfare, 1989).

The federal government also undertook a massive reform of Canada's tax system in 1988 (Muszynski, 1988). Its stated purpose was to make the tax system simpler and fairer. Although some improvements were made, such as the conversion of many deductions to credits, overall the impact of tax changes over the past decade has been regressive. The problem of the partial indexation of tax brackets and tax credits has already been mentioned. In addition the federal tax reduction for low- and middle-income taxpayers was eliminated and the federal government adopted the Goods and Services Tax, a regressive tax on the sales of almost all goods and services sold in Canada.

In keeping with its desire to transform Canada's income security system into a system that supports only people "in need," in 1989 the federal government introduced "clawbacks" on payments of family allowances and old age security, the flat rate benefits that went to families with children and elderly Canadians regardless of income. For several decades these programs had represented the commitment of Canadians to horizontal equity, or to the support families with children as a social good, and to elderly people because of their contribution to Canadian society. They represented transfers from families without children to those with children, and from working to non-working Canadians. In addition, they were seen as important mechanisms for assuring economic stability through maintaining consumer demand.

The Conservative government also mounted a serious strategy to reduce unemployment insurance beginning with a clawback on benefits paid to high-income earners despite the fact that they had paid premiums to insure against the risk of wage loss. The protection provided by unemployment insurance has been progressively eroded over the past fifteen years, but the most significant changes took place in 1990 as a result of the passage of Bill C-21. This significantly increased the minimum number of insurable weeks required to qualify, reduced the number of benefit weeks, raised the penalties for quitting a job, getting fired, or refusing a job, and reduced the benefit-wage replacement ratio (Campbell, 1992: 33). The net result of these changes has been to shift the cost of dependency in an economy with high unemployment to provincial social assistance programs.

After several years of reductions in the real value of child benefits paid to families with children, the Conservatives finally abolished universal family benefits in 1992. The 1992 budget announced that family allowances and the refundable and non-refundable child tax credits would be replaced with a unified and graduated income-tested benefit going only to low- and middle-income families. In so doing it has given Canada the distinction of being the only advanced industrial country that does not provide any tax or transfer support to families regardless of income.

Just as the federal government often unilaterally established social programs in the forties, fifties, and sixties, it was also the federal government that unilaterally reduced its role in social provision over the past decade. Another major cutback was in federal transfers under the Canada Assistance Plan (CAP). The CAP is the federal plan for sharing the cost of the provincial safety net of last resort (National Council of Welfare, 1991). Since it was created in 1966 the CAP has been paying 50 per cent of the costs of provincially run social assistance (or welfare), child-care subsidies, homemaking programs, and child welfare services. It was established to bring together under one program funding that was previously provided under a fragmented system of categorical programs such as for the blind or seniors. Because of CAP funding the provinces set up unified programs that eliminated many categorical distinctions and provided income or services to people solely based on need measured by a "needs test." By 1991 the federal government was paying about half of the total of $12 billion for welfare income and services in Canada. The 1990 federal budget announced that the federal government would impose a limit on the amount it would transfer to the provinces of Alberta, British Columbia, and Ontario. Instead of funding 50 per cent of everything paid out by the province, thenceforth the federal government would limit the increase in payment under the CAP to the three richest provinces to 5 per cent a year for the next two fiscal years.[8]

This measure has had a devastating impact on these three provinces but especially on Ontario, which experienced the brunt of the recession of the early 1990s. Unemployment increased, and with the federal cutbacks in unemployment insurance the demand for provincial welfare mushroomed. The cumulative losses to the three provinces affected were estimated to be $4 billion by 1992-93 (Ontario, 1992: 103). As a result of this change the federal share of social assistance in Ontario dropped to approximately 28 per cent by 1992-93. According to Ontario this cutback alone accounted for 29 per cent of Ontario's much denounced annual operating deficit.

EQUALIZATION

The federal Equalization Program was introduced in 1957. Equalization was designed to ensure that provinces have sufficient revenues to provide reasonably comparable levels of public services at reasonably comparable levels of taxation. The commitment to equalization is based on both equity and efficiency principles. In equity terms it is based on a commitment to the idea of equal opportunity for all Canadians in the same circumstances regardless of province to receive similar levels of services. It is also justified on efficiency grounds because unequal benefits and/or tax burdens can lead to a labour mobility and other inefficiencies within the nation. The federal government spent $8.5 billion (1991-92) on direct unconditional equalization payments to poorer provinces to bring their fiscal capacity closer to the national average (Economic Council of Canada, 1991: chapter 4). Three provinces, Ontario, Alberta, and British Columbia, are not eligible for equalization payments because their fiscal capacity is above the equalization standard.

In 1982 the federal government imposed a ceiling on the growth of its equalization payments. The ceiling was reached in 1988-89. From then to 1991-92 the provinces lost an estimated $3.3 billion in equalization payments they would have otherwise received. An important consequence of this ceiling is that it undermines the commitment to equalization or interregional sharing, a cornerstone of Canadian federalism and a key element of the Canadian welfare state.

In addition, implicit equalization elements are made in many other transfers from the federal government to the provinces in health, education, income security, and social services. For example, unemployment insurance is a major form of implicit equalization for the Atlantic provinces, which consistently experience above average rates of unemployment. These implicit forms of equalization exceed the transfers of direct equalization payments.

Although equalization is an important expression of social solidarity and interregional redistribution, it is useful to keep in mind what Québec sovereignists have argued for many years: the impact of equalization on poorer provinces should not be overstated. Even after equalization there is a wide variation in the level and quality of services available to Canadians in different provinces and regions. Moreover, federal cutbacks, especially in unemployment insurance, will have a large impact on the Atlantic provinces, which have depended on it to support seasonal industry workers. This erosion of federal equalization payments has little to do with constitutional or administrative decentralization.

DECENTRALIZATION AND NATIONAL STANDARDS

The federal government has played a declining role in social provision relative to the provinces since the 1970s. Overall consolidated federal/provincial government expenditure grew from 31 per cent of GDP in 1965 to 46 per cent in the late 1980s, but the provinces accounted for a much larger proportion of this growth (*ibid.*: 59). This was the result of new or expanded programs in health, education, and social services, in many cases spurred on by the federal government's cost-sharing carrot. In a more recent analysis of trends in social spending, the Caledon Institute of Social Policy estimates that from 1958-59 to 1990-91 provincial social spending increased thirteen times while federal social spending increased six times (Battle and Torjman, 1993). A similar pattern exists with respect to the growth of consolidated government revenue, in part a reflection of the transfer of significant tax points to the provinces by the federal government in the 1970s.

This continued shift in the locus of power from the federal government to the provinces has raised concerns about the maintenance of national standards. The development and maintenance of national standards, particularly in health and social services, has been an important rationale for a strong federal role in social provision. Before the establishment of national programs such as unemployment insurance, the CAP, medicare, and the Canada/Québec Pension Plan, there was considerable variation in social provision across the country. Decentralization, especially with the erosion of equalization, is perceived by many social policy advocates to be a threat to strong national standards.

This interest in national standards is not shared by all Canadians. For Québec the idea of the federal government as the enforcer of national standards is ludicrous both because Québec's standards have often been higher and because it is the expression of unacceptable meddling in provincial affairs. But even outside Québec there is concern that the role of the federal government in the maintenance of national standards is overstated and, in any case, in serious decline. The federal government has much less control over national standards than is conventionally assumed.

Ottawa has no control over how unconditional equalization payments are spent by the provinces. In shared-cost programs such as the Canada Assistance Plan, legislative standards exist in the form of program criteria to which provinces have to conform to be eligible, such as the application of a needs test. But there is considerable variation in social assistance benefit levels across provinces and differences in the application of essentially discretionary criteria for eligibility (National Council of Welfare, 1994). The closest thing to a firm national standard is the program criteria under the Canada Health Act. Here the provinces must meet certain requirements, such as universality and portability of insured health services, to be eligible for federal cash transfers. Through EPF the federal government funds the provinces to pay for part of the cost of provincially run programs of insured health services, extended health care, and post-secondary education. EPF transfers include both cash and a tax-point transfer where the federal government agrees to reduce tax rates so that provinces can occupy the vacated tax room. Because of the restraint imposed on increases in the cash component of EPF, it is estimated that cash transfers to the provinces will be elimi-

nated completely within a decade. Besides shifting the cost of these programs to the provinces, this effectively undermines the ability of the federal
government to impose financial penalties on the provinces for violations of
the Canada Health Act for such things as patient extra-billing by doctors or
the imposition of user fees (Maslove, 1992: 62).[9]

It is also worth noting that Canadian cost-sharing programs can be distinguished from shared-cost programs in other nations like Australia and
the United States in that they have comparatively few conditions and national standards (Economic Council of Canada, 1991). Indeed, it is in part
because of the weakness of the federal government in imposing national
standards, and its increasing unwillingness to improve social provision,
that during recent constitutional debates social groups turned to other
methods, such as rights-based approaches, especially the Canadian Charter of Rights and Freedoms provisions on legal rights (s. 7) and equality
rights (s. 15). Success in challenges based on the equality rights provisions
of the Charter have encouraged social advocates to call for a more comprehensive social charter that would specify basic rights to income, food,
and housing.[10]

THE RECENT CONSTITUTIONAL AGENDA

Over the past decade and a half Canadians have endured several intense
constitutional debates. In the most recent rounds it was clear that the Canadian public would rather have the status quo.[11] But national reconciliation was perceived to be necessary in light of long-standing claims by
Québec for a unique status within Confederation. In 1982 the federal
government patriated the constitution without Québec's consent, and
Québec was perceived to have suffered a humiliating defeat (Clarkson and
McCall, 1991).

With the ultimate rejection in 1990 of the Meech Lake Accord, which
had been intended to bring Québec back into the constitutional fold,
Québec felt its unique status within Canada was not respected even sym-
bolically by the rest of Canada. By this time confidence in the ability of
Québec to go it alone had risen sharply. Even members of the traditionally federalist business elite in Québec supported the idea of independence
if Québec could not get a satisfactory offer from the rest of Canada. The
Québec Liberal Party staked out its position in the Allaire Report of 1990,
which suggested that federalism was no longer an asset to Québec and

called for a massive transfer of responsibility from the federal government to Québec. The only areas of responsibility it would have seen Ottawa continue to hold were defence, customs and tariffs, currency and common debt, and equalization. Premier Robert Bourassa subsequently appointed an all-party commission (the Bélanger-Campeau Commission), which adopted a similar analysis of the failings of federalism and suggested that Canada come up with an offer Québec could not refuse.

The federal government staked out its position in its 1991 report, *Shaping Canada's Future*. Under threat from Québec, since the Québec National Assembly had passed legislation requiring a referendum on the constitutional question by October of 1992, the federal position proposed a significant limitation on the power of Ottawa. Under the rubrics of "serving Canadians better," "recognizing areas of provincial jurisdiction," and "streamlining government," the central thrust of the proposals was to disentangle the federal government from social provision where the provinces could provide alternatives and to devolve and decentralize responsibility for social programs to provincial governments.

These proposals were framed as a way of offering the provinces what they wanted – more control over programs within their jurisdiction. But the offer could also be seen as a logical extension of actions that have led to a withering of the strong federal spending power and a profound retreat on the part of all governments from social provision (Doern and Purchase, 1991: 14). At the core of the federal government's plan was a restructured and reduced federal welfare state.

The Charlottetown Accord represented a significant modification of the federal position. In it there was no significant transfer of power to the provinces although there was a transfer of responsibility for the administration of labour market programs – a shared jurisdiction – to the provincial level for reasons of administrative efficiency. Public opposition to the Charlottetown Accord, which was defeated in a national referendum in the fall of 1992, resulted from the perception that it would reduce federal leadership in social policy and the ability of Ottawa to maintain national standards. For example, allowing provinces to opt out of federal programs, which was part of the Accord, was regarded as an example of the inability of the federal government to impose critical national programs, such as day care. These criticisms were somewhat curious given the evident unwillingness of the federal government to initiate a national day-care policy in the first place.

What remains after the defeat of the Accord is not clear. The failure gave impetus to the desire on the part of many people in Québec for out-right sovereignty. The election of the Bloc Québécois as the official op-position in Ottawa in 1993 was in part because of the dissatisfaction un-leashed in Québec as a result of the failure of Meech and the inadequacy of the Charlottetown Accord. However, it also seems clear that the elec-tion of the Parti Québécois in Québec in September of 1994 had more to do with the desire to unseat the Liberals than with a commitment to sov-ereignty.[12]

Given the failure of Meech and Charlottetown and the political liabil-ity associated with constitutional issues, there is very little likelihood of a willingness on the part of politicians to open up the formal constitutional change process in the near future. Nevertheless the need remains. If there is to be a constitutional reconciliation, it appears that the federal govern-ment will have to cede to Québec powers that English-Canadian federal-ists believe are necessary for Canada to fulfil its national destiny. The na-ture of the Charlottetown Accord demonstrated that the provinces are unwilling to come up with a solution that would grant Québec special status within Confederation, an idea often referred to as "asymmetrical federalism." Each province has its own list of demands for more control and the federal government risks opening a floodgate of demands from other provinces if it grants to Québec power over areas that it wants. The solution may be not in any formal reconciliation or change in constitu-tional relationships but rather in further institutional accommodation within the existing constitution. After all there was no formal domestic constitutional amending procedure from 1867 to 1982. Yet Canada proved a remarkably adaptable federation with the locus of power shifting back and forth over time in response to changing political and economic circumstances. Canada may be unwilling to grant Québec *de jure* or con-stitutional recognition of its distinct status, but it surely is willing to grant it *de facto* recognition. The Charlottetown Accord would have provided some clearer definitions of responsibilities, but non-constitutional changes have been the means by which Canada has achieved accommodations with the provinces in the past and will continue to be the way of the fu-ture.[13] The danger for Canada remains that Québec, in its desire to achieve its national destiny, will not be able to accept the constitutional status quo and will take the route of sovereignty.

With respect to social policy, however, the main issue is not the con-stitutional division of powers, except of course for Québec, but the future of the federal government's spending power. The federal spending power has already been substantially eroded. The future presents us with a very different federal government than we have had over the past forty years.[14] Soon after the federal Liberals were elected in 1993 they launched a social security review that was to reform Canada's income security programs dramatically. While the Minister of Human Resources Development, Lloyd Axworthy, stated his desire to make Canada's income security system more effective in tackling child poverty and in assisting people to get jobs, the Minister of Finance, Paul Martin, stated on a number of occasions that the main purpose of social security reform is to reduce federal expenditures. Reforms to be introduced in 1993 were postponed because of provincial dissatisfaction with proposals that had not been made public and because proposals for major social policy reform were considered unwise in the midst of a Québec election. By the fall of 1994 the federal social security review appeared considerably less ambitious than at the outset. A discussion paper proposed to reduce UI coverage for repeat users of unemployment insurance, to change the financing of provincial education programs, and possibly to expand or modify federal child benefits. The federal agenda for reform is driven principally by the desire to make significant cuts in federal spending and the federal deficit.

In this context the provinces will play the main role in social policy development in the near future. A key aspect of future reform efforts may focus on disentanglement or a rationalization of programs provided by different levels of government. For example, the EPF program has been irrational from the start and has very little political benefit for the federal government for the amount of spending involved. Both the federal government and the provinces are involved in the funding and delivery of labour market training, which leads to overlap and inefficiencies. There are also irrationalities associated with CAP cost-sharing of welfare that could be resolved by dividing support for children from support for adults and expanding the federal government's child tax benefit while ceding to the provinces the sole responsibility for the support of adults.

THE ECONOMIC RATIONALE FOR WELFARE STATE EROSION

The erosion of federal programs and the rebalancing of the locus of power over social policy can be understood in several ways: as changes in federal commitments; as responses to increased pressure from the provinces, especially Québec, for decentralization; and as responses to changes in the economic and political environment.

As I have argued, there has been a major change in federal commitments since 1984 and the election of the Progressive Conservatives to national office (Mishra, 1990). This change has been based on a conservative or neo-liberal vision of the state in response to the pressures of global competition. The erosion of Canada's welfare state is a central part of the strategy by Canadian business to introduce more flexibility into Canadian labour markets (Muszynski, 1994). The logic of restraint is closely associated with how social policy is perceived to affect labour markets. Faced with increased competition, business has identified inflexibility in the labour market with respect to wages, staffing levels, and the deployment of labour as a key problem inhibiting Canada's ability to compete. And it perceives the welfare state as the principal villain. The problems from the business point of view are high benefit levels, the lack of incentives to move from income security to employment, the high cost of universal programs, and, of course, the high taxes associated with financing social provision.

This perspective has been given intellectual credibility by economists, who as a profession have almost universally rejected the tenets of Keynesianism, especially the notion that economic efficiency can be compatible with social equity. Courchene, for example, echoes a familiar theme in arguing that there is an overriding economic determinism influenced by fiscal limits, technology, productivity, trade constraints, and socio-demographic realities, which requires a substantial restructuring of the welfare state in Canada (Courchene, 1987: 20-22). On balance, he argues, the Canadian welfare state has traded off efficiency (or positive adjustment to new technology and trade) for greater equity (or security of income protection in instable markets). Canada's economic success, he concludes, will depend on its ability to shift the balance of this trade-off to the side of efficiency or adjustment. The goals of this restructuring are greater efficiency of economic allocation, more decentralization, and more private-sector provision of social services. A key element of this approach is to restructure income security programs to provide benefits only to people "in need," that is, people with low incomes. The abolition of universal family allowances, for example, is justified by reference to an explicit desire to eliminate poverty by more efficient targeting of scarce social policy dollars. The main thrust of this approach is to reduce social spending and the required taxation to support it on the grounds of economic efficiency.

The Canada-U.S. Free Trade Agreement is not so much the villain as the catalyst for reform. It has focused attention on the asymmetry in social protection and taxation in the United States and Canada. As Courchene bluntly reminds us, "an east-west transfer system does not square well with a north-south trading system" (Courchene, 1991: 142). It is important to remember again, however, that the pressures of global competition were there before the federal Conservatives were elected in 1984. Although the Conservatives were explicitly committed to this strategy, previous Liberal governments were similarly committed to welfare state restructuring along the same lines. Indeed, as I have argued, the move toward a more restrictive welfare state was initiated in 1975 by the federal Liberals in response to economic pressures experienced at that time. And there is little reason to believe that the federal Liberal government elected in October, 1993, will be capable of resisting the pressure to reduce social spending despite its generally acknowledged commitment to maintaining the social safety net.

Although there is ongoing pressure by the provinces, especially Québec, to hand over programs to provincial governments, these pressures are minor compared to the pressures on both federal and provincial governments, especially by business, to restructure the welfare state. Recent federal actions may be read mostly as a conservative response to economic changes, global competition, and rising deficits. The provinces, even those run by NDP administrations, are forced to act by the same logic. The logic appears economic but is in a more profound sense political (Chorney et al., 1992: 6). High budget deficits and levels of taxation are perceived to be incompatible with high international bond ratings and a desirable investment climate. The new reality of global economic integration has made it extremely difficult for individual nations, particularly small and open trading nations like Canada, to pursue independent and especially generous domestic social policies. In this context there has been a substantial weakening of the Keynesian idea of domestic demand management and the commitment to social protection.

A RECONFIGURED CANADIAN WELFARE STATE

Federalism and a strong federal government were important in the evolution of the Canadian welfare state. But then as now, other political and ideological factors played a more decisive role (Banting, 1982: ch. 3). Simply reinforcing the role of the federal government will do little in the face of powerful social and economic forces favouring a society that conforms to market logic rather than the logic of equality, caring, and solidarity. Similarly, the redistribution of federal powers or spending to the provinces or to Québec alone will do little to stem the tide of welfare state erosion unless there is a significant restructuring of political and economic visions and priorities.

It is not clear that decentralization would in itself substantially undermine the Canadian welfare state. At this point the provinces are no less progressive than Ottawa in their social policy visions. Indeed, many are more visionary. In 1993 Ontario released its report *Turning Point* that outlined a strategy to replace that part of provincial welfare that went to the support of children with an income-tested provincial child benefit. By extending child-related income supplementation to the working poor, the proposal would have introduced a major new income supplementation program into Ontario's income security system and eliminated welfare for many families. In pursuing this strategy the province was seeking to implement the visionary framework for welfare reform outlined in *Transitions*, the 1988 report of the Ontario Social Assistance Review Committee. The proposal was abandoned in 1994 in the face of severe fiscal restraint.

New Brunswick released its discussion paper, *Creating New Opportunities*, in December, 1993, outlining two pilot projects. One, N.B. Works, is a joint federal-provincial initiative over a six-year period to test the impact of providing intensive education, training, and job experience to social assistance recipients. While the proposal focuses on providing employment supports, the discussion paper also states the need for major income security reform in general terms. The experiments in New Brunswick are heralded as the new wave of thinking in welfare reform.

The most significant recent proposal for reform emerged from Newfoundland. In December, 1993, the Economic Recovery Commission released an information paper, *Proposal for a New Income Supplementation Program*, as part of its Strategic Economic Plan. This proposal is for a radical restructuring of federal and provincial income security programs in Newfoundland including reform of UI, and is very similar to those made in 1986 by the Royal Commission on Employment and Unemployment.

These proposals signal important new directions for income security reform in Canada. But it is useful to remember that the Canadian welfare state has never been overly generous or exemplary. We are justly proud of our national health insurance system, but it also supports a largely private medical system whose major beneficiaries are doctors and drug companies. We are proud of our education system, but it also streams working-class children, women, and Aboriginal people into low-skill and wage jobs. We want to defend national standards for social assistance and social services and reverse Bill C-69, which restricts CAP payments to Ontario, Alberta, and B.C., but often forget that the welfare system that CAP supports is demeaning, bureaucratic, and reinforces dependency. In Québec, which has had effective control of much more of its social protection system than any other province, social provision is considered to be superior in many cases to that which exists in the rest of Canada. But recent welfare reform in Québec has focused on getting people off welfare by coercive and punitive means. In the language of welfare state theory, Canada's welfare state is liberal/residualist: it has a weak commitment to full employment; it tends to rely much too heavily on low-level means/needs-tested social assistance; and it has high levels of private insurance provision that restrict coverage and benefit levels for pensioners and people with disabilities (Esping-Anderson, 1990: ch. 1).

Although it is easy to understand why we may want to defend social programs against the cutbacks made by governments trying to contain their deficits and debts, it is also useful to look more closely at what specifically is good about social provision and what is less desirable. Just as the ongoing crisis in Canadian federalism offers us the opportunity to rethink what relationships we want to have among ourselves as citizens of the same nation, it also provides us with an opportunity to rethink the relationships we want between the market and the state.

The welfare state has at least two important and apparently contradictory goals. One is to improve welfare by equalizing the distribution of income and reducing poverty; the other assures equality of status by conferring citizenship rights to support and services. From a political economic perspective, the notion of "decommodification of labour" is central to the understanding of what the welfare state does. As Esping-Andersen argues, only when citizens command resources outside the labour market can they freely resist the compulsion to work under any circumstances. Thus it is essential for solidarity to be established among workers so that they will not underbid others who through collective effort have achieved wage improvements, or take jobs during strike actions: "The social rights, income security, equalization, and eradication of poverty that a universal welfare state pursues are necessary preconditions for the strength and unity that collective power mobilization demands" (*ibid.*: 16). Decommodification can only arise from the collective provision of income security, health care, and social services outside of the market by the state or by social movements themselves.

It is in this context that the importance of universality must be understood. While there is intuitive appeal to the currently dominant idea that the welfare state should be more efficient and redistributive in targeting its "scarce" dollars on the poor, redistribution may not be the most important goal of the welfare state. Programs restricted to the poor tend to have the least political support and are, therefore, subject to the most negative political pressure. In Thatcher's Britain and Reagan's United States, the programs targeted on low-income earners were subject to the most restraint, while the social insurances that tend to benefit the middle classes expanded despite intentions to the contrary (Goodin and Le Grand, 1987). This suggests that the real alternative we face is not more redistributive programs focused on need and fewer universal programs; the alternative is likely to be fewer income security programs of any sort. If the alternative is (in the extreme) no welfare state at all, then the idea of a purely redistributive welfare state is the result of the pure logic of neoclassical abstraction with no basis in political or social reality. Goodin and Le Grand argue that if the objective of the welfare state is an egalitarian one, the beneficial involvement of the non-poor, or universality, might not be the best mechanism for achieving it, but it is still better than a selective welfare state.

For Scandinavian social democrats, the welfare state has always been much more a political resource for building social solidarity than an instrument of redistribution (Esping-Andersen, 1985). By protecting all people from the vagaries of markets, social protection builds political alliances between often disparate groups and engenders support for the rule of democratic politics over markets and private power. A welfare state that is primarily redistributive may sound desirable from the point of view of social justice, but it undermines this solidarity and ultimately undermines support for social democratic parties. In doing so it reinforces a business agenda and highly inequitable market distributions. This is one reason why selectivity or targeting on the poor is so desirable to conservatives.

The paradox that troubles so many people is why anyone interested in creating a fairer, more equitable society would favour universality, which is so evidently ineffective in improving distribution. The answer is in an understanding of the dynamics of politics. Progressives can be opposed to a redistributive welfare state strategy precisely because they know it will jeopardize the struggle for a more equitable society in the long run. Welfare states are not merely technical mechanisms of redistribution; they are instruments for empowering groups in society, and they can substantially modify the extent to which market logic determines our lives.

The new economic order is reconfiguring our lives, but the nature of the change is being determined by a conservative and limited vision of what welfare states do and what levels of equality and well-being are possible. An alternative vision exists largely among the wide variety of popular groups who make claims on the state to engage in social protection against market forces and private power. This vision does not share the view that there is an inevitable trade-off between greater economic efficiency and social justice. The focus of claims made on the state by these popular groups represents a fundamentally different vision of the welfare state from that of the politically conservative, business-oriented right.

They focus on supports for substantially altered social relations of power, between men and women, between Aboriginal people and white Canadians, between people with disabilities and people without disabilities, between labour and management, and they emphasize the creation of a more equitable primary distribution of income. The struggle for universal child care is critical in this regard because it is an essential element of a framework to free women from the limitations they face as people and as workers who are forced into being the primary if not exclusive caregivers and nurturers of our children (Gunderson and Muszynski, 1990). The struggle for Native self-government is critical because it would allow Aboriginal people to define and run their own systems of social protection. Universal disability insurance programs are essential to blind people who are often pitted against each other for scarce resources (Muszynski, 1992). Reformed labour regulation is central to the task of building a stronger institutional basis for labour participation and influence in economic management. These claims for social protection are not focused on giving more to the poor; they are focused on creating a society where all Canadians have rights to protection and support. In this vision of equality, high wages and universal social provision are fully compatible with economic efficiency, labour market flexibility, and success in world trade.

The idea that high wages, social equity, and effective social protection are compatible with a high degree of international competitiveness hinges on a rejection of the idea that competition is based solely or even mostly on lowering factor costs. The alternative, which is the core lesson of the

Japanese model, is competition based on continuous innovation and pro-ductivity improvements. This alternative is well articulated in Canada by the Ontario Premier's Council in its reports – *Competing in the New Global Economy* and *People and Skills in the New Global Economy*[15] – and by the Ontario NDP government in its industrial strategy paper, Working To-gether for Economic Renewal (Ontario, 1992). This approach stands in stark contrast to the one that has dominated federal policy over the past decade, that lowering factor costs, including the costs of social protection, was essential within the context of freer trading regimes (Drache and Gertler, 1991).

In the Scandinavian nations where social democratic governments have been consistently elected, this broad conception of the welfare state has been the most effectively institutionalized. These states have demon-strated a degree of economic success that undermines tradition neo-classi-cal notions of efficient allocation. Their historical success lies in institu-tional arrangements that effectively managed a political solution to the problems of equity and allocation (Mishra, 1990).

THE COUNTER-MOVEMENT FOR SOCIAL PROTECTION

I have argued that the history of the welfare state is a history of struggle by social movements to counter the socially destructive effects of markets (Polanyi, 1944; Block, 1990). Welfare state effort cannot be judged by its redistributive effort alone. It is about building social solidarity and build-ing support for the struggle to reduce the status of labour as a commodity. Paradoxically, this approach appears to lead to more social equity than so-cial policies exclusively designed to give more to the poor. I have also ar-gued that, contrary to conservative assertions, this project can be compat-ible with a productive and competitive economy; indeed, it may even be essential to it.

The battles by progressive groups in Canada against the Canada-U.S. Free Trade Agreement and the North American Free Trade Agreement were in large measure battles for the primacy of social and politically de-termined priorities over market priorities. These battles failed, but the war continues. The dramatic effects of globalization require that social policy be rethought. Although the conservative agenda has dominated for many years, the pressures of a changed economy have also spawned new move-ments for social protection that are helping to redefine an alternative welfare state agenda. In addition, the closed nature of the failed constitutional accords has moved many social groups to argue for a place in the constitutional debate. A wide variety of popular groups in Canada outside Québec have come together in a unified manner under the banner of support for a social charter or the entrenchment of social rights in the Canadian constitution, such as the right to public health care or the right to adequate income and housing. The entrenchment of such rights was viewed as the essential *quid pro quo* for an economic agenda that is creating social misery. What is important about this movement and these demands is not so much what such a charter would produce, but that it would help define an important sense of shared identity. This is critically important when Canada as a nation is threatened by continental economic integration and by the forces of global economic competition.

The values underlying a social charter debate highlight these differences. Canadians see themselves as more caring and more willing to share among themselves (Taylor, 1991). These differences in values are clearly manifested in terms of the different welfare state approaches that exist between the U.S. and Canada. Canadians are more committed to collective provision than Americans. The most obvious example is Canada's national health insurance program. By contrast, the American approach to health insurance appears to most Canadians both irrational, in terms of its cost, and uncivilized (Lindorff, 1992). And it is not only health insurance. Canada's system of child-related benefits for lower-income families stands in contrast to the lack of support for families with children in the United States (Kamerman and Kahn, 1988). Canadians are also committed to sharing between individuals, groups, and regions in the form of equalization, while the United States does not have such a tradition. These commitments are viewed with such importance that popular groups wanted constitutional assurance that they would not be sacrificed on the altar of corporate competition. The fact that this identity coalesces around the welfare state is an important insight into where future struggles are likely to take place.

For Québec, constitutional issues remain at the forefront of the struggle for autonomy. For Québec sovereignists, autonomy can be gained only in the context of independence. But the nationalist vision for Québec expressed as a desire for special status within Canada or for outright sovereignty does not embody a commitment to a radically different form of welfare state. The recent attraction of sovereignty to many Québec business leaders and conservatives suggests that sovereignty is the issue, not more social equity in Québec.

Constitutions are obviously important; they are about the rules governing power and setting norms in society. But the substance of any constitutional issue will not be resolved by virtue of any particular constitutional framework. Significant policy differences will reflect the representation of power in society. And in Québec, as in Canada outside of Québec, the struggle by popular movements for recognition of their legitimate demands for income, power, dignity, land, and democracy will be the real stuff of defining progressive social policy.

NOTES

1 The brief history of constitutional responsibility for social policy in Canada is drawn principally from the definitive Canadian text on the subject (Banting, 1982: ch. 4).

2 The adoption of the federal family allowance program in 1944 (the flat-rate benefit to families with children) did not require a constitutional amendment and was upheld by the courts as falling within the federal government's right to enact programs for the "peace, order, and good government" of Canada.

3 The Canada Pension Plan, which was established in 1965, was not established in Québec. Instead, Québec chose to set up its own Québec Pension Plan with approximately the same design characteristics. A big issue for Québec was its desire to control the investment potential of the pension fund.

4 For example, the report of the Québec Commission of Inquiry on Health and Social Welfare (the Castonguay-Nepveu report); *Report of the Royal Commission on the Status of Women in Canada* (1970). This set out the framework for the reorganization of health and social services in Québec in the early 1970s that was widely regarded as by far the most progressive in Canada.

5 See especially *Poverty in Canada* (1971), the report of the Senate Committee on Poverty; *Income Security* (1971), the report of the Québec Commission of Inquiry on Health and Social Welfare (the Castonguay-Nepveu report); *Report of the Royal Commission on the Status of Women in Canada* (1970).

6 The framework for this had been set out in the federal White Paper, *Income Security for Canadians* (1970).

7 This is Ken Battle, then director of the National Council of Welfare, now president of the Caledon Institute of Social Policy, writing under a pseudonym.

8   This was subsequently extended to 1994-95 and is expected to be permanent because of the fiscal consequences to the federal government.

9   The claim by Liberal leader Jean Chrétien in 1993 during the Conservative leadership campaign that the Liberals will preserve medicare and never impose user fees was purely political rhetoric given that the federal government will lose its leverage over provincial health systems within the decade.

10   However, there are many problems with this approach (Mandel, 1991).

11   A poll conducted by the federal government one year before the referendum on the Charlottetown Accord clearly indicated little public interest in constitutional reform.

12   The Parti Québécois received 44.8 per cent of the popular vote compared to 44.3 per cent for the Liberals. The support for sovereignty consistently falls below support for the Parti Québécois.

13   For example, through administrative accommodation Québec opted out of the Canada Pension Plan in the 1960s and set up its own successful Québec Pension Plan. And it has more recently opted out of the federal Canadian Labour Market Board and set up its own system of labour market boards.

14   A formal review of federal-provincial fiscal arrangements will need to be conducted within the very near future.

15   For an analysis of the importance of these reports, see the collection of essays in Drache (1992).

REFERENCES

Banting, Keith G. (1982). *The Welfare State and Canadian Federalism.* Montreal and Kingston: McGill-Queen's University Press.

Battle, Ken, and Sherri Torjman (1993). *Federal Social Programs: Setting the Record Straight.* Ottawa: Caledon Institute of Social Policy.

Blank, Rebecca M., and Maria J. Hanratty (1993). "Responding to Need: A Comparison of Social Safety Nets in Canada and the United States," in David Card and Richard Freeman, eds., *Small Differences that Matter: Labour Markets and Income Maintenance in Canada and the United States.* Chicago: University of Chicago Press: 191-231.

Block, Fred (1990). *Postindustrial Possibilities: a Critique of Economic Discourse.* Berkeley: University of California Press.

Campbell, Robert M. (1991). *The Full Employment Objective in Canada, 1945-85.* Ottawa: Economic Council of Canada.

Campbell, Robert M. (1992). "Jobs ... Job ... Jo ... J ... The Conservatives and the Unemployed," in Frances Abele, ed., How Ottawa Spends 1992-1993. Ottawa: Carleton University Press.

Canada, Department of Finance, (1992). The Budget 1992.

Chorney, Harold, John Hotson, and Mario Seccareccia (1992). The Deficit Made Me Do It! Ottawa: Canadian Centre For Policy Alternatives.

Clarkson, Stephen, and Christina McCall (1991). Trudeau and Our Times: Vol 1. The Magnificent Obsession. Toronto: McClelland & Stewart.

Courchene, Thomas (1987). Social Policy for the 1990s. Toronto: C.D. Howe Institute.

Courchene, Thomas (1991). "Toward a Reintegration of Social and Economic Policy," in G. Bruce Doern and Bryne B. Purchase, eds., Canada at Risk? Toronto: C.D. Howe Institute, Policy Study 13.

Doern, G. Bruce, and Bryne B. Purchase (1991). "Whither Ottawa?" in Doern and Purchase, eds., Canada at Risk?

Drache, Daniel, ed., (1992). Getting On Track. Montreal and Kingston: McGill-Queen's University Press.

Drache, Daniel, and Meric S. Gertler (1991). The New Era of Global Competition. Montreal and Kingston: McGill-Queen's University Press.

Economic Council of Canada (1991). A Joint Venture.

Esping-Andersen, Gosta (1985). Politics Against Markets: The Social Democratic Road To Power. Princeton, N.J.: Princeton University Press.

Esping-Andersen, Gosta (1990). The Three Worlds of Welfare Capitalism. Princeton, N.J.: Princeton University Press.

Goodin, Robert E., and Julian Le Grand (1987). "Not Only The Poor," in Goodin and Le Grand, eds., Not Only the Poor: The Middle Classes and The Welfare State. London: Allen and Unwin.

Gray, Gratton (1990). "Social Policy by Stealth," Policy Options, 11, 2 (March): 17-29.

Guest, Dennis (1980). The Emergence of Social Security in Canada. Vancouver: University of British Columbia Press.

Gunderson, Morley, and Leon Muszynski (1990). Women and Labour Market Poverty. Ottawa: Canadian Advisory Council on the Status of Women.

Haddow, Rodney S. (1993). Poverty Reform in Canada 1958-1978: State and Class Influences on Policy Making. Montreal and Kingston: McGill-Queen's University Press.

Kamerman, Sheila B., and Alfred J. Kahn (1988). Mothers Alone. Dover, Mass.: Auburn House.

Lindorff, Dave (1992). Market Place Medicine. New York: Bantam.

Mandel, Michael (1991). "Rights, Freedoms, and Market Power: Canada's Charter of Rights and the New Era of Global Competition," in Drache and Gertler, eds., *The New Era of Global Competition*.

Maslove, Allan (1992). "Reconstructing Fiscal Federalism," in Frances Abele, ed., *How Ottawa Spends: The Politics of Competitiveness 1992-93*. Ottawa: Carleton University Press: 57-77.

Mishra, Ramesh (1990). The Welfare State in Capitalist Society. Toronto: University of Toronto Press.

Muszynski, Leon (1985). "The Politics of Labour Market Policy," in Bruce Doern, ed., *The Politics of Economic Policy*. Toronto: University of Toronto Press.

Muszynski, Leon (1988). *Is It Fair?: What Tax Reform Will Do to You*. Ottawa: Canadian Centre for Policy Alternatives.

Muszynski, Leon (1992). *Comprehensive Disability Income Security Reform*. Toronto: Roeher Institute.

Muszynski, Leon (1994). "Defending the Welfare State and Labour Market Policy," in Andrew F. Johnson and Stephen McBride, eds., *Continuities and Discontinuities in Social Policy*. Toronto: University of Toronto Press.

National Council of Welfare (1989). *Social Spending and the Next Budget*.

National Council of Welfare (1991). *The Canada Assistance Plan: No Time For Cuts*.

National Council of Welfare (1994). *Welfare Incomes*.

Ontario (1992). *1992 Ontario Budget*.

Ontario, Industry, Trade, and Technology (1992). *Working Together for Economic Renewal*.

Polanyi, Karl (1944). *The Great Transformation*. Boston: Beacon Press.

Social Planning Council of Metropolitan Toronto (1985). "The Rise and Fall of the Canadian Welfare State," in Daniel Drache and Duncan Cameron, eds., *The Other Macdonald Report*. Toronto: Lorimer.

Taylor, Charles (1991). "Shared and Divergent Values," in Ronald L. Watts and Douglas M. Brown, eds,) *Options for a New Canada*. Toronto: University of Toronto Press: 53-76.

Vaillancourt, François (1985). "Income Distribution and Economic Security in Canada," in Vaillancourt, ed., *Income Distribution and Economic Security in Canada*. Toronto: University of Toronto Press.

Wolfe, David (1984). "The Rise and Demise of the Keynesian Era in Canada: Economic Policy 1930-1982," in Gregory S. Kealy, ed., *Readings in Canadian Social History*. Toronto: McClelland & Stewart: 46-78.

CHAPTER THIRTEEN

Retrenching the Sacred Trust: Medicare and Canadian Federalism

Miriam Smith

MEDICARE IS CANADA'S MOST POPULAR SOCIAL PROGRAM. The health care system often stands as the symbol differentiating Canada from the United States and as an indication of the willingness of Canadians to use the state to achieve collective ends – in this case, accessible, universal, portable, and comprehensive medicare. At the same time, however, the medicare system in Canada is widely believed to be in crisis, in particular because of rising costs. Provincial governments blame the federal government for failing to fund medicare, while the federal government claims that the high level of the federal deficit justifies retrenchment in the health care sector.

The shape of Canadian political institutions has a profound impact on the way choices are made in medicare policy-making. Two features of Canadian political institutions are critical to understanding policy-making in this area. The first is parliamentary government. Unlike the American system of checks and balances, which can create legislative gridlock, parliamentary systems concentrate power in the executive. Because of the fusion of executive and legislative authority, the executive cannot be easily stymied by opposition from the legislature. This effect is heightened in Canada because of the relatively high turnover of MPs in the House of Commons, the relative lack of resources of MPs, and the well-developed system of party discipline that reduces the possibility of a caucus revolt that could torpedo the executive's initiatives. This system gives the executive the relative freedom to pursue a concentrated policy agenda, free of obstruction from the legislative branch. This concentration of authority potentially facilitates changes in social policy – either expansion or retrenchment – depending on the policy goals of the party in power.

The second important institutional constraint on social policy-making in Canada is federalism, which divides authority between levels of government. In the case of social policy, this often means that policies fall under provincial jurisdiction while responsibility for program funding is shared between provincial and federal levels of governments. The particular institutional arrangements for decision-making and funding between the federal government and the provinces have an important impact on the possibilities for the federal government to pursue changes in social policy. These particular institutional designs provide political opportunity structures for parties and other actors who are committed to the pursuit of certain policies.

The impact of federalism on social policy expansion and retrenchment is complicated and contested in the political science literature. On the one hand, federalism is thought to work against both the expansion and retrenchment of social policy because of the multiple veto points in the system. The gridlock built into the American system at the national level is found in Canada between federal and provincial governments, which, in this view, prevents concerted action. On the other hand, some argue that federalism has been an advantage to the expansion of social policy because the division of jurisdictions has permitted provincial experimentation with social policy. In this chapter, I will examine these arguments as they apply to the establishment, consolidation, and retrenchment of medicare in Canada. With respect to retrenchment, I will argue that the combination of parliamentary governance and the particular features of federal arrangements in medicare increases the federal government's scope for unilateral retrenchment in the medicare field.

HEALTH CARE AND THE DIVISION OF POWERS

The constitutional division of powers laid out in the British North America Act did not anticipate the modern state's responsibility for public health. As the Rowell-Sirois *Report* (1940) pointed out, "In 1867 the administration of public health was still in a very primitive state, the assumption being that health was a private matter and state assistance to protect or improve the health of the citizen was highly exceptional and tolerable only in emergencies" (Rowell-Sirois, 1940: 33-34). Much public health activity was carried out by local and municipal authorities, which were under provincial jurisdiction. Under the BNA Act, all matters of "a merely local or private nature" were assigned exclusively to the provinces. In addition, the BNA Act, in section 92(7), explicitly gave the provinces the exclusive authority to legislate for the establishment, maintenance, and management of hospitals, asylums, and charities (other than marine hospitals). The only federal responsibilities in this area were ancillary to other federal jurisdictions such as navigation, immigration, shipping, trade and commerce, Indians, public works, and defence. By the interwar period, the Dominion Department of Health had been established to administer federal statutes on public health relating to narcotics, food and drug safety, leprosy, medical patents, and public works. In addition, a Dominion Council of Health brought together the provincial and federal ministers of health to coordinate federal and provincial activities (*ibid.*, 32-33).

However, the main lever of federal influence over the development of the medicare system has been the federal spending power. In the BNA Act, the federal government was assigned a virtually unlimited authority to tax and spend. Through the use of this power, the federal government has intervened in areas of provincial jurisdiction such as health care. Thus, the federal government may force the provinces to adhere to uniform national standards and may shape the substance of policies that fall under provincial jurisdiction. National standards in medicare, therefore, are enforced through the use of the federal spending power.

FEDERALISM AND SOCIAL POLICY

There is substantial debate in the literature on the relationship between federalism and social policy. This literature can be divided into two groups – that which argues that federalism constrains the growth of social programs and that which claims it has a neutral effect or even facilitates it.

Some claim that federalism constrains the development of social policy by dividing jurisdiction between levels of government. Depending on the division of jurisdictions, more than one level of government may have to agree to the establishment of social programs or to changes in such programs, once established. Despite the best efforts of one level of government to establish a social program, its efforts can be frustrated by another level of government. Indeed, defenders of federalism have often pointed to this aspect of federalism – divided government – as its great strength. Divided government – checks and balances, in American parlance – increases citizens' control over government, prevents one centre of power from dominating the political system, and divides the state against itself in ways that create obstacles to state intervention. For just this reason, supporters of social program expansion have often criticized federalism as a system that restrains the growth of social programs.

Such critiques of federalism were prominent in English-speaking Canada during the thirties. To many, the effects of the Great Depression pointed to the need for the expansion of social programs. Canadian federalism posed an obstacle to such expansion because the judicial decisions of Canada's highest court at the time – the Judicial Committee of the Privy Council – placed responsibility for many types of social programs (including unemployment insurance) in provincial jurisdiction. While some social policies were determined by the court to fall under provincial jurisdiction, the provinces lacked the fiscal resources to establish such programs. Indeed, the fiscal crisis of the provinces during the thirties rendered program expansion difficult. According to English-speaking critics of the JCPC, the court misinterpreted the original intentions of the framers of the constitution in placing some types of social policy in provincial jurisdiction (Cairns, 1971: 301-45).

Reinterpretations of the JCPC's role in devolving social policy to the provinces, however, have stressed that it was not so much JCPC decisions that prevented federal action during the thirties as it was lack of political will among the federal parties and lack of political support in either English Canada or Québec for social program expansion. For example, the Bennett government's 1935 "New Deal," a package of measures that would have established unemployment insurance, a national marketing board, and federal regulation of minimum wages and hours of work, was struck down as *ultra vires* federal jurisdiction in 1937. However, it is far from clear that the Conservative Prime Minister, R.B. Bennett, had the support of his cabinet and caucus for these measures. Bennett's successor, Liberal Prime Minister Mackenzie King, was similarly lukewarm about such proposals. As several studies have concluded, if the federal government had been strongly committed to such measures, it probably could have found ways to circumvent the JCPC's decisions; instead, the Liberal government took the initiative in referring the cases to the court, thus passing a political hot potato from the government to the judiciary (Mallory, 1954; Simeon and Robinson, 1990: 78-87).

In contrast to the very negative English-Canadian interpretation of the division of powers in social policy, Québec commentators have stressed the JCPC's role in defending the integrity of the division of powers. Generally, Québec governments have favoured provincial control of social policy. During the Duplessis era and before, provincial control was a means of averting large-scale state intervention in social policy, much of which was under the control of the Church. Following the Quiet Revolution of the sixties, social policy was seen as an important lever of control and development for the Québec state (Vaillancourt, 1988). Québec governments sought a greater role for the provincial level of government in the development of social policy in constitutional negotiations. At Victoria in 1971, for example, Québec pushed the federal government to development more flexible arrangements permitting an independent Québec role in some social policy areas (such as pension policy), and aimed to limit the reach of the federal spending power in areas of provincial jurisdiction in the 1980-81, Meech Lake, and Charlottetown rounds of constitutional negotiation (Rocher, 1992a: 87-98; Rocher, 1992b: 23-36).

Comparative studies of the effects of federalism on social policy have tended to conclude that federalism has a conservative impact on social policy expansion. Banting's comparative analysis of Canada's income security programs found that federalism had a moderately restraining impact on the development of income security (Banting, 1987). However, analyses of the health care field specifically have found that federalism has been neutral in the development of medicare. In a comparative analysis of the development of health policy in Canada and Australia, Gwendolyn Gray, for example, argues that the partisanship of government and the determination of politicians to enact (or not enact) medicare was more important than the impact of federalism itself (Gray, 1991). Others who have examined the development of the Canadian system have argued that, while federalism certainly affected the development of health policy, it did not prevent it or slow it down significantly (Tuohy, 1993). In an ardent defence of Canadian federalism, Pierre Trudeau took the position that federalism was an advantage in establishing and expanding programs such as medicare. In Trudeau's view, provincial jurisdiction permitted opportunities for provincial experimentation with social programs that then spread to other provinces (Trudeau, 1968). Trudeau rested his case on medicare, which began in one province (Saskatchewan) and was eventually established in all provinces.

Debates about the effect of federalism on social policy expansion have recently been extended to the question of how social policies are changed once they are established and, in particular, to the politics of social program retrenchment (Pierson, 1994). In the aftermath of the economic crisis of the seventies and the restructuring of the eighties, social policies in advanced capitalist countries have been under strain. In some countries such as Canada and the U.S., budget deficits have created new pressures on social spending. In addition, there has been a shift to the right, evidenced not only by the election of conservatives and conservative parties but also in the new-found commitment of such parties to break with the post-war consensus on social policy. In some cases, such commitments were overt – as in the case of Reagan in the U.S. and Thatcher's Conservatives in Britain. In the Canadian case, the popularity of certain programs, particularly medicare, placed electoral limits on the open advocacy of social policy retrenchment (Pierson and Smith, 1993). Nonetheless, as will be shown below, the Progressive Conservative government found less visible ways to carry out its commitment to social policy retrenchment in what has been called "the politics of stealth" (Gray, 1990: 17-29).

Just as federalism shapes the political opportunity structure for social policy establishment and expansion, so, too, it creates obstacles and opportunities for governments committed to retrenchment in social policy. In part, the federal government's retrenchment opportunities depend on the particular institutional arrangements between levels of government in the original program design. In other words, the extent to which federalism facilitates or creates obstacles to program retrenchment varies across policy areas. In his examination of the Canada Pension Plan, for example, Banting found that the institutional structuring of federalism in this policy area tended to impede radical change in either direction – expansion or retrenchment (Banting, 1985: 48-74). Unlike medicare, pensions are a concurrent jurisdiction with provincial paramountcy; changes to the Canada Pension Plan require the consent of two-thirds of the provinces with two-thirds of the population (as well as a *de facto* Québec veto to keep the QPP consistent with the CPP). This arrangement tends to forestall radical policy change and to inhibit further expansion.

In the medicare field, however, the particular institutional arrangement of federalism has facilitated retrenchment. The way in which medicare was established has left the federal government in a strong position to impose the hard choices on provincial governments. While in the area of pension policy, the entanglements of the provinces in the decision-making process create formidable obstacles to reform, with medicare the structure of the program makes it easier for the federal government to change the formula governing funding and to force the provincial governments to bear the burden of increasing health care costs. If the struggle over pensions in Canada has been a classic left-right debate over universalism vs. targeting, public debates over Canadian health policy have been fundamentally shaped by federal-provincial relations. Because health insurance is popular, both levels of government try to claim political credit for the program while imposing the rising costs of the program onto the other. Thus, debates over health care have not been about retrenchment but about which level of government is responsible for funding health care (Charles and Badgley, 1987: 50; Taylor, 1987: 83).

Furthermore, because the consent of the provinces is not required for changes to health care funding, the federal government has a relatively free hand in changing the program. When combined with the other salient feature of Canadian political institutions – parliamentary governance – the federal government does not face opposition from within the legislature. In addition, the federal budgetary process and the complexity of the system of federal-provincial transfers create obstacles to mounting opposition to the federal cuts. In addition, interest groups in medicare are concentrated on the provincial level, and what Caroline Tuohy (1988 has called the "diffuse consumer interest" of the clients of the medicare system is very difficult to mobilize due to collective action problems.

MEDICARE: FROM ITS ESTABLISHMENT TO THE CANADA HEALTH ACT

Federalism provided particular institutional opportunities for governments at both provincial and federal levels committed to the establishment of medicare. At both levels of government, the establishment of medicare required the election of political parties committed to medicare. At the provincial level, the election of the CCF government in Saskatchewan provided the political will for the pursuit of hospital insurance in 1947 and health insurance in 1961. Provincial jurisdiction over health care allowed the pioneering CCF government of Tommy Douglas to establish hospital insurance. The federal government's spending power permitted a federal role in financing the plan and in creating incentives for other provinces to follow the Saskatchewan lead. After a long political battle the federal government established a cost sharing plan for hospital insurance in 1957, and by 1961 all provinces had entered the plan (Taylor, 1987). Again, in the field of health insurance, Saskatchewan was a pioneer, bringing in health insurance after a doctors' strike in 1961. Following the advent to the Liberal leadership of Lester Pearson, the Liberal government became an advocate of medicare and put into place a shared-cost program in 1966.

The institutional arrangements between levels of government for financing medicare – provincial delivery and a federal financing role through the use of the spending power – stand in contrast to the federal-provincial relations in other fields of social policy such as income security. Social insurance programs such as contributory pensions and unemployment insurance also fell under provincial jurisdiction. In both cases, the federal government asserted a role for itself through constitutional amendment rather than through exercising the spending power. In the case of unemployment insurance, the 1940 amendment transferred jurisdiction to the federal government, while for pensions an amendment provided for shared jurisdiction with provincial paramountcy. Each of these arrangements provides a different political opportunity structure for the expansion and retrenchment of programs.

Within a decade of the establishment of health insurance, both levels of government had become disenchanted with the financing arrangements. The original financing formula was a series of conditional grants to the provinces for hospital and medical care insurance. Prior to 1977, provinces had to meet certain conditions to qualify for federal funding. These conditions were: public administration, comprehensive services, access to insured services, universal coverage, and portability of benefits. In return, the federal government provided 50 per cent of the national per capita costs of insured services (*ibid.*: 42-43). The important point here is that the federal government was committed to paying half of actual health care costs and could steer provincial health programs in line with national objectives, ensuring the provision of roughly similar services in all parts of the country through the conditionality of federal funding.

By the mid-seventies, however, several problems had emerged. First, the federal government had no way to control health care costs as the relevant spending decisions were made by provincial governments. The incentive for cost containment was reduced as the provinces were spending "fifty-cent dollars" on health care. In turn, the provinces complained that federal funding of hospital and medical care insurance distorted provincial health care priorities by funding only two types of health care programs – hospital and medical care insurance (Taylor, 1989: 89).

These concerns led to the negotiation in 1977 of a new formula – Established Programs Financing (EPF) – governing health care and post-secondary education transfers to the provinces. EPF established a per capita block grant from the federal government to the provinces. The grant was linked to a three-year rolling average of increases in per capita GNP. In addition, the federal government offered tax points equivalent to one-half of the existing federal contribution. Tax points are a percentage of personal and corporate income tax levied by the federal government. In transferring a percentage of income tax to the provinces, the federal government was in effect transferring to the provinces the capacity to levy and to benefit from that percentage of taxation in the future. The original transfer of tax points equalled one-half of the 1976 federal transfer for health care and post-secondary education. Of course, the actual value of tax points in a given year fluctuates, depending on factors such as the state of the economy. EPF also contained equalization payments for poorer provinces to increase their tax point yield to the national average.

Thus, transfers to the provinces after 1977 were comprised of two components: cash transfers and tax points. It is important to note that eligibility for tax point transfers was unconditional whereas conditions under the original medicare legislation still applied to the per capita grant (Charles and Badgely, 1987). The new formula loosened the link between federal funding and the actual cost of medicare. Under the pre-EPF system, the federal government had paid 50 per cent of the actual costs of medicare; in contrast, under EPF, the cash grant portion of the federal transfer was linked to growth in GNP, rather than to growth in actual health care costs. In addition, although the transfer was supposed to be divided between post-secondary education and health care with one-third of the total transfer (cash grant plus tax points) allocated to post-secondary education and two-thirds to health care, in fact, the transfer was not tied. The federal government allowed the provinces to treat the transfer as general revenue and left the spending decisions in the hands of the provinces (Maslove, 1992: 59).

The federal government had intended the new financing formula to restrain costs and to decrease the federal contribution. The transfer portion of the payments escalated by the three-year average rate of increase in GNP, in effect, a decremental cut because inflation rates in the health care sector were higher than the general rate of increase in the Consumer Price Index. However, because the rate of inflation in the late seventies rose faster than actual health and education spending, the federal share of provincial spending on health care actually increased after EPF. Total EPF spending (including post-secondary education) resulted in an estimated $1.5-$1.8 billion more in transfers to the provinces than they would have received under the pre-EPF formula (Parliamentary Task Force on Federal-Provincial Relations, 1981; Brown, 1986: 111-32).

That the complexity of the intergovernmental financing arrangements in the policy field contributed to the "invisibility" of information can be seen in the fact that, post-EPF, each level of government blamed the other for mounting health care costs. The provincial governments claimed that the federal government was underfunding the system while the federal government claimed that the provincial governments were diverting the transfers to other uses, a charge later found to be without foundation (Charles and Badgely, 1987: 51-52). In addition, when EPF (and the accompanying taxation agreements) was renewed for 1982-87, the federal government eliminated the revenue guarantee at a loss of an estimated $5 billion to the provinces for the period (Taylor, 1989: 84). As medicare costs increased, financial pressures on provincial governments opened the door to creeping privatization (increased extra-billing by doctors and user fees in some provinces).

Extra-billing and user fees undermine the basic principles of medicare and lead ultimately to a two-tiered health care system in which those who can afford to pay have better access to certain types of services (depending on the extent and type of user fees and on the medical specialties most prone to extra-billing). Ultimately, both practices can lead potentially to a situation in which some regions of the country might not have universal access to certain medical services.

While such measures did not affect large numbers of health care consumers, pressure mounted on the federal government to enforce its own conditions for federal financing. The federal government was seen as the guarantor of universal and accessible health care. The question was: how was the federal government to withhold funding from governments that violated the principles of medicare in this manner? In principle, the federal government, the enforcer of national standards in medicare, should have been able to withhold federal funding if provinces violated the principles of medicare. However, as federal bureaucrats discovered, neither the original medicare legislation nor EPF provided a formula for the federal government to enforce conditionality by withholding funds. Under EPF, tax points in any case could not be withheld from the provinces; the tax point portion of federal funding had already been transferred to the provinces and could not be easily taken back from provinces that permitted user fees or extra-billing. In principle, however, the cash grant portion of the grant could be withheld. Yet, neither the medicare legislation nor EPF contained a formula for the dollar-for-dollar withholding of federal fund-ing. The only way to bring recalcitrant provinces to heel was to withhold the entire cash grant portion of the transfer, a measure that not only would be disproportionate penalty but that also would throw provincial health care financing into chaos.

To solve this problem, the Liberal government passed the Canada Health Act (1984), which strengthened and clarified the federal condi-tions for health care financing. The Act established clear criteria govern-ing conditionality and provided for financial sanctions proportionate to the actual extent of user fees and extra-billing permitted by the provinces. These conditions only applied to the cash portion of the federal transfer. The Act also required that the provinces clearly state the federal financing role in medicare in public documents, thus increasing the federal govern-ment's visibility in this field. Finally, the Act provided that if provinces adopted binding arbitration (not required in the Act), they must permit the award to be debated in the legislature. This last change was made to accommodate the doctors who felt that public debate in the legislature would aid their cause (Taylor, 1987).

The Canada Health Act outraged both doctors and provincial govern-ments. The provinces argued that they had not been consulted, that the Act infringed provincial jurisdiction for health care, and that it did not solve the underfunding problem. Doctors also objected to the Act as an infringement of their entrepreneurial freedom (Canada, House of Com-mons, 1983-84). As Caroline Tuohy has pointed out, the passage of the Canada Health Act is a striking example of the defeat of a powerful and concentrated interest group – doctors – in favour of a diffuse consumer interest (Tuohy, 1988: 267-96).

This intervention must be seen in the light of party politics of the pe-riod. While the Canada Health Act was supported by all three federal par-ties (including the Mulroney Tories in opposition), the Act embodied several principles critical to the Liberal government's vision of national unity. The Act confirmed the Liberals' willingness to intervene in areas of provincial jurisdiction and to use the federal government as an instrument to build national identities. The Liberals centralizing version of Canadian federalism had reached its zenith in the 1980-82 period with the debate over the patriation of the constitution, the entrenching of a Charter of Rights, and the National Energy Program. By 1984, the government was close to the end of its mandate and had retreated from its centralizing and nationalizing bent in the areas of economic and energy policy. The Can-

329

ada Health Act allowed the government to reassert the nationalizing role of the federal government in social policy at no financial cost. While there were powerful actors arrayed against the bill – doctors and provincial governments – these interests were not in a position to threaten its passage. Unlike the CPP, the federal government was not obliged to consult the provinces about changes to the rules governing medicare (Courchene, 1985: 3-5). While the doctors testified at the public hearings held on the bill, they had no avenues of protest against a determined executive. Their only recourse was to pressure provincial governments; indeed, the outcome of the Canada Health Act in Ontario, for example, was a six-day doctors' strike over the extra-billing issue. Thus, the consequences of the doctors' dissatisfaction fell not on the federal government but on the provincial governments who were responsible for negotiating fee schedules with the doctors. Finally, the Canada Health Act was overwhelmingly popular with Canadians, although, unfortunately for the Liberals, they lost the partisan advantage on the issue when the federal Tories supported the Act (Canadian Institute of Public Opinion, May 10, 14, 1984; Tuohy, 1988: 295-96; Watson, 1985). In Brian Mulroney's words, "As far as the Conservative party is concerned, Medicare is a sacred trust which we will preserve" (cited in Taylor, 1987: 443).

RETRENCHING THE SACRED TRUST

While Liberal attempts to curtail federal responsibility for health care costs were only partly successful, the Conservatives quickly showed that the federal government's unilateral capacity to alter the complicated and obscure EPF formula could be used to the advantage of retrenchment. In 1985, the Minister of Finance restricted federal transfers under EPF to GNP increases less 2 percentage points. The 1989 budget accentuated this trend by changing the indexing formula to GNP increases less 3 percentage points (National Council of Welfare, 1990: 32). The 1990 budget went even further by freezing the cash component of EPF expenditure at 1989-90 levels, a freeze that was continued in the 1991-92 budget and extended through 1994-1995. These changes will save the federal government an estimated $2.34 billion over the five-year period beginning in 1991 (Battle and Torjman, 1993: 6; Table One).

Despite the obvious implications of these cuts for provincial governments and for consumers of medicare, there was very little public outcry

TABLE ONE: FEDERAL HEALTH CARE CONTRIBUTIONS, 1978-1992
(s MILLIONS)

	CASH	CASH AS % OF TOTAL	TAX POINTS	TAX POINTS AS % OF TOTAL	TOTAL CONTRIB.
1978-79	3,466	59.3	2,378	40.7	5,844
1979-80	3,859	58.7	2,720	41.3	6,579
1980-81	3,980	55.6	3,174	44.4	7,156
1981-82	4,283	54.3	3,605	45.7	7,888
1982-83	4,060	50.1	4,053	49.9	8,113
1983-84	5,564	56.6	4,269	43.4	9,833
1984-85	6,330	59.4	4,331	40.6	10,661
1985-86	6,386	57.5	4,726	42.5	11,112
1886-87	6,621	55.7	5,258	44.3	11,878
1987-88	6,558	53.2	5,771	46.8	12,329
1988-89	6,622	49.8	6,671	50.2	13,294
1989-90	6,934	49.2	7,165	50.8	14,109
1990-91	6,370	44.4	7,972	55.6	14,342
1991-92	6,058	41.8	8,454	58.3	14,511

Sources: Calculated from Health and Welfare Canada, *Estimates: Part III Expenditure Plan*, 1986-87: 2-23; 1987-88: 2-21; 1988-89: 2-21; 1989-90: 2-21; 1990-91: 2-52; 1991-92: 2-53. Numbers may not add because of rounding.

over the changes. While provincial governments complained that their funding for medicare was being cut by the federal government, such objections have not mobilized public opposition. In part this is because the complicated funding formula, which makes it difficult for the public to assess the claims and counter-claims of federal and provincial governments.

In addition, interests organizations in the medicare field that might have opposed such cuts are organized along the lines of provincial jurisdiction because of the provincial responsibility for the delivery of medicare. Even if such groups choose to bring their views to Ottawa, the budget process itself is fairly well insulated from interest group pressures unless such groups are able to mobilize public opinion against the government, as in the case of seniors' opposition to the deindexation of the old age security pension in 1985. Nation-wide groupings opposed to medicare cuts, such as the Canada Health Coalition — a broad alliance of labour, anti-poverty, church, and seniors' groups that support increased health care funding, universality, and a strong federal role in funding medicare – have been unable to mount an effective national opposition to the defunding of medicare. Interest groups are more cohesive at the provincial level, but, even there, powerful groups such as the doctors were defeated in their Ontario strike (Tuohy, 1989: 141-60).

Moreover, the effect of the cuts is not only to reduce the funding available to provincial governments for financing medicare but, more importantly, to erode the federal government's ability to enforce the conditions of the Canada Health Act. The (conditional) cash portion of the federal transfer has decreased relative to the (unconditional) tax portion. In 1991-92, cash transfers accounted for only 41.8 per cent of total federal spending on health care, down from 57.5 per cent in 1985. As well, if this decremental cut continues, the cash portion of the federal transfer will soon be eliminated. In one estimate, cash payments to Québec will disappear in fiscal 1996-97, payments to Ontario in 2002-03, and for other provinces and territories by 2010 (National Council of Welfare, 1991: 19-23, 30-35).

The effect of these cuts can be seen in Table One, which outlines the cash and tax components of the federal contribution for health care from 1978 to the projections for 1991-92. This table shows that the cash transfer portion of federal expenditure was declining until 1982-83. In 1983-84, the cash transfers increased, reaching a peak in 1984-85. As the federal cash funding declines as a proportion of total federal expenditure, the federal government's ability to enforce the conditions of the Canada Health Act also declines.

The effects of Ottawa's weakening grip on health care can be seen in recent battles between the federal and provincial governments over health spending. In the face of declining federal funding and rising medicare costs, provincial governments have several options. First, they can attempt to eliminate the federal cash contribution to medicare (while it still exists) in exchange for more tax points. This strategy is favoured by Québec and some western provinces. If this were to succeed, the portability, universality, and comprehensiveness of coverage across the country could be jeopardized in the long run as the federal government would have no lever for the enforcement of national standards. Second, the provinces can attempt to cut costs or raise taxes in the face of the fiscal crunch. NDP governments, in power in B.C., Ontario, and Saskatchewan, are pursuing this option. And, finally, the provinces can permit extra-billing and user fees.

For all provinces, regardless of their commitment to a federal or provincial role in financing or their stance on user fees and extra-billing, re-structuring the delivery of medicare has become critical to cost containment. Hospital services have been consolidated and cut, and procedures and services have been de-insured as "medically unnecessary." As the Canada Health Act sets out conditions for "medically necessary" services, provinces can avoid their obligations under the Act by defining certain procedures or services as unnecessary (Fuller, 1993: 14-19). De-insurance creates *de facto* user fees in the system that are less visible to the public than outright fees or extra-billing by doctors.

However, if the experience of the Canada Health Act is any guide, the creeping privatization of the system will focus the political responsibility for the erosion of medicare squarely back on the shoulders of the federal government. The Mulroney government was willing to cut medicare as long as the complexity of the funding arrangement shielded these cuts from public scrutiny. If user fees and extra-billing begin to appear once again in the system, however, the federal government will be held responsible. While such privatization affects only a very small proportion of health care consumers, the symbolic effect of the erosion of national standards is potent indeed, especially for a Liberal government supposedly committed to the preservation of national standards in social programs.

Thus, conflicting dynamics are at work in this policy area. On the one hand, the complexity of funding and the executive's unimpeded ability to impose relatively invisible funding cuts opens the door to retrenchment. Eventually, however, the fiscal strain in the medicare system opens the door to privatization. As the provinces take the first steps in the direction of privatization, the federal strategy is forced out into the open. Because of the popularity of universal and accessible health insurance, no federal government can afford to pay the political price of dismantling it (Leslie, 1993: 1-86).

In each of the provincial systems, different factors affect the provincial responses. The western premiers seek market solutions in part to outflank the growth of the Reform Party. As was so often the case in the past, Ontario finds itself favouring a strong federal role, this time under the auspices of a social democratic government strongly committed to universality in social policy.

CONCLUSION: HEALTH CARE AND FEDERALISM

In considering the interaction between Canadian federalism and social policy, one must be sensitive to the particular institutional arrangements between levels of government in particular policy areas. The dynamics of program expansion and retrenchment vary across policy areas because of the variety of institutional arrangements governing program financing and delivery between levels of government. These particular institutional arrangements are in themselves the products of the phase of social policy establishment and expansion. Arrangements put into place during one historical period provide opportunities and set limits on the kinds of change that are likely at another historical period (Banting, 1987; Pierson and Smith, 1994).

In policy areas such as pensions, where provincial agreement to financing formulas is required, the political opportunity structure for program change of any kind – expansion or retrenchment – narrows. In fields such as medicare, where the federal government can act unilaterally, the concentration of authority in the Westminster model of parliamentary governance creates political opportunities for determined governments to alter program structure. Furthermore, because of the complexity of federal-provincial transfers, cuts can be shielded from public scrutiny, thus allowing the federal government to pass the buck to provincial governments.

However, in medicare there are political limits on the extent to which unilateral federal retrenchment can succeed. As the federal government loses control over the conditionality of the program, this opens the door to a renewal of the debates over extra-billing and user fees that originally led to the implementation of the Canada Health Act. Medicare is still resoundingly popular with the public. Outside Québec, there is strong public support for the federal role in the maintenance of national standards in social programs generally and medicare specifically. In the constitutional debates over the Meech Lake and the Charlottetown Accords, critics often claimed that constitutional change would undermine the federal role in maintaining national standards in social programs. If federal defunding results in creeping privatization of medicare, then the experience of the Canada Health Act suggests that a public backlash against medicare cuts will occur. User fees and extra-billing have more potential to mobilize public opposition to federal defunding than do the complexities of the EPF formula.

A final question remains. To what extent has the defunding of medicare become irreversible? Could a future federal government reassert the federal role in medicare with ease? Just as the EPF formula allows the federal government to defund medicare through the budgetary process, so, too, the federal government could choose to increase the cash grant portion of the funding and thus restore the federal role. The main obstacle to a reassertion of the federal role is the fiscal pressure created by the federal deficit and debt.

REFERENCES

Banting, Keith (1985). "Institutional Conservatism and Pension Reform," in Jacqueline S. Ismael, ed., *Canadian Social Welfare Policy: Federal and Provincial Dimensions*. Montreal and Kingston: McGill-Queen's University Press: 48–74.

Banting, Keith (1987). *The Welfare State and Canadian Federalism*. Montreal and Kingston: McGill-Queen's University Press.

Battle, Ken, and Sherri Torjman (1993). *Federal Social Programs: Setting the Record Straight*. Ottawa: Caledon Institute of Social Policy.

Brown, Malcolm C. (1986). "Health Care Financing and the Canada Health Act," *Journal of Canadian Studies*, 21, 2: 111–32.

Cairns, Alan (1971). "The Judicial Committee and its Critics," *Canadian Journal of Political Science*, 4: 301–45.

Canada (1990–91). *Estimates: Part I The Government Expenditure Plan*.

Canada (1991–92). Estimates: Part I The Government Expenditure Plan.

Canada, Health and Welfare Canada (1986–92). *Estimates: Part III Expenditure Plan*.

Canada, House of Commons (1983–84). *Minutes of Proceedings and Evidence of the Standing Committee on Health, Welfare and Social Affairs Respecting Bill C-3, Canada Health Act*. 2nd session of the 32nd Parliament 7.

Canadian Institute of Public Opinion (1984). *Gallup Report*.

Charles C., and Robin F. Badgley (1987). "Health and Inequality: Unresolved Policy Issues," in Shankar A. Yelaja, ed., *Canadian Social Policy*. Waterloo, Ont.: Wilfrid Laurier University Press: 47–64.

Courchene, Thomas (1985). "The fiscal arrangements: focus on 1987," in *Ottawa and the Provinces: The Distribution of Money and Power*. Toronto: Ontario Economic Council.

Fuller, Colleen (1993). "A Matter of Life and Death: NAFTA and Medicare," *Canadian Forum*, October: 14–19.

Gray, Gratton (1990). "Social Policy by Stealth," *Policy Options*, 11, 2: 17–29.

Gray, Gwendolyn (1991). *Federalism and Health Policy: The Development of Health Systems in Canada and Australia*. Toronto: University of Toronto Press.

Leslie, Peter (1993). "The Fiscal Crisis of Canadian Federalism," in Peter M. Leslie *et al., A Partnership in Trouble: Renegotiating Fiscal Federalism*. Toronto: C.D. Howe Institute: 1–86.

Mallory, J.R. (1954). *Social Credit and the Federal Power in Canada*. Toronto: University of Toronto Press.

Maslove, Allan M. (1992). "Reconstructing Fiscal Federalism," in Frances Abele, ed., *How Ottawa Spends: The Politics of Competitiveness, 1992-93*. Ottawa: Carleton University Press: 57–78.

National Council on Welfare (1989). The 1989 Budget and Social Policy.

National Council of Welfare (1991). *Funding Health and Higher Education: Danger Looming*.

Parliamentary Task Force on Federal-Provincial Relations (1981). *Fiscal Federalism in Canada*.

Pierson, Paul (1994) *Dismantling the Welfare State? Reagan, Thatcher and the Politics of Retrenchment*. Cambridge: Cambridge University Press.

Pierson, Paul, and Miriam Smith (1993). "Bourgeois Revolutions?: The Policy Consequences of Resurgent Conservatism," Comparative *Political Studies*, 25, 4: 487–520.

Pierson, Paul, and Miriam Smith (1994). "Shifting Fortunes of the Elderly: The Comparative Politics of Retrenchment," in Theodore R. Marmor *et al., Economic Security and Intergenerational Justice*. Washington: Urban Institute: 21–59.

Rocher, François (1992a). "La consécration du fédéralisme centralisateur," in Claude Bariteau *et al. Les objections de 20 spécialistes aux offres fédérales*. Montréal: Éditions Saint-Martin: 87–98.

Rocher, François (1992b). "Quebec's Historical Agenda," in Duncan Cameron and Miriam Smith, eds., *Constitutional Politics*. Toronto: James Lorimer: 23–36.

Rowell-Sirois Commission (1940). *Report of the Royal Commission on Dominion-Provincial Relations*. Ottawa, Queen's Printer.

Simeon, Richard, and Ian Robinson (1990). *State, Society and the Development of Canadian Federalism*. Toronto: University of Toronto Press.

Taylor, Malcolm G. (1987). *Health Insurance and Canadian Public Policy*, Second edition. Montreal and Kingston: McGill-Queen's University Press.

Taylor, Malcolm (1989). "Health Insurance: The Roller Coaster in Federal-Provincial Relations," in David P. Shugarman and Reg Whitaker, eds., *Federalism and Political Community*. Peterborough, Ont.: Broadview Press: 73–92.

Trudeau, Pierre (1968). "The Practice and Theory of Federalism," in Trudeau: *Federalism and the French Canadians*. New York: St. Martin's Press: 124–50.

Tuohy, Carolyn (1988). "Medicine and the State in Canada: The extra-billing Issue in Perspective." *Canadian Journal of Political Science*, 21, 2: 267-96.

Tuohy, Carolyn (1989). "Health Care in Canada," in William M. Chandler and Christian W. Zollner, eds., *Challenges to Federalism: Policy-making in Canada and the Federal Republic of Germany*. Kingston: Institute of Intergovernmental Relations: 141-60.

Tuohy, Carolyn (1994). "Social Policy: Two Worlds," In Michael M. Atkinson, ed., *Governing Canada: Institutions and Public Policy*. Toronto: Harcourt Brace Jovanovich: 275-306.

Vaillancourt, Yves (1988). *L'évolution des politiques sociales au Québec, 1940-1960*. Montréal: Les Presses de l'Université de Montréal.

Watson, William G. (1985). "Health Care and Federalism," in Ottawa and the Provinces: The Distribution of Money and Power, II. Toronto: Ontario Economic Council: 40-57.

CHAPTER FOURTEEN

Federalism and Training Policy in Canada: Institutional Barriers to Economic Adjustment

Rodney Haddow

"THE REAL ECONOMIC CHALLENGE," FOR ANY NATION, "IS TO increase the potential value of what its citizens can add to the global economy, by enhancing their skills and capacities and by improving their means of linking those skills and capacities to the world market" (Reich, 1991: 8). Such is the hypothesis of Robert Reich's most recent best-seller on the political economy of contemporary capitalism. Reich, appointed Secretary of Labor by President Clinton after publishing the book, was not expressing an isolated view. There is an increasing consensus among economists and politicians in many countries that improving human capital, especially by training workers better, is the key to future success in the global economy. In its 1989 report, Canada's Advisory Council on Adjustment, for instance, identified "improvements in basic education and training, as well as lifelong re-education and retraining, as among the most critical steps Canada must take to enhance its international competitiveness" (Canada, Advisory Council on Adjustment, 1989: xviii).

If a well-trained work force is the key to future success in the world marketplace, Canada's prospects are uncertain. Private spending on training in Canada, according to the best available statistics, lags considerably behind comparable expenditures by our European and Japanese competitors (Ontario Premier's Council, 1990: 91-92, 196-98). This "training deficit" has existed for many years and has received considerable attention. It has been explained, variously, as a by-product of Canada's traditional reliance on immigration as a source of skilled labour; of a business culture that is preoccupied with short-term profitability; and of the lack of corporatist bargaining arrangements between business and labour, which have presided over much more extensive commitments to training elsewhere (Porter, 1965: 49; Campbell, 1992: 42-45).

This chapter argues that training policy in Canada is also powerfully shaped by another dynamic: a complex and fractious relationship between federal and provincial authority. In the contemporary period, when Canada requires labour market measures that will facilitate effective adjustment to global economic pressures, this relationship represents an important additional barrier to responsive policy-making. It is frequently suggested that social program development in Canada during the post-war years was retarded by the constitutional division of social policy-making authority (Banting, 1982: 81-82). Similarly, it will be argued here, competing jurisdictional claims, policy-making capacities, and program goals have always plagued federal-provincial relations on training and represent important barriers to a coordinated and comprehensive adjustment of Canadian training programs to the new policy imperatives.

The main task of this chapter is to analyze federal-provincial relations surrounding the Canadian Jobs Strategy – (CJS) and the Labour Force Development Strategy (LFDS) – the main training initiatives of the Conservative government of Prime Minister Mulroney – and to examine the role of training policy in the Charlottetown round of constitutional discussions and in federal-provincial discussions since the Accord's demise. The implications of these developments for future developments in the training sector are discussed at the end of the chapter.

CONTESTED TURF

A responsibility that government was not anticipated to assume in 1867, training was not among the enumerated powers listed in the British North America Act. Provinces, especially Québec and the more affluent English-speaking ones, have nevertheless claimed authority over training, viewing it as an extension of their exclusive right, under section 93 of the BNA Act, to "make laws in relation to education." But as federal interest in training grew in the post-war era, the senior government justified its interventions by referring to its generally accepted responsibility to oversee the economy; constitutionally, this claim was reinforced by allusions to the federal spending power, its unrestricted right to spend money on matters affecting any "particular class of individuals" (Dupré, 1973: 13, 26).

Over the years, these competing positions have been accommodated through a complex intergovernmental relationship. The provinces administer the educational institutions (usually community colleges) in which most training takes place in Canada. When training programs first became a priority in the 1960s, this created a bias in favour of expanding "institutional training" (provided by accredited training colleges) over "industrial training" (provided on the job by employers). Provincial education bureaucracies are much more vitally interested in the former than the latter because administration of the colleges is their main responsibility (*ibid.*: 76-77). This preponderance of institutional training is radically at variance with the pattern in most other countries (Muszynski, 1985: 265) and has fostered criticism by business that much training – designed and delivered by educators, far away from the settings where it will be used – does not meet the real needs of firms (Business Council on National Issues, 1986: 9; Canadian Chamber of Commerce, 1990: 8-9).

Federal involvement in training has been based on its ability to allocate sums of money and to set detailed guidelines for their expenditure. In part because of the provincial interests referred to above, from the 1960s onward this mainly meant setting guidelines for the expenditure of federal money in provincial training institutions. Ottawa bureaucracies have periodically altered these financing arrangements. Because this has usually caused, or threatened to cause, significant disruption in provincial training institutions, such shifts in federal policy usually precipitated interjurisdictional confrontations. These periodic federal initiatives, and provincial responses to them, have been the most important forces shaping the conflictual history of Canadian training policy.

THE HISTORICAL SETTING: TVTA AND AOTA

Federal involvement in financing technical education commenced in 1919, but it remained modest until passage of the Technical and Vocational Training Assistance Act (TVTA) in 1960 (Dupré, 1973: 14). In the late 1950s Canada experienced rapidly rising rates of unemployment at the same time as there were many job vacancies. Stimulating job creation, a Keynesian solution to unemployment, would clearly not fill the vacancies; there was a deficiency of required skills (Campbell, 1987: 129). Accordingly, Diefenbaker's Conservative government established TVTA, which permitted the federal government to pay for 50 per cent of the costs of provincial training programs; the federal government attached few conditions to the expenditure of these moneys. Within very broad limits, provinces could offer whatever training courses they wanted and had substantial influence over who was enrolled in courses.

TVTA presided over a substantial expansion of training facilities in Canada during the 1960s. Nevertheless, TVTA had some other, less desirable, consequences. First, because it was a 50-50 cost-sharing measure, the richer provinces were much more able than their poorer cousins to make use of it; they could more easily match federal grants offered by the legislation. Second, federal authorities were concerned that training offered in provincial institutions was not addressing the real needs of industry: reflecting the "educationist" prejudice of provincial authorities, programs focused too much on providing academic upgrading and basic skills, rather than specific job-related ones; even when they did the latter, federal officials wondered if the right kind of job-related skills were being acquired (Dupré, 1973: 43-46).

In 1966, consequently, the federal government replaced TVTA with the Adult Occupational Training Act (AOTA); instead of sharing the costs of provincial training, the federal government would "purchase" the training directly from whatever "seller," including provincial institutions, it preferred. It would pay the entire cost of training but would in principle also entirely control its content. The new approach was supposed to allow the federal government to provide more training in poorer provinces simply by increasing its purchases there. It could also assure that training was of the right kind by specifying what courses it wanted to buy and by selecting persons to enrol in them (*ibid.*: 50-53).

Provincial governments were not consulted in advance about AOTA, and they attacked it bitterly. The discretion sought by the federal government represented unwanted uncertainty for the provinces. If the federal government altered its training purchases from one year to the next, this could have sudden and unpredictable consequences for provincial institutions. And federal officials could use their purchasing power to transfer some training to the private sector. This, of course, would lead to a corresponding reduction in funding for provincial institutions (Muszynski, 1985: 265). For the more affluent provinces, these problems were compounded by knowledge that the senior government fully intended to use AOTA to transfer training resources toward the erstwhile low-spending jurisdictions.

The latter federal objective was largely achieved. By the early 1970s federal training expenditures no longer favoured the affluent provinces (Dupré, 1973: 114-15). Provinces were much more successful, though, in blunting federal ambitions in other areas. Under pressure, federal authorities committed themselves to making no sudden reductions in purchases from provincial institutions; for this reason, and because of federal officials' own inhibitions about providing on-site training, AOTA, once in operation, maintained provincial institutions in the dominant position as purveyors of training. Equally importantly, the provinces – led by militant Ontario – were able to position themselves as the exclusive brokers for training dollars in the provinces; under AOTA provincial bureaucracies acquired the right to mediate the relationship between federal authorities and trainers, gaining considerable influence over how the former spent its money and how the latter structured its courses (*ibid.*: 103-05). Provincial influence was also exercised through participation in Manpower Need Committees (MNCs), consisting of federal and provincial training officials; the MNCs permitted provincial input into federal training plans at an early stage of development: the general parameters of federal purchases in each province would be written into federal-provincial training agreements, and the MNCs and their sub-committees would oversee the agreements' implementation.[1]

THE NATIONAL TRAINING ACT

In this form, AOTA survived until 1982, when Prime Minister Trudeau's last Liberal government replaced it with a National Training Act (NTA). The new Act was the first, and the most ephemeral, of three federal efforts in the 1980s and 1990s to alter fundamentally its relationship with the provinces in the training field. In each case, the federal government has attempted to use its role as a course purchaser to assert greater control over its training expenditures, permitting them to be adapted more effectively to changing economic needs. As in the 1960s, provincial bureaucracies have sought to protect their interests, above all their institutions, in the face of federally imposed uncertainty.

The NTA preserved the buyer role for the federal government, but attempted to strengthen the federal hand in dealing with provincial sellers. This influence would be used to achieve the goals of the federal Manpower Department's Dodge Report, released in 1981 (Muszynski, 1985: 275-76). That Report complained that federal training dollars were still funding too much basic educational upgrading and that not enough was being done to provide more advanced skills desperately needed by industry. To improve this situation, Dodge recommended, the federal government should encourage more private-sector involvement in training – by increasing training in industry and by consulting more with business about the goals of training programs (Employment and Immigration, 1981: 176-77).

Accordingly, the NTA created a Skills Growth Fund to help provinces expand their training capacities in a number of "national occupations" in which a skills shortage was thought to exist; these would be specified by federal authorities. The NTA also included two new initiatives in industrial training: General Industrial Training and Critical Trade Skills Training. These permitted the federal government to deal directly with private employers, weakening slightly the long-standing exclusive brokerage role of the provinces. But during NTA's brief history federal authorities remained unable to shake their spending free of the tentacles of provincial institutional interests. The sum of advanced skills training in institutions was no greater in 1985, when NTA was terminated, than it had been in 1981, and industrial training expenditures rose only modestly, from 15 per cent to 17 per cent, as a proportion of all federal outlays during the life of the program (McBride, 1992: 135-36; Smith, 1984: 185).

CONSERVATIVE TRAINING POLICY SINCE 1984:
A CONTRADICTORY AGENDA

A truly decisive departure from the policy legacies of the 1960s had to await the election of a Progressive Conservative government in 1984.[2] 1960s. The Canadian Jobs Strategy (CJS), the Tories' first reform, launched in 1985, broke with the web of institutional linkages that had guaranteed provincial influence over federal training expenditures. The Conservative approach to training reflected two aspects of the market-oriented liberalism that typified most of its public policy: the focus on private sector leadership and budgetary restraint associated with its economic policy and a preference for social benefits targeted at the most needy (Prince and Rice, 1989: 251, 265).

Traces of this liberalism are pervasive. Both the CJS and the Labour Force Development Strategy (LFDS), its successor in 1989, went much further than the NTA in emphasizing market sensitivity and private-sector involvement in training; they both also presupposed that expenditures on training from the federal Consolidated Revenue Fund would have to be curtailed as part of the government's policy of budgetary restraint.

Despite these consistent themes, Tory training policy did not lack for contradictions. First, it never clearly defined what a more market-sensitive training policy should entail. There was some desire, in keeping with the Dodge Report, to concentrate on relatively advanced critical skills in short supply in the economy; the recent interest in "human capital" as a key to global competitiveness reinforced this tendency. But the selectivist preferences of Conservative social policy pulled policy in a quite different direction: toward concentrating on the very rudimentary skills that are easiest to provide to groups traditionally on the periphery of the labour market. In the Canadian Jobs Strategy, at least, this latter tendency predominated.

There were other contradictions. The CJS and the LFDS took quite different approaches to enhancing private-sector involvement in training. The CJS involved a "pluralist" image of private-sector involvement; the LFDS substituted a "corporatist" one. And since mechanisms created by the CJS survived its eclipse in 1989, these often sit uneasily beside new institutions designed for the LFDS.

Both initiatives implied a reduction of provincial influence over federal training expenditures: the private sector will be consulted where provinces were before. But here there are contradictions with initiatives pursued by the Conservative government in other areas. A key ingredient of the Charlottetown Accord was a federal offer to cede to the provinces a leading role in labour market policy, especially training, and a federal willingness to reduce its role in the sector survived the Accord's collapse. Constitutional discussions, proceeding on the level of summit relations between the two levels of government, have taken a direction at variance with the thrust of the CJS and LFDS.

The tumult that has characterized federal-provincial relations in training policy since 1984 reflects this complex and contradictory setting: federal policy has been far from consistent in design, and provinces have resisted, with various degrees of success, federal efforts to reduce their policy role. The more powerful among them have sought to regain at the constitutional level, or in bilateral administrative relations, what federal policy intended to take away from them; weaker provinces have had fewer resources for this strategy. Consequently, the federal-provincial training relationship is increasingly taking on a quite different complexion in different provinces. The balance of this chapter examines these developments in federal-provincial training relations.

CANADIAN JOBS STRATEGY

In February, 1985, the provinces accepted a federal statement of principles that was supposed to lay the groundwork for the Canadian Jobs Strategy; it stressed the need for training that "is economic in orientation with emphasis on small business and entrepreneurship" (McBride, 1992: 147). But when the detail of the CJS were announced in June of 1985, specifying how private-sector involvement would be enhanced, the provinces found many reasons to be concerned (*ibid.*: 150).

Curtailing Provincial Authority to Accommodate the Market

The private-sector focus of the CJS was responsible for many provincial complaints. To increase the role of business in directing federal training dollars, the CJS sought to diminish the influence of provincial bureaucracies and their colleges. As noted earlier, under AOTA the provinces had secured an important role for themselves in directing federal training by positioning themselves as exclusive brokers between the federal purchaser and the supplier of training (usually a provincial college), and by using Manpower Needs Committees and their sub-committees, staffed by federal and provincial officials, to negotiate and administer training agreements for the provinces. Through these mechanisms, provincial officials could leave their imprint on the overall direction of training and could secure stable demand for their college systems.

The CJS substantially abandoned these mechanisms. A distinction was introduced between "direct" and "indirect" federal training purchases; only the latter, which declined to less than 60 per cent of all expenditures by 1990 and to less than half in 1993 (Employment and Immigration Canada, 1992a: 57-58), involved direct coordination with the provinces and agreement to a training plan. The increasingly important indirect route left provincial authorities in a less secure position. Here, federal Canada Employment Centres (CECs) would sign training agreements with private parties, which might include individual firms requiring new skills, firms willing to supply specific training, non-profit organizations, or sectoral or local committees usually dominated by interested businesses. The parameters of indirect training — what training would be provided and where — would be set out in detail in agreements with the private parties. It might be agreed that some of the training should be purchased from provincial community colleges, but increasingly large parts of it were instead purchased from private-sector trainers. Federal officials had long felt that private training was cheaper and more sensitive to market need than were public colleges, burdened as they were with high overhead costs and union-induced higher wages. By 1989 CECs were also devolving more decision-making authority to private sector committees organized along sectoral or regional lines. These business-dominated bodies, called Community Industrial Training Committee (CITCs) in Ontario, as well as other bodies, would receive federal sums and exercise considerable discretion about where to spend it. Because of its lower costs and, perhaps, because of the ideological preferences of committee members, most of whom represented the business community, these bodies also redirected large sums from provincially dominated public institutions toward private trainers. As indirect training dollars made their way to private trainers, they stimulated substantial growth in this sector, just as federal dollars had stimulated growth in provincial public institutions in the 1960s.[3]

The texture of the government-business links fostered by the CJS conformed to a pluralist pattern: the focus was relatively desegregated, concentrating on firm-level relations with business, especially small business, and broader structures remained modest in scope, reflecting the business dominance typical of pluralist policy environments. Such broader structures had only modest or inconsistent representation from labour and other interests.

Every aspect of these indirect purchasing arrangements represented a major blow to the provinces. Direct purchases had provided provincial colleges with a secure supply of training dollars, overseen by friendly provincial bureaucracies; as these purchases declined, the colleges' circumstances became much more precarious. As we will see below, federal spending on training decreased in real terms in the mid- to late 1980s. Consequently, to the extent that indirect purchases ended up in the private sector, public institutions found themselves receiving a smaller part of a shrinking pie. In training agreements with the federal government, provinces – especially Québec and Ontario – did receive some guarantees that direct purchase levels would not fall below certain specified levels (McBride, 1992: 152), but the shift toward the indirect route was nevertheless dramatic.

In principle, provincial colleges could hope to recapture indirect purchases by "chasing them down" at the CECs, and in the private-sector committees. This could be done by convincing these bodies to purchase their training in public institutions rather than at private alternatives.

Some provincial college systems thus developed a very entrepreneurial approach to suppliers of indirect purchasing dollars in their catchment area and were able to limit the damage to their finances. Ontario, for instance, opened Ontario Skills Development Offices in the community colleges, with a mandate to contact firms requiring training and to arrange with the firms and with the local CEC that their training needs be met within the college system. But even Ontario experienced a noteworthy loss of revenues for its public institutions.[4] In other provinces, such as Nova Scotia, colleges were slow to adapt to the new environment; the resulting devastation to college finances led to substantial layoffs and program curtailment.[5] Provinces complained bitterly that, having built up provincial community college systems two decades earlier with its money, the federal government was now strangling them.[6] Only Québec was relatively immune to this development. In its training agreement with Ottawa, according to federal officials, Québec ensured that only a small part of indirect federal training dollars in the province went to private trainers.

Even where colleges were relatively successful in recapturing indirect purchases, they and their allies in provincial bureaucracies resisted the new arrangements. The need to bid for training dollars from a plethora of changing sellers whose demands often altered significantly at short notice, created enormous complications for provincial institutions accustomed to planning curriculum and staff development in a predictable financial setting and not used to facing low-budget competition from the private sector.[7]

The growth of private-sector training posed yet another problem for the provinces: to receive federal funds on an ongoing basis, private trainers must be certified by provincial governments. Provincial training offices frequently argue that they lack the resources to undertake this assessment effectively; their natural loyalty to their colleges leads them to suspect that the cheaper training available in private institutions is inferior in quality, and they argue that they lack the resources to ensure that adequate standards are maintained (*ibid.*: 157). Finally, some private training is completely beyond the grasp of provincial authority: a large component of training is now provided through temporary arrangements with individual employers or contractors, and the provinces have no role in supervising these measures.

The Impact of Selectivism

A private-sector orientation was not the only feature of the CJS that created friction with the provinces. The Conservative government's market ethos inspired reforms of social programs, such as pensions and family benefits, to concentrate benefits on those most in need. Similarly, the CJS targeted federal training initiatives "particularly [to] those at a disadvantage in the labour market" (Employment and Immigration Canada, 1985: 4). Target groups thought to be included in this "most needy" category included women seeking re-entry to the labour market, Natives, disabled persons, visible minorities, and social assistance recipients; additional provisions existed for youths and workers in declining industries and depressed communities (Employment and Immigration, 1992a: 26-54). There is much speculation in the provinces that federal officials gave the CJS a selectivist focus to make it more appealing to a Conservative cabinet considering deep cuts in the department's budget (McBride, 1992: 150).

The equity focus was very much reflected in program expenditures. The two largest components of the CJS, accounting for $983.9 million of expenditures in 1989-90, were "Job Development," targeted at the long-term unemployed, especially the disabled, and "Job Entry," designed to assist people, especially women and students entering the labour force for the first time. Two other components, "Skills Investment" (for workers facing technological obsolescence) and "Community Futures" (for communities hit by layoffs), were not directed at the equity categories but also had a strong orientation to helping the most needy. They expended $235.7 million in 1989-90. Only the "Skills Shortages" category clearly had more of an efficiency orientation, as it was designed to provide the economy with talents in short supply; it absorbed only $267 million in 1989-90 (Supply and Services Canada, *Estimates*, 1991-92: part II, 24).[8]

The CJS's equity priorities had several negative implications for the provinces. First, some provincial officials complained that the preferences were a straitjacket, denying access to the scarce supply of federal training dollars to those unlucky enough not to belong to a target group. This concern about rigidity also applied to other features of the CJS designed to secure federal control of its dispersements. "Skills Shortages" exclusively directed training dollars to skills deemed by the federal government to be in short supply; and under "Job Entry" candidates for training had to have been unemployed for twenty-four of the previous thirty weeks to qualify for training dollars; the latter provision was only modified, after considerable provincial complaint, in 1988 (Employment and Immigration Canada, 1988: 26). In general, the CJS went much further than NTA had in setting detailed conditions for federal training dollars, and it was far removed from the virtual open-endedness of the programs of the 1960s. Each new restriction created administrative problems for provinces, limiting their ability to match available federal funds to what their institutions were able to offer.[9]

By 1986 it was clear that much CJS training, especially when it was aimed at the target groups, provided minimal skills, which at best prepared trainees for low-paying employment at the entry level of the labour market. Newspapers reported stories about CJS funds being used to provide training in donut shops and restaurants (Globe and Mail, July 4, 1988: A1). Widespread criticism also emerged that training funds were simply being used as wage subsidies by low-wage employers (ibid.; Mahon, 1990: 85). In interviews, federal officials denied that this was an intended consequence but conceded that it was the most likely kind of training to be useful to these target groups, given their precarious history of labour market attachment. They also acknowledged that inexpensive training provided in short courses was much easier to find among the newly favoured private trainers.

The poor quality of much CJS training created additional friction with the provinces. The human capital perspective stresses the importance of training of a more sophisticated kind; this view increasingly found allies in the provinces, many of which have departed from their traditional "educationist" preference for basic training. In 1990, for instance, Ontario's Premier's Council complained that "the CJS places an overwhelming emphasis on short-term, entry-level employment training" resulting in a "gap in federal training programs relative to the long-term needs of industry." Ontario's own training measures, by contrast, were thought to offer more resources for higher quality training (Ontario Premier's Council, 1990: 111).

The Impact of Fiscal Restraint

A final source of discord over the CJS, and one that clearly aggravated all of the others, was the curtailment in federal spending on training after 1985. In constant (1986) dollars, federal outlays on labour market programs declined significantly under CJS, from $1.80 billion in 1985–86 to $1.63 billion in 1988–89; the number of persons trained under CJS similarly declined, from 470,500 in the former year to 425,296 in the latter (see Table One). Clearly, the government's dedication to training was weaker than its commitment to deficit reduction. Federal politicians justified the decreased spending by suggesting that economic growth in these years resulted in fewer people in need of training. But this argument is unpersuasive if, as the human capital argument suggests, the real purpose of training is to facilitate long-term economic adjustment, not to alleviate short-term need.

LABOUR FORCE DEVELOPMENT STRATEGY

In April, 1989, the federal government announced a new training initiative, entitled the Labour Force Development Strategy. The LFDS again redefined federal priorities in response to new political pressures being experienced by the Conservative government in the wake of the free trade debate and to new thinking within the Employment and Immigration Canada (EIC) bureaucracy. The views of the provinces – especially Québec – did have an impact, but on another level: as the federal government assembled a new constitutional proposal in 1991, Ottawa offered the provinces an important expansion of their jurisdiction over labour market policy; after the 1992 referendum, it continued to offer the provinces more authority in the training field. The resulting confusion about long-term federal plans for training has caused further turmoil in federal-provincial relations in the sector.

Origins

During the autumn, 1988, election campaign Canadians were captivated by a debate about the merits of the Conservative government's Free Trade Agreement (FTA) with the United States. The opposition parties warned of the potential job losses in Canadian industries that would face new competition from American firms; they pointed out that adjustment programs to replace these jobs and retrain displaced workers were relatively underdeveloped in Canada. The Conservatives responded with promises that passage of the FTA would be combined – after the election – with adjustment measures to facilitate the mobility of capital and labour from sectors hurt by free trade to new sectors aided by it (Mahon, 1990: 73).

There was a second political purpose of the LFDS: a continuing thirst in the Conservative government for fiscal restraint and for redeploying expenditures along more market-enhancing lines. After 1984 a number of government-sponsored studies – including the Macdonald Royal Commission and Claude Forget's Commission of Inquiry on Unemployment Insurance – criticized UI as wasteful and as creating disincentives to work (Royal Commission on the Economic Union, 1985: vol. 2, 814-16; Commission of Inquiry on Unemployment Insurance, 1986: 115-25). Though for quite different reasons, business and labour had also long been critical of the UI system. The government therefore sought politically acceptable ways of reducing the availability of unemployment insurance for income support and of increasing its use for more productive uses, such as training. If it succeeded, the government could realize the additional advantage of reducing outlays for training from its core revenue source, the Consolidated Revenue Fund (CRF) (Mahon, 1990: 74-75).

A third influence on the LFDS was bureaucratic. According to interviewed sources, leading EIC officials, including Deputy Minister Arthur Kroeger, visited a number of European countries that devoted much greater resources to training; they found that a common parameter of these commitments, in such countries as Germany and Holland, was extensive participation by business and labour in corporatist bodies that designed and directed training policy. Upon returning to Ottawa they wrote a paper, suggesting that the creation of similar mechanisms here might foster a "training culture," leading business and labour to contribute more of their own resources to improving skills. The Conservative government, increasingly reluctant to allocate incremental public revenues to training, found the idea very appealing that private-sector alternatives might be found.

The LFDS was announced in April, 1989. It redirected $800 million from the UI fund toward developmental (training) uses; the money was made available by reducing benefit periods for various categories of UI claimants. The UI fund had been used previously to finance training and job creation but to a much more limited extent. To help guide the use of this new training resource, the LFDS would include "a major consultation process with [the federal government's] partners in labour, business, provincial and territorial governments, education training institutions and other spheres" (Employment and Immigration Canada, 1989: 13). Consultation, it was hoped, would foster recognition that "the primary responsibility for the skills training of employed people rests with employers

351

and workers" (*ibid.*: 5), thus stimulating the training culture sought at EIC.

Consequently, the Canadian Labour Market Productivity Centre (CLMPC), an Ottawa research institution operated jointly by national business and labour organizations, was asked to undertake the consultation exercise. The provinces complained that they were largely left out of the consultation exercise (Mahon, 1990: 93). A March, 1990, report by the Centre announced agreement within its two constituencies on the importance of training for Canada's economic future (CLMPC, 1990a: 4-8); in another report in July, the Centre proposed the creation of a National Training Board, consisting predominantly of business and labour and given the responsibility "to oversee and provide guidance and direction on all national training policies and programs" (CLMPC, 1990b: 5).

In January, 1991, the federal government obliged, announcing the creation of a Canadian Labour Force Development Board (CLFDB) made up of twenty-two non-governmental representatives. Business and organized labour would dominate the Board, with eight members each and with its co-chairs; there would also be single representatives from each of four social action groups – women, the disabled, visible minorities, and Natives – and two representatives from training providers (Employment and Immigration Canada, 1991: 4). Initially, the Board's relation to federal training expenditures would be purely advisory, but it would "gradually take on increasing responsibility for setting national training priorities ... and for developing the annual expenditure plan for Developmental Uses under the Unemployment Insurance Act" (*ibid.*).

The CJS had opened federal training policies to private-sector involvement, but along narrowly circumscribed lines: individual firms signed training agreements directly with EIC offices, and relatively low-level committees in specific sectors and communities, generally dominated by business, could allocate parts of the EIC training budget according to agreed criteria. The new CLFDB structure envisaged private-sector direction on a much broader scale: non-governmental actors could eventually provide direction for all federal expenditures and programs in the training field. With its potentially broad mandate and national scope and its dominance by equal numbers of representatives of national business and labour organizations, the CLFDB very much resembled the corporatist arrangements that EIC officials had witnessed in Europe. As more details of the Board structure were unveiled later in 1991 this would become even more apparent. And it was at this point, too, that the implications of the Labour Force Development Strategy for the provinces finally began to be clarified.

The Interjurisdictional Design

In December, 1991, as its first main accomplishment, the CLFDB formally launched *A Proposal to Establish Local Labour Force Development Boards, inviting provinces to cooperate with it and* EIC to create a network of private-sector-led provincial and local boards, to complement the national one. Creation of this network – which continued after the Liberals won the 1993 election – proceeded slowly and inconsistently across the country; in part this is because of difficulties in mobilizing business and labour participation; it is also, however, partly a result of fractious federal-provincial relations. Provincial governments found that the CLFDB's proposed structure had significant implications, many of them negative, for their future role in the training field.

A first basis for provincial suspicion had little to do with the proposal itself but concerned the national business and labour organizations that dominated the Board and prepared the proposal. They clearly supported a strong federal role in training. The business and labour co-chairs of the Board warned the Beaudoin-Dobbie constitutional committee, almost coincidentally with the release of the local boards proposal, that "if the field of training is redivided in a way that excessively diminishes the federal role, existing programming will be less coherent, less useful to clients, and less productive.... There is an important role for the federal government in the field of training that stems both from the federal government's responsibility for economic management and the desirability of coordinated Canada-wide labour markets and labour market programming" (CLFDB, 1991a: 15). And, as we will see below, the same national business and labour organizations that dominated the Board also helped to stiffen federal resolve about labour market jurisdiction in the summer of 1992. Not surprisingly, then, provincial officials often see the Board as an extension of federal government influence over their training structures.

The three-tiered network of boards proposed by the CLFDB reflected the centralism of its authors, granting to the national board important prerogatives over provincial and local structures. The CLFDB would "develop national guidelines for the establishment of [provincial and local] boards and their operation" (CLFDB, 1991b: 10). Indeed, as provincial boards slowly emerged in some provinces, they often found themselves the beneficiaries of unwanted but firm advice from the CLFDB, especially its co-chairs, about the composition of provincial and local boards: they should be identical in composition to the federal Board, with equal numbers of business and labour representatives, who would be in a predominant position. The national Board also examined the procedures used by some provincial board constituencies to select board members, assuring themselves that boards acquired an acceptable balance of representatives from different sectors of business and labour and from various demographic groups.

The main responsibility envisaged for the provincial boards was expected to be to "review ... and approve local board plans within the national framework set by the CLFDB" (ibid.: 8), implying that provincial boards would serve as conduits of national Board influence at the local level. The federal Board would also "monitor local board performance to ensure compliance with national guidelines" (ibid.: 10). The crucial responsibility of local boards would be to spend money: they would draw up training plans, under national and provincial guidance, and fulfil them by purchasing training in their locality; as with the private-sector bodies set up under the CJS, they could allocate funds between private and public institutions as they saw fit. Despite this autonomy and the supposed control of these bodies by private sector actors, there was much room for EIC's influence: "The actual administration of the contract to operationalize the training plan for federal funds will be the responsibility of the appropriate Employment and Immigration Canada regional office. The contract will include provisions to ensure local board compliance with CLFDB national guidelines" (ibid.:11).

One development that accompanied the LFDS presumably pleased the provinces: after several years of decline under the CJS, total federal expenditures on training initially rose as a result of the LFDS, from $1.62 billion in constant (1986) dollars in 1989-90 to $2.36 billion in 1992-93; the number of Canadians trained with federal dollars also rose from 464,346 in the former year to 593,812 in the latter (see Table One). Nevertheless, few observers in the provinces gave the government much credit for this. The LFDS actually reduced federal disbursements from its Consolidated Revenue Fund, from $1.31 billion (in 1986 dollars) in 1988-89 to $986 million in 1992-93. The contribution of the UI fund to training, by contrast, rose from $320 million to $1.37 billion (again, in 1986 dollars) over the same period. Since the cutbacks on UI that accompanied the LFDS eliminated federal financial contributions to the UI fund, the extra training outlays therefore come from a resource increasingly referred to as "belonging" to business and labour, since they now exclusively pay for it. Meanwhile, the federal government reduces expenditures from its CRF.

TABLE ONE: FEDERAL GOVERNMENT LABOUR MARKET EXPENDITURES
AND NUMBER OF PERSONS TRAINED, 1985-93 (IN 1986 $)

PROGRAM EXPENDITURES ($ MILLIONS)*

	CONSOLIDATED REVENUE FUND	DEVELOPMENTAL USES (UI FUND)	TOTAL	NUMBER TRAINED
1985-86	1,442.0	362.9	1,804.9	470,500
1986-87	1,485.4	333.2	1,818.7	434,222
1987-88	1,407.7	303.9	1,711.6	426,507
1988-89	1,310.8	320.8	1,631.6	425,294
1989-90	1,307.4	355.0	1,662.4	464,446
1990-91	1,242.3	477.1	1,719.4	453,556
1991-92	1,111.6	1,127.7	2,239.3	548,439
1992-93	986.3	1,373.7	2,360.0	593,812
1993-94**	992.7	1,374.7	2,367.4	639,000
1994-95**	942.3	1,373.7	2,316.0	639,000

*Expenditure figures include those for job creation as well as training; these have been combined since the inception of the CJS. Figures exclude operating costs.

** Figures for 1993-94 are forecasts; those for 1994-95 are estimates. All others represent actual expenditures.

Sources: Expenditure and enrolment figures are derived from Supply and Services Canada, *Estimates*, part II, various years. Expenditures were adjusted for inflation using Consumer Price Index tables from the *Bank of Canada Review*, Various dates: Table H11.

Furthermore, the UI funds seems to have exhausted its capacity to generate more revenues for training; as Table One shows, training expenditures from the UI fund stagnated at 1992-93 levels during the next two fiscal years, and are unlikely to rise in the foreseeable future, in the wake of the February, 1995, budget; CRF funding also stagnated for two years before being cut drastically (by $600 million) in the 1995 budget.

One feature of the change from CRF to UI financing is particularly disturbing to the provinces: UI funds are devoted exclusively to indirect purchases. Consequently, as they replace CRF resources in federal training outlays, "EIC will continue the trend of reducing the direct purchase of training in favour of [indirect] purchase-of-training options" (Canada, Supply and Services Canada, *Estimates, 1992-93: part II, 16). Indirect purchases have already overtaken direct purchases in some, if not all, provinces, eroding further the provinces' ability to protect their colleges and to have a significant voice in directing training expenditures through the training agreements. Anticipating this development, the provinces issued a joint statement in November, 1989, demanding that greater security of funding be provided under* LFDS *for their colleges* (Mahon, 1990: 110).

Federal reliance on the UI fund presents another problem for the provinces: UI monies are to be spent exclusively on persons eligible for UI benefits. Consequently, since UI funds overtook CRF funds in the 1991-92 fiscal year, federal training has increasingly been concentrated on this group, forcing provinces to absorb the cost of training others. Federal officials refer to this new division of labour as a "partnership" with the provinces, but it is one that is often resented by provincial officials.

The LFDS also continues many aspects of the CJS that provinces found objectionable. Federal officials in many provinces allocate more resources to private training and there is good reason to believe that much federal training still provides the kinds of rudimentary skills emphasized by the CJS, since the new strategy again targets benefits at four equity groups (women, the disabled, visible minorities, Aboriginals). As before, these groups can most readily benefit from rudimentary training and private trainers can most easily provide it.

An additional complication caused by the transition from the CJS to the LFDS is that the new system of local boards has yet to be reconciled with the network of community training committees and other private-sector committees created under the CJS. The CLFDB's local boards document was unclear about the anticipated relationship between these old and new structures (CLFDB, 1991b: 14). The issue has not been resolved in many provinces. Many members of the old structures resist their replacement by the new boards because of their perceived success, because sectoral training needs may not be adequately addressed by local boards, and because of a reluctance among business members to abandon authority to local boards where decision-making power would have to be shared equally with organized labour.[10] Some provincial officials complain that adding a new layer of local boards to the existing ones will create a confusing array of purchasing institutions, making even more unmanageable the work of provincial training institutions; in the smaller provinces the addition of new bodies is thought likely to stretch the capacity of private-sector constituencies to find qualified persons for available committee positions.

Finally, the LFDS is burdened by other features of federal-provincial training arrangements that emerged over the years. The larger and more affluent provinces complain that federal training programs duplicate their own, and the distribution of federal funds, which favoured the affluent provinces in the early 1960s, now does the opposite. In fiscal 1992-93, Ontario claimed that it received only 26 per cent of federal training money, though 38 per cent of the nation's labour force resided in the province (*Globe and Mail*, August 7, 1993, A1).

Implementation

The tensions listed above have made the provinces unenthusiastic partners in creating new boards. Nowhere has there been smooth progress toward the creation of provincial and local boards; and the ability of the CLFDB, backed by the federal government, to move forward with its preferred option has largely depended on the capacity for resistance at the disposal of individual provinces. Where provinces have traditionally asserted their prerogatives in the training field and allocated considerable of their own funds (Ontario, British Columbia, Alberta, and, above all, Québec), there has been little headway, or structures have emerged in a form radically at variance with the federal design.

Québec's break with the CLFDB structure has been complete. It has refused to acknowledge any authority for the federal board in the province. Québec has nevertheless independently committed itself to greater private-sector involvement in training. In June, 1992, the province created a Société québécoise de développement de la main d'oeuvre, dominated by business and labour representatives (Johnson, 1994: 255), with a mandate to direct provincial training programs. In an August, 1993, agreement with Québec, Ottawa delegated to the Société, and to local and sectoral boards under its direction, the authority to oversee federal training purchases in Québec. In effect, the federal government accepted an entirely provincially organized network of boards as a substitute for its own. Human Resources Development Canada (HRDC), which assumed control of federal training programs from EIC in 1993, will still influence dispersement of its training funds through the training agreements and through local HRDC purchasing relationships with local boards, and Ottawa secured the right to appoint members to the Société's board (*Globe and Mail, August 4, 1993: A1). But this agreement did not provide the* CLFDB with any influence in Québec, and it remains to be seen whether the arrangement will permit a harmonious relationship between the federal purchaser and provincially directed boards.

The CLFDB has also encountered resistance in Ontario, though that province is less interested in excluding the federal government from the field. In December, 1991, the Ontario government created the Ontario Training and Adjustment Board (OTAB), with a private-sector composition similar to that of the CLFDB, and a mandate to direct training policy in the province. OTAB had been proposed by the province's private-sector-led Premier's Council on Technology (Ontario Premier's Council, 1990: 118-19). OTAB immediately assumed direct control over most of Ontario's training programs, in contrast with the federal model that envisaged more modest powers for both federal and provincial boards. Like Québec's Société, OTAB is a provincial crown agency and is exclusively accountable to the province. Early in 1992, the federal and Ontario governments and the CLFDB issued a statement on local boards, which they committed themselves to creating jointly. The local boards will be answerable to the federal and provincial boards, respectively, for training programs under federal and provincial governments (Ontario, 1992: 4-5). Whether these entirely separate responsibilities can be integrated remains unclear; certainly, there is no chance that OTAB will respond to the "national frameworks" envisaged by the CLFDB.[11]

British Columbia and Alberta, again working from positions of relative strength, have also stymied the federal design. As in Ontario, B.C. has created a structure that will be accountable to the provincial government, and will not be integrated with the CLFDB in the manner envisaged by the latter; B.C. also has not committed itself to establishing local boards. Alberta has shown little interest in cooperating with the federal board to create a provincial private-sector training equivalent; it apparently does not intend to have such a board established within the province.

Among the six smaller and poorer provinces, much more dependent on federal training dollars, the federal design has better prospects. Under the CLFDB's sponsorship, provincial boards have been created in all four Atlantic provinces. These boards are not provincial government agencies. In New Brunswick, for instance, the board was set up as an independent company, and it has a much closer relationship with the federal government than with the province. But even here the picture is far from rosy, from a federal viewpoint. Training bureaucracies in at least two of these provinces – Nova Scotia and New Brunswick – have strongly resented the federal Board's (and HRDC) efforts, often viewing them as a simple extension of the CJS. New Brunswick has resisted the creation of local boards, seeing them as tools for HRDC's employment centres around the province, and it is still unclear if local boards will be created there; in both New Brunswick and Nova Scotia, harmonization of federal and provincial training initiatives under private-sector guidance is far from assured.[12]

Business and Labour

With governments now opening training to the influence of corporatist boards dominated by business and labour, these private actors will have a role in shaping the future of training programs at both levels of government. But between business and labour there is reason to expect more discord than harmony, and little commitment to a shared agenda. These disagreements were revealed in the CLMPC consultations in 1990 and in subsequent private-sector discussions in Ontario. Business representatives advocated board decision-making structures that constrain as little as possible the traditional prerogatives of firms to determine their own training needs; individual firms, they believe, are the best judges of their skill requirements. Business also resisted the equality granted to labour on the CLFDB and on provincial and local boards. They often see no reason why all labour seats should be held by union members, since most workers are not unionized.[13] Most importantly, business has evidenced little desire to increase its spending on training, yet creating a willingness to do precisely this was the *raison d'etre* of the new corporatist structures. Many government officials think that business remains reluctant to allocate more of its own resources to training. The Canadian Federation of Independent Business, which appears to be particularly reluctant, has repeatedly challenged Statistics Canada figures suggesting that Canadian business, especially small business, spends much less on training than its counterparts in other OECD countries (Canadian Federation of Independent Business, 1992: ii). Most business groups also oppose the creation of a mandatory training tax on business (commonly called a "grant/levy"), with a provision for rebates to firms that meet training expenditure targets. They prefer more voluntary options, such as tax deductions for businesses that train.[14]

Labour, by contrast, wants training to be adaptable and of high quality, and wants use it to enhance labour mobility and wage levels. It supports tighter standards and more centralized control of training expenditures to assure that business meets these standards. Unions have successfully insisted on equal representation with business and on union control of all labour seats on boards. Finally, they support a compulsory training tax on business but are reluctant to see taxes paid by workers used to finance training in private firms (Canadian Labour Market Productivity Centre, 1990a: 260-61; Ontario Training and Adjustment Board, 1992: 13, 22; interviews with labour officials).

The creation of corporatist decision-making structures for training has therefore added yet another layer to the institutional complexity that has always plagued the policy sector in Canada; to the barriers created by federal-provincial conflicts is now added the tensions between business and labour, apparently unable to overcome their traditionally adversarial relations and don the cooperative spirit required of participants in corporatist policy networks. In this context, the uncertainties introduced by the constitutional debate since 1990 represent an unwelcome additional burden.

THE CHARLOTTETOWN ACCORD AND ITS AFTERMATH

The collapse of the Meech Lake Accord in June, 1990, engendered a powerful mood of anger in Québec and a rekindling of *indépendantiste* sentiment there. The Meech document had responded to Premier Bourassa's five minimum conditions, laid out in 1985, for Québec's giving its consent to the Constitution Act. These conditions had indeed been minimal. Since the 1960s Québec had demanded constitutional recognition of its "exclusive jurisdiction" over training programs (Québec. Ministère du Conseil exécutif, 1991: 23); but this demand, and most others for extensions of Québec's authority, were absent from Bourassa's position. Reflecting the frosty political climate in Québec after the demise of Meech, the Québec Liberal Party's Allaire Report and the National Assembly's Bélanger-Campeau Commission Report both demanded a sweeping transfer of powers from Ottawa to Québec; training was one of these powers. Bourassa made it clear that he would settle for less than these demands (Conway, 1992: 148), but the federal government knew that any new constitutional package would have to offer new powers to Québec. Since Ottawa wanted to avoid asymmetry in its offer, all other provinces would have to receive the same terms.

Consequently, Ottawa's September 24, 1991 recommendations for renewing the constitutional reform process included a proposal that "section 92 of the Constitution Act, 1867 be amended to recognize explicitly that labour market training is an area of exclusive provincial jurisdiction" (*Globe and Mail*, September 25, 1991: A7). The proposal created surprise and dismay among many officials in EIC and in the CLFDB's new bureaucracy. They wondered how it could be reconciled with a continuing federal role in training. Nevertheless, EIC and the CLFDB apparently were not consulted about the proposal and their views had no evident impact on federal constitutional thinking.[15]

More important reservations about the transfer were expressed by some anglophone provinces. During the summer of 1992 it became evident that they were not unanimous in wanting to take up responsibility for training. The three English-speaking provinces that had long joined Québec in resisting federal authority over training – Ontario, Alberta, and B.C. – were happy to assume the role. Elsewhere, especially in the Atlantic region, there was less enthusiasm: federal training dollars would be hard to replace, even with reasonable compensation from Ottawa. The final text of the Charlottetown Accord, released on August 28, therefore made the transfer optional: "At the request of a province, the federal government would be obliged to withdraw from any or all training activities and from any or all labour market development activities, except Unemployment Insurance." On the other hand, a province could insist that Ottawa "maintain its labour market development and training programs and activities in that province" (Canada, 1992: 9-10). Training officials from the poorer provinces were only partly satisfied with this option; in interviews, they argued that with only poorer and less populated provinces remaining in federal training programs, these programs would likely deteriorate over time.

Other reservations were expressed by national business and labour groups. As was noted above, the CLFDB co-chairs jointly endorsed a continuing federal role in training. During July, 1992, national business and labour groups convinced the federal government to qualify its withdrawal from training in an important way. The June version of the constitutional proposal had already specified that provinces taking over training "should be obliged to ensure that labour market development programs are compatible with the national policy objectives" (Status Report, 1992: 9), without indicating how these objectives would be established or what legal standing they would have. After considerable pressure from business and labour groups, according to informed sources, an additional paragraph was added to the Charlottetown Accord proposing "a constitutional provision for an ongoing federal role in the establishment of national policy objectives for the national aspects of labour market development." This was followed by a lengthy list of factors to be considered in establishing objectives, which would be debated in Parliament (Canada, 1992: 10). It remained unclear, however, how these objectives would be enforced.

Such uncertainties were not ended by the Charlottetown Accord's defeat in the October 26, 1992, referendum. Afterwards, Québec's Manpower Minister continued his province's demand for a federal withdrawal (*Globe and Mail*, November 6, 1992: A6). The federal Employment Minister, Bernard Valcourt, responded that the Charlottetown proposal was now dead and that the federal government therefore would continue its role in the field and proceed with the LFDS (*Globe and Mail, November 12, 1992: A10; January 15, 1993: A4*).

Nevertheless, Québec continued to press its case. On June 22, 1994, the federal government responded by offering to transfer four important parts of its role in labour market policy to the provinces. These included control over most direct and indirect course purchases now made by HRDC and an important role in strategic planning of what skills should be given priority in the training system. The federal government, under the proposal, would retain some role in this strategic planning, and would also continue to offer employment counselling and employment availability information through its Canada Employment Centres; it would also retain a role in job creation and some related activities. In the wake of the proposal, HRDC undertook negotiations with each province about its possible implementation in their jurisdictions. What the precise role of each government would be if the agreement is implemented remains unclear as these discussions proceed.

CONCLUSION: TOWARD ADMINISTRATIVE ASYMMETRY?

What does the future hold for the respective roles of the federal and provincial governments in the training field? The contradictory nature of recent developments makes it difficult to be sure. Since 1982 the federal government has often tried to free itself from provincial influence over its training expenditures; in constitutional negotiations and in its 1994 proposal, however, it has displayed a quite contradictory willingness to cede to the provinces authority over labour markets.

The available evidence does, however, warrant some prognostication. First, unless comprehensive constitutional review resumes soon, it is unlikely that the federal government will entirely abandon its role in labour market policy because this field is close to the federal government's core economic responsibilities. The HRDC bureaucracy also remains an important ally of an ongoing federal role and, as we have seen, national business and labour federations hold a similar view.

But recent developments also reveal other patterns. Under both Conservative initiatives the eventual outcome of federal-provincial conflict differed from one province to the next. This is also likely to be true of discussions about the June, 1994, offer. Where provincial capacity to resist federal policy was high – above all in Québec and Ontario, and to an extent in Alberta and B.C. – the resulting federal-provincial arrangements in the training field accommodated provincial authority in important ways. The emerging pattern, then, would seem to be one of *de facto* jurisdictional asymmetry: what the federal government determined to avoid in constitutional negotiations is nevertheless emerging on the plane of administrative practice. In some provinces, federal authority has been compromised significantly, and provincial authority is likely to increase even more in the future; in others, the federal role will remain substantial.

Québec has been particularly successful in stymying the senior government, reflecting its centrality to the broader constitutional crisis. It supplanted the LFDS within the province with a process dominated by institutions entirely of its own creation. Québec has also rejected Ottawa's June, 1994, offer, demanding that all labour market programs be transferred to its jurisdiction. While not rewarded so impressively, Ontario also made some headway. Its training agreements limited the rise of private training to a degree and it had the resources to assist its colleges in recapturing indirect training dollars; it is quite likely to take up fully the powers offered to it by Ottawa in 1994. In the Maritimes, the picture is quite different. Provincial training officials feel a pervasive vulnerability in the face of federal initiatives. As noted earlier, for instance, Nova Scotia's college system was hurt badly by the CJS, and there is a mood of resentment toward federal authority there and in New Brunswick. Nova Scotia, in particular, is hesitant about expanding its authority over training.

Will future Canadian training policy provide Canadian workers with the skills they need to succeed in an increasingly competitive international markets? Here, one must express some doubt. The federal government allocated significant new sums of money to training during the early 1990s by restricting the generosity of unemployment insurance benefits and diverting the resulting savings into training. But this new money was partially offset by substantial reductions in expenditures from the Consolidated Revenue Fund (CRF), as the government sought to eliminate its budgetary deficit. The UI fund has now probably reached its limit as a source of new money. This seems to be confirmed by the stagnation of UI funding for training at 1992-93 levels for the subsequent three years, while CRF funding was again cut severely in 1995. Equally importantly, the early history of the CLFDB suggests that the private-sector is unlikely to increase substantially its training expenditures; business and labour also have divergent visions of the proper design of training policies.

Finally, the turbulent relationship between federal and provincial governments – the central focus of this chapter – represents an important barrier to effective policy-making. Federal and provincial bureaucracies continue to entertain different definitions of the appropriate focus of policy – the kind of training to be provided and the relative merits of private and public institutions – and federal policy-makers themselves have not adopted consistent approaches to these questions. The two also have not yet reached agreement on the appropriate role of each in the labour market field. In the contemporary period, the federal and provincial governments have proceeded only haltingly, and with no assurance of success, toward a coordinated training strategy based on a corporatist model. The prospects for a comprehensive and economically adaptive national training strategy are not encouraging.

NOTES

1   These arrangements are described by Wayne Doggett, director, Nova Scotia Department of Vocational and Technical Training, in a submission to the Senate Sub-Committee on Training and Employment, May 13, 1987, Issue 7: 42-43. See also Dupré (1973: 205) for a discussion of similar arrangements in the early 1970s.

2   Developments in federal-provincial relations in the training field during Brian Mulroney's terms of office as Prime Minister were discussed with twenty-seven relevant individuals, including training officials from the federal, Ontario, Nova Scotia, and New Brunswick governments, and with labour and business representatives in each of these jurisdictions. The follow-

ing discussion is based on these anonymous interviews, as well as the printed sources acknowledged in the notes.

3   There is some discussion of these arrangements in McBride, (1992: 152); otherwise, this section is based on interviews.

4   See McBride (1994: 285); Senate Sub-Committee on Training and Employment, submission by Ms. Terry Dance, Chair, Community Outreach, George Brown College, May 11, 1987, Issue 5: 82-83; interviews.

5   Senate Sub-Committee on Training and Employment, submission by Doggett, May 13, 1987, Issue 7: 41.

6   *Ibid*, for Nova Scotia views. For New Brunswick, *ibid*, submission of Jean-Guy Finn, deputy minister, New Brunswick Department of Advanced Educations and Training, May 15, 1987, Issue 9: 140-41. For similar views among Ontario and Manitoba officials, see McBride (1992: 153).

7   All of the sources indicated in note 6 make this point; but New Brunswick's Finn does so particularly eloquently in his submission *ibid.*: 144.

8   The CJS included one other component, "Innovations," which spent only modest sums of money ($32.2 million in 1989-90); it provided "financial assistance for pilot and demonstration projects which test new solutions to labour market programs." Employment and Immigration Canada (1985: 18).

9   Senate Sub-Committee on Training and Employment, submission of Finn: 141; *ibid.*, submission of Doggett: 44.

10   In public consultations, Ontario's CITCs expressed a desire not to be eliminated when the new local boards come into being, or to have themselves become the local boards; see Ontario Training and Adjustment Board (1992: 27-28). Also, "many representatives from CITCs and businesses across Ontario expressed concern that organized labour, which represents only one-third of the labour force, would speak for all workers in Ontario." *Ibid.: 17.*

11   For more information on the local boards arrangement in Ontario, see McBride (1994); Haddow (1992: 17-18).

12   On the Nova Scotia and New Brunswick cases, see Haddow (1992: 28-33).

13   For business views on these questions, see CLMPC (1990a: 250, 255-58); OTAB (1992: 12-14). The Ontario community discussions process found, for instance, that "The business community and CITCs objected strongly to the District Labour Councils' view that organized labour should represent all workers, union and non-union." (*ibid: 13). Similar views were expressed by national, Nova Scotia, and New Brunswick business leaders in interviews.*

14   In the Ontario consultations, "The majority of business representatives did not support the notion of an employer training tax" (Ontario Training and Adjustment Board, 1992: 22). Similar views were expressed in interviews. See also Canadian Labour Market Productivity Centre (1990a: 249-50).

15   In June, 1992, Arthur Kroeger, Deputy Minister of Employment and Immigration, sent a memo to departmental staff about the constitutional proposals. He was obviously aware of the alarm that the proposals had caused, writing that "I know that the coming months will be difficult for EIC staff," and that senior departmental officials would "make every effort to ensure that your interests receive full recognition" (Employment and Immigration Canada, 1992b: 2).

REFERENCES

Banting, Keith (1982). *The Welfare State and Canadian Federalism*. Montreal and Kingston: McGill-Queen's University Press.

Business Council on National Issues (1986). *Social Policy Reform and the National Agenda*.

Campbell, Robert (1987). *Grand Illusions*. Peterborough, Ont.: Broadview Press.

Campbell, Robert (1992). "Jobs ... Job ... Jo ... J ... The Conservatives and the Unemployed," in Frances Abele, ed., *How Ottawa Spends, 1992-93*. Ottawa: Carleton University Press.

Canada (1992). Consensus Report on the Constitution. August, 28.

Canada, Advisory Council on Adjustment (1989). *Adjusting to Win*.

Canada, Commission of Inquiry on Unemployment Insurance [Forget Commission] (1986). *Canadian Jobs Strategy*.

Canada, Employment and Immigration Canada (1981). *Labour Market Development in the 1980s* [Dodge Report].

Canada, Employment and Immigration Canada (1985). *Canadian Jobs Strategy*.

Canada, Employment and Immigration Canada (1988). *Response of the Government to the Second Report of the Standing Committee on Labour, Employment and Immigration*.

Canada, Employment and Immigration Canada (1989). *Success in the Works*.

Canada, Employment and Immigration Canada (1991). *Canadian Labour Force Development Board*.

Canada, Employment and Immigration Canada (1992a). *Statistical Bulletin for the Canadian Jobs Strategy*.

Canada, Employment and Immigration Canada (1992b). "Subject: Prospective Constitutional changes," memorandum to EIC employees from Arthur Kroeger, June 16.

Canada, Royal Commission on the Economic Union and Development Prospects for Canada [Macdonald Commission] (1985). *Report*.

Canada, Senate (1987). *Proceedings of the Sub-Committee on Training and Employment.*

Canada, Supply and Services Canada (Various dates) *Estimates.*

Canadian Chamber of Commerce (1990). *Positions on Selected National Issues, 1988, 1989 & 1990.*

Canadian Federation of Independent Business (1992). Upgrading at Work: the Extent and Cost of On-the-Job Training in Smaller Firms in Canada.

Canadian Labour Force Development Board (1991a). *The CLFDB Response to the Federal Proposals for Constitutional Change with Respect to Labour Market Training.*

Canadian Labour Force Development Board (1991b). A Proposal to Establish Local Labour Force Development Boards.

Canadian Labour Market Productivity Centre (1990a). *Report of the CLMPC Task Forces on the Labour Force Development Strategy.*

Canadian Labour Market Productivity Centre (1990b). A Framework for a National Training Board.

Conway, John (1992). *Debts to Pay.* Toronto: Lorimer.

Dupré, J. Stefan *et al.* (1973). *Federalism and Policy Development.* Toronto: University of Toronto Press.

Haddow, Rodney (1992). "The Political Economy of Labour Market Reform in Ontario, New Brunswick and Nova Scotia," paper delivered at Atlantic Political Science Association Conference, Halifax.

Johnson, Andrew (1984). "Towards a Neo-Corporatist Labour Market Policy in Québec," in Johnson *et al.*, *Continuities and Discontinuities.* Toronto: University of Toronto Press.

Mahon, Rianne (1990). "Adjusting to Win? The New Tory Training Initiative" in K. Graham, ed., *How Ottawa Spends, 1990-91.* Ottawa: Carleton University Press.

McBride, Stephen (1992). Not Working. Toronto: University of Toronto Press.

McBride, Stephen (1994). "The Political Economy of Ontario's Labour Market Policy," in Johnson *et al. Continuities and Discontinuities.*

Muszynski, Leon (1985). "The Politics of Labour Market Policy," in G. Bruce Doern, ed., *The Politics of Economic Policy.* Toronto: University of Toronto Press.

Ontario (1992). *Local Boards: A Partnership For Training.* [Published jointly with Employment and Immigration Canada].

Ontario Premier's Council (1990). *People and Skills in the New Global Economy.*

Ontario Training and Adjustment Board (OTAB) (1992). *Community Discussion: Training and Local Boards.*

Porter, John (1965). *The Vertical Mosaic.* Toronto: University of Toronto Press.

Prince, Michael and James Rice (1989). "The Canadian Jobs Strategy: Supply Side Social Policy," in K. Graham, ed., *How Ottawa Spends, 1989-90*. Ottawa: Carleton University Press.

Québec. Ministère du Conseil Executif (1991). Québec's Traditional Constitutional Positions, 1936-1990. Working Paper.

Reich, Robert (1991). The Work of Nations. New York: Vintage Books.

Smith, Douglas (1984). "The Development of Employment and Training Programs," in A. Maslove, ed., *How Ottawa Spends, 1984*. Toronto: Methuen.

Status Report (1992). "Status Report on the Multilateral Meetings on the Constitution. Rolling Draft as at June 11, 1992 – End of Day."

CHAPTER FIFTEEN

Regional Development: A Policy for All Seasons

Donald J. Savoie

REGIONAL DEVELOPMENT IS A RELATIVELY NEW POLICY FIELD in Canada. Indeed, the federal government had no explicit policy of regional development from Confederation to the late 1950s. It has since, however, made up for lost time. From its modest beginnings, regional development policy has seen many dramatic twists and turns over the past thirty-five years. Rarely have political leaders been satisfied for very long with the various new approaches introduced. To be sure, the search for a panacea, for a quick fix, has been a factor, as has the need to update the policy to reflect changing economic circumstances. But the desire by Ottawa to secure visibility and due credit for federal money spent has been equally important – if not more so – in defining and redefining Canadian regional development policy.

The purpose of this chapter is to review briefly the historical evolution of Canada's regional development policy and how intergovernmental relations in the field have developed and to speculate on future policy directions. It seeks to provide a broad perspective by looking not only at the substance of the policy but also at the forces that have shaped regional development efforts and federal-provincial relations. Since the various programs Ottawa has put in place over the years have largely been discussed elsewhere, this chapter will serve rather as a backdrop to provide a better understanding of how and why Canadian regional development policy and federal-provincial relations have evolved the way they have.

AN ALPHABET SOUP

Though the matter had been debated many times in royal commission reports and at federal-provincial meetings, it was the 1960 budget speech that unveiled the first of the many measures Ottawa has developed to combat regional disparities (Bickerton, 1990; Savoie, 1992). The budget permitted firms to obtain double the normal rate of capital-cost allowances on most of the assets they required to produce new products – if they located in designated regions (Careless, 1977). The thinking behind this initiative was that "footloose" industries could be attracted to slow-growth regions. However, the thinking neglected to note the fact that well-run "footloose" industries can locate anywhere they like, but "where they like" is usually where they are now (Higgins, 1992: 28). Shortly after, Parliament passed the Agriculture Rehabilitation Act (ARA) in an attempt to rebuild the country's depressed rural economy (*ibid.*). ARA was a federal-provincial effort designed to increase the productivity of small farmers by providing assistance for alternative use of marginal land, developing water and soil resources, and setting up projects to support people in non-agriculture natural resources industries. The initiative was soon found wanting, largely because it was not sufficiently flexible and lacked a clear geographical focus.

ARA thus begot FRED (Fund for Regional Economic Development) in 1966. FRED did have a clear geographical focus. It was concentrated in five designated regions with widespread low incomes and major problems of economic adjustment. Typically, a FRED plan provided for industrial development measures, employment-development activities, and industrial infrastructure. Soon, however, FRED was found wanting from both a technocratic and political perspective. More is said about the political perspective later. As for the technocratic view, senior government officials felt that FRED made little provision for coordinating a growing number of federal and federal-provincial initiatives in the economic development field. They were also convinced that in concentrating as it did on some of the poorest regions in the country, FRED was far too restrictive to meet the challenges of the 1970s (Brewis, 1978: 220).

FRED thus gave way to the Department of Regional Economic Expansion (DREE). Established in 1969, it introduced two new major programs. One was designed to attract private-sector investment to slow-growth regions through cash grants. The other – labelled the Special Areas Program – was designed to promote faster industrial growth. In the case of the latter, twenty-three areas were designated and each became the subject of a federal-provincial agreement. DREE borrowed from François Perroux's growth pole concept – or at least thought it did – to give life to its Special Areas Program. Perroux had argued that economic activity tends to concentrate around certain focal points. Growth, he wrote, "does not appear everywhere and all at once, it reveals itself in certain points or poles, with different degrees of intensity; it spreads through diverse channels" (Perroux, 1969: 179). The federal government embraced Perroux's views mainly because it seemed to describe Canada's situation well. For senior DREE officials, the main difference between Ontario and the Maritimes was that Ontario had major urban centres with vigorous economic growth to which people from northern Ontario could move. The Maritimes had few cities capable of strong growth and providing employment; consequently, many people remained in economically depressed rural areas. The growth pole concept, it was believed, would create new opportunities at selected urban centres. Economic growth would take place through movement and change within regions, rather than between regions.

Within a few short years, DREE decided to scrap its Special Areas Program. The reason given was that the approach was too "restrictive," that its concentration on a limited number of areas incurred the risk of overlooking economic development opportunities elsewhere. Henceforth, DREE would "pursue viable" opportunities whether they were in urban or rural areas, though it would be preferable if they were located in slow-growth regions, and priority status would still be given to these. In 1973, the department introduced a new approach – the General Development Agreement (GDA) (Savoie, 1981). It was remarkably flexible, capable of supporting virtually any imaginable type of government activity. Negotiated by Ottawa with all provinces except Prince Edward Island (which was already covered by the fifteen-year FRED plan), a GDA provided a broad statement of goals for both levels of government to pursue, outlined the priority areas, and described how joint decisions would be taken. GDAs were enabling documents only and did not in themselves provide for specific action; projects and precise cost-sharing arrangements were instead presented in subsidiary agreements that were attached to the umbrella-type GDAs.

From a strictly administrative point of view, all nine GDAs were basically similar. Each had a ten-year life span; each stipulated that DREE and the provincial government in question would, on a continuing basis, review the socio-economic circumstances of the province; and each outlined a similar process for joint federal-provincial decision-making. They differed only in cost-sharing for subsidiary agreements. Under the GDA approach, DREE was granted the following authority to share the cost of a subsidiary agreement: up to 90 per cent for Newfoundland, 80 per cent for Nova Scotia and New Brunswick, 60 per cent for Québec, Manitoba, and Saskatchewan, and 50 per cent for Ontario, Alberta, and British Columbia (Savoie, 1981). The variety of projects supported under the various GDAs was truly remarkable. Virtually every economic sector was covered, particularly in the Atlantic provinces. GDAs sponsored, among many others, projects in tourism, urban development, fisheries, recreation, mineral development, rural development, agriculture, forestry, industrial development, communications, cultural infrastructure, and ocean-related industries (Savoie, 1981; Savoie, 1992).

By the late 1970s, however, DREE was being assailed from a number of quarters, particularly from central agencies in Ottawa. For one thing, the country's economic picture had changed since DREE was first established. The term "stagflation" had crept into the economic vocabulary and Canada's industrial heartland – that is, the economy of southern Ontario and Montreal – was getting "soft" (Canada, 1981a). The Liberals lost the 1979 election and the Conservative Clark government's tenure in office was too short-lived to reform regional development policy in any meaningful way. Returned to office in 1980, the Trudeau government quickly set out to revamp Ottawa's economic development policies, in particular those related to regional development. Underpinning the new economic thinking was the view that "regional balance was changing as a result of buoyancy in the west, optimism in the east, and unprecedented softness in key economic sectors in central Canada" (*ibid.*). The economic prospects associated with resource-based megaprojects in Atlantic Canada (Sable Island and Hibernia) and the West gave rise, at least in part, to the new thinking. The solution was to encourage a "good" investment climate and market access in the West and East, where large investments were bound to take place, and to put in place measures to draw resources from declining industries and move them into growth sectors in central Canada.

So DREE begot MSERD and DRIE. Both new departments were established in 1982, with MSERD (Ministry of State for Economic and Regional Development) designed to play a central agency role by coordinating line department activities and DRIE (Department of Regional Industrial Expansion) designed to deliver a regional industrial program based on a "development" index (Canada, 1983: 1-2). The index established the needs of individual regions, as far down as a single census district, with all regions arranged in four tiers of need. The first tier, which covered 58 per cent of the population, covered the most developed regions of the country, while the fourth, which included 5 per cent of the population, covered the regions with the greatest need (based on level of employment, personal income, and provincial fiscal capacity). The thinking behind this initiative was that the private sector everywhere in Canada needed government assistance to locate, to expand, or to modernize. MSERD became responsible for the GDAs and quickly began replacing them with a "new and simpler set of agreements with the provinces, involving a wider range of federal departments" (Canada, 1982). The agreements were labelled "Economic and Regional Development Agreements" (ERDAS), but in time they came to resemble very closely the GDAs they replaced. The one important difference was a provision that would allow the federal government to deliver directly certain programs and initiatives rather than always having the provincial governments deliver them, as was the case with the GDAs.

During his brief tenure as Prime Minister, John Turner declared his intention to streamline federal government operations, which in his opinion had become "too elaborate, too complex, too slow and too expensive" (*Globe and Mail*, July 2, 1984: 5). He abolished two central agencies, including MSERD and turned responsibility for the ERDAS over to DRIE.

Brian Mulroney came to office in 1984 determined to "inflict prosperity on Atlantic Canada" (Savoie, 1992: 98). Though slow off the mark, the Progressive Conservative government tried after several months in office to redirect more DRIE funding to slower-growth regions. Within a few years, however, it became clear that the government would have to overhaul its regional development policy completely. The four Atlantic premiers, as well as many business groups in the Atlantic region, became extremely vocal in their criticism of Ottawa's regional policy. DRIE was accused of being extremely bureaucratic and not sufficiently concerned with the economic difficulties of the Atlantic provinces. In addition, the resource-based megaprojects never materialized in Atlantic Canada or in the West, and the "unprecedented softness" in central Canada suddenly disappeared. Indeed, by the mid- to late 1980s the Ontario economy, if anything, was overheating. Atlantic premiers made the case that DRIE, by focusing many of its efforts in central Canada, was exacerbating the regional disparities problem. They argued that it was "better to have no federal regional programming at all than to have DRIE [and] DRIE programs favouring central Canada" (Savoie, 1987: 20). In any event, Mulroney – as politicians are wont to do – wanted to put his own personal stamp on government policy, particularly on regional development, which is a high-profile and particularly popular policy field in slow-growth regions.

DRIE thus begot three new agencies. In unveiling the Atlantic Canada Opportunities Agency (ACOA), Mulroney declared: "We begin with new money, a new mission and a new opportunity. The Agency will succeed where others have failed" (*Halifax Sunday Herald*, June 7, 1987: 1). He gave ACOA $1.05 billion of new money over five years and also transferred part of DRIE's budget – about $1 billion – over five years. The newly appointed ministers and deputy ministers of ACOA declared early on that the agency would have "no Ottawa bureaucracy to answer to" (*Fredericton Daily Gleaner*, June 8, 1987: 3). They designed a new program labelled Action, essentially a continuation of incentives programs to the private sector first introduced as early as the pre-DREE days. The one important difference is that the Action program is far more flexible in terms of both the type of projects and the sectors that qualify for assistance. ACOA also took over the ERDA agreements and renamed them Cooperation agreements. They, too, are remarkably similar to earlier agreements, whether ERDAS or GDAS.

Mulroney's powerful Alberta minister, Don Mazankowski, also saw little prospect in working with DRIE, which was no more popular in the West than in Atlantic Canada. Mazankowski was determined to bring to the national agenda the need to diversify the western economy and pressured the government to announce an ACOA-type agency for western Canada. Several weeks after he had unveiled ACOA, Mulroney went to Edmonton to announce a new Western Diversification (WD) department (Canada, 1987). This time, he announced that the new department would be allocated $1.2 billion of new money, as well as responsibility for DRIE's budget in western Canada and the western ERDAS. Like ACOA, WD looked to modify an existing government program to launch its Western Diversification initiative. The department redesigned the Western Transportation Industrial Development Program, made it considerably more flexible, and provided for increased levels of assistance. The new incentives program is targeted to the private sector and makes funding available to firms investing in new projects or willing to expand existing facilities. The program's overarching objective is to diversify the economy of western Canada (Savoie, 1992).

On July 15, 1987, yet another special agency was created to promote economic development – this time in northern Ontario. Federal Economic Development for Northern Ontario Region (FEDNOR) launched three new programs shortly after it was established, all of which were designed to support private-sector investment in the region (Canada, 1989: 6)

A new industry department – the Department of Industry, Science and Technology (DIST) – was established to replace DRIE. DIST would retain regional development responsibilities for Ontario and Québec and assume sectoral responsibility for Canadian industry. It immediately scrapped DRIE's tier system and launched new programs and initiatives designed to strengthen Canada's competitive trading position. The department's focus, much to the delight of many of its senior officials, would become national and sectoral in scope rather than regional.

Still, DIST was being asked to assume responsibility for federal regional development programs in Québec. Ottawa decided to replace Le Plan de l'Est, a program dating back to DREE days but scheduled to expire in March, 1988, with a new province-wide agreement to develop Québec's regions. It signed a five-year $820 million ERDA subsidiary agreement with the Québec government. Ottawa agreed to contribute $440 million and Québec $380 million. With DIST having federal responsibility for the agreement, the funding was increased by an additional $283 million in 1989. The agreement divides Québec's regions into two broad categories: the central regions and the peripheral or resource regions. The central regions were awarded a larger share of the funds – $486 million. The resource regions consist of eastern Québec (Bas-St-Laurent, Gaspésie), the North Shore, the North-Centre (Lac St-Jean), the western region (Rouyn-Noranda), and the northern region (Abitibi). The central regions cover the rest of Québec (Canada, 1988).

REGIONAL DEVELOPMENT FROM A FEDERAL-PROVINCIAL PERSPECTIVE

Any attempt to understand the evolution of Canada's regional development policy strictly from the perspective of changing economic circumstances would be seriously off the mark. Indeed, many forces have shaped and reshaped it, not least of which is federal-provincial relations – and all this entails, including the issue of visibility in government spending and partisan politics.

Canada's constitution does not assign to either level of government explicit responsibility or powers for economic development or for combatting regional economic disparities. Provincial governments have a major function in economic development because they own natural resources and control most determinants of human resources and land use. The federal government has created for itself a major role, essentially on the basis of its spending power. Equalization payments, income transfers, and shared-cost agreements with the provinces all derive from Ottawa's spending power. In addition, the federal government holds jurisdiction over such matters as foreign and interprovincial trade and chartered banking, and it shares with the provinces jurisdiction over agriculture and immigration.

Thus, from a constitutional perspective, close federal-provincial coordination is required simply because both levels of government have assumed important roles in regional development. In any event, many practitioners of regional development tend to put aside these constitutional niceties, arguing that a classical view of federalism may be appropriate for other policy fields, but not for regional development. As regional development becomes more complex, they point out, so does the interdependence of government actions. Measures to promote regional development must be multidimensional and, by their very nature, cut across jurisdictional lines; otherwise, the efforts of one government could well work at cross purposes to those of the other. One former senior federal government official explained that "regional economic disparity is economic, not constitutional" (Savoie, 1992: 17).

The federal government has hardly needed to impose itself on the provinces in the regional development field. Indeed, several provinces, notably the four in Atlantic Canada, have insisted over the years that Ottawa play a lead role in regional development. The pressure to include a new constitutional provision in the 1982 Constitution Act, committing Parliament and the government of Canada to the principle of equalization payments and to the promotion of equal opportunities and economic development throughout the country, came from the provinces and not from the federal government. Federal officials now report that in the face of such pressure they set out to "contain" provincial demands by insisting that any constitutional provision for equalization or regional development be drafted in the "broadest" of terms. They were successful, as section 36 of the 1982 Constitution Act merely commits the government of Canada to the principle of equalization. A number of provincial governments came back to the fore in the negotiations that led to the Charlottetown Accord. This time they were much more successful. The failed Accord committed the "Government of Canada to making equalization payments so that provincial governments have sufficient revenues to provide reasonably comparable levels of public services at reasonably comparable levels of taxation ... to ensure the provision of reasonably comparable economic infrastructures of a national nature ... [and] to promoting regional economic development to reduce economic disparities" (Canada, 1992: 3).

This is not to suggest that the federal government has always had to be brought to regional development negotiations kicking and screaming. The original impetus for federal involvement in the field came from royal commissions at the national level and subsequently from the federal government itself. One of the legacies of the Trudeau government was the view, now widely held by many Canadians, that striking an appropriate regional balance in the country's economic development is an important tenet of national unity. Trudeau, it will be recalled, stressed that the problem of regional development was as threatening to national unity as the language issue.

The debate in Canadian politics has rarely been over whether or not the federal government should be involved in regional development. Even neo-conservatives and those who abhor government intervention in the economy accept that Ottawa must, or at least will, play such a role. Tom Courchene, a leading proponent in Canada of the neo-classical school, has stated: "I have no illusions that governments will stand idly by and allow the unfettered market to call the adjustment tune. They will intervene [in the name of regional development]" (Courchene, 1984: 513). Right-of-centre politicians may argue against federal regional development programs while in opposition, but they quickly change their tune once in power, as many Conservative cabinet ministers did in 1984.

Rather, the debate has centred on the geographical application of Ottawa's approach: which region is in, which is out, and how the federal government should intervene. When Pierre Trudeau declared war on regional disparity and argued that "economic equality is just as important as equality of language rights," he was thinking about the economic problems of eastern Québec and Atlantic Canada. His powerful Québec minister and the first minister of DREE, Jean Marchand, argued that if the bulk of federal regional development funding – at least 80 per cent – was not spent east of Trois-Rivières, then Ottawa's efforts would fail (Savoie, 1992: 244). He went even further, insisting that federal programs, such as special areas and regional incentives, needed a limited geographical application or their value would be severely diluted. As it was, the Special Areas Program designated such "growth-pole" communities as Hawke's Bay and Come-by-Chance, communities as far removed from what François

Perroux had envisaged as one could imagine. Still, observers agree that Marchand was successful in limiting DREE's programs to carefully selected regions, though those designated for industrial incentives included all of the Atlantic provinces, eastern and northern Québec, parts of northern Ontario, and the northernmost regions of the four western provinces. The regions designated accounted for about 30 per cent of the Canadian labour force. Parts of Ontario, Alberta, and British Columbia were designated more as a gesture to ensure that these provinces would not feel completely left out of a federal government program. The fear was, given their relatively strong fiscal positions, that they might establish their own incentive programs, thereby greatly inhibiting the new federal initiatives.

It was not long before strong political pressure was put on Marchand to extend DREE programs to other regions. Cabinet ministers and MPs from the Montreal area frequently made the point that Montreal was Québec's growth pole and that if DREE were serious about regional development, then it ought to designate Montreal under its industrial incentives program. Montreal's growth performance rate was not keeping pace with expectations, particularly those of the large number of Liberal MPs from the area. The city's unemployment rate stood at 7.0 per cent in 1972, compared with 4.6 per cent for Toronto. Further, Québec's economic strength, it was argued time and again, was directly linked to Montreal, and unless new jobs were created there little hope was held for the province's peripheral areas. Montreal required special measures, it was argued, to return to a reasonable rate of growth. In the end, Marchand agreed. A special region, known as "region C," was designated. It consisted of southwestern Québec, including Hull and Montreal, and three counties of eastern Ontario (Canada, 1972: 21).

The changes, however, stipulated that the special designation should only apply for two years. Thus, in late 1976, DREE Minister Marcel Lessard once again pressed his colleagues to designate Montreal for special regional industrial incentives. The Parti Québécois had come to power, which resulted in a sudden downturn in private investment and rumours that head offices of major companies were leaving Montreal. Cabinet agreed once again to a special designation for Montreal, but in so doing secured a commitment from the DREE Minister that he would look at the possibility of designating other regions, including northern British Columbia and the Northwest Territories. The pressure to push and pull the incentives program to more areas of the country remained strong. By the time DREE was disbanded, the program covered fully 93 per cent of Canada's land mass and over 50 per cent of the population (Savoie, 1992: 210). DRIE, DREE's replacement, sought to solve the problem once and for all when its first minister, Ed Lumley, rose in the Commons and declared that he had come up with a program that he could recommend to "all Members of Parliament and all Canadians." He announced that the new Industrial and Regional Development Program (IRDP) "is not a program to be available only in designated regions. Whatever riding any Member of this House represents, his or her constituents will be eligible for assistance" (Canada, 1983: 1-2). In brief, the program would apply everywhere in Canada, including Toronto, Calgary, and Vancouver.

The pressure to extend federal regional development efforts to a wider geographical focus did not come only from within the federal cabinet, the government caucus, or Parliament. No sooner was DREE established than provincial governments, especially the premiers of slow-growth provinces, began to call on Ottawa to extend its Special Areas Program to more communities. But they met a strong-willed Jean Marchand, who resisted provincial pressure at almost every turn. He explained: "The more you extend it – special areas – the more you weaken it.... We have to stick to our guns" (Canada, 1970: 2:62). Marchand, together with his powerful deputy minister, Tom Kent, had a "take it or leave it" approach that did not sit well with provincial governments. Atlantic premiers in particular called time and again for a closer form of federal-provincial cooperation and asked the Prime Minister to intervene. They pointed out that DREE was introducing ambitious measures for their provinces, invariably in areas of provincial jurisdiction but with very little consultation.

The federal government, fresh from a near defeat at the hands of Robert Stanfield in the 1972 general election, responded by scrapping the Special Areas Program and introducing the GDA approach. Marchand and Kent were also transferred to other departments. The GDA approach was everything the Special Areas Program was not. It was a highly flexible instrument that called for close federal-provincial cooperation and was available to all provinces. It could support initiatives in any city, town, village, or hamlet in any province and in any sector. In hindsight, we now see that the GDA constituted a fundamental shift in both the substance of regional development policy and in federal-provincial relations.

That the GDAs and their replacements (the ERDAs and the cooperation agreements) are flexible instruments has been well documented elsewhere and there is no need to repeat the findings here (Savoie, 1981). What is perhaps less well known is that these broad enabling documents have placed the provincial governments in the driver's seat in shaping regional development programs. In many ways, the introduction of the GDAS reversed the kind of relationship the federal government had with the provinces under Marchand and Kent. The provincial governments henceforth would propose initiatives to which the federal government would react. In many ways, Ottawa acted and continues to act like a Treasury Board vis-à-vis the provinces – it reviews proposals from provincial governments, accepting some and rejecting others. Admittedly, the poorer provinces, contributing only 20 per cent of the cost, were never in a position to adopt a cavalier posture toward the federal government. Nevertheless, even they were in an enviable bargaining position. If DREE refused to support a particular proposal, the province simply came back with another. Though the agreements also allowed the federal government to make proposals, this did not often occur.

The GDAS and their replacements redefined in a fundamental fashion the nature of Canadian regional development policy. Indeed, one can argue that Canada has not had a genuine policy in this area since the days of Marchand and Kent. What we have had instead are ten provincial economic development policies supported with federal funds. Federal programs are available in all regions and Ottawa pumps regional development funding into all ten provincial governments. Tourism efforts in Ontario, Alberta, and British Columbia, for example, have all been supported by federal funds through regional development agreements. There are many similar examples, including funds earmarked to assist economic development planning in Ontario and industrial development in British Columbia.

At the risk of repetition, Canadian regional development policy has, over time, been pushed and pulled to cover virtually every area and community of the country. The process began in the mid-1970s and has accelerated ever since. During the 1980s, the rest of Canada caught up to Atlantic Canada in the level of business assistance the federal government provided. Outside the Atlantic region, business assistance per capita more than doubled to $252 between 1980 and 1987, while it fell to $133 in Atlantic Canada. The situation is now such that one of ACOA's main concerns in early 1991 was that its Action program was "uncompetitive" with federal assistance offered to the private sector in other regions. The Action program now must compete with attractive federally funded regional development incentive programs available in Québec, parts of Ontario, and western Canada (Savoie, 1990: 47).

But this only tells part of the story. ERDA agreements, WD in the West,

FEDNOR in northern Ontario, DIST in Ontario and Québec, ACOA in Atlantic Canada, along with tax incentives, now make billions of dollars available annually everywhere in the country to an array of projects in the name of regional development. Indeed, few projects anywhere are ineligible for funding. If nothing else, this has given regional development a bad reputation and many would argue that it has become the main factor contributing to the "Canadian disease" – regional envy.

One keen student of Canadian politics recently noted that "the first thing a foreign observer must learn about Canadian politics is that it is not about right and left, it is about east and west." He added that "the political culture of Canada may be defined as a profound sense of regional grievance married to a discourse of entitlement. Sixty-four per cent of Canadians feel their province gets back less in federal spending than the taxes sent to Ottawa. Nearly three-quarters of Canadians feel that the federal government favours one region of Canada over the others, and very few feel that their region is the one favoured" (French, 1990: 2).

By having broad enabling agreements with the ten provinces and the territories, Ottawa is, in effect, inviting them to compete for federal funds for regional development. No provincial government is about to pass up such an invitation. The provincial and territorial governments have responded with a variety of projects and a sense of ownership in Canadian regional policy. Provincial governments, including those representing Canada's wealthiest provinces, have applauded Ottawa's regional development efforts ever since the 1970s. Alberta's Premier Lougheed, for example, was a strong supporter of the GDA approach at federal-provincial conferences (Canada, 1978: 289, 384). In fact, most premiers took turns at these conferences to register similar support. Those from slow-growth regions are particularly enthusiastic, if only because the agreements constitute a pool of new money to tap for virtually any conceivable economic development project. The one exception was DRIE, which was perceived in Atlantic Canada at least as being tilted too much in favour of central Canada. The argument that it was "better to have no federal regional programming at all than to have DRIE programs favouring central Canada" speaks volumes about the Canadian disease.

The federal government has, as we saw earlier, altered its regional development policy on many occasions. The changes, if anything, have served to disperse federal efforts ever more widely. And Ottawa has never tried to scrap the broad federal-provincial regional development agreements since it introduced the GDA approach in 1973.

Federal concerns have centred on changing economic circumstances, in particular the growing weaknesses of some sectors and regions, notably in central Canada in the early 1980s. More important, however, is the struggle to "gain credit, status and importance and to avoid discredit and blame" (Simeon, 1972: 185). It is not too much of an exaggeration to say that the issue of visibility has been, from an Ottawa perspective, the single most important factor in shaping Canada's regional development efforts. Regional economic development is a high-profile activity, more often than not placing governments in a positive light. Accordingly, it provides an attractive target for government competition for status. Not only is it highly visible, but it is also an area where the roles of each level of government are determined more by politics and spending than by formal jurisdiction.

Ottawa's decision to designate Montreal as a special region shortly after the Parti Québécois came to power reflected the city's deteriorating economic circumstances. However, the decision was also taken to demonstrate to Québécois that federalism and the federal government could work on their behalf. Indeed, the Trudeau government became convinced during its last mandate that there was an urgent need to re-establish more direct relations with Canadians in all regions and to strengthen the federal position in relation to the provinces. On being returned to power in 1980, Trudeau and some of his most senior ministers believed that the pendulum of power had swung too far in favour of the provinces. Trudeau set out, therefore, to repatriate the constitution and to assert the superior position of the federal government. To strengthen the hand of the central government, the government turned to the energy policy and regional economic development. Trudeau, in his last major speech on federal-provincial relations as Prime Minister, reflected on what had gone wrong. "The balance swung too far. With opting-out provisions, tax points transfers, cash transfers and shared-cost programs for which the federal government rarely got any of the credit ... the federal government risked losing its already limited amount of direct contact with the public" (Canada, 1984: 11).

Early in the last Trudeau mandate, senior cabinet ministers spoke openly about the problem, and the GDAs, in particular, became the target for criticism. Federal Fisheries Minister Roméo LeBlanc commented that he had great difficulty in seeing federal funds transferred to provincial governments to support provincially designed and implemented fisheries initiatives under federal-provincial agreements, while he himself could not obtain funds from the federal Treasury Board to implement urgently required federal initiatives (*Moncton Times*, February 11, 1977: 1). The Deputy Prime Minister, Allan MacEachen, summed up the visibility issue in this fashion: "The visibility of each order of government in a federation is part of the overall issue of intergovernmental balance" and complained that provincial governments employed federal funds to give themselves a higher political profile (Canada, 1981b: 11). DREE's own minister, Pierre De Bané, simply added fuel to the fire. He constantly referred to a public opinion survey showing that when Ottawa delivers a program directly, 95 per cent of respondents are aware that the federal government is responsible for it, but when the program is delivered through a federal-provincial agreement, only 15 per cent know that the federal government is involved (*Globe and Mail*, August 13, 1981: 1). He refused to renew a GDA-subsidiary agreement with Manitoba simply on the grounds that Ottawa was not getting sufficient political credit for its expenditures. He also completely overhauled the Prince Edward Island comprehensive plan to enable the federal government to deliver some projects directly. He finally launched a major policy review that eventually led to the abolition of DREE and to new federal-provincial agreements – the ERDAS – to replace the GDAS.

The government document explaining the new approach makes it clear that it was trying to deal as much with federal-provincial concerns as with emerging economic circumstances. It pointed out that the federal government would "give priority within its own areas of jurisdiction" (Canada, 1981a: 10). While it recognized the importance of bringing harmony to economic development planning and programming, it argued that "joint implementation of economic development programming may not always be desirable" (*ibid.*: 11). Ottawa insisted on delivering directly a number of the initiatives sponsored by the ERDAS. Almost half of the programs under Phase III of the Prince Edward Island comprehensive development plan were earmarked for direct delivery. In the case of Québec, the Trudeau government announced toward the end of its mandate over $100 million of regional development projects, all of which were to be delivered by federal departments.

Not unexpectedly, provincial reaction to the new direct delivery approach and to the new organization was negative. A federal-provincial conference on the economy was held in Ottawa shortly after the new policy was announced and observers were unanimous in reporting that it degenerated into a counterproductive and acrimonious session (see, for example, *Globe and Mail*, February 5, 1982: 1). Provincial governments denounced the new approach. They were convinced that competitive federalism had replaced cooperative federalism and that regional development had become an important part of the battleground.

However, one by one, the provinces also signed new ERDA agreements with Ottawa. Not doing so meant forgoing federal cost-sharing of certain initiatives – those that, for various reasons, the federal government could not or did not wish to deliver. Still, negotiations for the various ERDAS were in most instances difficult and lengthy. In the case of Québec, for example, the provincial government only agreed to sign an ERDA after the Liberal government in Ottawa was defeated. The provincial Minister of Justice, Pierre-Marc Johnson, explained that "negotiations had bogged down with the previous Liberal government, but things changed radically when the Progressive Conservatives came to power. They [the new government] have a different way of looking at things and [respect] Québec's jurisdiction" (Montreal *Gazette*, December 15, 1984: 2).

The Mulroney government came to office committed to bringing about national reconciliation. Mulroney explained that "our first task is to breathe a new spirit into federalism. I am convinced that the serious deterioration of federal-provincial relations is not exclusively the result of the constitutional deficiencies. Centralistic and negative attitudes are much more to blame" (Progressive Conservative Party, 1984: 4). He also reported that his government would look to the provinces for solutions to regional development rather than impose centrally designed policies and programs. The provinces jumped on Mulroney's pledge and requested that program delivery under federal-provincial agreements revert to the provinces, as in the past. The federal cabinet agreed and for a few years at least did away with the federal direct delivery component found in many ERDA subsidiary agreements.

In the early days of Mulroney's first mandate, the federal cabinet made every effort to make close relations with provincial governments a top priority. The fact that Mulroney's own party also held power in the four Atlantic provinces, Ontario, Alberta, and Saskatchewan certainly helped. The regional development field was specifically identified for closer federal-provincial cooperation. Both levels of government agreed to establish a joint federal-provincial task force on regional development. In addition, the federal government made immediate plans to transfer much of the responsibility for delivering regional cash-grant programs to provinces.

However, harmonious federal-provincial relations, at least in the case of regional policy, were short-lived. To be sure, the task force was established and a report was tabled. It has had no visible impact, however. The idea of transferring to the provinces responsibility for the delivery of incentives programs to the private sector also proved short-lived. Senior federal officials, believing that ministers would eventually have a change of heart, dragged their feet on the matter, insisting that more in-depth analysis was required. They were right – and key cabinet ministers like John Crosbie began to oppose the transfer of program delivery to the provinces after only a year in office. As before, the issue of political visibility, of Ottawa's getting due credit for federal money spent, proved the decisive factor in preventing the transfer. This prompted a senior federal official to observe "plus ça change, plus c'est pareil" (cited in Savoie, 1992: 18).

By the end of its first mandate, the Mulroney government had lost all interest in transferring responsibility to the provinces. For one thing, the political landscape had changed. Liberal governments were getting elected in Ontario, Prince Edward Island, Newfoundland, and New Brunswick. Federal cabinet ministers responsible for these provinces became less inclined to transfer funds to provincial governments to enable them to deliver programs. The establishment of regional development agencies ACOA, WD, and FEDNOR confirmed the federal intention to stake out a highly visible presence in regional development programs. Although the report that led to the establishment of ACOA recommended that the regional incentives programs could be more efficiently delivered by the provinces, this avenue was rejected by the Mulroney government.

Federal-provincial agreements are still under the agencies but, in the case of ACOA, Ottawa has increasingly pointed to the need for a federal direct delivery component. WD, meanwhile, has not attached a high priority to these agreements and at one point considered scrapping the ERDA process altogether. The federal cabinet would not permit this, with western ministers arguing that the only way the ERDAs could be scrapped in western Canada would be to do away with all such agreements across the country. Despite the concern with visibility, $240 million of new funding was made available in early 1990 for new subsidiary agreements in western Canada to be spent over five years (Canada, 1990: 12). It was also made clear that federal departments were expected to be directly involved in developing these agreements and that they were to deliver directly certain initiatives.

The situation is different in Québec in that federal regional development measures are implemented under a federal-provincial agreement and not through federal agencies. The agreement is managed jointly by the federal Department of Industry, Science and Technology and by the Office de planification et de développement du Québec. The provincial government delivers the great majority of the projects under the agreement, which in fact operates much like previous spatial (or regional, as opposed to sectoral) subsidiary agreements did under ERDA and even under the GDA approach. The special political situation in Québec, where both major provincial parties are completely divorced from federal parties, and the particularly close working relationship that Prime Minister Mulroney and Premier Bourassa enjoyed explain the apparent lack of concern with visibility in this instance. For Mulroney, the political battle in Québec was not with other federal parties, but with the forces of sovereignty. Having gained Bourassa's support on this front, Mulroney saw little merit in risking it over the visibility issue.

LOOKING TO THE FUTURE

Since the early 1970s Canadian regional development policy has been nothing if not flexible. If one were to look to the constitution to see who is doing what in the field, he or she would get very little appreciation of how things actually work. The constitution and the formal division of responsibility are no guide. Even federal policy no longer provides much of a guide. The federal-provincial regional development agreements are broad enabling documents that essentially permit both orders of government to strike deals bilaterally in any policy field. The result is that Canada has ten different policies, some of which hardly qualify as regional development or, for that matter, as policy at all. Simply striking deals to clean up the Halifax harbour or to promote tourism in Ontario and Alberta or to build the Victoria Convention Centre in British Columbia do not add up to a policy. There is neither a geographical focus nor a coherent purpose. The federal government has, in this respect, simply become a kind of Treasury Board to which all the provinces apply for funding various projects. When Ottawa gets fed up with playing this role, as it periodically does, it simply declares that it will deliver some of the initiatives directly or it reduces spending in the field.

In trying to be all things to all regions, Canadian regional development has thus lost its way. It is floundering from one project to another and, in the process, contributing substantially in its own right to the politics of regional envy. And the policy has lost its way at a particularly bad moment. Ottawa faces a trying fiscal position. Its accumulated debt now stands at over $546 billion and something like 35 per cent of its annual revenues are now required to service the debt. Federal sources of revenue have been pretty well tapped to the limit, with several tax increases in recent years and the introduction of the Goods and Services Tax (GST) in January 1991. Rather than a fundamental rethinking of Canadian regional development policy – which is clearly needed – there will no doubt be pressure to cut back spending in light of the failures of the past and Ottawa's difficult fiscal situation.

There are also powerful new forces at play. Globalization, including trade patterns arising under the Canada-U.S. Free Trade Agreement, and NAFTA, could well redefine the relationship various regions have with one another. The "National Policy" that was at the core of every government's economic program for over a century was discarded in the mid-1980s. That policy, as it is well known, sought to create and strengthen East-West ties. It became widely accepted that the policy largely favoured the economies of Ontario and Québec, in particular that of southern Ontario, and that its impact on the rest of the country was discriminatory. It will be recalled that the Ontario government fought a rearguard action on the Canada-U.S. Free Trade Agreement.

As Ontario, Alberta, and British Columbia – the "have" provinces – adjust to hemispheric free trade and other global economic forces, they may well begin to hang question marks alongside programs designed to maintain Canada's East-West links, whether in the form of transfer payments to individuals or of federal regional development programs. For instance, it may well become more important for Ontario to secure measures to undercut Michigan's cost structure than to maintain East-West links. The global economic forces will also have a major impact on the evolution of the political economy of Canada's regions. As they become inserted differently into the global economy, their links with the outside world will "become more important relative to their economic linkages within Canada...." In this sense, Canada becomes less able to act as the giant "mutual insurance company" that Premier Allan Blakeney once called it (Simeon, 1990: 12). In such a political economy, "it may well become harder to sustain the political commitment in wealthier provinces to interregional redistribution" (ibid.).

Indeed, the global economy itself may well contribute to regional fragmentation and decentralization. Global pressures, the argument goes, will increasingly constrain federal policy instruments such as monetary, fiscal, trade, and redistributive policies (Courchene, 1990). The result is that areas of provincial jurisdiction such as education and infrastructure will become the key instruments to promote regional economic development. The fact that some provincial governments are less capable of financing such measures will matter less and less.

If history is any guide, we will likely see a move soon within the federal government to restructure its regional development policy. The pressures to reduce the size of government, to relegate it to a decision-making body only with respect to regional development, are such that Industry Canada, ACOA, WD, and FEDNOR will shortly be replaced by new departments and institutions. We should remember that most politicians long to leave their own imprint on government. Few areas offer them as many possibilities to do so as does reorganization. It allows them to point to tangible evidence that they were able to clean up the mess their predecessors left behind.

History also tells us that a new organization will not be based on a new approach or even a new policy. Regional development will likely continue to be the preserve of broad federal-provincial agreements and some form of financial incentives to the private sector. Funding levels will probably be reduced, but the programs will go on. It is unlikely that any government will completely embrace a dominant theory of an all-encompassing approach to support the operations of departments and agencies concerned with regional development. Pragmatism will continue to carry the day. In other words, "if you can do something for that region or that province, then for God's sake do something for mine."

REFERENCES

Bickerton, James P. (1990). *Nova Scotia, Ottawa and Politics of Regional Development*. Toronto: University of Toronto Press.

Brewis, T.N. (1978). "Regional Economic Development in Canada in Historical Perspective," in H. Lithwick, ed., *Regional Economic Policy: The Canadian Experience*. Toronto: McGraw-Hill Ryerson.

Canada, House of Commons (1970). *Minutes of Proceedings, Standing Committee on Regional Development*.

Canada, Department of Regional Economic Expansion (1972). *Annual Report 1971-72*.

Canada, Secrétariat des conférences intergouvernementales canadiennes (1978). Conference fédérale-provinciale des premiers ministres. Ottawa (13-15 février).

Canada, Department of Finance (1981a). Economic Development for Canada in the 1980s (November).

Canada, Department of Finance (1981b). *Federal-Provincial Fiscal Arrangements in the Eighties* (April 23).

Canada, Office of the Prime Minister (1982). "Reorganization for Economic Development – News Release" (January 12).

Canada, Department of Industry, Science and Technology (1983). "Speaking Notes – The Honourable Ed Lumley to the House of Commons on the Industrial and Regional Development Program" (June 27).

Canada, Office of the Prime Minister (1984). Speech by the Prime Minister at the Colloquium Organized by Laval University Concerning the Reform of Federal Institutions. (March 30).

Canada, Office of the Prime Minister (1987). "Western Diversification Initiative – News Releases" (August 4).

Canada, Department of Industry, Science and Technology (1988). *Canada-Quebec Subsidiary Agreement on the Economic Development of the Regions of Quebec* (June 9).

Canada, Department of Industry, Science and Technology (1989). *The FEDNOR Review.*

Canada (1990). *Part III - Expenditure Plan, Western Economic Diversification Canada 1990-91 Estimates.*

Canada (1992). *Consensus Report on the Constitution* (August 28).

Careless, Anthony (1977). *Initiative and Response: The Adaptation of Canadian Federalism to Regional Economic Development.* Montreal and Kingston: McGill-Queen's University Press.

Courchene, Thomas J. (1981). "A Market Perspective on Regional Disparities," *Canadian Public Policy*, 7, 4.

Courchene, Thomas J. (1990). "Global Competitiveness and the Canadian Federation," paper prepared for the University of Toronto Conference on Global Competition and Canadian Federalism (September 15).

French, Richard D. (1990). "The Future of Federal-Provincial Relations ... if Any," paper presented to the Institute for Public Administration of Canada. National Capital Region (June 14).

Higgins, Benjamin (1992). *Entrepreneurship and Economic Development: Moncton and Cape Breton.* Moncton: Canadian Institute for Research on Regional Development.

Perroux, François (1969). *L'économie du XXe siècle.* Paris: Presses universitaires de France.

Progressive Conservative Party (1984). "Background notes for an address by Brian Mulroney, P.C., M.P." Toronto (August 28).

Savoie, Donald J. (1981). *Federal-Provincial Collaboration: The Canada-New Brunswick General Development Agreement*. Montreal and Kingston: McGill-Queen's University Press.

Savoie, Donald J. (1987). *Establishing the Atlantic Canada Opportunities Agency – A Report Prepared for the Prime Minister*. Office of the Prime Minister (May).

Savoie, Donald J. (1990). *ACOA: Transition to Maturity*. Moncton: Canadian Institute for Research on Regional Development.

Savoie, Donald J. (1992). *Regional Economic Development: Canada's Search for Solutions*, Second edition. Toronto: University of Toronto Press.

Simeon, Richard (1990). "Thinking About the Constitutional Future: A Framework," paper presented for the C.D. Howe Institute (December), mimeo.

CHAPTER SIXTEEN

Conflicting Trends in Canadian Federalism: The Case of Energy Policy

Michel Duquette

THIS CHAPTER, BASED ON THE CANADIAN LITERATURE ON energy and on new data gathered from a five-year survey, analyzes the experience of Canadian federalism in the energy sector. As a starting point, I suggest that major changes in the international environment, both North American and world-wide, brought about a breakdown of this country's traditional equilibrium between provincial and federal jurisdictions over energy through centre-periphery conflicts. The resulting policies led, in a first period from 1973 to 1982, to an exaltation of a nationalist self-sufficiency approach to energy development, which deeply affected the balance of power between the federal government and the provinces. In contrast, from 1983 onward, a deeper conflict between regions and layers of government, as well as a stabilized international environment, brought about a major change in policy, characterized by decentralization, favouring a more "consociational" regime through a process of mutual forbearance and accommodation.

RECONCILING TWO DIVERGENT BODIES OF LITERATURE

Among the widely accepted views in the Canadian political literature on intergovernmental relations, two main theoretical streams can be identified, both rooted in the political economy field of research and in partisan politics. The last twenty years in Canadian political life have been characterized by a growing controversy among political actors as well as analysts. On the one side and as early as 1959, H.G.H. Aitken's work on the "new staples" led him to perceive the important implications of direct foreign investment on federal-provincial relations in Canada (Aitken, 1959). A decade later, Levitt suggested that the particularist economic strategies of the provinces, specifically those that benefit from a rich resource base, favour centrifugal tendencies that are conducive, in her words, to a "silent surrender" to American capital (Levitt, 1970).

By the middle of the decade, Canadian nationalists or "nation-building" advocates, strongly influenced by dependency theorists, keep insisting, outside as well as within the federal government, on the actual "foreign economic control" from U.S. multinational corporations as the result of a "balkanization" of the political system.[1] The 1980 Bertrand Report followed the same line of analysis, arguing that high levels of concentration in the oil industry, from drilling and refining operations to wholesale distribution, restricted market competition and damaged the public interest.

In the late seventies and on the eve of the National Energy Program (NEP), Stevenson justified the necessity of a strong federal involvement in the economy from a rather pessimistic point of view. In his words, Canada was little more than a loosely tied Confederation of petty states, envious of each other and eager to compete on the international market for whatever source of foreign investment was available in order to expand their own income base. This allowed for cartel practices in an oligopoly-dominated economy (Stevenson, 1979).

One might question to what extent such a literature served as a justification after the fact for the nationalistic path followed by Ottawa's decision-makers in energy policy, a paramount sector of this country's industrial strategy from 1973 on. However, more plausible factors may be found in the domestic political arena, from the Canada-U.S. controversy around the Mackenzie Valley pipeline project in the late seventies (Pearse, 1974) to the pressures exercised by a new class of Canadian energy developers in the West in favour of further Canadianization of their industry (Niosi and Duquette, 1987), and even in the very style of a Trudeau regime that was committed to broad international recognition. Nevertheless, it has been accepted that the renewed influence of traditional variables in the Canadian political system, as well as the introduction of new variables such as, in the seventies, Alberta's and Québec's own industrial strategies based on energy resource development, were due to an unstable international environment triggered by the two oil shocks of 1973 and 1979.

Quite interestingly, Stevenson was also the first analyst to acknowledge, in the last decade, the deepening of a centre-periphery cleavage in Canada.

A political gap seemed to widen between the diversified economy of Ontario and the resource based economy of the West, while another cleavage appeared in central Canada between a dominant and highly industrialized Ontario and a weaker, less modern Québec with fewer natural advantages. This appealing hypothesis, it seems, allows for revealing comparisons between Canada and related situations in the Western Hemisphere. In that respect, the contribution of the late Stein Rokkan may prove useful in reconciling recent surveys on the making of a national policy at the federal level (Doern and Toner, 1985; Duquette, 1988b; Gingras and Rivard, 1988; Leslie and Watts, 1989) with another independent body of literature, mainly dealing with provincialism and interactions between local entrepreneurs and provincial development strategies.

While Richards and Pratt (1979) recounted the main features of "Prairie capitalism," in particular the Lougheed policy of industrial diversification in the early seventies, Nelles (1974) and McKay (1983) analyzed the rise of energy development in Ontario and Bliss (1987) portrayed a class of entrepreneurs with rising ambitions in the West. Starting from the Rokkan's paradigm of centre-periphery cleavages that shape national politics, Leslie and Watts (1989) noted a mounting provincial ascendency in federal politics in the previous five years of Tory government.

Rokkan's concepts of centre and periphery refer to three sets of relationships. The first is territorial and has political implications. Privileged locations within the national territory and major urban networks of financial, administrative and industrial importance establish ties with other regions where towns are essentially outposts of the urban economy servicing the rural population. A second type is economic. The centre benefits from its international exposure to commerce and technological innovation. By contrast, the periphery remains a loose network of communities whose survival is overwhelmingly dependent either on resource development or on the allocation of subsidies from the state in a variety of equalization payments and social programs (Rokkan and Urwin, 1982). Inequality is at the very core of the whole economy. It may happen that inequality is reduced by successful regional development strategies, but it cannot be suppressed. Centres tend to grow more steadily over the years, given a more diversified economy with wealthy entrepreneurs and a sophisticated lobbying network merging into the nation's political structure. Westerners' complaints about unequal representation in the Senate as well as in the Commons are a traditional debate in Canadian politics. Finally, the last set of relationships involves issues of ethnic-cultural coexistence

393

and even dominance. French-speaking Québec and the English-speaking provinces are bound to accommodation and compromise if national unity is to be preserved. Here again, cultural or language policies may try to bridge differences, but they never completely succeed in suppressing this last cleavage.

In smaller or less populated countries with powerful neighbours, Rokkan adds, the weight of the centre-periphery cleavage is even greater and poses a challenge to unity. Such countries are historically dependent on the inflow of political, economic and cultural resources from the outside (Rokkan et al., 1970: 123).

Canadian Confederation in 1867 was, in Weberian terms, a covenant between local states, each with a distinctive cultural and political identity, for specific political and economic purposes. The driving force was essentially defensive: to counteract rising U.S. influence with protectionist policies to consolidate East-West relations in a national territory. In the twentieth century, development takes place and continental patterns of trade, mainly in resource development, progressively challenge that goal. Regional centres emerge from wealth. Increasing integration in the international environment generates elite factions clustered in mass parties. These in turn tend to echo complaints about unequal access to wealth in the regions, diverging perceptions of national objectives and further integration with neighbouring countries. National unity and a viable political development of the polity can only evolve from the capacity of the whole system to avoid confrontation on basic issues and to foster national cohesion on common grounds.

To this task, two theoretical sets of policies are possible. On the one hand, "nation-accentuating" policies initiated by the elites from the centre will try to foster the metropolitan settlement within the peripheral territory through new fiscal capabilities and the takeover of the natural resources for the benefit of the majority. On the other hand, counter-elites from the periphery will likely support a more consensual policy, where deliberate compromises by elites circumscribe and limit the extent to which political power can be wielded by the centre. If the content of such counter-policies is as diffuse as one might expect from a rather loosely tied coalition of diverse regional interests, they nevertheless imply that a limit is thus imposed on the capacity of the centre to manipulate the whole system (Daalder, 1973).

THE PROVINCIAL COMMITMENT TO ENERGY POLICY

Until the early seventies a major objective of energy policy in Canada had been to foster a strong petroleum and gas industry through pricing and tax incentives that were more generous than those available outside the resource sector. Both provinces and the federal bureaucracy promoted industry and encouraged economic growth in western Canada. Such a policy, however, imposed higher direct costs on other parts of the country, as prices varied considerably over regions. It also left the federal government with little revenue from the gas and petroleum or power industries. In such conditions, the constitutional responsibilities of the provinces over natural resources were strengthened, allowing Alberta, Ontario, and Québec to put forward their respective energy programs in oil extraction and refining or hydro and nuclear power.

Resource development lies within provincial jurisdiction and experience showed that the provinces invariably favoured maximum resource extraction in the shortest possible time and on the largest possible scale. Ontario in 1906 and Québec in 1944 embarked on ambitious hydroelectricity projects. Ontario eventually diversified its electrical network through the installation of a very ambitious nuclear power program, based on the CANDU heavy-water and natural uranium technology developed in the post-war period by Atomic Energy of Canada Limited (McKay, 1983).[2] On the other hand, Québec and Ottawa struggled in late 1977 over the issue of nuclear development in the context of a larger confrontation (Bothwell, 1988). Because Québec refused to commit itself to the installation of further nuclear power facilities from AECL, the construction of the Laprade heavy-water plant was interrupted. The province essentially relied on its hydroelectric potential for energy development.

The case of Alberta is more relevant to this study, because it pioneered the development of today's institutional arrangements between government and industry. As a far less populated province, Alberta chose to adopt the main features of systems developed in energy-producing American states, such as Texas. Simple licensing regulations provided the province with the means to maintain surveillance and control over general exploration activity without intervening in corporate strategy.[3]

Further regulations were put forward by the Manning government with the Gas Resources Conservation Act of 1949, in order "to prevent federal encroachment over provincial resources" (Fry, 1981: 42 ff.). The Alberta Gas Trunk Line was established, not as a public utility firm but rather as a consortium of private investors supported by public funds, and under provincial legislation. AGTL was expected to facilitate gas distribution to consumers all over the province as well as to potential importers in the United States. Thus, Edmonton gained control over a highly profitable activity in a rapidly expanding intercontinental market that eventually linked the province's gas and oil fields with customers located as far away as California. In that era of business expansion, Alberta's interest in new foreign costumers and markets grew. Under the Lougheed Tory government from 1971 on, Alberta's ambitions shifted to industrial diversification and urban development, a task at which the province devoted considerable money from the multi-billion-dollar Heritage Fund.[4] As a growing periphery, Alberta did nothing more than follow the path of Québec's Quiet Revolution of the sixties. In the short term, Edmonton's industrial strategy was bound to clash with a federal energy policy essentially devised, in the Trudeau years, by politicians from central Canada. A heated debate was to break out sooner or later around the main issues of control over energy resources and local industrial development.

A NATION-ACCENTUATING ENERGY POLICY: THE NEP

The constitution gives overriding responsibilities to Ottawa for interprovincial and international trade and commerce. It also entrusts the federal government with the responsibility of stimulating the industry in the name of national development. Nevertheless, analysts agree that the 1961 National Oil Policy of the Diefenbaker government turned down most nationalist demands expressed by the Gordon Commission on Canada's Economic Prospects, and displayed a preference for natural continental patterns of supply in which Canadian and U.S. crudes could be freely used in the best markets. In practice, the Montreal market was reserved for overseas sources of supply, while Alberta's production grew by expanding in Ontario and British Columbia markets and by marked penetration of accessible U.S. markets (Doern and Toner, 1985: 79). Such an energy policy was synonymous with a high level of compatibility among the demands of the industry, the strategies pursued by the resource-producing provinces, and the federal bureaucracy responsible for the national interest of Canada. Although more a consequence than a cause, this policy corresponded with an era of international wealth, from which Canada benefited through this open-door economic strategy. The energy crisis changed all that, as it did in most Western countries. In West Germany, for example, it favoured increasing planning from the federal government and encroachment on the jurisdiction of the *Länder* (Rokkan and Urwin, 1982: 236).

By exerting increasing pressures over domestic consumers – Ontario, Québec and the Maritimes – the oil shock imposed substantial changes in policy definition and implementation. The 1976 Liberal electoral victory and its subsequent return to power in 1980 can be interpreted as a powerful provincial response to a growing external threat. In this context, the federal government was given the mandate to emerge as a major entrepreneur through new pricing practices and subsidies to megaprojects. In the name of self-sufficiency, Ottawa wished to isolate the domestic energy sector from an unstable international environment and gain control over the reserves. As early as 1974, specific programs aimed at protecting the importers of foreign oil in eastern Canada were followed by a comprehensive policy in 1976 with an array of new measures for the energy sector (Canada, 1976). From its establishment in 1975, Petro-Canada was intended to play a major role in price regulation and policy implementation and began taking over foreign-owned firms such as British Petroleum and Petrofina.

The entire policy was fully consistent with the nation-building theory, a very appealing theoretical approach to many French- and English-speaking Canadian intellectuals and decision-makers in the mid-seventies. It was obviously, in Rokkan's terms, a nation-accentuating policy. The fact remains that, in the Trudeau years, new political elite leaders from Ontario and Québec took firm control of the federal government. They gave little weight to the recriminations of the peripheral provinces about this encroachment on provincial jurisdiction in resource development. Thus, Ottawa began debating with Alberta about energy resource control and even wrestled with Québec, a large but rather poor province, over the issue of local self-determination. Their political program clearly created a majority consensus in central Canada for almost ten years, but it slowly widened the gap between central and peripheral provinces.

Behind the politicians, a sophisticated bureaucracy was thriving, mainly through the establishment of new federally sponsored programs for economic or regional development. Energy was of considerable interest to them. The oil crisis provided both the justification and the rationale for intervention. The Foreign Investment Review Agency (FIRA) began scanning projects that involved foreign investors, but rules were seldom enforced until the second oil shock. Nevertheless, conflicts arose between the government bureaucracy and corporate culture (Sawatsky, 1987). Some have even suggested that the self-interest of a highly specialized and technically able bureaucracy, as a class of state entrepreneurs, is to be held responsible for the whole conception of the policy (Foster, 1982).

From central Canada, the federal policy of the National Energy Program, established in 1980, looked impeccable. In constitutional terms, no new ground was broken. The NEP simply meant that the federal level of government was fully conscious of its responsibilities in price regulation, interprovincial trade, and frontier development. But if the NEP's intention was "to avoid confrontation on basic issues" and to "foster national cohesion," in Rokkan's terms, it led to a bitter clash.

THE TRIUMPH OF PROVINCIALISM

The oil industry did not foresee the coming of a National Energy Program that would feature regulations curtailing exports to foreign countries, the development of Arctic offshore energy resources, and an ambitious Canadianization program involving grants based on the nationality of ownership (Canada, 1980). Grants, under the management of the Canada Oil and Gas Lands Administration (COGLA), could amount to 80 per cent in any project where Canadian participation would be at least 50 per cent of the joint venture (Canada, 1982: 17). Holdings were subject to a retroactive 25 per cent back-in, giving the Crown the right and power to buy a quarter of any petroleum or gas found on federal Crown lands. This rule applied to pre-NEP discoveries as well as to new ones. The taxes were heaviest on firms that were drilling on provincial lands and firms that exported south (Carmichael and Stewart, 1983: 19). On the other hand, domestic prices were kept significantly lower than international prices to avoid disturbances in the eastern consumer market. The difference between international and domestic prices until 1983 resulted in a huge transfer of wealth from the Prairies to the eastern consumer provinces.

The NEP sent the energy-producing provinces and the industry into panic. The policy, with its original tax system and new criteria for subsidies — such as Canadianization — diverted considerable money from the industry and from the provinces, thus fostering the interventionist capacities of Ottawa, not only in the energy sector but in the economy as a whole. For the most ambitious firms, state intervention meant that they could now move into market dominance by shrewd use of public policy.

With the NEP, that strategy was picked up and refined to near perfection by companies such as Dome Petroleum. In the two years from 1981 to 1983, Dome was the largest recipient of federal support with $615 million, while public-owned Petro-Canada and private-owned Canterra and Norcen received $576 million, $199 million, and $111 million, respectively (Canada, 1982: 17).

Few foreign firms were allowed in the new Petroleum Incentives Program (PIP), although rules loosened after 1982. At first, only Gulf, Mobil, and Esso Canada, a subsidiary of Exxon, qualified for the program. In these conditions, Canadian ownership over the reserves jumped from 25 per cent in 1980 to 35 per cent in 1983 and 40 per cent in 1985. Offshore drilling activity flourished from generous grants for North Atlantic projects as well as for others in the Beaufort Sea, and this activity resulted in significant but expensive oil and gas finds. However, given the international environment, war in the Middle East, and an increasing oil glut, the whole policy proved unsuccessful in financial terms. The growing federal deficit actually put an end to the NEP ambitions. The recession opened the way to a more pragmatic and modest approach to energy development.

The trend toward centralization implicit in the NEP was resented by corporate and provincial actors and denounced as a unilateral policy of forced unification at the expense of the actual balance of power within the Canadian constitutional tradition. The harshest criticisms even suggested that, while it set up a crusade for national unity, the federal government had second thoughts. It only wished to tap into oil revenue. Above all, there was a growing similarity of views among the industry (Canadian as well as foreign-owned), the producing provinces, and the American government against the NEP's interventionism. Even though Canadian firms, in relative terms, had the most to gain from the policy, they shared with the multinational corporations the fear of further state monitoring of their activities. As for the provinces, they obviously rejected federal involvement in a provincial activity. In Washington, complaints from American-owned corporations operating in Canada against the pro-Canadianization discriminatory regulations of the NEP, particularly about the national treatment criteria applied to Canada/U.S. investment practices, began to favour anti-Canadian attitudes and increased protectionist measures against Canadian gas and electricity exports to the U.S.

In the "national treatment" sense, current Canadian investment policies, as reflected in the National Energy Program, are discriminatory in that U.S. and other foreign-owned firms are treated less favourably than Canadian firms.... The NEP is a very serious derogation from the OECD's 1976 declaration on national treatment, even taking into account the interpretative statement made by the Canadians at the time of their initial adoption of this declaration.[5]

In 1981, as American and European-owned oil firms voiced their complaints to the OECD Committee on International Investment and Multinational Corporations, new funds were allocated to the Canadian Petroleum Association (PAC) representing multinational corporations, for the establishment of a powerful lobby in Ottawa. The lobby launched an impressive advertising campaign. Its initial position was uneasy. It could hardly engage in rhetorical combat with Ottawa on an issue such as Canadianization. It held fire on the NEP's principles and showed instead a more friendly attitude toward Ottawa. In sharp contrast, Canadian-owned firms in the Independent Petroleum Association of Canada (IPAC) harangued the government and were ostracized from official circles until the Tories came back to power. This gave the multinational firms an occasion to benefit from Ottawa's generous PIP grants in drilling projects off the Newfoundland coast and in the Arctic.

But the PAC and the IPAC had more ambitious goals. They were aiming for a major change in policy. Fully aware of the former Prime Minister's flat opposition to public ownership in the oil industry and even to state planning, the lobby came in close contact with Joe Clark, still leader of the Tories but back in opposition. On corporate issues, Clark was a typical Alberta MP and remained among the most conservative members of his party. Other rising Tory figures, such as Pat Carney in the West and Sinclair Stevens in Toronto, began campaigning from coast to coast against the NEP. So swift was the establishment of a consensus over the whole issue that, in August 1984, a 'counter energy policy' was publicly announced.[6] Brian Mulroney, as new leader of the party, confirmed the mandate and sided with the westerners' vision of energy development. Little else could be expected from a Québecer with strong ambitions in the federal arena but a weak political base in his native province. Québec had been assumed to be a Liberal fortress. But Québec shared with the West a deeply ingrained sense that the current federal economic strategy and, more specifically, protectionist policies such as the NEP, invariably favoured Ontario industry (Dunn, 1989).

The producing provinces, Alberta, Saskatchewan, and British Columbia, also participated the new coalition. All three were ruled by Conservative or Social Credit leaders. All three felt that the Liberals had no credibility whatsoever in energy policy. As natural leader of the West, Alberta's Premier Peter Lougheed voiced his firm opposition to the NEP and to the centralizing trend underlying the policy. While the western periphery was organizing against the Liberals, the Parti Québécois, still resentful of the Liberals in the aftermath of the 1980 referendum campaign, joined the coalition and poured resources into the Tory election campaign in 1984. The outcome of the election, with the Conservatives winning 202 ridings out of 276, showed that public opinion was tired of constant federal-provincial conflict, increasingly associated with a rather bleak economic situation and the chill in U.S.-Canadian bilateral relations. The Mulroney victory was a black day for Canadian nationalists, sending both Liberals and centralizing policies to the opposition benches for the next decade. The periphery had succeeded in reversing a powerful trend toward economic nationalism initiated ten years earlier.

Not surprisingly, an entirely new approach to federal-provincial relations, consistent with consociational theory, was put forward by the Mulroney government. It resulted in an energy policy respectful of provincial jurisdictions and more concerned with regional development in the energy-producing areas. Steps were taken to deregulate oil and gas exports to the U.S. A gas pipeline section was built to northern Alberta to help producers increase cash flow with more exports, given the high prices on the international market (Bliss, 1987: 557). Deregulation of the domestic market was impeded, however, by the existence of an array of federally funded programs in oil substitution. Ottawa simply put an end to most of them over a two-year period (Gingras and Rivard, 1988). Deregulation went ahead, albeit slowly.

Late in 1985, Ottawa opened discussions with the Maritimes on issues of offshore energy development. Although constitutional rulings clearly supported federal authority, the government did not hesitate to surrender not only major potential revenues to the provinces of Newfoundland and Nova Scotia, but also important measures of policy and administrative control. The Venture gasfield off Sable Island, already in operation, fell under Halifax jurisdiction. In late 1988, Ottawa and Québec reached an agreement over power and gas exports to the U.S., allowing the province to conclude significant contracts with utility firms in the Northeast U.S. Some lamented that these various accords permitted provincial ascendency, which eventually could be applied over constitutional rights in the

Pacific. However, through these various compromises, Ottawa was able to achieve consensus with most provinces (seven out of ten)[7] over the controversial free trade issue (Shoyama, 1989). Considering the importance of establishing such a common front – a condition specified by American negotiators at the beginning of talks – it seems clear that the two projects (rapprochement between the federal government and the provinces and rapprochement with the U.S.) were linked in the package of Tory policies (Duquette, 1988a). The relinquishing of state monitoring over energy activities and the parallel abolition of FIRA – a paramount symbol of economic nationalism – are other indicators of this trend.

With the 1985 Western Accord, the Tory government implemented what it called a national reconciliation policy toward the provinces and the industry. Shifting away from the Liberal government's energy policy, the Accord abolished the entire taxation system of the NEP. The wellhead special tax on oil was gradually eliminated and prices were deregulated. Tax exemptions on the income of smaller Canadian-owned firms were established in order to support a fragile economic sector faced with recession. It is estimated that the new fiscal regime resulted in a net transfer of about $3 billion annually to the industry (Senate of Canada, 1985: 4). The federal government's share of upstream oil and gas activity was drastically reduced to 4.6 per cent in 1986, from a peak of 26 per cent in 1982 (Canada, 1987: 123). With such a reduction in federal taxation, the industry could look forward to better days. While a barrel of oil at $27 in 1985 conceded to the producing firm $7.82 in net benefit, an $18 dollar barrel yielded $7.85 in 1987. Finally, on aspects of privatization, Petro-Canada was newly endowed with an Executive Board comprised of prestigious industrialists, with a mandate to act like any private firm on the market.

Other developments suggest an alignment with international practices as well as the erosion of the Canadianization principle. It is quite true that corporate takeovers have been important in recent years. In July, 1986, Canadian Home Oil was sold to Interprovincial Pipelines for $1.1. billion, excluding holdings in the U.S. but including Sovereign Oil & Gas in the U.K., a very profitable development firm in the North Sea. Canadian-owned Nova, former AGPL, sold its share in Husky to Hong Kong investor Li Ka Shing for $484 million. Smaller Canadian firms such as Sulpetro of Calgary and Ocelot, which had high expectations under the NEP but ended up crippled by debt, were auctioned in 1987 to Imperial Oil (Exxon) and Mosbacher of Texas.

Ottawa then issued a Solomon-like judgment, when a major player of the NEP era, heavily indebted Dome Petroleum, was offered to potential buyers. Canadian-owned Trans-Canada Pipelines offered $5 billion for the firm. The American gas industry leader Amoco bid $5.4 billion and won out, despite nationalist lobbying and political pressures. The final offer for $5.8 billion was finally accepted in late 1987, but not without some resistance from all parties, including Canadian shareholders, and from foreign as well as domestic creditors. Yet Dome's Canadian subsidiary Encor was excluded from the Amoco deal and went to TCP. Sceptre, a company engaged in Prairie gas exploration, was partially owned by the Québec government. The acquisition of new shares by Québec's retailer Gaz Métropolitain, also a firm involving significant public ownership, was clearly an indication of easterners' interest in resources. Otherwise, Québec's energy policy encouraged oil substitution by residential and industrial users (Québec, 1988: 20).

Such examples suggest the end of Canadianization in energy policy. Not until 1988 was there any statement on Canadianization, although energy developments in the field were numerous and significant. Increasingly, Ottawa favoured criteria of financial health over nationalist preoccupations. National treatment was applied to any firm operating in the sector. Petro-Canada, although still involved to some extent in Atlantic offshore drilling, went ahead with its retail market development program – an activity seen by Ottawa as more profitable than exploration. Large Canadian firms received no special treatment. Heavily indebted ones were sold, in whole or in part, to foreign investors. Otherwise, financially sound corporations or cooperatives were still protected from takeovers. Special tax exemptions were offered to smaller Canadian-owned firms faced with recession, while Canadian investors from other provinces bought extra shares in these, an indication of continuity of the principle of national ownership. All this generosity could be of some help to Canadian producers facing the new challenges posed by the Canada-U.S. Free Trade Agreement (FTA).

ENERGY DEVELOPMENT UNDER THE FTA

With the FTA, Canada and the United States agreed, first, to a complete phase-out of tariffs over ten years. Second, most restrictions in the trade of agricultural goods along with subsidies were to be abolished, mainly on meat and grain. Third, the price of oil, gas, and power offered to the other partner was expected to be the lowest on the market, allowing for an increase in energy trade between them. Fourth, a gradual but significant liberalization of access to public markets and to commercial services, including finance, was to occur. Finally, supplier guidelines and bilateral institutions were to be defined and implemented in order to settle conflicts on matters of foreign investment.

Energy must be considered as one of the primary achievements of the FTA. A long-standing tradition of free movement of energy resources between the provinces and the U.S. inevitably faced protectionist measures from time to time. Canada, as the second largest energy producer in the OECD and the largest per capita producer in the Western world, has always been the primary supplier of natural gas to the U.S. Both California and the Midwest have been major clients for Canadian natural gas since the fifties. Canada supplies 13 per cent of American imports of oil and petroleum products as well as 100 per cent of gas imports. Canadian gas exports must be able to meet the huge American demand and, in this perspective, one can better understand the protectionist objectives of the NEP. It was imperative to the federal government that Canada not compromise its more vulnerable eastern Canadian market to the demands of the American Midwest and that U.S. energy sales benefit the national economy and not only the revenue of the producing provinces (Economic Council of Canada, 1988: 13).

With growing American demand for hydrocarbons and electricity, it seems that virtually all the bilateral obstacles to energy trade have been lifted with the FTA. In the case of world shortages, the U.S. is guaranteed more secure access to continental energy sources. It is likely that Mexico, with its immense oil and gas resources, will be called upon to play a major role in the establishment of a strategic energy supply system in the case of a world-wide market disruption.[8] The proportional access clause (article 904 [a]) of the FTA introduced further constraints on the imposition of quantitative export restrictions: "... the restriction does not reduce the proportion of the total export shipment of a specific energy good made available to the other Party relative to the total supply of that good of the Party maintaining the restriction...."

The Canadian oil industry, given its limited resources, was vulnerable to this clause. Few safeguards in the text would guarantee the protection of diminishing Canadian reserves. Worse, Ottawa was forbidden to look for a better return on its resources in other markets in the case of higher international prices. Many even feared the issue would become a sore point between the two partners. The government had no direct answers to these fears but insisted that, by securing such a huge export market, the FTA rendered possible the development of Canadian resources in need of huge investments, particularly in the remote Far North (Canada, 1988: 9).

Has the FTA contributed to changes in the patterns of supply, investment and trade? The main outcome was the approval by the National Energy Board (NEB) of exports to the U.S. of ten exajoules of natural gas from the northern territories. This decision was the first step in the extension of the new northern Alberta gasline to the Mackenzie Delta. According to data for the 1989-92 period, there was a slight (5 per cent) increase in the volume of exports, although the data indicate that benefits did not increase, given lower prices on the market. Further increases are less likely to occur in the short term, as existing gaslines operate at full capacity. Otherwise, the FTA does not seem to have shifted trade patterns between Canada and the U.S., as each country had already adjusted its energy regulations to market forces. These, along with the shift in energy policy previously implemented by Ottawa, were thus far more important than the FTA, as is openly admitted by the NEB (1989).

On the other hand, electricity production and exports have been drastically reduced in the last four years due to unfavourable water flows resulting from dry weather. Volumes of interruptible power supplies to the U.S. fell drastically although, consistent with the FTA provisions, guaranteed supplies were preserved. This is an accomplishment of the FTA *per se. Shortages also pushed prices up, although not significantly, given this short-term crisis. Canadian power producers obviously chose to maintain the attractiveness of the market through competitive prices for their American customers, having in mind the promising contracts that were under negotiation. The strategy, helped by heavy rains, paid back; by 1993, growth had resumed.*

Québec has concluded a significant twenty-year contract for the supply of about $17 billion worth of power generation to New York state, to begin in 1995. This agreement follows another $8 billion contract among the same parties signed in 1988. Directly related to the FTA, both arrangements are strong examples of Québec's commitment to the FTA. However, the implementation of the multi-billion-dollar James Bay II megaproject faces strong opposition from the Cree nation in northern Québec, and further delays have been imposed by the NEB on questions related to the environment. The whole issue has met with mounting demands from opponents, such as the Audubon Society and the Sierra Club, which have powerful environmental lobbies in Washington. Although the Cree are split into two political factions – a radical one around chief Matthew Coon Come, who claims political autonomy for the whole James Bay area and calls for an end to hydro projects, and a moderate one, possibly around Abel Kitchen, president of the Cree Company – the outcome of the conflict is difficult to predict. Aboriginal claims over northern Québec have become, along with the summer, 1990, Mohawk uprising, issues of importance to Québec.

More importantly in the long term, recession in the U.S. and in Canada as well as growing concerns about the environment and the protection of wildlife have challenged the viability of major hydro projects. It is no surprise that such preoccupations have fuelled heated debates in communities in Vermont and other New England states over the last three years. As an example, the Maine Public Utility Commission, under intense public pressure, put an end in March, 1989, to the $4 billion contract signed earlier by Hydro-Québec and the Central Maine Power Corporation. As far as energy is concerned, one must admit that the much-expected trickle-down effects of the FTA have been rather disappointing for Québec.

In the West, after much delay, 1990 saw the approval by the NEB of a major construction project by TransCanada Pipelines, aimed at upgrading transport facilities across the provinces as well as south of the border. British Columbia, also plagued by low water flows, partly shifted electricity generation from hydro to natural gas to preserve guaranteed sales to the U.S. The major event of 1990, a sudden increase in demand and production from September onwards, also illustrates the influence of international factors on the industry, namely the Persian Gulf crisis. Prices rose abruptly following Iraq's invasion of Kuwait. As an important producer, Canada was asked by the International Energy Agency to participate in a joint effort to expand the strategic reserve in the case of war in the Middle East. Short-term revenues helped increase cash flow for the industry, but no special drilling projects were undertaken. Benefits, rather, helped to service the corporate debt (Canada, 1991). This was obviously the consequence of the poor performance of domestic oil production in 1989, when Canadian exports of crude oil were slashed in half. In 1990, exports to the U.S. did not increase because most new wells put into operation were emitting natural gas and oil. Imports from the North Sea and from OPEC countries (aside from Kuwait and Iraq) experienced a sharp increase. For crude oil, given these conditions, the FTA is likely to remain a neutral factor in the foreseeable future.

The growth of the domestic oil and gas trade to the eastern provinces, it must be noted, is structurally impeded by insufficient capacity as well as high transportation prices. Growing imports in late 1990 and early 1991 were a result of this situation. This has forced Québec-based Gas Métropolitain to seek arrangements with American gas transportation firms from Houston, Texas, to maintain the level of supply. Ontario also increased oil imports from the Midwest, partly in response to the partial destruction of the Syncrude facilities in Saskatchewan in late 1989 and their closure for repairs. At first glance, such developments point to strengthened North-South integration patterns in the energy sector, if not elsewhere, and a stabilization of the traditional coast-to-coast axis. As a general conclusion, it can be seen that structural changes in the energy industry have increased market integration, not only between Canada and the U.S. but also within the world market, OPEC as well as non-OPEC.

Other secondary factors, related to the state machinery and federal-provincial relations, may also be playing a role. Slow procedures on the part of the federal NEB with regard to new projects initially designed by the provinces, such as James Bay II and Soligaz, indicate that other, institutional domestic constraints are challenging the FTA.[9]

HYDRO DEVELOPMENT AND THE ABORIGINAL ISSUE IN QUÉBEC

Canada's wealth in hydro energy is considerable and only partially exploited. The constitution of 1867, amended in 1982, recognizes that the development of this wealth is a matter of provincial jurisdiction. In the case of Québec, its exploitation of this resource has to be understood in the context of nationalism, as hydroelectric development contributes to economic autonomy. As elsewhere, Québec government decision-makers regard natural resource development, and in particular energy-related development, as part of a program of political affirmation and economic expansion.

The main problems with power development in northern Québec are both social and political. The 1975 James Bay Agreement between the Québec government and the Inuit and Cree of northern Québec was a daring and innovative gesture, which has never been imitated in Canada or the United States. Québec granted political and economic space to the Inuit and Cree. Generously intentioned, the James Bay Agreement was meant to set the Cree back on the path to the future.

Québec was upset by the federal government's threat, voiced by Environment Minister Jean Charest in 1992, to intervene in an area of provincial jurisdiction, namely the development of James Bay. This is not the first time that Ottawa has given in to the temptation to intervene in an area that the constitution unambiguously grants to the provinces (Duquette, 1992a: 84). There is no doubt that the British North America Act (1867) gave the provinces ownership of and control over natural resources, and this has always guaranteed the provinces significant revenue as well as providing a major tool of economic development. Federal tactics to direct and control resource development have therefore always focused on the federal spending power and on federal jurisdiction over categories affected by such development. For example, there is federal jurisdiction over international and interprovincial trade, which has allowed the federal government to set export quotas and, to some extent, even to control production itself.

Unlike the American states, Canadian provinces enjoy substantial autonomy, not only in regulating and issuing permits but also in the production, distribution, and management of resources. Canadian provinces are fully in charge of the energy sector within their boundaries, either as owners of what lies beneath the ground or as owners of Crown corporations entrusted with the development of electrical or fossil resources. In Canada, as in the United States, the federal government remains jointly responsible for industrial development in this sector, for it enjoys an inalienable power to spend, a principle that made possible the creation of Petro-Canada.

On the other hand, electricity production, mainly based in Québec and Ontario, is beyond the reach of federal regulators. The federal government prefers to rely on expertise already accumulated on the provincial level, and to divest itself of responsibility for a sector already being developed. The United States did this in the case of Texas oil. The recognized presence of regional government in the energy sector, and the expertise of its civil servants, may create a precedent. This is what took place in Québec and Ontario as these provinces undertook the development of their hydroelectric resources at a time when the federal government had not yet intervened in the area (Ontario in 1906, Québec much later, in 1944).

There is no doubt that the hydro energy sector gives rise to overlapping jurisdictions because of the constitutional division of powers. Every grand project has an impact on the environment (Duquette, 1992b: 235-57). It is hardly surprising that, as the owner of islands in James Bay and as the party responsible for studying the region's flora and fauna, Ottawa may require guarantees from Québec that the animal species under federal jurisdiction will not be hurt by the effects of a project not within Ottawa's ambit. In the name of public health, the problem of methylmercury in the newly created lakes might concern it as well.

The constitution, however, does not grant Ottawa the power to stop a hydroelectric facility if a province satisfies reasonable safety conditions in implementing the project. The federal government's responsibility for protecting Native peoples is weakened by the fact that the provinces also enjoy prerogatives in this area. Moreover, Québec and its northern Natives in 1975 signed a formal agreement to develop jointly the subarctic region of Québec on the basis of new rules that both accepted.

In federal-provincial relations, the major test will be whether or not Québec can exercise to the fullest its capacity for economic development, of which its northern territory is obviously an integral part. Non-Aboriginal Québecers and Aboriginals, in a spirit of mutual recognition, will have to come to an arrangement over the manner in which this development is implemented.

CONCLUSION

A first conclusion can be drawn from the experience of the last twenty years in energy policy. In Canada, if nationalizing policies go too far through forced centralization and eventually constitutional reform, whatever their rationale, they will be perceived by the periphery as internal colonialism. Control over energy resources is a case in point. The whole equilibrium of the polity may be in jeopardy. On one hand, separatism may rapidly gain ground in public opinion, as it did in Alberta and Québec in the late seventies. On the other hand, provinces may also try to "escape" economically what they believe to be the heavy burden of federalism by overwhelmingly committing their industrial strategy to the logic of foreign markets and globalization.

It is likely that, if centrifugal tendencies evolve into diverging paths of development for the regions and a marked weakening of the political centre, balkanization will occur. In this case a minimal consensus among élites over basic issues would give way to particularism. Here again separatism is strengthened. Comparative experience suggests that the whole history of Switzerland, the Netherlands, Belgium, and Canada, among other federal or regionally designed countries, swings between these two poles.

Energy policy in Canada is particularly illustrative of attempts undertaken by both levels of government within the federal system to deal with the territorial and economic cleavages of Rokkan's matrix. Over the last ten years, the shift in policy from one extreme to the other may be indicative of the difficulties encountered by policy-makers in pursuit of over-ambitious and politically divisive goals, given a changing international environment and, more importantly, an already fragile political equilibrium between central and peripheral provinces.

It is too early to predict if the new political trend, which is perceived by some as an aggressive ascendency of the peripheral provinces at the expense of federal authority, will pave the way to a balkanization of the country. Given the uncertainty over the federal government's implementation power on issues of interprovincial commerce and free trade arrangements with the U.S. concerning energy resources, the potential for provincial-federal frictions and disputes remains high. Yet, the case of energy suggests the contrary. The resource-producing provinces and Ottawa are in full agreement over basic issues such as joint support to the industry and new field developments in oil and gas in Alberta, Saskatchewan, British Columbia, Nova Scotia, and Newfoundland. As far as Québec, Newfoundland, or New Brunswick are concerned, power exports to the U.S and eventually other areas of the world are all the more welcome.

A second conclusion concerns the potential internationalization of domestic political issues, previously dealt with at the provincial, interprovincial, and federal levels of government. Such is the lesson, it seems, that can be taken from the Québec Cree lobbying in New York state and New England and from their alliance with American environmentalists. Hereafter, sensitive issues of energy development will be decided and debated where the market lies – in New York City, Albany, Montpelier, and Boston. This is, in the political arena, an immediate consequence of global economic integration. Further limitations on trade may and probably will be imposed by the mounting deficit that the U.S. experiences with Canada, mainly in the energy sector.

NOTES

1   From 1972 to 1976, the NDP exerted strong influence on the minority gov-

ernment of Trudeau; it is largely acknowledged that the balance-of-power position of the NDP was responsible for the evolution of the Liberal regime towards economic nationalism, with the establishment of Petro-Canada in 1975 and the new energy policy of self-sufficiency in 1976.

2   For a comprehensive history of Ontario energy development from its origins, see Nelles (1974).

3   Limited permits allow the firm to undertake drilling in concessions. Such restricted leases leave remaining areas as Crown reserves, which may be sold by auction through sealed bids at a later time. Alberta receives three kinds of charges from the industry: initial payments from Crown reserves, annual rentals payable on leases, and royalties levied as a percentage of the wellhead value of the resource when it is extracted. Other limits are imposed on drilling, in order to prevent waste. Finally, pro-rationing of the total output required among wells, another measure inspired from the Texas precedent, is used to adjust the output to changes in total demand and prices on the international market.

4   In 1979 the Heritage Fund amounted to some $14 billion and was responsible for a spree of industrial initiatives in Alberta as well as in neighbouring provinces.

5   Interview with David R. MacDonald at the Centre for International Relations, New York, September 22, 1981.

6   At the beginning of the election campaign, a package of new Tory policies was released in Prince Albert, Saskatchewan, in July, 1984. Thus the Prince Albert 12 Documents served as the first draft of future political orientations for Canada. Though no reference was made to free trade with the U.S., energy policy was given a lengthy consideration.

7   Ontario, Manitoba, and Prince Edward Island opposed the agreement.

8   In such a sensitive and controversial sector as mutual energy supply in a time of crisis, the artisans of the FTA have proven to be more cunning than original. In effect, should Canada, in the event of shortage, claim its right to limit its energy exports to the United States, it must nevertheless guarantee its regular proportion of the reduced Canadian supply. In this sense there could be no circumstances that would justify special rights over imports or exports.

9   Soligaz, originally designed in 1986 to allow for a stable supply of natural gas liquids from Alberta to Québec, has been faced with strong opposition from Ontario's industry and doubts about profitability. It has been delayed several times at the NEB and does not appear to be on its short-term agenda. This has prompted a prospecting spree in the Québec lowlands from a consortium comprised of Québecois and Australian interests and the American Bow Valley prospecting firm, for a total investment of about $30 million (*Maga-*

zine Affaires Plus, April, 1991).

REFERENCES

Aitken, H.G.H. (1954). "The Changing Structure of the Canadian Economy with Particular Reference to the Influence of the United States," in Aitken *et al.*, *The American Economic Impact on Canada*. Durham, N.C.: Duke University Press.

Bertrand, Robert J. (1980). *The State of the Competition in the Canadian Petroleum Industry*. Ottawa: Supply and Services Canada. Bliss, Michael. (1987). *Northern Enterprise: Five Centuries of Canadian Business*. Toronto: McClelland & Stewart.

Bothwell, Robert (1988). *Nucleus: the History of Atomic Energy of Canada Limited*. Toronto: University of Toronto Press.

Canada (1976). *An Economic Strategy for Canada*. Ottawa: Energy, Mines, and Resources.

Canada (1980). *The National Energy Program*. Ottawa: Supply and Service Canada.

Canada (1982). COGLA (Canada Oil and Gas Lands Administration). *Petroleum Incentives and Administration, Report*. Ottawa: Energy, Mines, and Resources.

Canada (1987). *Energy in Canada*. Ottawa: Energy, Mines, and Resources.

Canada (1988). *Energy and Free Trade*. Ottawa: Energy, Mines, and Resources.

Canada (1991). *Canadian Petroleum Market*. Ottawa: Energy, Mines, and Resources.

Carmichael, E., and J.K. Stewart (1983). *Lessons from the National Energy Program*. Montreal: C.D. Howe Institute.

Doern, Bruce, and Glen Toner (1985). *The Politics of Energy*. Toronto: Methuen.

Dunn, Sheilagh M. (1987). "The Free Trade Initiative and Regional Strategies," in Leslie and Watts, eds., Canada: The State of the Federation: 57-76.

Duquette, Michel. (1988a). "Politiques canadiennes de l'énergie et libre-échange – ou le sacrifice d'Iphigénie," *Etudes internationales*, XIX, 1: 5-32.

Duquette, Michel (1988b). "Libéralisme ou nationalisme dans la politique énergétique canadienne?" in D. Brunelle and Y. Bélanger, eds., *L'ère des libéraux*. Québec: Presses de l'Université du Québec.

Duquette, Michel (1992a). *Énergie et fédéralisme au Canada*. Montréal: PUM.

Duquette, Michel (1992b). "A Two-Year Assessment of the Canada-U.S. FTA. International and Domestic Factors Affecting Energy Trade," in Stephen Randall, ed., *Facing North Facing South*. Calgary: University of Calgary Press: 235-57.

Economic Council of Canada (1988). *Open Borders: An Assessment of the Canada-U.S. Free Trade Agreement*. Ottawa.

Foster, Peter (1982). *The Sorcerer's Apprentices: Canada's Super-Bureaucrats and the Energy Mess*. Toronto: Collins.

Fry, Earl H., ed., (1981). *Energy Development in Canada: the Political, Economic, and Continental Dimensions*. Provo, Utah.: Brigham Young University, Centre for International and Area Studies.

Gingras, Yves, and Jacques Rivard (1988). "Energy R&D Policy in Canada," *Science and Public Policy*, XV, 1: 35-42.

Leslie, Peter M., and Ronald L. Watts, eds., (1989). *Canada: The State of the Federation*. Kingston: Institute of Intergovernmental Relations.

Levitt, Kari (1970). *Silent Surrender. The American Economic Empire in Canada*. New York: Liveright.

McKay, Paul (1983). *Electric Empire: The Inside Story of Ontario Hydro*. Toronto: Between the Lines.

National Energy Board (1989). *Annual Report*. Ottawa.

Nelles, H.V. (1974). *The Politics of Development: Forests, Mines, and Hydro-Electric Power in Ontario, 1849-1941*. Toronto: Macmillan.

Niosi, Jorge, and Duquette, Michel (1987). "La loi et les nombres: le Programme énergétique national et la canadianisation de l'industrie pétrolière," Canadian Journal of Political Science, XX, 2: 317-36.

Pearse, Peter H., ed. (1974). *The Mackenzie Pipeline: Arctic Gas and Canadian Energy Policy*. Toronto: McClelland & Stewart.

Québec (1988). *An Energy Policy for the Nineties*.

Richards, John, and Larry Pratt (1979). *Prairie Capitalism: Power and Influence in the New West*. Toronto: McClelland & Stewart.

Rokkan, Stein, A. Campbell, P. Torsvik, and H. Valen (1970). *Citizens, Elections, Parties*. Oslo: Universitetsforlaget.

Rokkan, Stein, and Derek Urwin (1982). *Economy, Territory, Identity: Politics of West European Peripheries*. London: Sage.

Sawatsky, John (1987). *The Insiders: Power, Money, and Secrets in Ottawa*. Toronto: McClelland & Stewart.

Senate of Canada (1985). Third Report of the Senate Permanent Committee on Energy and Natural Resources. No. 19.

Shoyama, Thomas K. (1989). "The Federal-Provincial Social Contract," in Leslie and Watts, eds., *Canada: The State of the Federation*: 159-66.

Stevenson, Garth (1979). *Unfulfilled Union*. Toronto: McClelland & Stewart.

CHAPTER SEVENTEEN

Federalism, Environmental Protection, and Blame Avoidance

Kathryn Harrison

THE RENEWED SALIENCE OF ENVIRONMENTAL ISSUES IN RECENT years has given rise to environmental policy initiatives by both the federal and provincial governments and, not coincidentally, to increased intergovernmental conflict. Federal-provincial disputes have emerged over the Québec government's James Bay hydro development, the Al-Pac pulp mill and the Oldman River Dam in Alberta, and the Rafferty-Alameda Dam in Saskatchewan, to name but a few. As a result, questions concerning the appropriate balance of federal and provincial roles in environmental policy have assumed increasing prominence. This chapter examines how the current division of federal and provincial responsibilities for environmental protection evolved during the 1970s and 1980s, and speculates about future directions.

In light of recent conflicts concerning the environment, it is striking that there were remarkably few intergovernmental disputes over environmental matters until recently. As late as 1989, scholarly publications praised the cooperative atmosphere of federal-provincial relations in the environmental field (Dwivedi and Woodrow, 1989). The degree of intergovernmental cooperation with respect to environmental protection during the 1970s and early 1980s was particularly noteworthy in contrast to the often hostile climate of federal-provincial relations in other fields, including energy policy and constitutional reform, during the same period.

What happened in recent years to disrupt that climate of intergovernmental harmony? It is argued here that the low level of intergovernmental conflict from the early 1970s to the late 1980s reflected the fact that the federal government did not challenge provincial dominance in the environmental and natural resources field. Prior to the late 1980s, the federal government played a largely supportive role of conducting research, offering technical expertise, regulating mobile source emissions, and gently encouraging the provinces to adopt consistent national standards (Thompson, 1980). In contrast, provincial governments assumed the role of front-line protectors of the environment – setting standards for environmental and effluent quality, issuing permits for individual sources, and enforcing both provincial and federal standards.

This chapter argues that the balance of federal and provincial roles and the tenor of federal-provincial relations in the environmental field have evolved in response to trends in public opinion concerning the environment. Federal (and provincial) jurisdictional assertiveness in recent years can be attributed to electoral incentives to claim credit from the public during a period of heightened attention to environmental issues. In contrast, previous federal deference can be seen as an effort to avoid blame from industries resistant to environmental regulation during a period of public inattentiveness. Provincial jurisdictional sensitivities are attributed to efforts to maintain control of natural resources and thus cater to those same interest groups.

EXPLAINING INTERGOVERNMENTAL CONFLICT AND COOPERATION

Two explanations for the historically weak federal role in the environmental field traditionally have been offered: constitutional constraints and provincial resistance. Many authors have suggested that the federal government has played a limited role because it is constrained by limited constitutional authority (Dwivedi, 1974: 180; Lundqvist, 1974: 135; Alhéritière, 1972: 571; Webb, 1983: 1-4). As discussed below, there is little disagreement that the provinces have strong claims to jurisdiction over the natural resources within their borders. In contrast, federal jurisdiction over the environment is both indirect and uncertain. The problem with the constitutional constraint argument, however, is that uncertain authority has not always stopped the federal government before. Why would the federal government display such self-restraint with respect to the environment, when it did not do so with respect to health care, post-secondary education, or oil-pricing?

Legal scholars have been more inclined to argue that the federal government has taken a limited view of its own environmental powers (Saunders, 1988: 28-29; Percy, 1984: 86; Muldoon and Valiante, 1988: 26; Tingley, 1991: 132). For instance, Franson and Lucas have suggested that "the excuse of constitutional difficulties [has been] used as a smokescreen" by the federal government (Franson and Lucas, 1977: 25). Legal scholars generally attribute federal timidity to an unwillingness to confront the provinces, which tend to be highly protective of their jurisdiction over natural resources (Lucas, 1986: 39; Thompson, 1980: 22; Saunders, 1988: 21; Muldoon and Valiante, 1988, 27; Rabe, 1989: 262). Again, however, it is noteworthy that the federal government has not been so reluctant to provoke the provinces in other fields. For instance, when an opportunity arose to tax windfall profits from the oil industry in the late 1970s, the federal government did not hesitate to challenge provincial authority with respect to natural resources. One is left to wonder why provincial resistance in the environmental field was so successful during the same period.

These two explanations also fail to account for the disruption of cooperative federal-provincial relations in the environmental field that occurred in the late 1980s. Clearly, there was no change in the constitution to account for increasing federal jurisdictional assertiveness.[1] Nor is there evidence that the provinces let down their guard concerning natural resources. The one factor that has received too little attention to date in the literature on federalism and environmental policy is public opinion concerning the environment. While not denying the existence of either constitutional uncertainty or provincial resistance, this chapter argues that an explanation for federal and provincial roles in environmental protection is not complete without considering governments' electoral incentives to extend or defend their jurisdiction over the environment in the first place.

Two kinds of questions in public opinion polls offer insights concerning public attitudes toward the environment. First, the degree of public concern is indicated by close-ended questions, such as those asking respondents to rank the severity of environmental problems. Second, the salience of environmental issues is revealed by open-ended questions asking respondents to identify the "most important problem" facing the country today. Although the two measures have tended to move together over the last two decades, trends in the salience of environmental issues have been much more pronounced, suggesting that although there may be a high level of latent public concern for the environment, environmental issues are not always top of mind for most people.

Since the late 1960s, there have been two cycles of public attention to the environment. Environmental concerns rose to prominence for the first time in the late 1960s, coinciding with the first Earth Day (Parlour

and Schatzow, 1978). However, public concern for the environment subsequently declined nationally from the early 1970s to the mid-1980s.[2]
Thereafter, the trend began to reverse, concluding with a surge in environmental concern in the late 1980s and culminating in the second Earth
Day (Bakvis and Nevitte, 1992). The prominence of environmental issues
again subsided with the onset of a recession in the early 1990s.[3]

When environmental concerns are prominent on the public agenda, as
was the case in the late 1960s and late 1980s, federal and provincial governments alike face strong incentives to claim credit from voters by responding to public demand with environmental protection initiatives.
However, when the salience of environmental issues is low, as was the
case in the period between the first and second green waves, the diffuse
benefits and concentrated costs associated with environmental protection
present important obstacles to government action (Wilson, 1975; Weaver,
1986). Because each member of the general public who benefits from improvements in environmental quality has a relatively small stake in the
outcome, people tend to be inattentive to governments' particular environmental policies. In contrast, industries that stand to bear the costs of
environmental regulations remain not only attentive but adamantly resistant. Environmental regulation holds the promise of making more ene-
mies than friends, and a government motivated to avoid electoral blame
would be expected to take a more restrictive view of its jurisdiction.
Thus, the absence of electoral incentives, rather than constitutional constraints or provincial opposition *per se*, may explain why the federal government did not pursue a larger role in environmental protection
throughout the 1970s and early 1980s (Harrison, 1993).

Why, then, have provincial governments been so eager to defend their
environmental jurisdiction, even during periods of low salience? A crucial
difference between the federal and provincial perspectives is that the
provinces are the owners of Crown resources within their borders. Although both orders of government would be expected to respond prefer-
entially to the concentrated interests of resource development industries
rather than the diffuse interests of the beneficiaries of resource conservation during periods of public inattentiveness, in the provinces' case, their
ability to do so is inextricably tied to their authority to control the terms
of resource exploitation. Thus, the provinces would be expected to defend their jurisdiction over natural resources even during periods of low
salience, though not so much to protect them as to manage their exploitation.

THE CONSTITUTIONAL CONTEXT

Since pollution was not a prominent issue in 1867, it is not surprising that responsibility for environmental protection was not explicitly allocated to either the federal or provincial legislatures by the BNA Act. In light of this omission, both federal and provincial authority with respect to environmental protection is derivative of other fields of jurisdiction explicitly mentioned in the constitution. Since almost every aspect of human endeavour has some environmental impact, "The powers that may be used to combat environmental degradation are liberally sprinkled through the heads of power given to each level of government" (Franson and Lucas, 1976: 251). The result is a substantial degree of overlap between federal and provincial powers.

Sources of Provincial Authority

Provincial governments have extensive authority to protect the environment in their capacity both as owners of public property and as legislators. With respect to the former, the constitution confers on the provinces ownership of public lands within their borders. As noted by Thompson and Eddy, that "ownership confers a form of jurisdiction over resources that is scarcely less far-reaching than legislative jurisdiction" (1973: 76). In particular, the provinces have extensive proprietary authority to conserve and protect their natural resources within their borders (Gibson, 1973).

The provinces also have important sources of legislative authority over natural resources, the most significant being that concerning "property and civil rights." The combination of proprietary powers and legislative jurisdiction over property and civil rights gives the provinces authority to legislate with respect to both publicly and privately owned resources within the province. However, an important limitation of provincial jurisdiction is that a province cannot control sources of environmental contaminants beyond its borders that affect the quality of the environment within the province (*Interprovincial Cooperatives*, 1975).

Sources of Federal Authority

The constitutional position of the federal government with respect to the environment is less clear. Like the provinces, the federal government has extensive authority with respect to its own property. Federal ownership is extensive offshore and in the northern territories, but much less significant within the provinces. As a result, federal proprietary powers cannot support comprehensive federal policies to protect the environment within provincial borders.

Indirect federal authority to protect the environment is associated with a number of specific subject areas, such as fisheries, navigation, and agriculture. Environmental jurisdiction associated with those powers is circumscribed, however, because federal actions taken under them must relate to the particular constitutional subject. In that respect, the federal power over fisheries is of greatest interest, since the fact that most water pollutants are harmful to fish gives the federal government considerable latitude to control water pollution using its fisheries power (Lucas, 1982).

Federal powers that have the potential to support a more comprehensive role in environmental protection include trade and commerce, criminal law, and "peace, order, and good government." Although the limits of each are unclear, the extent of federal authority concerning the environment under the residual power to make laws for the peace, order, and good government of Canada is particularly controversial. Most critics agree that some federal role is justified to address discrete interjurisdictional spillovers (LaForest, 1972). However, proponents of greater federal involvement argue that the environment is a subject that is inherently interjurisdictional and thus within federal jurisdiction (Gibson, 1969; Emond, 1972). Others oppose such expansive interpretations of federal powers by arguing that environmental protection is not a coherent subject in the constitutional sense, and that assignment of a matter so pervasive to one level of government or the other would have profound implications for the Canadian federal system (Landis, 1970; Tremblay, 1973; Beaudoin, 1977; Lederman, 1975).

Judicial Review

There are surprisingly few indications of how the courts will interpret federal powers concerning the environment. However, two recent decisions by the Supreme Court offer considerable support for federal jurisdiction over environmental matters.

In the 1988 *Crown Zellerbach* decision, a majority of the Court accepted marine pollution as a valid subject under "peace, order, and good government" with surprisingly little discussion and apparently few reservations (Saunders, 1988: 19). While the dissenting opinion argued that allocating matters of environment protection exclusively to the federal government "would effectively gut provincial legislative jurisdiction," the minority nonetheless clearly envisioned extensive federal jurisdiction with respect to the environment (*R. v. Crown Zellerbach*, 1988: 53). Following this decision, one prominent legal scholar observed that "Large chunks of the broad 'environment' subject now appear to be fair game for federal legislators" (Lucas, 1989: 183).

Perhaps the most significant constitutional case to date was the 1992 Supreme Court decision concerning the Oldman River Dam. In unanimously upholding the constitutionality of a federal environmental assessment regulation, the Court embraced a broad interpretation of federal authority concerning the environment. The decision was not, however, unanimous on questions of administrative law. While the Court maintained the traditional requirement that federal legislation must relate to a particular constitutional head of power, it nonetheless condoned federal reliance on narrow heads of power, such as navigation, as an indirect means to promote environmental protection (*Friends of the Oldman River Society*, 1992: 45). The Court also noted in passing that "In any event, [the federal regulation at issue] falls within the purely residuary aspect of the Peace, Order and good Government' power" (*ibid.*: 49).

The federal government clearly faces two limitations concerning its jurisdiction over the environment. First, many federal powers with respect to the environment are indirect. A second and arguably more important constraint on federal powers is uncertainty. The courts might find comprehensive federal jurisdiction within the criminal law, trade and commerce, and peace, order, and good government powers, but the limits of federal authority remain unclear twenty years after the passage of the first generation of contemporary environmental statutes. The courts cannot be blamed for this persistent uncertainty; they have had few opportunities to clarify federal environmental jurisdiction. The persistent jurisdictional uncertainty reflects the fact that the federal government has taken a limited view of its own powers, and thus has not provoked many constitutional tests.

THE FIRST GREEN WAVE

Public consciousness of pollution problems in the Western Hemisphere grew throughout the 1960s, prompted by a series of high-profile events, including discovery of the impact of DDT on wildlife and oil spills off the coasts of England and Santa Barbara, California. By 1970, Canadians were confronted by environmental problems closer to home, when the tanker *Arrow* ran aground in Chedabucto Bay off Nova Scotia and when mercury contamination of waterways prompted extensive fishing bans. As public interest in pollution grew in the late 1960s, federal and provincial politicians also turned their attention to environmental protection.

This first green wave witnessed a dramatic change in federal politicians' attitudes toward their environmental jurisdiction. Prior to the late 1960s, federal cabinet ministers resisted occasional calls from the opposition for a federal response to pollution problems by arguing, for instance that, "the conservation of natural resources within the provinces is primarily a provincial responsibility" (House of Commons, 1953: 1491). However, in the face of public demand and opposition pressure in the late sixties and early seventies, they underwent a change of heart and passed nine environmental statutes, in addition to creating a Department of the Environment to administer them (Dwivedi, 1974). The Canada Water Act, passed in 1970, was the flagship of the package of federal environmental statutes introduced during the 28th Parliament. It was followed by, among others, the 1970 amendments to the Fisheries Act, which authorized uniform national effluent standards to control water pollution, and the Clean Air Act of 1971.

At the same time, provincial governments also were scrambling to satisfy public demands for pollution control. During this period, all ten provinces passed environmental protection statutes, with some preceding the federal initiatives (most notably, British Columbia and Ontario) and others trailing. Provincial reactions to the federal proposals also varied. Although there was quiet support for federal legislation among the smaller provinces, the four largest provinces – Ontario, Québec, British Columbia, and Alberta – openly resented what they depicted as unnecessary federal intrusion in provincial jurisdiction. As a result, federal-provincial relations concerning environmental protection during this period were characterized by tension and conflict (Dwivedi and Woodrow, 1989). Intergovernmental accommodation was facilitated, however, by the existence of an institutional forum for ministerial discussions, the Canadian Council of Resource Ministers, which was renamed the Canadian Council of Resource and Environment Ministers (CCREM) during this period.

THE FEDERAL RETREAT

When the economy took a turn for the worse in the early 1970s, the environment was soon displaced on the national agenda by bread and butter issues like inflation and unemployment. Federal and provincial governments thus confronted the formidable challenge of implementing their new environmental protection statutes in a less supportive political environment than that which gave rise to them.

The pace of legislative activity in the environmental field declined sharply after 1971. At the federal level, there was sufficient momentum in the early 1970s to carry through two additional statutes already under development: the Ocean Dumping Control Act and the Environmental Contaminants Act. Thereafter, although minor amendments were made to the Fisheries Act in 1977 and to the Clean Air Act in 1980, no new environmental legislation was passed until 1988.

It is not entirely surprising that legislative activity declined in the early 1970s, since the recently enacted statutes offered ample tools to combat pollution. The task at hand was to implement them. However, the promise of the first wave of federal environmental statutes was not fulfilled. The water quality provisions of the Canada Water Act, which had been hailed as the centrepiece of federal environmental protection efforts, simply were never implemented. The federal government made greater progress in implementing the Fisheries Act, but even there, national regulations were issued for only six industries under the Act, though twenty had originally been planned (Edgeworth, 1973: 5). In comparison, over fifty broad industrial categories were regulated during the same period under the U.S. Clean Water Act.

During this period, the balance of federal and provincial roles in environmental protection shifted back toward the provinces. By the mid-1970s a clear division of responsibilities emerged, with the federal government developing national guidelines but leaving their implementation and enforcement to the provinces (Giroux, 1987). The origins of this arrangement lay in long-standing agreements concerning the federal Fisheries Act, in which the federal government delegated administration of the Act to all but the Atlantic provinces (Parisien, 1972). That informal delegation of responsibility for enforcement was clarified and extended to other federal environmental statutes by a series of federal-provincial accords signed in the mid-seventies. All provinces but Québec, British Columbia, and Newfoundland signed bilateral accords with the federal government, which set out mutually agreed roles for the federal and provincial governments in the environmental field.[4] The federal government was to develop national discharge guidelines in consultation with the provinces, while the provinces were to "to establish and enforce requirements at least as stringent as the agreed national baseline requirements." In turn, the federal government agreed not to take action to enforce its own regulations unless the provinces failed to do the job.

In theory, delegation of responsibility for implementation of national standards to the provinces was conditional. In practice, however, despite a record of widespread and persistent non-compliance with federal standards, the federal government rarely intervened. Even in provinces where the accords expired or were never signed, provincial governments were given priority in enforcement (Huestis, 1985: 53; Webb, 1983: 5-187).

By 1979, the federal government further withdrew from the commitment to establish national standards, nominally assuming the mantle of advocate rather than regulator (Henley, 1985). Standard setting under the Fisheries Act ground to a halt.[5] By 1984, Environment Canada's annual report noted that federal "Regulatory powers are used sparingly as a last resort" (Environment Canada, 1984: 1).

While, like the federal government, most provinces faced little electoral pressure to aggressively pursue environmental protection during the 1970s and early 1980s, they did have incentives to defend their jurisdiction over natural resources. In light of federal deference in the environmental field, they had little to fear. It is thus not surprising that, as observed by Woodrow, "the early 1970s seemed to witness federal-provincial relations with regard to pollution control and environmental management turn its face from confrontation to co-existence" (1977: 480). The turf battles that accompanied the passage of the Canada Water Act subsided as the federal government assumed a welcome supporting role of providing research and technical expertise to the provinces and facilitating consensus on national standards.

In explaining the cooperative character of federal-provincial relations during this period, much has been made of the institutional form of CCREM, in which federal and provincial ministers participated as equals, with the chair rotating among them (Whittington, 1974; Jenkin, 120-24). However, in light of federal deference to provincial jurisdiction during this period, the absence of federal-provincial conflict can be seen more as a reflection of the fact that there was little to fight about than as a tribute to the mechanisms available to resolve intergovernmental conflicts. As

Skogstad and Kopas (1992) have noted, federal and provincial governments were equally willing to turn a blind eye to widespread non-compliance with environmental standards.

The short-lived burst of federal government concern for the environment around 1970 did have lasting impacts. Federal leadership prompted
many provinces to adopt comparable standards based on national guidelines (Franson, Lucas, and Lucas, 1982: 22) – though they did not necessarily enforce them. In addition, Environment Canada's regional officials
occasionally succeeded in pressuring individual provinces to tighten permit conditions or prosecute persistent violations, and on rare occasions
federal officials pursued unilateral enforcement action (Nemetz, 1986).

Ultimately, however, federal officials' impact on provincial standards
was limited by the provinces' willingness to accept federal input. It was as
if the federal government volunteered to conduct an orchestra, without
any guarantee that the musicians would be playing the same tune. When
the musicians were eager to play together, the conductor provided a valuable service. But when they were intent on playing solo, all the baton-
waving in the world could not produce a symphony.

THE SECOND WAVE

In the second half of the 1980s, public fears concerning the environment
were rekindled by reports of a seemingly endless series of ecological disas-
ters, including Bhopal, Chernobyl, and the *Exxon Valdez*. In addition, the
discovery of a hole in the stratospheric ozone layer and emerging evidence of global warming contributed to a growing recognition that environmental issues are global in scope. Within Canada, the 1980s brought
discovery of a toxic "blob" in the St. Clair River, detection of dioxins in
pulp mill effluents, and a PCB warehouse fire at Saint-Basile-le-Grand,
among others.

Brown reports that Environment Canada's own public opinion polls
revealed an important shift in Canadians' attitudes concerning the environment as early as 1984 (Brown, 1992: 31). However, it was not until the
late 1980s that heightened public interest in the environment was
reflected in a dramatic surge in salience of the environment in national
opinion polls, only to be followed by an equally rapid decline with the
onset of a recession in the early 1990s.

In many respects, the governmental response to the second green wave was a replay of the first. Brown and Siddiq (1991) report an average increase in provincial expenditures on environmental protection of 6.6 per cent per year between 1985 and 1989, more than three times the overall rate of growth in provincial expenditures. The federal government also was increasingly active concerning the environment. Reminiscent of the early seventies, the increased federal presence in the environmental field provoked federal-provincial tensions.

An important difference between the first and second green waves was the role played by environmentalists. The early seventies had witnessed the birth of dozens of local environmental associations, which were ill-prepared to participate in the first round of environmental policy-making (Woodrow, 1977: 124). By the late eighties many of those groups had matured to become professional organizations with respectable, if not extravagant, budgets.

With the possible exception of environmentalists in Ontario and Québec, many Canadian environmentalists distrusted the provinces more than the federal government, to the point of labelling them "the environmental ogres of our time" (Buttle, 1990: B4). Although far from satisfied with federal policies, they sought the reassurance of overlapping federal and provincial jurisdiction. Their ability to achieve that goal was reinforced by significant changes in the environmental policy-making process. In the late 1980s, federal consultation processes traditionally limited to federal and provincial governments and regulated industries were expanded to include environmental groups (Hoberg, 1993). Environmentalists thus were able to provide a voice for diffuse public concerns and, in so doing, to serve as a counterpoint to industry and provincial resistance to federal initiatives.

The Canadian Environmental Protection Act

When Tom McMillan was appointed Environment Minister in 1985 after the disastrous tenure of Suzanne Blais-Grenier, his first order of business was to repair both his own department's morale and the new Conservative government's reputation at a time of growing public concern for the environment. McMillan responded by asserting a stronger federal role in environmental protection in the form of new legislation that placed renewed emphasis on uniform national standards.

Like the Canada Water Act before it, the Canadian Environmental Protection Act (CEPA), proclaimed in June 1988, was offered as the centrepiece of a new federal environmental strategy (Lucas, 1989; Giroux, 1989; Tingley, 1991). In addition to consolidating several existing environmental laws, the new statute proposed to strengthen significantly the federal government's role in toxic substance control. CEPA rejected the supplementary federal role envisioned by earlier environmental statutes.

As with the Canada Water Act two decades earlier, provincial resistance was strongest from Ontario, Alberta, British Columbia, and especially Québec. In response to Québec's continuing concerns, a committee of federal and provincial officials proposed the concept of "equivalency," an arrangement in which federal regulations under CEPA could be revoked in a particular province if the federal government and that province agreed that the province's own regulations were equivalent to federal standards. The proposed federal legislation was amended accordingly after second reading to authorize equivalency agreements.

Ironically, provincial efforts to resist federal involvement in the environmental field resulted in a more intrusive statute. In introducing equivalency amendments in the face of opposition demands for an ever stronger federal role, the federal Minister included a number of statutory conditions on equivalency. Thus, although equivalency was envisioned by the provinces as a mechanism to limit federal involvement within their jurisdiction, as adopted, it has the potential to inject an element of hierarchy into the federal-provincial relationship, since any province seeking equivalency agreements must agree to be held accountable to federal conditions (Duncan, 1990: 55). Not surprisingly, many provinces are wary of the potential for federal oversight of provincial policies, and only one equivalency agreement was signed in the first six years following the passage of CEPA.

Lucas (1989: 184) has aptly characterized CEPA as a turning point in federal environmental policy. The late 1990s will reveal whether CEPA will sustain a stronger federal presence in environmental protection or succumb to the fate of the Canada Water Act. However, the early indications suggest a path closer to the latter. Although the federal government fulfilled its promise to evaluate forty-four categories of priority substances within five years of the publication of the Priority Substances List, as of July, 1994, it had issued control regulations for only one. A parliamentary review of the statute was scheduled for completion in 1994-95, and there are indications that Environment Canada will seek relaxation of the existing conditions on equivalency (Environment Canada, 1993, vii).

The Green Plan

Despite his own Québec nationalism, Lucien Bouchard, McMillan's successor as Environment Minister, continued to emphasize the need for a strong federal role, in particular, the need for national environmental standards (Bouchard, 1989). At the height of public concern for the environment in the summer of 1989, Bouchard received cabinet approval to develop an ambitious five-year environmental agenda for Canada. Extensive public consultations on the so-called Green Plan were held in parallel with private discussions with the provinces, many of which were uneasy about the secretive federal plan.

The Green Plan was finally released in December 1990 (Canada, 1990). Among other commitments, the federal government promised to spend an additional $3 billion on the environment over the next five years, although that soon was extended to six years. The Plan can be viewed essentially as a spending program, with heavy emphasis on programs that win friends, such as national parks, new research centres, and educational programs, and significantly less emphasis on coercive regulations, which tend to make enemies among both regulated industries and the provinces (Hoberg and Harrison, 1994). In fact, the Alberta business community, which had been hostile to the Plan's development, openly praised the final product (Carlisle, 1990: 12). Provincial officials also breathed a collective sigh of relief. An Ontario official recalled, "Our first reaction was, 'is that all there is?'" while an Alberta counterpart described the Green Plan as a "paper tiger" (confidential interviews).

In the first year of the Green Plan, the federal government maintained a high profile by announcing some seventeen initiatives projected to cost more than $1 billion. However, actual budgets fell short of original projections as the cabinet's commitment waned in the face of declining public pressure on the environment (Toner, 1994).

Environmental Impact Assessment

Although the passage of CEPA had already disturbed the long-standing federal-provincial détente in environmental matters, the impact of a subsequent series of court decisions concerning environmental assessment was much more profound. In 1989, the Federal Court ruled that the federal government was required under the terms of its own Environmental Assessment and Review Process (EARP) guidelines to conduct an environmental review of two dams being constructed by the Saskatchewan government on the Rafferty and Alameda rivers. The decision was significant because it previously had been assumed that the federal government could exercise discretion in interpreting its own guidelines. However, the Court ruled that by using inflexible terms such as "shall" to describe ministerial responsibilities in a formal regulation, the federal government had, in effect, regulated itself and, short of revising the regulation, would thus have to abide by its own Guidelines Order.

The combined effect of the *Rafferty-Alameda* and subsequent *Oldman Dam* decisions was to force the federal government to acknowledge and exercise its considerable jurisdiction over the environment. Although a 1992 Supreme Court ruling in the Oldman Dam case subsequently restored some federal discretion to perform environmental reviews, in the intervening three years the federal government was forced to operate under the assumption that it could be compelled to perform an environmental review of virtually any project that impinged on federal jurisdiction. As a result, although only thirty-three full environmental reviews were performed by the federal government in the fifteen year period from 1974 to 1989, there were twenty-four reviews in the first year alone after the Rafferty-Alameda decision (Ross, 1992: 323).

It warrants emphasis that the expansion of the federal role in environmental assessment following the Rafferty-Alameda and Oldman Dam decisions was not the result of a federal power grab. Rather, at the behest of environmental groups, the courts thrust jurisdiction upon a reluctant federal government. Indeed, Canadians were given a rare opportunity to see a federal Minister at a loss for words because he was granted more extensive powers vis-à-vis the provinces than he had sought (Howard, 1990, A5). Moreover, the federal government time and again vigorously opposed environmentalists' legal arguments that it should apply its own law.

Both federal and provincial governments were frustrated in the aftermath of the EARP litigation. The federal government resented the loss of control of its agenda to environmental groups and the courts, while the provinces resented the uncertainty introduced by belated federal reviews of projects that they had already approved. However, the nature of the EARP decisions greatly limited the ability of the two levels of government to resolve their differences through compromise. In granting citizens enforceable claims to federal actions, the courts effectively empowered private litigants to drive a wedge between the federal and provincial governments.

The fact that these events occurred during a period of unprecedented public concern for the environment may explain the federal government's unwillingness to accede to provincial pressure to amend the EARP regulation. Instead, the federal government proceeded with legislation to replace the regulation altogether. The resulting Canadian Environmental Assessment Act (CEAA) received royal assent in June, 1992.

Led by the Alberta government, the provinces displayed unprecedented consensus in their opposition to the federal legislation. Their objectives were threefold. First, the provinces argued that federal involvement was unnecessary since they were already doing the job. Provincial bureaucrats and politicians alike complained of a federal "cherry-picking syndrome," arguing that the federal government sought involvement only in the few prominent cases that capture the public's attention.

Second, many provinces were highly defensive of their jurisdiction concerning natural resources. It was significant that the most prominent EARP disputes, including the Rafferty-Alameda and Oldman dams and the James Bay hydroelectric development, challenged the provinces' authority to develop their own Crown resources. As the Alberta Forestry Minister stated, "We fought hard for control of the resources in this province, and we're against the federal government coming into this process through the side door" (*Western Report*, 1989: 30).

Finally, as one provincial official put it, "The bottom line is not environmental protection here, but economic development" (confidential interview). The potential invasiveness of federal environmental jurisdiction was brought home by the efforts of environmental groups to use the EARP regulation to block dozens of major projects in virtually every province. The provinces' desire to control the pace and direction of economic development within their own jurisdictions spurred them to present a common front in opposition to federal proposals. In the end, although the federal government agreed to amendments to make consultation with the provinces mandatory under certain conditions, it denied all of their more substantive proposals, including ones for a form of equivalency in the environmental assessment field.

The Canadian Council of Ministers of the Environment

Although the intergovernmental tensions provoked by renewed federal involvement in the environmental field were reminiscent of the late 1960s, the scope of conflict was much broader in the late 1980s. In the face of legal claims by environmental groups for federal assessments, federal and provincial governments no longer were able to resolve their disputes behind closed doors. The scope of conflict expanded within governments as well, as environmental questions moved beyond the bounds of environment departments to intergovernmental affairs. As anticipated by Smiley (1979), provincial officials specializing in intergovernmental affairs tended to be less inclined to cooperate with the federal government than their counterparts within the provincial ministries of the environment.

As in 1970, the late 1980s witnessed a rejuvenation of the federal-provincial Council of Ministers. The Council was reorganized, relocated (to Winnipeg), and renamed the Canadian Council of Ministers of the Environment (CCME) in 1988. CCME responded to the passage of CEPA by drafting a Statement on Interjurisdictional Cooperation, in which the federal, provincial, and territorial governments agreed to cooperate "in the spirit of partnership" (Canadian Council of Ministers of the Environment, 1990).

It is noteworthy that jurisdictionally defensive provinces like Alberta and Québec not only agreed to sign the Statement, but were among its strongest proponents. By 1990, after the passage of CEPA and the Supreme Court's *Crown Zellerbach decision, federal involvement in the environmental field was accepted by all provinces as inevitable. Jurisdictionally defensive provinces thus reverted to a second-best strategy of precluding federal unilateralism by immobilizing the federal government with consultations. As one of the architects of the Statement on Interjurisdictional Cooperation explained, "if some guy moves into your basement and you can't evict him, you at least try to keep him in the basement"* (confidential interview).

It remains to be seen whether the cooperative or obstructive impulse in the multilateral Statement on Interjurisdictional Cooperation will prevail. Its very existence signals a degree of acceptance by each level of government of the other's presence in field, as well as broad commitment to harmonize federal and provincial programs. On the other hand, in light of at least some provinces' intent to preclude federal unilateralism, the Statement may prove more effective as a rhetorical weapon in federal-provincial disputes than as a benchmark for federal-provincial cooperation.

WHITHER OR WITHER THE FEDERAL ROLE?

Federal-provincial relations in the environmental field have been cooperative for the most part in the last two decades largely because the federal
government has not provoked the provinces by testing the limits of its environmental jurisdiction. The extent of the federal government's hesitance concerning its constitutional jurisdiction has varied over time, however, in parallel with trends in public opinion.

For decades prior to the late 1960s, the federal government resisted
sporadic calls for federal involvement in pollution control. However,
when public interest in the environment surged in the late 1960s, the
same politicians who had deflected calls for a stronger federal role only a
few years earlier began to talk tough about the need for national standards.
When public attention subsided in the early 1970s, politicians' enthusiasm
for environmental protection also diminished. Between 1972 and 1985,
when environmental issues virtually disappeared from public opinion
polls, federal politicians gradually retreated from their earlier assertions of
authority.

Finally, as the public rediscovered the environment in the late 1980s,
so, too, did their elected representatives. Federal politicians again expressed confidence in the constitutional basis for a strong federal role in
environmental policy and renewed their efforts to establish uniform national standards. This resurgence of the federal role was hastened by court
decisions concerning the federal environmental assessment regulation,
which effectively forced the federal government to acknowledge the
breadth of its environmental jurisdiction and, more importantly, to exercise it. Thus, while the federal government was advancing tentatively on
its own in response to growing public demand in the late 1980s, environmental groups used the courts to give the federal government a powerful
push.

The temptation to resist imposition of concentrated costs is ever-pre-
sent in all democratic political systems. However, in the Canadian context, federalism provided a convenient means of escape from jurisdiction
that presented politically difficult regulatory responsibilities. It is significant that the avenue through which the federal government retreated
from implementation of its early environmental statutes during the 1970s
and early 1980s was delegation to the provinces. Yet, rather than trying to
pass the buck right back to the federal government, many provinces were
highly motivated to defend their jurisdiction over natural resources be-

cause it is so closely related to their authority to pursue resource-driven economic development. Thus, as the salience of environmental issues rose and fell, the balance of federal and provincial roles in the environmental field shifted accordingly.

An implicit assumption in much of the literature on Canadian federalism is that both levels of government invariably seek to expand or at least to exploit fully their jurisdiction (see Norrie, Simeon, and Krasnick, 1986: 123; Cairns, 1988: 150-51).[6] But, in the environmental field, intergovernmental competition for jurisdiction over environmental protection has been the exception to the rule. The apparent hesitance of the federal government in environmental policy forces reconsideration of the common assumption that governments compete to extend their jurisdictional grasp. In light of potential political costs and benefits, federal and provincial politicians can be expected to perceive some fields of jurisdiction as worth fighting for and others worthy of surrender without a fight. Moreover, the possibility that governments can use the federal system to avoid responsibility for environmental protection cautions against the optimism of authors who have argued that two heads of power are better than one (Gibson, 1983; Nemetz, 1986; Thompson, 1980).

The 1990s represent a potential turning point with respect to federal and provincial roles and their relationship with one another in the environmental field. While aggressive federal statutes passed during the second green wave herald a new era of federal activism, which could shift the current balance away from the provinces, the record of non-implementation of the environmental statutes of the early 1970s suggests that the new federal commitments must be viewed with some scepticism. Will CEPA herald a more activist federal role in environmental protection, or does the disappointing rate of progress in its first six years suggest a fate closer to that of the Canada Water Act? Will Green Plan dollars provide the kind of federal leverage over provincial programs afforded by traditional shared-cost programs or merely sustain the federal government's traditional research and technical support function? Finally, will the Canadian Environmental Assessment Act sustain a prominent federal role in environmental assessment or restore ministerial discretion to defer to both polluters and the provinces?

Although public concern for the environment remains high, the prominence of environmental issues has subsided since the late 1980s. Many of the same conditions that prompted the federal retreat in the 1970s are replicated in the 1990s. The crucial difference this round could be the watchdog role of environmental groups. Environmentalists now routinely have a place at the table in government-sponsored consultations, and they will also retain considerable legal resources with respect to environmental assessment. But their effectiveness in preventing a federal (and provincial) retreat in the years to come ultimately will depend on their ability to mobilize support from a public increasingly preoccupied with other concerns.

NOTES

1   It is true that the Supreme Court decisions in the *Crown Zellerbach* and *Oldman River* cases during this period clarified the extent of federal authority within the existing constitution. However, well before the first of these decisions, the federal government had already disrupted intergovernmental harmony by introducing the Canadian Environmental Protection Act.

2   Unfortunately, Gallup did not report responses to the "most important problem" question between 1969 and 1972, when other indicators, such as trends in Canadian media coverage and in public opinion in the U.S., suggest the salience of environmental issues peaked. In 1972, pollution was cited as the most important problem by 5 per cent of respondents. Thereafter, the fraction of respondents citing pollution declined to the point where it was not even mentioned by Gallup in conjunction with this question between 1976 and 1987. (See, for instance, "Concern with Pollution Drops Among Canadians," *Gallup Report*, February 26, 1975.) Although a relatively high degree of residual concern was revealed by close-ended questions asking respondents how serious they perceive environmental problems to be, even there, the percentage responding "very serious" declined steadily from 63 per cent in 1970 to a low of 51 per cent in 1985 (*Gallup Report*, May 28, 1990.)

3   The fraction of respondents identifying the environment as the "most important problem" facing the country peaked in July, 1989, at 16.5 per cent, when the environment was the top-ranked problem, and thereafter declined to 2 per cent by late 1991. (See *Gallup Report*, October 3, 1991).

4   The Canada–New Brunswick Accord for the Protection and Enhancement of Environmental Quality is reprinted in Standing Committee on Fisheries and Forestry, *Minutes and Proceedings of Evidence*, June 8, 1977, 29A: 51.

5   A revision of the pulp and paper regulations, which was ready for review by the Privy Council Office, and a proposed regulation for the textile industry,

433

which was even further advanced, were abandoned when the advocacy approach was introduced in 1979.

6   An important exception is Young, Faucher, and Blais (1984).

REFERENCES

Alhéritière, Dominique (1972). "Les problèmes constitutionnel de la lutte contre la pollution de l'espace atmosphèrique au Canada," *La Revue du Barreau Canadien*, 50: 561-79.

Beaudoin, Gerald A. (1977). "La protection de l'environnement et ses implications en droit constitutionnel," *McGill Law Journal*, 23: 207-24.

Bouchard, Lucien (1989). *Notes for an address at the Symposium 'Le Saint-Laurent, un fleuve a reconquérir*, November 3.

Brown, M. Paul (1992). "Organizational Design as Policy Instrument: Environment Canada in the Canadian Bureaucracy," in Robert Boardman, ed., *Canadian Environmental Policy: Ecosystems, Politics, and Process*. Toronto: Oxford University Press.

Brown, M. Paul, and Fazley Siddiq (1991). "The Dimensions of Provincial Environmental Protection Spending," paper presented at the annual meeting of the Canadian Political Science Association, Kingston.

Buttle, Jeff (1990). "Cutback in environmental role feared," *Vancouver Sun*, May 10: B4.

Cairns, Alan (1988). "The Governments and Societies of Canadian Federalism," in Cairns, *Constitution, Government and Society in Canada: Selected Essays by Alan C. Cairns*, edited by Douglas E. Williams. Toronto: McClelland & Stewart.

Canada (1990). *Canada's Green Plan*.

Canadian Council of Ministers of the Environment (1990). Statement of Interjurisdictional Cooperation on Environmental Matters.

Carlisle, Tamsin (1990). "Mixed Reactions in Alberta over Green Plan," *Financial Post*, December 28: 12.

Duncan, Linda F. (1990). "Trends in Enforcement: Is Environment Canada Serious about Enforcing its Laws?" in Donna Tingley, ed., *Into the Future: Environmental Law and Policy for the 1990s*. Edmonton: Environmental Law Centre (Alberta) Society.

Dwivedi, O.P. (1974). "The Canadian Government Response to Environmental Concerns," in Dwivedi, ed., *Protecting the Environment: Issues and Choices — Canadian Perspectives*. Vancouver: Copp Clark.

Dwivedi, O.P., and R. Brian Woodrow (1989)."Environmental Policy – Making and Administration in a Federal State: The Impact of Overlapping Jurisdiction in Canada," in William M. Chandler and Christian W. Zollner, eds., *Challenges to Federalism: Policy-making in Canada and the Federal Republic of Germany*. Kingston: Institute of Intergovernmental Relations.

Edgeworth, Les (1973). "Canada's Approach to Environmental Pollution Control for the Pulp and Paper Industry," paper presented by F.G. Hurtubise to the 15th EUCEPA Conference, Rome, May 7-12.

Emond, Paul (1972). "The Case for a Greater Federal Role in the Environmental Protection Field: An Examination of the Pollution Problem and the Constitution," *Osgoode Hall Law Journal*, 10: 647-80.

Environment Canada (1984). *Annual Report, 1983-84*.

Environment Canada (1993). Environment Canada Regulatory Review. Environmental Protection Program: A Discussion Document.

Franson, M.A.H., R.T. Franson, and A.R. Lucas (1982). *Environmental Standards: A Comparative Study of Canadian Standards, Standard Setting Processes and Enforcement*. Edmonton: Environment Council of Alberta.

Franson, Robert T., and Alastair R. Lucas (1976). *Canadian Environmental Law*. Vancouver: Butterworths.

Franson, Robert T., and Alastair Lucas (1977). "Legal Control of Hazardous Products in Canada," in Science Council of Canada, *Canadian Law and the Control of Exposure to Hazards*. Ottawa: Science Council of Canada.

Friends of the Oldman River Society and The Queen in right of Alberta et al. (1992) DLR, 88: 1-60.

Gibson, Dale (1969). "The Constitutional Context of Canadian Water Planning," *Alberta Law Review*, 7: 71-92.

Gibson, Dale (1973). "Constitutional Jurisdiction over Environmental Management in Canada," *University of Toronto Law Journal*, 23: 54-87.

Gibson, Dale (1983). "Environmental Protection and Enhancement under a New Canadian Constitution," in Stanley M. Beck and Ivan Bernier, eds., *Canada and the New Constitution*. Montreal: Institute for Research on Public Policy.

Giroux, Lorne (1987). "Delegation of Administration," in Donna Tingley, ed., *Environmental Protection and the Canadian Constitution*. Edmonton: Environmental Law Centre (Alberta) Society.

Giroux, Lorne (1989). "Les nouvelles technologies et le régime de la protection de l'environnement au Canada: la nouvelle loi canadienne sur la protection de l'environnement," *Les Cahiers de Droit*, 30: 747-76.

Harrison, Kathryn (1993). *Passing the Buck: Federalism and Canadian Environmental Policy*, Ph.D. dissertation, University of British Columbia.

Henley, Doreen C. (1985). "The Advocacy Approach," in Linda F. Duncan, ed., *Environmental Enforcement: Proceedings of the National Conference on the Enforcement of Environmental Law*. Edmonton: Environmental Law Centre (Alberta) Society.

Hoberg, George (1993). "Environmental Policy: Alternative Styles," in Michael Atkinson, ed., *Governing Canada: Institutions and Public Policy*. Toronto: Harcourt Brace Jovanovich.

Hoberg, George, and Kathryn Harrison (1994). "It's Not Easy Being Green: The Politics of Canada's Green Plan," *Canadian Public Policy*, 20: 119-37.

House of Commons (1953). *Debates*. January 30: 1491.

Howard, Ross (1990). "Oldman dam ruling stuns federal officials – Bouchard noncommittal, calls decisions 'interesting,'" Globe and Mail, March 15: A5.

Huestis, Lynne B. (1985). "Pilot Study Report, S. 33 Fisheries Act," Department of Justice, Federal Statutes Compliance Project. December.

Interprovincial Cooperatives Ltd. et al. v. The Queen in Right of Manitoba (1975). DLR 53: 321-59.

Jenkin, Michael (1983). *The Challenge of Diversity: Industrial Policy in the Canadian Federation*. Ottawa: Science Council of Canada.

LaForest, Gerard V. (1972). "Interprovincial Rivers," *Canadian Bar Review*, 50: 39-49.

Landis, Henry (1970). "Legal Controls of Pollution in the Great Lakes Basin," *Canadian Bar Review*, 48: 66-157.

Lederman, W.R. (1975). "Unity and Diversity in Canadian Federalism: Ideals and Methods of Modernization," *Canadian Bar Review*, 53: 597-620.

Lucas, Alastair R. (1982). "Constitutional Law – Federal Fisheries Power – Provincial Resource Management and Property and Civil Rights Powers – *Fowler v. The Queen* and *Northwest Falling Contractors Ltd. v. The Queen*," *University of British Columbia Law Review*, 16: 145-154.

Lucas, Alastair R. (1986). "Harmonization of Federal and Provincial Environmental Policies: The Changing Legal and Policy Framework," in J. Owen Saunders, *Managing Natural Resources in a Federal State*. Toronto: Carswell.

Lucas, Alastair R. (1989). "The New Environmental Law," in R. Watts and D. Brown, eds., *Canada: The State of the Federation, 1989*. Kingston: Institute of Intergovernmental Relations.

Lundqvist, L.J. (1974). "Do Political Structures Matter in Environmental Politics? The Case of Air Pollution Control in Canada, Sweden, and the United States," *Canadian Public Administration*, 17: 119-42.

Muldoon, Paul, and Marcia Valiante (1988). *Toxic Water Pollution in Canada*. Calgary: Canadian Institute of Resources Law.

Nemetz, Peter (1986). "The Fisheries Act and Federal-Provincial Environmental Regulation: Duplication or Complementarity?" *Canadian Public Administration*, 29: 401-24.

Norrie, Kenneth, Richard Simeon, and Mark Krasnick, (1986). *Federalism and Economic Union in Canada*. Toronto: University of Toronto Press.

Parisien, Richard W. (1972). *The Fisheries Act: Origins of Federal Delegation of Administrative Jurisdiction to the Provinces*. Ottawa: Environment Canada.

Parlour, J.W., and S. Schatzow (1978). "The Mass Media and Public Concern for Environmental Problems in Canada," *International Journal of Environmental Studies*, 13: 9-17.

Percy, D.R. (1984). "Federal/Provincial Jurisdictional Issues," in Harriet Rueggeberg and A.R. Thompson, eds., *Water Law and Policy Issues in Canada*. Vancouver: Westwater Research Centre.

R. v. Crown Zellerbach Canada Ltd. (1988) 84 NR 1.

Rabe, Barry G. (1989). "Cross-Media Environmental Regulatory Integration: The Case of Canada," *American Review of Canadian Studies*, 19: 261-73.

Ross, Monique (1992). "An Evaluation of Joint Environmental Impact Assessments," in Monique Ross and J. Owen Saunders, eds., *Growing Demands on a Shrinking Heritage: Managing Resource-Use Conflicts*. Calgary: Canadian Institute of Resources Law.

Saunders, J. Owen (1988). *Interjurisdictional Issues in Canadian Water Management*. Calgary: Canadian Institute of Resources Law.

Skogstad, Grace, and Paul Kopas (1992). "Environmental Policy in a Federal System: Ottawa and the Provinces," in Robert Boardman, ed., *Canadian Environmental Policy: Ecosystems, Politics, and Process*. Toronto: Oxford University Press.

Smiley, Donald V. (1979). "An Outsider's Observations of Federal-Provincial Relations Among Consenting Adults," in Richard Simeon, ed., *Confrontation and Collaboration − Intergovernmental Relations in Canada Today*. Toronto: Institute of Public Administration of Canada.

Thompson, Andrew R. (1980). *Environmental Regulation in Canada: An Assessment of the Regulatory Process*. Vancouver: Westwater Research Centre.

Thompson, Andrew R., and H.R. Eddy (1973). "Jurisdictional Problems in Natural Resource Management," in W.D. Bennett et al., *Essays on Aspects of Resource Policy*. Ottawa: Science Council of Canada.

Tingley, Donna (1991). "Conflict and Cooperation on the Environment," in Douglas Brown, ed., *Canada: The State of the Federation, 1991*. Kingston: Institute of Intergovernmental Relations.

Toner, Glen (1994). "The Green Plan: From Great Expectations to Eco-Backtracking ... to Revitalization?" in Susan D. Phillips, ed., *How Ottawa Spends 1994-95: Making Change*. Ottawa: Carleton University Press.

Tremblay, André (1973). "La priorité des compétences provinciales dans la lutte contre la pollution des eaux," in Phillippe Crabbé and Irene M. Spry, eds., *Natural Resource Development in Canada*. Ottawa: University of Ottawa Press.

Weaver, R. Kent (1986). "The Politics of Blame Avoidance," *Journal of Public Policy*, 6: 371-98.

Webb, Kernaghan R. (1983). "Industrial Water Pollution Control and the EPS," unpublished background study prepared for the Law Reform Commission of Canada.

Western Report (1989). "Fjordbotten: No means No," December 25: 30.

Whittington, Michael (1974). "Environmental Policy," in G. Bruce Doern and V. Seymour Wilson, *Issues in Canadian Public Policy*. Toronto: Macmillan.

Wilson, James Q. (1975). "The Politics of Regulation," in James McKie, ed., *Social Responsibility and the Business Predicament*. Washington: Brookings Institution.

Woodrow, R.B. (1977). "The Development and Implementation of Federal Pollution Control Policy Programs in Canada, 1966-1974," Ph.D. thesis, University of Toronto.

Young, R.A., Philippe Faucher, and André Blais (1984). "The Concept of Province-Building: A Critique," *Canadian Journal of Political Science*, 17: 783-818.

Langsdale Library
University of Baltimore
1420 Maryland Avenue
Baltimore, MD. 21201

CONTRIBUTORS

Gérald Bernier is a member of the Political Science Department at the University of Montreal.

Kathy L. Brock is a member of the Political Studies Department, St. John's College, University of Manitoba.

Robert Campbell is a member of the Political Studies Department at Trent University.

Michel Duquette is a member of the Political Science Department at the University of Montreal.

Alain-G. Gagnon is member of the Political Science Department at McGill University.

Rodney Haddow is a member of the Political Science Department at St. Francis Xavier University.

Kathryn Harrison is a member of the Political Science Department at the University of British Columbia.

David Irwin is a member of the Political Science Department at the University of Montreal.

Radha Jhappan is a member of the Political Science Department at Carleton University.

Kenneth McRoberts is a member of the Political Science Department at York University.

Leon Muszynski is a social policy consultant at the Social Planning Council of Metropolitan Toronto.

Richard Nimijean is a Ph.D. candidate in the Political Science Department at Carleton University.

Ian Robinson is a member of the Political Science Department at Reed College, Oregon.

UNIVERSITY OF BALTIMORE - LANGSDALE

3 2056 00871 9977

François Rocher is a member of the Political Science Department at Carleton University.

Donald Savoie holds the Clément-Cormier Chair in Economic Development and is a member of the Department of Public Administration at the University of Moncton.

Jennifer Smith is a member of the Political Science Department at Dalhousie University.

Miriam Smith is a member of the Political Science Department at Carleton University.

Robert Vandycke is a member of the Sociology Department at the University of Montreal.

WITHDRAWN

DATE DUE

MAY 24 1999	
10/30/04	
OCT 0 ? RECD	

BRODART, CO.   Cat. No. 23-221-003